THE GLOBAL
INTERIOR

THE GLOBAL INTERIOR

MINERAL FRONTIERS
AND AMERICAN POWER

MEGAN BLACK

Harvard University Press

Cambridge, Massachusetts · London, England

Library of Congress Cataloging-in-Publication Data
Names: Black, Megan, 1987– author.
Title: The global interior : mineral frontiers and American power / Megan Black.
Description: Cambridge, Massachusetts : Harvard University Press, 2018. |
Includes bibliographical references and index.
Identifiers: LCCN 2018009507 | ISBN 9780674984257 (cloth : alk. paper) |
ISBN 9780674271197 (pbk.)
Subjects: LCSH: United States. Department of the Interior. | Mines and mineral
resources. | Mineral industries. | Imperialism. | United States—Foreign relations—1865–
Classification: LCC HD9506 .B46 2018 | DDC 333.8/50973—dc23
LC record available at https://lccn.loc.gov/2018009507

Contents

THE GLOBAL
INTERIOR

Introduction

I N FEBRUARY 1967, Secretary of the Interior Stewart Udall and his
signature bolo tie embarked on a two-week journey across the Middle
East. The tour included a stopover in Saudi Arabia, a locale far afield from
the American West where Udall, a politician from Arizona, famously led
a variety of land use projects in his capacity as the head of the U.S. Department of the Interior. Although his stated purpose in Saudi Arabia
was to discuss the seemingly apolitical topics of national park creation
and water desalination, he also undertook activities that the international community had come to see as deeply political: those dealing with
U.S. mineral interests abroad. Udall's main purpose in the Middle East,
for example, was to investigate the highly charged oil situation during the
tumultuous prelude to the 1967 Arab-Israeli war. He met with the
president of Aramco, the oil firm formed in the 1930s by the Standard
Oil Company, before having a private audience with King Faisal Ibn
Abdul Aziz—or that "old camel raider," as Udall privately referred to the
modernizing leader of the land—to affirm U.S.-Saudi oil relations. Arab
news media suspected as much, charging Udall with manipulating political and economic structures involving oil. To refute these accusations,
Udall insisted, with all due modesty and aw-shucks charm, that he was
just "an *innocent* Minister of the Interior who should be called Minister
of Natural Resources."[1] What could he—or the Interior Department, for
that matter—have to do with the politics of the world?

1

Stewart Udall walks with Sheik Hassan Machani, Minister of Agriculture, during his Saudi Arabian tour. Papers of Stewart Udall, Special Collections, University of Arizona.

A great deal, it turns out. The U.S. Department of the Interior is an arm of the federal government known today for managing natural resources and indigenous affairs, as well as overseeing the nation's public parks. It is widely understood to be an inward-looking engine of domestic policy. Yet this dismissal has concealed an expansionist trajectory that challenges even the most capacious frames for analyzing U.S. global engagement. The Interior Department oversaw an ever-widening quest for minerals that, far from adhering to standard political borders, began in indigenous lands of the American West, circled the Global South, plumbed the oceans, and eventually departed the atmosphere with the leap into outer space. The department, in short, operated in a global field. Although this field had been staked out over a century, Stewart Udall can help begin to trace its perimeter. For example, during his tenure, Udall not only ventured to the Middle East but also supervised the affairs of semi-sovereign indigenous nations. He oversaw the territories of Guam, Samoa, and Micronesia, which had fallen under Interior's jurisdiction since the New Deal. He undertook diplomatic missions to nations across

Africa, Asia, and Latin America where Interior had piloted natural resource programs since the earliest days of international development.
He managed the exploration and leasing of the continental shelf, a mineral-
rich expanse roughly the size of the Louisiana Purchase. And he advanced a space exploration agenda that involved both the colorful attempt
to mine the moon and, more consequentially, the creation of Landsat, a
satellite that could view Earth's resources. His reach, like that of the unassuming department he led, aimed tenaciously outward.

This book uses the Interior Department as a prism through which
to make sense of a paradox at the heart of American global power.
The United States has undertaken activities closely associated with
imperialism—the projection of political authority over other sovereign
entities in service of economic gain and ideologies rooted in race, gender,
and nation. Scholars have seen this process, which created asymmetrical
arrangements governing the people and nonhuman nature within those
geographic bounds, at play in American undertakings from continental
expansion in the nineteenth century to its various overseas involvements

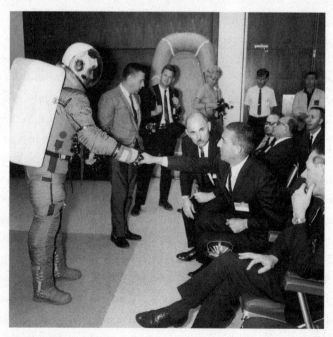

Udall reaches out to an astronaut at the Johnson Space Center in 1967. Papers of Stewart
Udall, Special Collections, University of Arizona.

in the twentieth century.[2] Yet everyday Americans do not think of the United States as an empire. This invisibility is a partial legacy of American exceptionalism, the widespread belief that the nation emerged from a wholly unique set of conditions, including its own anticolonial struggle with Great Britain, ensuring not only its incommensurability with other nations and empires but also its superiority to them.[3] However, when the innermost arm of the American state is revealed to have participated in and at times led expansionism in its many forms, one is confronted with the existence and persistence of American empire. I argue that the Interior Department, more than just standing as evidence of this broadly established historical condition, was a key mechanism for ensuring *and* obscuring the projection of American power in the world, from U.S. settler colonialism to its global hegemony during and after the Cold War. As the United States drew distinctions between domestic and foreign, exploitation and benevolence, and nature and politics—only to transgress those boundaries at will—the Interior Department oversaw important operations of power betwixt and between that allowed the nation to pursue its global dreams, dreams that were oriented with incredible consistency to extractive ends.

To discern this important arc in U.S. history, we must begin with the premise that the Interior Department's foreign orientation in the twentieth century was not a contradiction. Despite its apparent domesticity, Interior had always been, in fundamental ways, in a steady process of becoming a *global* Interior. One Interior official, Assistant Secretary of the Interior Vernon Northrop, hammered this point home in an address on October 24, 1952, appropriately enough, on United Nations Day. Northrop began his remarks by acknowledging that many Americans were surprised to learn of the department's extensive involvements in postwar international development. He gently corrected this misunderstanding. Interior, he countered, was in fact ideally suited to such far-reaching activities. As evidence, he pointed to the Interior Department's origins in nineteenth-century continental expansion. "Once it was the undeveloped West of the 1850s which constituted a primary reason for the establishment of this Department and conditioned its development," Northrop offered. "Now it is the underdeveloped areas of the free world of the 1950s." He concluded that Interior had the "know-how" needed to bring about "the opening of this new frontier."[4] Drawing on an intoxicating symbol deeply entwined with the history of American exceptionalism (the frontier), Northrop argued that Interior's history with continental expansion had prepared it for this new and global calling.

The Interior Department *was* born in mid-nineteenth century contests for the midcontinent. When lawmakers in Congress gave life to the Department of the Interior on March 3, 1849, they explicitly aimed to create the first arm of the federal government to oversee domestic affairs, a task that had previously fallen on states. The "interior" at the heart of the new department's mission was meant to signal, consciously and forcefully, the home, the domestic, and the American self. It was meant to wrest domestic meaning from foreign space. However, the interior also quickly came to designate a hinterland, an inner recess of resources awaiting utilization. One struck out for the interior to strike it rich.[5] After the Mexican-American War, U.S. formal sovereignty technically spanned from sea to shining sea, but the cultural and material landscape did not reflect this legal presumption. The Interior Department undertook the day-to-day work of U.S. settler colonialism, making expropriated lands ready for capitalist development on a vast geographic scale. At its founding, the federal engine of domestic policy pushed outward, incorporating people and landscapes. It is only when the continent has been so naturalized as the "United States," and indigenous sovereignty so subordinated to European sovereignty, that Interior appears as a domestic entity at all.[6] The Interior Department's domestication, at its moment of origin and in historical memory, ultimately laid important foundations for the domestication of U.S. settler colonialism writ large.

Interior's more "global" mineral pursuits in the twentieth century had crucial origins in the so-called closing of the American frontier in 1890. As U.S. officials increasingly if mistakenly declared an end to processes of westward settlement, the U.S. government faced an organizational crisis: what to do with institutions like Interior after executing, to a great extent, the task that they were called forth to do. In a bid for survival in the twentieth century, Interior leaders adapted, offering up their services in pursuit of new horizons. Although this survivalist impulse initially manifested in renowned and wide-ranging efforts in conservation, officials increasingly pinned their hopes on the specific possibilities of mineral resources.[7] Minerals opened new arenas of activity and impact for the Interior Department, in part because of their increasing value to industrial society and in part because another arm of the federal government seized control over biological resources: the Department of Agriculture. Most significantly, however, minerals (which constituted only 1 to 2 percent of the gross domestic product) mattered because they provided new frontiers, those defined less by territorial limits than terrestrial ones.[8] Minerals were thus not just a straightforward *motive* for expansion, as historians overwhelmingly suggest; they were also a vital *means* for it. They became a way for the Interior Department to venture into a disparate array of zones beyond American formal sovereignty, including territories, foreign nations, and earthly and extraterrestrial expanses, in a recurrent quest to prove bureaucratic worth. It was not just the idea of the frontier or its material bounty that galvanized regenerative processes of U.S. expansion, as scholars suggest, but also a machinery of governance dedicated to managing and extending it—a machinery that refused to fade into the sunset.[9] The histories of U.S. settler colonialism and U.S. global reach, widely understood to be separated by time and space, have thus been institutionally linked.

Interior's operations also fell between benevolence and exploitation, an equivocal modus operandi that U.S. officials consciously hoped would broaden American influence in the world. At its founding, the Interior Department was meant to be a civilian counterpoint to the military violence of federal action bent on securing the continent for American settlers and capitalist interests. It was meant to signal the softer side of American empire. In the twentieth century, this same operation of power proved to be exceptionally well suited to a world growing disenchanted with imperial structures. With the rise of anti-imperialism across the globe, territorial expansion closely associated with both military rule *and* raw material exploitation increasingly fell out of favor. In this new global milieu, the civilian Interior Department appeared once again to be a welcome corrective to U.S. military agencies associated with the nation's many foreign interventions in the Caribbean, Latin America, and Asia. Yet Interior still targeted minerals, themselves sticky symbols of imperial lust. Interior agents worked under the banner of assistance to offer technical expertise on minerals across borders, bringing them into the national fold and global market. Unlike territorial imperialism, this process did not alter political borders but rather worked within the constraints of other forms of sovereignty to bring in, to "interiorize," that which had been exterior.[10] Cooperation, not coercion, was its favored mode. Such activities unfolded alongside but on an even more sweeping scale than well-known material interventions despite the fact that the ends were similar. Because Interior balanced cooperation and exploitation, it confounds favored distinctions between "hard" and "soft" power in American foreign relations. Although scholars have argued that both modes furthered American hegemony, they did so through different means. And the means mattered. The former relied on military might and material intervention, while the latter undertook subtler campaigns rooted in winning hearts and minds. Interior's cooperative approach to extraction ultimately reveals that U.S. global reach could and did merge activities attributed to soft and hard power, taking advantage of a contradictory, illegible status in between them.[11]

Throughout, Interior officials were able to frame their global actions as apolitical because of their grounding in natural resource management. Another key claim of this book is that expansion and environmental management were deeply entangled, a convergence that warrants more sustained dialogue across subfields of history. Diplomatic and environmental historians have until recently struggled to speak to each other despite a shared interest in the way the United States has interacted with and shaped the world—a world configured predominantly by political boundaries in one vision and environmental features in the other. Bridging this gap, scholars have begun to reveal how environmental ideas and processes, from resource scarcity to climate change, became an object of international relations, as well as how environmental conditions shaped and were shaped by American foreign relations.[12] The Interior Department's outward calling provides important inroads between these viewpoints by first challenging the national frame often applied to American environmental management. America's nineteenth-century expansion produced key knowledges and practices of the environmental management apparatus within the American state, an apparatus that, like conservation itself, is all too frequently portrayed as exclusively domestic in orientation.[13] In discharging these duties, including the surveying, parceling, codifying, dispossessing, disposing, settling, and utilizing of land, Interior had by the twentieth century forged a powerful natural resource bureaucracy distributed across many specialized and separate bureaus. The fact that this particular know-how was conditioned by and supportive of the subjugation of indigenous peoples and foreign landscapes would be forgotten over time, as the department came to see and present itself as a neutral clearinghouse of scientific expertise.[14] Environmental management in the American state, despite appearances, was a partial byproduct of expansion.

In the twentieth century, Interior's environmental management would, in turn, shore up new forms of American expansion. The department therefore also makes visible a process by which environment itself became a means and *logic* of intervention. Interior officials claimed that because natural resources crossed borders, so should natural resource experts. Northrop, for example, on United Nations Day, maintained that "natural resources—land, water, and minerals—know no national boundaries."[15] National borders had, after all, become deeply politicized in a twentieth century marked by increasing global commitments to national sovereignty, typified by the founding of the United Nations in 1945. Part of the appeal and longevity of such claims rooted in borderless nature was that they could seem wholly separate from other troublesome categories, such as race and nation. Interior officials could and often did claim something to this effect: People and nations, that was politics. Land, water, and minerals, that was nature. It was this commitment to what scholars have revealed to be a fictive binary between politics and nature that allowed Stewart Udall to make a plea of innocence rooted in the fact that he was merely a minister of natural resources.[16] Ideas about nature and the environment—namely, that their facets were borderless—formed the basis of powerful arguments to depoliticize U.S. border crossings. Moreover, these claims had the effect of deterritorializing the American interior, projecting it onto a global screen. This *global* interior, in common noun form, signals a global vision of American power that Interior officials helped to imagine and implement.

In the process, Interior completed crucial spadework for the expansion of capitalism. This, in turn, has implications for how we understand the capitalist legacies of American empire and related activities that ensued outside the confines of military-backed rule—two contexts in which the

Interior Department was equally at home. In the nineteenth century, the department's routine preparatory efforts on the ground, or spadework, eased the extension of capitalist institutions in new arenas as a necessary precondition for incorporating territory. In the twentieth century, Interior personnel continued twisting the earth into a template for capitalist activity across national borders without altering those borders, instead working within other sovereign contexts to bolster American influence. Throughout, Interior helped survey the land, move the earth, and curtail the risks of investment. Cultivating long-standing rapport with industry, Interior cleared pathways for Phelps Dodge Corporation in Apache lands, Kennecott Copper in Alaska, Bethlehem Steel in Cuba, and Chevron in Sudan, as well as hundreds of oil firms in offshore drilling operations, to name an exemplary few. Although historians have long illuminated how public and private collusions enabled the spread of U.S. and multinational capital at home and abroad, they frequently emphasize the abstract arena of markets and finance. For capitalism to spread, however, landscapes also needed to be known and remade from the earth up, and Interior personnel were among the government agents who did precisely this. Such earthly renovations were vital political mechanisms facilitating American empire and capitalism's expansive unfolding.[17]

However, the department was not just an instrument of capitalist institutions, a point evident in both Interior's regulatory capacities and its detractors in the private sector. Interior had a role regulating the same activities it promoted in the name of broadly defined and constantly shifting public interests—or rather, settler interests—especially but not exclusively within U.S. borders. It set standards and limits regarding parcel sales, mine safety, material rationing, and environmental protection. Corporate representatives overwhelmingly pointed to this type of federal action in public statements, downplaying or omitting corporate reliance on the American government and U.S. taxpayer dollars for help penetrating new frontiers of profitable investment. They offered blistering critiques of state power, accusing Interior of interfering with industrial efficiency through the red tape unfurled by pro-labor, antimonopoly, and environmentalist policies. Such criticisms were misleading—with enemies like the Interior Department, we might ask, who needed *friends*?—but they nevertheless shored up a pervasive myth of antagonism between the sectors. They also helped to usher in free-market ideologies and neoliberal policies that favored deregulation in the late twentieth century, which in turn relieved corporations from obligations to redistribute wealth to the same American taxpayers who had shouldered costs associated with extraction across the globe.[18] Private industry, in sum, opposed not government involvement, but government regulation.

Ultimately, Interior's ambivalent role promoting and regulating capitalism facilitated the fanning out of extractive institutions, arguably in more enduring ways than if it had been a mere functionary of capitalism. This is because Interior's dual disposition allowed both parties to disavow their partnerships when convenient, especially in the wake of crises emanating from unfettered capitalism. For example, when the Teapot Dome scandal of the 1920s and the Santa Barbara oil spill of 1969 attracted rare national attention to public-private collusion, state and corporate representatives each condemned the other party. It was a sleight of hand, a ritual of finger-pointing that deflected attention from the spadework that united them and shared responsibility for problems tied to those activities. Such performances had the effect of simultaneously reassuring the public of state legitimacy and distracting the public from corporate misconduct. Interior's mantle of environmental regulation, meanwhile, often functioned as a bromide facilitating further extraction with troubling economic and ecological impacts. Regions from the Navajo Reservation to Sudan, for example, became sacrifice zones to extractive desires— frequently with the environmental stamp of approval from the Interior Department. If the department had been more overt in its commitments to private interests, it might have inspired less public trust. It might have cast into relief the ways in which public-private collusion in extraction frequently cut against the public good, catalyzing "slow violence," or the incremental tolls of racialized labor, debt crises, bodily contamination, toxic tailings, and global warming, all of which have disproportionately affected marginalized groups both within U.S. borders and across the Global South.[19] In short, public-private collusion was itself a key source of economic inequality and environmental degradation—of asymmetries closely associated with empire that lingered on long after empire's supposed demise.

Although Interior's trajectory over the twentieth century reveals continuities across time, which might suggest the inevitability of expansion, it was in reality highly contingent. Both inside and beyond the walls of the Department of the Interior building, Interior personnel from the top-brass officials to the deskbound pencil pushers made choices that often but not uniformly furthered the expansionist mandate. On the one hand, well-positioned and charismatic officials like the long-serving secretaries Harold L. Ickes in the New Deal and Stewart Udall outlined clear visions for the department's growth to shore up prospects for institutional continuation. They managed to rally political consensus and marshal funds in support of these visions, pulling levers that helped shift the tracks of departmental policy. This is not to suggest that all Interior leaders observed the same problems or posited the same solutions. Some leaders, for example, feared the depletion of resources, while others lamented the withdrawal of resources from private development. Nevertheless, both viewpoints overwhelmingly sanctioned pursuing new zones of extraction, a process that enabled conserving resources *at home* and bolstering private development *elsewhere.* On the other hand, and on a broader and more pervasive scale, Interior personnel across the sprawling organizational chart saw ways to apply their existing expertise in new contexts. To return to Northrop's evocative comments on United Nations Day, this "know-how" had been "conditioned" by expansion itself. The repertoire of expansion, handed down with modification from generation to generation, eventually garnered an appearance of technical and scientific neutrality that disguised its outward disposition.[20] The gradualness of this process also helps to explain how Interior personnel could so consistently frame and evaluate their interventions in benevolent terms. The extractive agenda, far from being understood as political maneuvering or exploitation, frequently appeared natural and good.

This contingency is also evident in the ways that Interior consistently engaged and responded to a broader cultural field defined by grassroots movements. In the twentieth century, the U.S. government confronted actors and organizations—anti-imperialist, Third World nationalist, environmentalist, and indigenous—that challenged and shaped extractive agendas in different ways. Public opinion mattered in the enactment of policy. Anti-imperialist critiques that gained traction across the globe in the 1930s and 1940s, for example, compelled U.S. decision makers to craft policies that aligned, at least nominally, with self-determination. The rise of a more militant strand of Third World nationalism in the 1960s made extractive operations overseas more tenuous and helped incentivize a turn to the continental shelf as a zone of mineral activity. A growing environmental movement, responding to disasters offshore and elsewhere, positioned extraction as ecological degradation, inspiring Interior officials to promote a satellite that would combat transborder ecological problems (while quietly prospecting minerals from the sky). Later, indigenous social movements fighting to protect their reservations' minerals brought greater scrutiny to the Interior Department's methods. Interior officials and technicians, in short, did not operate unilaterally or without friction.

The Interior Department's bid for survival through growth also came into conflict with other agencies of the federal government. Chief among these competing agencies was the frequently analyzed Department of Defense. Interior had systematically trailed the military, usurping functions from the Indian Service to territorial management, much to the chagrin of military officials. As arms of the government vied for funding and prestige, overlapping jurisdictions caused friction and galvanized campaigns for legitimacy. Yet defense agencies and other features of the military-industrial complex have attracted far more scrutiny than Interior for embedding the United States in foreign spaces.[21] Interior's struggles, meanwhile, were in many ways representative of those faced by other civilian agencies. The Department of Agriculture, for example, also jockeyed for power and funds, taking on new arenas of activity at home *and* abroad. It disseminated personnel in developing nations as part of technical assistance programs.[22] It is unsurprising that the Interior Department and Department of Agriculture, claiming expertise over different natural resources—roughly, mineral and biological—should have such interwoven fates. The Department of Agriculture had originated as an offshoot of the Interior Department in 1862, as would many other agencies.[23] In this sense, the fate of Interior—the pressure it faced to grow outward or risk obsolescence—is one consonant with that of the broader federal bureaucracy.

However, the Interior Department is also peculiar, a status that becomes apparent when turning to the global comparative frame. The Interior

Department in the United States has historically performed a radically different set of functions than the Ministries of the Interior across Europe and the formerly colonized world, on which it was directly modeled. Ministries of Interior have, for example, ensured matters of law and security, while the U.S. variant instead came to oversee natural resources and indigenous affairs, a distinction shared with other settler states like Canada and Australia (though the departments in these nations were eventually disbanded).[24] In the case of the United States and other settler states, the problems posed by settler colonialism, namely the capitalist accumulation and settlement of land within established territorial borders, required idiosyncratic mechanisms of governance. The origins and early undertakings of the U.S. Interior Department, in turn, unfolded alongside the broader centralization and professionalization of state bureaucracies in the late nineteenth century.[25] The Interior Department in the United States therefore *was* different from most other departments in the U.S. government and most other departments in governments across the world, for it had performed material and ideological work to domesticate the nation's settler expansionism. Consequently, the Interior Department and other peculiarities of settler colonial governance represent potentially fruitful sites for comparing empires around the world and considering ways in which America's expansionist trajectory, while frequently congruous with other empires in scope and content, was also distinct from them in certain aspects of its implementation.[26]

The story that follows begins with the nineteenth-century continental expansion that led some to herald the closing of the frontier. After Interior completed the task of parceling land, containing indigenous populations, and mapping natural resources needed to ensure the settlement of the continent, conservationists and other critics called for the department's closure on grounds that it was harmful to the nation. Interior survived the tumult by embracing this burgeoning ethos of conservation, while also following the U.S. military to overseas territories in the Pacific and Caribbean. In the wake of the Teapot Dome scandal, Interior underwent further renovation, and in the New Deal, Ickes enlarged Interior's mineral technocracy and assumed full authority over U.S. territories and island possessions. A crucible of global war merged these two agendas, as the U.S. government coveted minerals—rebranded "strategic minerals"—in territories such as Alaska and the Philippines. In the process, Interior officials honed an approach to minerals rooted in technical assistance. Building on this repertoire, Interior launched "cooperative" mineral programs throughout Latin American republics at the outbreak of the Second World War. Under the auspices of technical cooperation, Interior agents completed reconnaissance work on minerals that eventually became enfolded into the war effort, an activity that fit uncomfortably alongside the recent Good Neighbor Policy of nonintervention in the Western Hemisphere. U.S. officials built on these earlier arguments in the continuation of a mineral agenda in postwar international development with the launch of the Point Four program. Interior personnel oversaw geological reconnaissance and assisted American and multinational companies in participating nations. To justify departmental involvements in extraction abroad, Interior leaders argued that minerals belonged to all *and* were dangerously misunderstood by primitive peoples.

The second half of this book turns to zones that defied traditional understandings of territorial sovereignty. The Interior Department added the continental shelf to its jurisdiction in 1945. Attentions to this mineral-rich expanse did not crest until increasing politicization in mineral-rich regions throughout the Third World made a move offshore more desirable. Interior officials, like Stewart Udall, operated in both contexts, ambivalently linking the Third World and the move offshore. Udall, despite his vaunted environmental reputation, pushed for the intensification of offshore drilling operations until the infamous Santa Barbara oil spill cast doubt on departmental credentials, leading to the creation of the rival Environmental Protection Agency. In the age of the "new frontier," the Interior Department pursued minerals in outer space. After initial attention on lunar minerals, officials developed a satellite that could view Earth's resources and the remaining frontiers of the earth—particularly in nations participating in international development. Although Interior billed Landsat as a tool for developing nations to combat poverty, the world's largest extractive firms used the resulting images in far greater number.

This book ends with a shift in perspective to a grassroots social movement that directly challenged the Interior Department's sweeping ambitions. This change in viewpoint from the satellites'-eye view of Interior planners to a ground-level view of those impacted by the plans allows for a more nuanced picture of the halting contingency that underscored Interior's expansionism. With the escalation of the global energy crisis, Interior attentions turned once again to indigenous lands, revealed to hold vast amounts of uranium, coal, oil, and natural gas. One coalition of indigenous nations, self-labeled as the "Indian OPEC," mounted a resistance that challenged the Interior Department's natural resource management and insisted upon a shared history of exploitation between Native Americans and members of the Third World. Challenged by social movements like the Indian OPEC, and losing control of its mineral technocracy with the creation of the Department of Energy, the Interior Department fragmented and ultimately ceded much power. The ascendant Reagan administration further dismantled Interior through the appointment of the notorious and antigovernment James G. Watt to secretary of the interior. At the same time, Reagan redirected funds from civilian agencies to defense agencies, which would become the favored instrument for securing American mineral interests in the ensuing decades, most famously in the Middle East.

After a century and a half of existence, the Interior Department had achieved nearly global coverage. When the wide-ranging zones of Interior Department activities are brought into the same frame, one begins to see a pattern: Interior furthered American hegemony and capitalist extraction. Yet its actions across the globe easily fell from view both for contemporaries and historians. This invisibility was a partial result of the way in which the United States successfully upheld and, when convenient, disregarded apparent distinctions between foreign and domestic, exploitation and benevolence, and politics and nature. Such contradictions created blind spots facilitating a largely unchecked operation of American power. Interior was a domestic agency, so how could it shape the foreign? The department was civilian, so why would it inflict harm? It dealt with nature, so what could it have to do with politics? What becomes clear when the Interior Department is a prism of U.S. power in the modern era is that these contradictions were not incidental to the push of American power beyond its sovereign threshold, or to the spread of capitalism across the globe, but rather instrumental to them both.

CHAPTER ONE

The Closing of the Interior

The task of developing the immense resources of the archipelago
appeals most congenially to a nation descended from pioneers.

George F. Becker, U.S. geologist in the Philippines

AMERICA'S MID-NINETEENTH-CENTURY expansion was vexing, or at least Henry Foote thought so in the spring of 1849. From the perspective of the brazen senator from Mississippi, who would gain notoriety for drawing a pistol in defense of slavery in a heated congressional debate over the Compromise of 1850, the nation's expansive unfolding had advanced at a pace that far exceeded the capacities of the federal government to oversee it. In just three years, the United States had acquired a continental land base spanning from the Atlantic to the Pacific through the annexation of Texas, negotiations for Oregon, and war with Mexico and indigenous nations. "Some immense space of territory," Foote summarized, "is every year or two falling into our hands by some treaty effected with these children of the forest, which speedily becomes subject to all our general regulations for the disposition of the public domain." Foote left unuttered the state and settler-driven violence that belied this enlarged domain, but he did observe a fundamental problem of governance at its heart. The nation had grown from a population of 3 million to 20 million, with a "proportionate increase" in the nation's "territorial extent" and its attendant "resources." He thus reasoned that there must be "expansion in the governmental machinery itself."[1] On the evening of March 3, 1849, Congress would create such a federal machinery—it would give birth to the U.S. Department of the Interior.

One hundred years after the founding of the Interior Department, one of its leaders would obliquely reference this origin story in justifying the work of the department in a wider world. Vernon Northrop pointed to Interior's history managing the undeveloped West as explanation for its new role in the undeveloped world; its task, he offered, was once again to bring about "the opening of a new frontier."[2] This chapter begins in the nineteenth century in order to investigate these claims about Interior's past and its implied reverberations in the twentieth-century world. Charting the birth of the Interior Department in the wake of the Mexican-American War and its messy bureaucratic evolution in the first five decades of operation reveals that the Interior Department—which had come to appear as the innermost arm of the American state—was born *of* and *for* American expansionism. The Interior Department was, in reality, always *exterior*.[3] Interior oversaw indigenous peoples and expropriated lands that were, in important ways, *foreign*. It came to appear as a singularly domestic entity through forceful narratives of nation building that made the continental projection of the United States seem inevitable and the persistent racial and gendered hierarchies that made indigenous sovereignty appear to be of a lesser order than European sovereignty.[4] Throughout, Interior's relationships with both the military and private interests were enabling conditions, as well as sources of formidable tension. First, trailing behind the U.S. Army, Interior transformed lands expropriated from indigenous peoples and Mexico into properly American ones, a consciously civilian antidote to military power. Playing the self-styled role of passive administrator, Interior helped the nation to portray its forceful extension of sovereign power in the benevolent light of a civilizing mission. Second, Interior cleared the way for white settlers and private interests, creating conditions favorable in once-foreign lands to capitalist activities ranging from the development of individual small farms to the construction of railroads and the extraction of minerals.[5]

As America's continental expansion seemed more and more assured at the turn of the twentieth century, the Interior Department entered a period of uncertainty. When Frederick Jackson Turner heralded the close of the American frontier, however inaccurately, he was not just describing the culmination of America's westward settlement, as intended.[6] He was also implicitly memorializing the life's work of the Interior Department. Through its various bureaus, the Interior Department parceled the land, contained the indigenous populations, and mapped the resources that eventually signaled to Turner the end of an era. Even the 1890 census that prompted Turner's elegy had been compiled and distributed at the command of the secretary of the interior. Put differently, the humdrum of settler colonialism, its daily exertions and happenings, was the lot of the Interior Department. If the advance of settlement posed an existential crisis for the nation, one that scholars argue partially redirected American imperial ambition from the continent to overseas territories, then it also posed an organizational crisis for the department born of and for expansion.[7] In this moment of transformation, the Interior Department drew criticisms for being out of joint with a new era defined by different national interests, including the conservation of natural resources. Some critics, like conservationist Gifford Pinchot, went so far as to call for the closure of the Office of the Secretary.

Yet Interior persisted. Its leaders ensured institutional survival by redirecting the skill set of expansion to new contexts. First and most centrally, Interior leaders embraced—and Interior became the new institutional home of—the conservation movement. Although Interior had once maintained equal roles in population and natural resource issues, it increasingly consolidated expertise over natural resources and minerals in particular, which provided a more capacious arena in which to exert an institutional power devoted more and more to extraction. The fact that this resource "know-how" was conditioned by and supportive of the subjugation of indigenous peoples and lands would become almost entirely forgotten over time. Second, and related to the first, Interior personnel became indispensable to America's new projects of empire, beginning with the Philippines and Cuba. An exploration of Interior's role in insular affairs and resource surveys, particularly through the experiences of the geologist George F. Becker on the ground in the Philippines, reveals this constancy of purpose. Ultimately, although the Interior Department evolved from a constellation of clerks to a streamlined natural resource bureaucracy over the course of half a century, it also retained the outward disposition of its origins and early operations, allowing its staff to be enlisted to new fronts of U.S. global reach. Interior therefore reveals important continuities between continental expansion, conservation, and overseas imperialism stemming from the United States' deep attachment to settler colonial governance. Institutions like the Interior Department laid important foundations for the domestication of settler colonialism in the first place, rendering the nation's original empire effectively invisible. Interior helped uphold the fiction of an inward-looking national self, while the fiction of the inward-looking self, in turn, would make Interior's ongoing expansionism so difficult to see. In the end, Interior's domesticity, rather than its imperial projection, was its most astonishing achievement, for that domesticity was the product of systematic and painstaking efforts to disavow the U.S. settler expansion it oversaw.

Expansion

Before and after the founding of the American republic, white settlers fought and negotiated with indigenous peoples to claim land for settlement, but the process of expansion had yet to be backed by the full force of a system of governance. The British government had even attempted and failed to place limits on westward movement in the years leading up to the American Revolution. After securing independence from Britain, the new "Americans" expropriated land with increasing levels of coordination and violence, clearing pathways to white property ownership and capitalist development. They did so out of a faith in the racial, religious, and gendered superiority of European-descended settlers to indigenous peoples, but also out of a belief that indigenous peoples did not properly utilize the land. Western rationales that reduced nonhuman nature to potential economic gain and disregarded other approaches to nature as mere incompetence were therefore key drivers of settler expansion.[8] When hunger for lands suitable to cotton plantations, which would run on labor extracted from enslaved peoples, and gold mining in indigenous lands swept the new republic, the more locally driven process of encroachment gave way to federal engines of expansion. The southerner Andrew Jackson ran for president in 1828 on a settler-expansionist platform and, upon winning the election, petitioned Congress to advance legislation to dislodge indigenous peoples from ancestral lands in Georgia, Mississippi, and Alabama. This agenda materialized in the Indian Removal Act.[9] In the judicial branch, Chief Justice John Marshall issued a series of Supreme Court rulings, including *Cherokee Nation v. Georgia* (1831), which both enabled and constrained the process of removal by defining indigenous peoples, most equivocally, as "domestic, dependent nations."[10] The status upheld that indigenous peoples maintained a semi-sovereign authority that required the U.S. government to secure treaties to acquire land for its eventual disposal to white settlers. This combination of executive order, legislative action, and judicial decision catalyzed the removal of the Cherokee, Choctaw, Creek, Chickasaw, and Seminoles in the lethal Trail of Tears and ushered in an era of federal oversight of settler colonialism.[11]

This nascent federal apparatus of dispossession was in place when Manifest Destiny, the belief in America's providential right to span the continent, reached a fever pitch in the 1840s. A new order of expansionists in the Democratic party, including would-be president James K. Polk, eyed regions to the west in which to extend their prized institution of slavery, first in the newly independent Republic of Texas and eventually in distant California. Polk and the expansionists routed the protests of abolitionists against slavery's extension and Americans loath to incorporate nonwhite masses into the national framework, beginning a swift and comprehensive land grab culminating in the blood and bullets of the Mexican-American War. Despite the dogged resistance of the Mexican Army and indigenous nations that participated as belligerents on their side, the U.S. Army secured Mexican surrender in the Treaty of Guadalupe Hidalgo on February 2, 1848. The combination of the earlier Texas Annexation of 1845 and Oregon Treaty of 1846 with the new Mexican cession of 1848 added 1.2 million square miles to the United States (the Louisiana Purchase of 1803, by comparison, had added 820,000 square miles)—effectively projecting U.S. sovereignty across the continent.[12]

Almost immediately, the federal government apparatus began buckling under the weight of this radically augmented territory, as well as the people and resources attached to it. Expansion was especially taxing on the different cabinet-level departments.[13] Robert J. Walker, the proslavery expansionist from Pennsylvania who had helped propel the war and had been

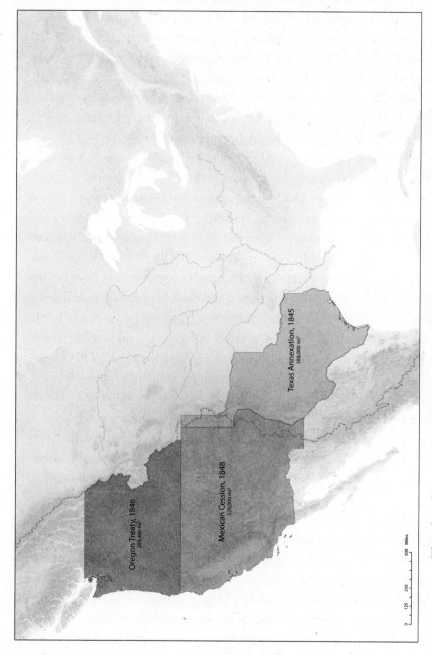

The enlarged domain of the United States leading up to the Interior Department's founding in 1849.

named the new secretary of the Treasury, pleaded with Congress for assistance. The General Land Office under his supervision, Walker claimed, faced an onslaught of legal battles emerging from heated land claims in the Mexican cession. The situation was particularly acute in mineral lands throughout New Mexico and California, where gold had been discovered several months earlier near Sutter's Mill, initiating a frenzied gold rush. Walker feared that arbitrating these land claims would lead to an endless parade of corruption charges aimed at his division.[14] Other concerns emerged for the leadership of the Indian Service under the War Department. A great deal more personnel, the secretary explained, would be required to conduct ongoing relations with American Indians of lands acquired from Texas and Mexico, a population estimated at 124,000 people. Many of these nations, including the Kiowa, Comanche, and Apache, would continue to assert sovereignty following a war that had been pivotally shaped by their involvement.[15] The Pension Office, meanwhile, was similarly overwhelmed by the responsibilities in paying out dividends due to the war's veterans, who had fought, killed, and given limbs to secure the nation's juridical reach beyond extant borders.[16] In short, continental expansion created a logistical and organizational problem. It had catalyzed a hurried piling on of federal responsibilities.

For Henry Foote, like other senators intent on inaugurating a new federal department, this vast increase of territory at the midcentury clearly required a new mode of governance. But in calling for a new department to manage the "domestic" or "interior" matters of the nation, they were also rethinking the relationship between foreign and domestic in American governance—or rather, they were calling attention to the gradual process by which this relationship had already begun to shift. Since the founding of the nation, domestic affairs had fallen largely under state rather than federal jurisdiction, even though the first Congress in 1787 had briefly considered installing a "Home Department" in the federal government.[17] By 1849, the bifurcation of foreign and domestic affairs along lines of federal and state power had largely, though not completely, been etched into the government system. For example, the pro–Interior Department senator from Virginia, James Murray Mason, pointed out that there already was a clear precedent for certain domestic matters falling under the discretion of the national level: the General Land Office and the Patent

Office, both proposed to be brought under the new department, and the Post Office, which was briefly slated to move there, dealt in domestic issues. Mason concluded that matters of "domestic interest" should fall under federal authority. Ultimately, part of what allowed the Interior Department legislation to move so quickly and seemingly without vigorous debate through the Senate and House was the fact that it recombined existing offices in one place rather than conjuring new mechanisms of government out of thin air. Critics, like the noted legislator and staunch defender of states' rights and slavery, John C. Calhoun, still found this rearrangement a distressing enlargement of federal power. The proposed department, he lamented, would cover "everything upon the face of God's earth," bringing together tasks "without the slightest connection."[18]

For Calhoun, who would lose the argument, the department was an ill-conceived repository for mismatched functions. Many historians have shared in Calhoun's evaluation. They have concluded that the Interior Department lacked internal coherence, a result of its hasty conception. Historian Leonard White, for example, maintained that the sprawling department was a "great miscellany" with "no semblance of unity."[19] Such disunity has all but cemented the popular conviction that the department did not enact a coherent mission or marshal meaningful power in the broader system of American governance. In truth, the Interior Department was not the most carefully devised state institution. It emerged at a time before American governance was a meaningfully organized bureaucracy.[20] Government officials hardly warranted the label "bureaucrats" in the context of a system strung together by Congress and a light distribution of clerks. Instead, government employees in the nineteenth century worked frequently on the local level, exacting fees for their individual services on behalf of the state. This fee-based system was, at the end of the century, supplanted by a new salaried and centralized form of federal power.[21] Even the first secretary of the interior, Thomas Ewing, had to admit befuddlement as to what the new department's full purpose actually was, since it had not been fully fleshed out by the rushed legislation. Yet, importantly, he also recognized that departmental duties would be organized around a central problem. "The number of private land claims, and questions arising out of our Indian intercourse," Ewing observed, "will be also greatly increased by the extension of our settlements to

Oregon and the accession of California and New Mexico."[22] Officials calling for the founding of the department were therefore not so much outlining a systematic vision for the future as they were responding to pressing stimuli in the moment. The stimuli influencing legislators were decisive: the exigencies of settler colonialism called for an apparatus to oversee its daily work.

These debates might seem to confirm an entrenched truism about the Department of the Interior—that it was and has been an internally directed arm of the American state. Yet a deeper analysis reveals contradiction at its founding. Beyond the fact that Interior was conditioned by an overt act of foreign relations—the Mexican-American War—the central purpose of the department once formed was to bring in and metabolize the territory that had been outside the nation just months before. Yesterday it was Mexico, today the United States of America. In short, calling Interior's agenda "domestic" worked to cover over the way in which the nation was venturing into the "foreign." It naturalized one of America's most systematic and violent projections of power beyond extant borders by renaming it the "interior." Interior would have a lead role in bridging the gap between foreign and domestic, in banishing the alternate sovereignties that had so recently been attached to the expropriated land. Put differently, in order for the American nation to truly span the continent at midcentury, in accordance with the legal declaration, the cultural and material landscape needed to be reordered. Interior therefore also narrowed the distance between theory and practice in settler colonialism.

Interior's two key capacities, in managing land and indigenous populations, straddled interior and exterior. First, after decades of painstaking negotiations and war, lands expropriated from other sovereign nations, including indigenous peoples and Mexico, were brought into singular unity as the public domain. The United States had long called lands expropriated from indigenous peoples the "public domain," but after an unequivocal continental war for territory, that designation became an ultimate euphemism for empire.[23] The fact that many of these regions, including Arizona, Dakota, Idaho, Montana, New Mexico, Utah, Washington, and Wyoming, would continue to be understood as territorial holdings overseen by territorial governors throughout the nineteenth century highlights the ongoing in-betweenness of their geopolitical status.[24] The process of disposing of or "privatizing" the public domain in these territories and eventual states would be haltingly slow. Guided by the Jeffersonian ideal of small farm plots, the General Land Office worked to populate the western expanse with white settlers. Through its network of land officers, surveyors, and funds receivers, the General Land Office "disposed" of land in the public domain. The Homestead Act of 1862 provided a legislative imperative to distribute acreage for individual families, "land for the landless." A national patchwork of farms was the ideal among government officials for its potential to bring once-foreign land into the fold of a unified nation, the American home.[25]

In disposing of land, the department both responded to and facilitated the advancement of private interests in the region. From the outset, it struggled to balance the regulation and promotion of capitalism. Minerals, in which Interior had a lead role, represented one ambivalent link between government and industry. Interior oversaw a transition from an era of government ownership of mines to private ownership, leasing and selling lands rich in minerals like copper, lead, or other ores to private operators.[26] Interior leaders supported extractive expansion on grounds that that land was an "unlimited" asset; extraction added valued materials to the national economy and propelled westward settlement.[27] Following the gold rush of 1849, countless operators advanced into the timber- and mineral-rich corridors of the West at a greater pace than the government machinery could regulate—spurred on by railroad interests desirous of materials to haul across an ever-expanding network of rails.[28] Some Interior officials eventually came to lament how ill prepared they were to regulate these same activities, which prevented some white settlers from accessing individual plots. Interior personnel also fretted over who was eligible to enter a mining claim, an issue that quickly dovetailed with citizenship and national belonging. In 1852, for example, the Interior secretary reported, "I beg leave to repeat the recommendations . . . that the privilege of mining be restricted to citizens of the United States."[29] The precedent of federal permissiveness helped to initiate an avalanche of mining interests that outpaced the juridical regime. The effect was a veritable giveaway. Mining acts of 1866 and 1872 did little to restrain the influx of extraction throughout the Mexican cession.[30]

Second, Interior also had growing jurisdiction over indigenous people and lands, which were targeted by the same private interests the department was helping to advance. Just as gold fever underscored the removal policies of the 1830s, the gold rush in California in the 1840s launched avaricious policies that resulted in the genocide of California Indians whose lands fell in the bull's-eye of the storied mineral veins. Decades later, the U.S. government and mining interests, including Phelps Dodge Corporation, targeted gold in the Sioux lands of the Black Hills and copper in the Apache lands of Arizona.[31] Some Interior Indian officials, driven by racism and greed, exploited their wards for personal gain, a legacy of the corruption stemming from the fact that many Indian agent positions were the product of patronage systems in governance.[32] Others watched such developments in the West with disgust, rebuking "evil-disposed whites" bent on "annihilating" the "defenceless (sic) Indians with impunity."[33] Eventually, calls to protect indigenous peoples from encroaching settlers reinforced the belief that they should be relocated to designated zones as part of the reservation system, a process spearheaded by the U.S. Army. Military campaigns frequently yielded racial violence and atrocities, most notably in the arduous "Long Walk" of the Navajo to Bosque Redondo, New Mexico, and the militia-led massacre of a Cheyenne village in Sand Creek, Colorado—even though the U.S. Army had been designated as a protector.[34] With remarkable consistency, the federal government removed indigenous peoples from lands known (through the efforts of surveying by army and Interior personnel and private interests) to be arable or mineral-rich to lands with less perceived potential—all on grounds that it was for their own safety.[35]

The push to relocate indigenous people on reservations had itself emerged from a shift in Indian policy from more martial to more administrative ways of managing dispossession. When Congress moved the Indian Service from the War Department to the Interior Department, they did so out of a growing conviction that "Christianity, knowledge, and civilization," as Robert Walker had summarized it, rather than military force should be the means of subduing the population. In Walker's view, like many others, Indian affairs now constituted a "domestic" matter and therefore should no longer remain the purview of the military.[36] Less associated with the "fortified outposts" of U.S. military-driven continental activity, the now-civilian Indian Service became the dominant arm of the nation's civilizing mission toward Native Americans.[37] This civilian-led civilizing project intensified under President Ulysses S. Grant's "Peace Policy," itself a response to calls in civil society for humanitarian reform of Indian affairs that, in conjunction with 1871 congressional legislation ending treaty making with indigenous nations, facilitated the forcible removal of indigenous nations from ancestral lands to reservations or their relegation to ancestral lands of greatly diminished size.[38] In superintending these reservations, the Indian Service quadrupled in size in the two decades after the Civil War.[39] Through mundane correspondence and paperwork, the civilian employees did the clerical labor of reservation building, a process aided over time by improved methods of registration, categorization, and enumeration—documenting, for example, the amount of bushels cultivated, clothing worn, and butter churned. Throughout, the Census Bureau, moved under the Interior Department at its founding, indexed the changing shape of America's population-settlement nexus.[40] The mundane efforts of Indian Service employees to register and relocate Native Americans worked in tandem with the brute force of the military campaigns to give the new indigenous land base its diminished and widely scattered shape.

Yet as the civilian Interior Department usurped functions previously overseen by the War Department, tensions arose and tempers flared. Army officials were not so content to have their jurisdiction in Indian affairs trampled on in service of the humanitarian reforms sweeping Washington. An 1878 *Harper's Weekly* magazine cover caricatured the growing acrimony between the Interior Department and the War Department over Indian affairs.[41] In the woodcut image, Interior Secretary Carl Schurz, a German-born reformer and erstwhile Republican senator for Missouri, and General Philip Sheridan, a veteran of the Civil War and Indian Wars, stand on either side of an unflappable American Indian carrying both a peace pipe (on the Interior side) and a tomahawk (on the War side). Schurz and Sheridan, with hands firmly in pockets, grimace at each other over their would-be ward, signaling the competing approaches to Indian affairs. Skulking behind Sheridan in the doorway is General William Tecumseh Sherman. Sherman, the man who had set Atlanta ablaze in the Union Army's march to the sea before devoting his life to fighting Indians, was one of the loudest advocates for the return of Indian affairs to the War Department. In 1876, Sherman had argued that the army commander could oversee the matter "in a better manner" than the civilian agents of Interior "because he has soldiers to support his authority." He added that contrary to popular perception, the army did not want war. In the occasional cases where "natural hostility" broke out between the clashing cultures, the army merely responded with its considerable skill in pacification. The army, Sherman insisted, though not convincingly enough to elicit the transfer of Indian affairs, had "always been the best friends the Indians have had."[42]

The infighting between the civilian and military arms of the state also bled into the realm of government surveying, another vital feature of continental expansion. The practice of surveying had long been a fixture of the U.S. Army, which investigated territories with parties of surveyors. This was a task shared in part with the General Land Office, which parceled land through surveyors-general. In the late 1860s, government officials began commissioning a greater number of civilian scientists to join survey parties to explore the American space in the making. A one-armed veteran of the Civil War, John Wesley Powell, was one larger-than-life agent of this errand, having made a name for himself by charting the treacherous mountain passes and the rapids of the Colorado River. In the mid-1870s, advocates in government and the professional sciences, including the National Academy of Sciences, lobbied for a new arm of surveying to be nested under the Interior Department. Powell himself supported civilian oversight, finding that military escorts heightened hostilities in Indian lands. He ultimately concluded that credentialed experts fitted with tools of science, not soldiers armed with "more terrible implements of destruction than ever before known," should be the ones tasked with exploring the land and resources of the nation.[43] The U.S. Army was angered at the usurpation of yet another of its key functions, one of perceived importance to ongoing military campaigns against Indians, by the upstart Interior Department.[44] Animosities even mounted *within* the Interior Department, as the General Land Office feared part of its surveyor-general work would be ushered into a rival bureau.[45]

Despite the criticisms, the civilian model prevailed. The U.S. Geological Survey was inaugurated in the Interior Department on March 3,

In "The New Indian War," Secretary of the Interior Carl Schurz, left, and General Philip Sheridan, right, spar over Indian affairs while General William T. Sherman looks on. A peace pipe is in the Indian's pocket on Schurz's side and a tomahawk is in the pocket on Sheridan's side. 1878. Harpers Weekly Collection, Prints and Photographs, Library of Congress.

1879, thirty years to the day after Interior was founded. This Geological Survey, headed by the Yale-educated civilian scientist Clarence King, would not only shore up white settlement through topographical mapping of landscapes but also the extraction of minerals on a vast scale through geological mapping of soils and rocks. Although government geologists explicitly aimed to identify minerals suited to economic exploitation, members of private industry threw in criticisms to match those of the army and General Land Office. Alexander Agassiz, a scientist and son of copper-mining magnate Louis Agassiz, argued that the work of surveying could be done much better by private industry: "There are not five hundred people or institutions whom they will do any good."[46] However, government geologists did help provide invaluable information to private industry, a point even Agassiz conceded decades later. Although much had been made of America's natural resource endowment, the Geological Survey aided mining investments by giving a clearer sense of resources' location and quality. Enlisting camp hands, "native" laborers, and teams of mules—all subsidized by federal revenues—these geologists conducted investigations that ranged from broad-strokes "exploration" to fine-grain "reconnaissance."[47] The Geological Survey became a relentless producer of geological knowledge for private industry with its myriad maps and reports. In the decades following the founding of the U.S. Geological Survey, the United States became a leading producer of virtually every mineral used in industry, an era that coincided with the nation's rise to manufacturing supremacy. The Geological Survey, in turn, would receive international renown for its part in shaping this industrial ascendance.[48]

Many arms of the Interior Department joined in the effort to help with the extension of white settlers and private industries from sea to shining sea, even if the relationships between and among them were at times uneasy. The Geological Survey and General Land Office, sometime competitors and sometime collaborators, worked with the Indian Service to define the shrinking parameters of indigenous reservations.[49] At the same time, Interior agencies that seemed to have nothing to do with expansion also contributed in important ways. In managing the new national parks, for example, including the new 2 million acre Yellowstone National Park founded in 1872, Interior helped to cleave terrains deemed aesthetically and culturally significant to the nation from the protections of indigenous sovereignty. The national parks opened these lands for westward-moving settlers and eastern tourists while foreclosing them to traditional use by indigenous peoples such as the Havasupai and Blackfeet, creating what the Lakota Sioux leader Black Elk had called "little islands" of the federal government. Indian Affairs agents aided the park administrators by arguing that the Havasupai needed to be separated from the Grand Canyon and their ancestral hunting grounds to learn the more "civilized" practices of agriculture.[50] Throughout, the Indian Office adopted increasingly sophisticated methods of compelling assimilation, from the management of Indian schools to measuring the intimate details of reservation life, to instill Christian values and capitalist virtues.[51]

These interagency protocols of dispossession were well underway when the Dawes Severalty Act of 1887 initiated one of the final and most comprehensive indigenous land grabs of the century. The legislation, also known as the General Allotment Act, authorized the parceling of indigenous communal holdings into individual plots before absorbing the "surplus" into the public domain. Proponents claimed that allotment would stem the tide of military conflict and private interests on indigenous lands. Yet the allotment policy was enclosure on a vast scale.[52] Although congressional action in allotment opened Native American lands to exploitation by white settlers, lawmakers did help curtail wholesale expropriation by establishing a system of leasing, which slowed free-for-all prospecting on Indian lands. New laws also limited federal or private action without tribal consent. However, the formal elevation of tribal consent turned out to be a mixed blessing. U.S. officials introduced "tribal councils," or federally defined indigenous governments, in part to smooth the process of land transfer by creating a legal entity with which to negotiate. The existence of tribal councils had the effect of rooting treaties and mining and timber leases more firmly in the rule of law.[53] All told, allotment dispossessed 90 million acres of indigenous lands, or two-thirds of the existing base. Looking back with nostalgia on this period, President Theodore Roosevelt would call this legislative overhaul a "mighty pulverizing engine to break up the tribal mass," clearing the way for the engines of industrialization.[54] The ends in allotment were quite as decisive and violent as previous military campaigns, even if the means were more banal and bureaucratic. These efforts, in turn, altered the landscape in ways that would lead some Interior personnel to declare an end to the American frontier.

Conservation

The United States' ascent to continental supremacy seemed nearly assured, according to the census of 1890. Calculating the rapidly growing settler population, a cumulative effect of Interior's efforts to spur westward movement and industrialization, had become such a backbreaking task that mere mortals could no longer do it. Instead, for the first time, Interior's census workers turned to an enigmatic new technology of population management, the Hollerith tabulator. This tabulating machine, the basis for the modern computer, would not have existed without the Interior Department or continental expansion; it was invented, patented, and first used by Interior personnel for the purposes of measuring nation building across expropriated lands.[55] Although the findings of the technologically elevated census were vast and varied, the omnibus section entitled "Progress of the Nation" would become its most binding legacy. This attachment to the overall findings formed the basis for Turner's famed analysis. Using an amalgam of statistics and maps, the report aimed to give concrete shape to the otherwise abstract process of American settlement in the century since the first census.[56] At the opening of the analysis, the superintendents observed that a frontier line no longer existed on the map. Registering this apparent shift, the census workers opted for celebration. They praised how nearly 2 million square miles of land had been at last "redeemed from the wilderness and brought into the service of man."[57]

The claim by the report, and later by Turner, that the frontier disappeared was deeply misguided. Most glaringly, the process of indigenous land dispossession was still ongoing, while white settlement itself remained uneven. Other Homestead Acts would be needed to spur on the latter through the early 1900s.[58] Moreover, when the frontier allegedly closed, public lands remained at 586 million acres, and even grew by 200 million acres by 1905.[59] However, in subsequent years, the idea of the frontier's closing captured the popular imagination, and Interior officials shared in many of these assumptions. Since the founding of the Interior Department, "frontier" had been an important symbol.[60] For Interior leadership at the turn of the twentieth century, celebratory overtures for eliminating the frontier were beset with anxious realization. The Interior Department's annual report of 1896 conveyed this mix of pride and anxiety over the work. Although the secretary of the interior boasted of the "great strides" taken to diminish the public domain, he also cautioned that lawmakers must "consider the question seriously before disposing of any more large areas of the public domain." He elaborated, "If the rate of disposition of the last thirteen years is continued for thirteen years to come, there will be little of the public domain outside of Alaska remaining in the possession of the Government."[61] The implication was that with the successful execution of its mandate to privatize the public domain, the shape of Interior's arena of activity would also shrink.[62] With the closing of the frontier, Interior's central capacities in the disposal of land became a potential liability.

The limits of continental expansion also helped illuminate limits of natural resources, a revelation that helped launch the conservation movement. Conservationism, an ethos with many intellectual sources, found well-positioned champions in President Theodore Roosevelt and his stalwart crusader of scientific forestry, Gifford Pinchot. It mandated rational planning to promote the wise and efficient use of land and natural resources—a multifaceted endeavor that encompassed agricultural, livestock, timber, water, and mineral resources.[63] Many conservationists and preservationists, like Pinchot and Sierra Club founder John Muir, exuded righteous indignation about the framework of disposal that dominated in the federal government in general and the Interior Department in particular. In the advance of settlers and private interests across the continent, conservationists increasingly saw profligate waste, while downplaying colonial violence. The Roosevelt administration implemented policies in the early 1900s that aimed to put an end to the "haphazard public law of the previous century"—precisely the framework under which the Interior Department had discharged its duties.[64] In short, the services Interior provided in settler colonialism would appear, in the moment of its apparent completion, to be both an anachronism and anathema.

In this changing tide, the Interior Department faced deep criticism and even calls for the abolition of key offices. Conservationists and Gifford Pinchot, in particular, were key agitators in this backlash against the Interior Department. Pinchot led a campaign to transfer the full range of duties tied to the prized Forest Service from the Interior Department to the Department of Agriculture. Since the Forest Management Act of 1897, the Interior Department had been entrusted with the power to set aside forest reserves as a partial bulwark against trespassing mining investors. Officials had taken steps to create a Forest Service under the General Land Office that would administer 47 million acres of land. In 1905, Pinchot lambasted the agency for consolidating legal expertise rather than a scientific knowledge of forestry. He further critiqued the way Interior's role supporting private industry cut against the protection of forests from encroaching interests.[65] He thought the forests would find better stewards in the Department of Agriculture, an appendage that had actually evolved from Interior's Patent Office four decades earlier (the result of an interwoven history between mechanized agriculture, hybrid seeds, and technical innovation).[66] The dilemma hinged on the determination of which arm of the federal government was best equipped to superintend biological resources—forestry, animal husbandry, and grasslands—increasingly understood to be separate from and often in direct conflict with activities related to mineral resources. Pinchot was ultimately successful in rallying consensus among well-positioned officials, and Congress reallocated the Forest Service to the Department of Agriculture. In the aftermath of this upheaval, the rancor in Interior over the loss of the Forest Service ran deep. Over the ensuing decades, various department leaders, including Harold Ickes and Stewart Udall, would fight to regain control over forestry but to no avail.[67]

Other critics in the U.S. government would recommend the dissolution of the Office of the Secretary altogether. This was one of the recommendations offered by the Keep Commission in its well-documented investigation into departmental affairs. Roosevelt initiated a commission in 1905 under the Assistant Secretary of the Treasury Charles Keep, known also as the Committee on Department Methods, to investigate the inner workings of the executive branch. The commission, on which Pinchot served, was asked to place its most glaring spotlight on Interior. After examining Interior operations of the past decades, the group uncovered corruption, disorganization, miscommunication, and inefficiency.[68] These claims were well founded, a legacy of the patronage system and misdealing in Indian affairs in particular. However, the department's greatest sin, according to the final report, was that it had prioritized private claimants over the public good. The Keep Commission members acknowledged that such "bad and unbusinesslike practices" had been "*necessary* a half century ago," but they lamented how such practices had "assumed binding force."[69] In response to such accusations, Secretary of the Interior Ethan A. Hitchcock countered that Interior had long fought to protect the "nation's heritage" with "every available rod," but "efforts made to release it from the grip of its despoilers have been met by every embarrassment human ingenuity could devise."[70] The truth was that Interior had both promoted and regulated, however clumsily, extractive industries. It had merely struggled to balance the interests of industry and the interests of white settlers in the process of settler colonialism.

Pinchot and the Keep Commission's greatest disgust with the Interior Department actually stemmed from changing ideas about what constituted the national interest. Whereas in the midcentury, government officials broadly positioned the *disposal* of land and resources as vital to the national interest, a necessary precondition for effecting American control of the continent, many would insist that the *conservation* of land and resources was vital to the national interest at the century's end. The anxiety about scarcity was a crude arithmetic, contingent on which resources were being debated; fear of future shortages of materials like oil, for example, could also mix with real anxieties about overproduction that accompanied the economic depressions from the 1870s to the 1890s.[71] Nevertheless, conservationists insisted there were limits to the landscape's material bounty. Unchecked privatization threatened to breach those limits. Throughout this recalibration of national interest, Interior's actions quickly shifted from being understood as dutifully serving the common good to selfishly cutting against it. The calls for Interior's closure on grounds of its corruption and duplicity represented a huge disavowal of the way in which transferring public lands into private hands was needed to give coherence to the nation in a frenetic era of continental expansion. In the era of conservation, Interior's disposal of such lands, which had always been detrimental to the interests of indigenous peoples and Mexico, merely came to be viewed as detrimental to the interests of a growing number of white settlers.

If conservation provided temporary impediments for the department, it also created vast and enduring opportunities at a time of massive state centralization. Many leaders in the Interior Department saw in the burgeoning conservation movement an arena in which to carry forth their existing skill set. For example, Frederick Newell of the Geological Survey drew upon previous experiences in hydrography and mineral engineering to spearhead a favorite attraction in the big tent of conservation, the proposed federal program of irrigation. Newell aimed to create with the irrigation program favorable conditions for agricultural, timber, and mineral production in the arid West. He eventually headed the massive government effort in reclamation through the construction of hydroelectric dams—an agenda that would secure $100 million from Congress.[72] In this energetic moment of legislative and executive enthusiasm for the wise-use cause, the Interior Department spawned new bureaus devoted to increasingly specialized expertise, such as the Reclamation Service (1907), the Bureau of Mines (1910), and the National Park Service (1916).[73] Interior shifted away from privatizing the public domain to managing public lands, though such lands would also continue to be privatized. Others would be held aside for their aesthetic value and historical significance, as in National Parks, or shared use, such as rangelands. This bureaucratic diversification, in turn, mapped onto a broader shift in American governance in which government employees became salaried, an important step on the path to the modern American state and a "resource management state."[74]

Interior's embrace of conservation might seem like a departure from old habits, but it was in many ways a continuation and even extension of those habits. This was because conservation was not expansion's opposite but rather its slower-moving counterpart. Conservation, like expansion, operated on a logic of growth and limits but did so on different temporal scales. As Pinchot had famously argued, conservation was the belief that a resource should provide "the greatest good of the greatest number in *the long run*."[75] American expansionism followed a virtually identical argument but did so without restraint concerning time. Conservation was, in this sense, expansion slowed down—even as certain features of conservation, like hydroelectric dams, would also work to accelerate growth.[76] Further challenging the notion that expansion and conservation were separate impulses, Ian Tyrrell has recently illuminated the transnational origins and imperialist aims of conservation.[77] What was ultimately so consonant between continental expansion and the conservation ethos was that the latter still viewed land as a supply of natural resources yet to be exploited, a vision that resembled the earlier justification for settler expansion on grounds that indigenous peoples did not properly utilize nature. A cartoon parodying the way public land grants functioned as a Trojan horse ushering mining, timber, and reclamation interests into new regions tapped into this problem. The image emblazons "mineral rights" over mountains, "water power" over cascades, and "timber rights" over forests, showcasing the deeply entrenched perception that material landscapes inherently awaited extraction, a perception shared by even the most sanctimonious of the conservationists in an era of increased industrialization. In short, the inability to see the problem of resource scarcity as one tied to continental expansion and its exaltation of capitalist development shaped a federal conservationist platform that was always already expansionist.

Perhaps because conservation could so easily function as expansion by other means, the department was never seriously under the threat of elimination with the apparent closing of the American frontier. Calls to abolish parts of the Interior Department went unheeded by a recalcitrant Congress backed by Republican interests that favored not conservation but rather disposal.[78] Interior leaders thus curried the necessary political support by continuing a tenuous balancing act between advancing and regulating private interests, supporting industry with varying degrees of eagerness and patience, disposal and conservation. In this sense, conservation was also expansionist in that it was a means of conserving and redirecting the capacities of settler colonial bureaucracies like the Interior Department to new horizons. At heart remained a repertoire of expansion bent on capitalist utilization. These knowledges were *already* proving indispensable to the task of managing key facets of America's *overseas* empire. Conservation at home, put differently, was conjoined with expansion elsewhere, as Interior

"The dummy homesteader; or, the winning of the West," cartoon featuring a giant statue labeled as "U.S. Public Land Grant," which, like a Trojan horse, ushers mining, timber, and water "grafters" and "monopolists" into public lands. The image conveys a utilitarian view of nature, in which environment is carved up for different interests in "mineral rights," "water power," and "timber rights." 1909. Puck Collection, Prints and Photographs, Library of Congress.

ventured to the Pacific and Caribbean, the largely invisible process to which we now turn.

Imperialism

In 1899, George Ferdinand Becker was doing what he did best. He was helping to open new lands to American power and private industries. Throughout his twenty-year career with the U.S. Geological Survey (having joined the year it was founded in the Interior Department), Becker had investigated minerals across the American West, including the famed mercury deposits of the New Almaden region in California.[79] Although Becker had made countless surveys of "unexplored" terrains, this was the first time that he was doing so from the back of a gunboat. Becker was in the Philippines under the escort of the Military Governor General Elwell Stephen Otis, conducting a survey of the mineral resources of the island of Mindanao while the U.S. military waged war with Filipino insurgents. The previous May, Admiral George Dewey had destroyed the Spanish fleet in Manila Bay as part of the Spanish-American War, in which the United States had intervened to support anti-imperialist insurrections led in Cuba by Máximo Gómez and in the Philippines by Emilio Aguinaldo against Spanish colonial rule. After securing the surrender of the Spanish, however, the United States refused to deliver the promised liberation. This refusal launched a separate Philippine-American War, pitting Filipino fighters against the U.S. military. In making sense of his and the United States' involvements in the Philippines, Becker framed the struggle as an extension of U.S. settler colonialism. "The opposition which the natives have made to our occupation of the islands," Becker explained, "has aroused the doggedness of our Teutonic race; and the task of developing the immense resources of the archipelago appeals most congenially to a nation descended from pioneers."[80]

George Becker's work in the Philippines illustrates a through-line between U.S. continental expansion and U.S. imperial rule overseas. In his own words, Becker clearly transposed the mythology of the American frontier onto the as yet foreign space of the Philippines. In juxtaposing the "natives" with the "Teutonic race" and "pioneers," Becker drew upon the prevalent late nineteenth-century discourse of civilization famously advanced by Theodore Roosevelt, a close interlocutor of Becker's who had just reached new levels of fame with his Rough Riders' charge in the Battle of San Juan Hill in Cuba. One year after that spectacle, Roosevelt wrote to congratulate Becker both for his faith in the "effect upon the national character of expansion," *and* for his work as a "trained and upright observer" of "the exact facts on the ground" in the Philippines.[81] Roosevelt's comments signaled the extent to which Becker—more than just reenacting the frontier myth in keeping with the mandates of the "strenuous life"—possessed a skill set deemed indispensable to the project of expansion. Becker agreed with Roosevelt that he had "peculiar qualifications" stemming from his experience in Interior's Geological Survey, which had performed "compatible" work in the United States and the mineral-rich territory of Alaska.[82] Such training allowed him to help develop the "immense resources" of the Philippines. Thus, when setting out for the Philippines, Becker drew upon long-standing methods such as enlisting camp hands and "native" laborers, hiring pack trains, and outfitting the team with measuring instruments and other supplies. He compiled reports on the geology and mineral resources of the archipelago as though it were the uncharted expanse of the American continent.[83] A repertoire of U.S. settler colonialism, in short, helped to underwrite U.S. imperialism at its formal launch in the Pacific.

The Interior Department, like its employee George Becker, adopted important if widely overlooked roles in this projection of American power overseas. The work took on predictable forms in population and natural resource management. As a starting point, U.S. Indian policy shaped U.S. imperial policy in the new territories at the level of law and legislation, and racial attitudes toward Indians influenced if did not fully determine attitudes toward Filipinos, Cubans, and Puerto Ricans.[84] Drawing on personnel and procedures from the Indian Service, Interior staffed and shaped the commonwealth governments. The bureaucratic apparatus superintending Indian affairs was thus also a bridge between continental and overseas expansion. For example, Interior spawned in the Philippines a new Bureau of Non-Christian Tribes, which would oversee the effort to assimilate and subdue an array of ethnic groups.[85] At the same time, Interior's Geological Survey was dispatched on the heels of the U.S. military to generate an on-the-ground portrait of the islands and their natural resources. The teams, in turn, explored and mapped the "interior," a designation meant to describe a region beyond reach of coastal surveys with untold natural resources.[86] In this way, the "interior" at the heart of the department's agenda was extended beyond the continent. It became a highly transportable canvas on which to project extractive desires.

Minerals were important prizes in this extended interior, a fact that runs somewhat against historical wisdom. Classic accounts of U.S. territorial imperialism have illuminated both economic incentives, especially the desire for markets for American manufactured goods, and cultural ideologies rooted in race, gender, and religion in explaining the nation's intervention in the affairs of the Caribbean and Pacific. Of the clear economic motives for expansion, raw material exploitation, particularly that of minerals, appears as a marginal concern, in part because America's own overproduction—the overflowing of oil wells, the swelling of mines—was cited by many Americans like Secretary of State William Seward as a chief motive for pursuing territories overseas. Such ideas of American mineral abundance also reinforced the exceptionalist myth that unlike European nations, short on territory and finite minerals, the United States did not face the same pressures to expand overseas that galvanized, for example, an imperial "scramble" in Africa.[87] Yet alongside the lust for markets and the civilizing mission, one given global heft by contemporary calls to lift up "primitive" peoples as part of the "White Man's Burden," Interior Department personnel also were centrally preoccupied with accessing resources. As one report aptly summarized, the Geological Survey "does not let much grass grow under its feet as is evidenced by the report . . . upon the mineral resources of our recent acquisition."[88] This is not to say people associated with the Interior Department uniformly supported these resource pursuits or the extension of U.S. power. Carl Schurz, the former Interior secretary depicted in the woodcut with General Sheridan, joined the Anti-Imperialist League founded after U.S. refusal to relinquish control to the Philippines, arguing, "If Washington were alive today, I think that he would feel more at home with Aguinaldo than in our army."[89] Overseas empire was an altogether different affair, in Schurz's peculiar humanitarian sensibility, from continental expansion.

Despite such critiques and America's seeming mineral abundance, Interior officials targeted minerals for both military and capitalist purposes. Becker's excursions in the Philippines speak to the way civilian efforts supported and rested uncomfortably alongside military strategy. Throughout his migrations, Becker observed numerous resources of interest, including the fertile agricultural lands that produced hemp for rope, copra for soap, and an assortment of dyewoods. In an article Becker wrote for *Scribner's* entitled "Are the Philippines Worth Having?" he pointed to these resources as evidence to quell popular uncertainty about incorporating the archipelago. Yet his training as a geologist leant his observations especially in the direction of mineral potential. He argued that the Philippines' minerals were "considerable" if not astonishing. The Philippines' gold resources, for example, were no Colorado or California, sites of the storied booms that had driven America's westward expansion, but they *were* akin to the gold of the Carolinas and Georgia (which had helped propel the earlier indigenous land dispossession culminating in the Trail of Tears).[90] Most impressive of the Philippines' minerals was lignite coal, strewn across the archipelago in Luzon, Mindanao, and Cebu's Mount Uling ("Coal Mountain" in Visayan), where petroleum had also been detected. Becker argued that coal in particular could form a reliable fuel basis for U.S. naval vessels. He observed that these same coal sources had fueled the insurgents' steamers and would thus be highly suitable for U.S. coaling stations in keeping with the strategy for maintaining U.S. military presence in the Pacific.[91]

Becker's activities, like those of the Interior Department that would follow him, were meant to affect civilian neutrality, but they instigated violence. Becker sought to maintain the image of President William McKinley's policy of "benevolent assimilation," which insisted upon the freedoms and rights of Filipinos under U.S. rule by supporting the introduction of "civil government." Although he greatly admired military methods, and insisted civilians should learn from them, he urged the creation of a new "Home Government" (presumably a companion to the Interior Department) to develop programs for roads, hygiene, and schools.[92] Becker represented this kind of civilian alternative, though his scientific exploration also yielded the kind of brute death-dealing associated with military force. This becomes apparent in an event on June 16, 1899, that Becker recounted in correspondence to Roosevelt, then governor of New York. Accompanied by a military escort, Becker visited a lignite deposit at the mouth of the Talabe, a stream in northeastern Negros. In the early hours of the next morning, shots were fired around the camp in an ambush. Becker explained to Roosevelt that a group of as many as 300 Filipino insurgents, "armed with spears or bolos" and led by a captain named Vincente Ornedo, attacked the American crew and their indigenous collaborators. After forty-five minutes of conflict and a fuselage of bullets by the U.S. Army, fifty-three of the Filipino raiders were dead, including Ornedo. It quickly became apparent, upon finding a list of names on the leader, that the raid targeted indigenous informants rather than the American survey team. One such informant was missing and presumed dead after the house he was hiding in was found empty and splattered with blood. The violent encounter reminded Becker of an earlier incident in which an indigenous engine driver who helped him and other military personnel was "cut to pieces in the presence of his wife" as punishment. Becker explained that the event had been so "impressed upon [his] memory" because the man was going to provide details on the minerals of the island, which, as result of his untimely death, Becker failed to get.[93]

If Interior personnel pursued minerals for strategic considerations, blurring boundaries between military and civilian purposes, they also did so to shore up capitalist profits. Becker was explicit in his reports that ascertaining facts about the distribution of coal, copper, gold, and other minerals in the Philippines was meant to create conditions so that "capital can be intelligently directed to investment."[94] American companies would have much to gain in making the decision to invest in the Philippines. In addition to the mineral prospects, part of what made the Philippines so conducive to mining investments, in Becker's evaluation, was the availability of "hands to perform work." Reducing the peoples of the Philippines to the anatomical levers that performed "rude labor," Becker outlined detailed taxonomies of racial difference, sorting "Mestizos, Malay, Talgo, Pangasinanes, Macabebes, Visayas, and the Moros of Jolo" into positions of inferiority to the Anglo-Saxon race—a point the expert in earth and rocks consistently made in public forums to champion U.S. imperialism in the Philippines.[95] If the Filipinos declined to undertake these tasks, Becker offered, there remained "an abundance of other Asiatics available" to take their place. Becker also offered that opportunities abounded for white Americans seeking employment and adventure in the Philippines, including roles as mining foremen. He promised that white men would not have to work "cheek by jowl" with "men of darker colors."[96] Rather, Anglo-Saxons would have good opportunities in management, while Filipino and other Asian workers would serve as unskilled labor. In short, Becker celebrated the extent to which U.S. capitalists could rely on racialized labor in extracting valuable minerals and other commodities.

Becker's racism built expressly on attitudes toward America's indigenous population, even as he held up U.S.-indigenous relations as evidence of American benevolence in the Philippines. Before American audiences, Becker compared the Filipinos and indigenous Americans by borrowing from the settler colonial trope of the vanishing Indian; he observed that some tribes of the archipelago, like the "dwarf Nigritos," were "rapidly dying out."[97] He also commented on "intertribal relations" in the Philippines. Like intertribal relations with American Indians, Becker argued, "nothing but conquest will ever unify" the indigenous peoples of the archipelago.[98] Before Filipino audiences, he reassured locals that the United States treated its indigenous population most fairly. In two articles in the *Manila Times* and the *Filipina Republica,* one translated into Spanish, Becker directly countered the idea circulating across the islands that the United States had exterminated Native Americans. On the contrary, he argued, many indigenous communities were growing. He singled out the "civilized" Osage nation in "beautiful" Indian territory, offering that they were "without doubt the richest community in the world" for their allotment of land and prosperous ranches (a number of white trustees began murdering Osage allottees on oil-rich lands for the titles in the 1920s). Although some tribes had diminished, Becker acknowledged, this was due to epidemics of smallpox and measles, as well as Indians' natural proclivity to drink in excess. The U.S. Army, through its "justice and kindness," had protected indigenous peoples from encroaching white settlers—an argument that harkened back to General Sherman's earlier claim that the army was the best friend the Indians ever had.[99] As evidence, Becker pointed to the U.S. government's recent intervention on behalf of unspecified Indians near San Francisco, California, whose lands had been taken over by white settlers. In an already dubious argument, this detail was perhaps the most egregious given that particular region's history. To clear the way to gold in the first years of the gold rush, two-thirds of the population of some California Indians had been exterminated. It was one of the clearest cases of genocide toward U.S. indigenous populations, done in the name of capitalist greed.[100]

Across the world in the Caribbean theater, the effort to create conditions favorable to capitalism was perhaps even more readily apparent. Immediately following U.S. victory against Spain, General Leonard Wood, a Rough Rider who became the first U.S. military governor of Cuba and would later lead murderous raids in the Philippines, called for a survey of the mineral resources of the island, long renowned for its gold and copper extracted under Spanish colonial rule. Secretary of the Interior Ethan A. Hitchcock agreed to send the geologists David T. Day, C. Willard Hayes, and T. W. Vaughan to survey the island in the spring of 1899 and again in the spring of 1901. The latter team of Hayes and Vaughan arrived on the coattails of the signing of the Platt Amendment, which affirmed the United States recognized Cuban independence but maintained the right to intervene at will. They zigzagged across the island to study iron, manganese, and copper, reaching from Santiago and the North Coast to Guantánamo Bay, mapping every province of Cuba.[101] The resulting report offered a thorough account of the current mining conditions, paying particular attention to iron ore, which had been mined since 1884.[102] Three *American* firms, including the Pennsylvania Steel Company, later bought out by the behemoth Bethlehem Steel, controlled all of the island's mining operations under local-sounding subsidiaries, like the Cuban Steel Ore Company. The Cuban miners under their charge had unearthed 3.4 million tons of ore to be shipped to the United States. Cuban ores increased from representing 5 percent of America's total imports in 1884 to representing 75 percent of its total imports in

1897, the year before the U.S. military arrived in Cuba.[103] All told, the three American companies invested $8 million in Cuba, paying into the U.S. Treasury more than $2 million.[104]

Despite such developments, the U.S.-based steel firms faced obstacles that the government sought to eliminate in the new American territories. First, the terrain itself was difficult to navigate. Lacking infrastructure made moving across the island, beset with heavy rains and humidity, difficult or even impossible. Projects to build roads and rails, like the railroads some of the American companies had taken initial measures to build, were needed in a more systematic fashion. Physical limitations had been met with the obstinacy of the Spanish government, which had passed laws that allowed American companies into Cuba in the first place but then proceeded to tax them heavily.[105] The Spanish officials, moreover, failed to maintain accurate information on mineral reserves. U.S. geological reports of Cuba lamented how it had been difficult for interested parties to get reliable information from the friendly but disorganized "Latin race."[106] One report elaborated, "The most painstaking seeker after truth is baffled by the chaotic state of Government records as regards mining properties on the island."[107] This political bog, matched with the physical obstructions, had made these regions "positively inaccessible" to mining investors and operators.[108]

Such inscrutable conditions would not do at the dawn of U.S. overseas empire. The American approach to securing territory, whether across the continent or overseas, hinged on enlisting federal agents to clear pathways to private capital. The Interior Department had performed this task since 1849. Half a century later, that task seemed to have renewed meaning and significance. "Capital, ever on the lookout for that in which it may 'safely invest,'" the Interior geologist David T. Day explained, had arrived in Cuba with the expectation that companies would have access to the untapped resources of the new territory.[109] Although some affiliated with private industry had been skeptical of the way government could clear pathways to resources, many would benefit from its effort. Becker, for example, sent one of his early reports on the Philippines directly to Agassiz, who had earlier claimed government surveyors would do few members of industry any good.[110] Alongside American investments in hemp and copra, companies bankrolled mining operations there. One year after the first reports surfaced from Becker, for example, the Tidewater Coal Company invested in coal in the archipelago. The Consolidated Mining Company and Union Carbide would follow in the next decades.[111] Other skeptics of the Interior Department had also benefited from its imperial ventures, if not exclusively for profits, including Gifford Pinchot. Aided by the findings of U.S. surveyors in the region, Pinchot had left for the Philippines in 1902 to launch new scientific forestry investigations in America's own "tropical backyard"—another firm reminder that conservation and empire went hand in hand.[112] The Interior Department had helped forge the path into this distant interior, even as the American mineral endowment seemed assured. Consequently, as Day had cheerily observed in his report, the prospects for capitalist development in overseas territories were rosy, for "the promoter is now abroad in the land."[113]

THE U.S. INTERIOR DEPARTMENT emerged from specific exigencies tied to America's mid-nineteenth-century settler colonialism. It marked a rethinking and rewiring of American governance in order to streamline federal capacities for incorporating the territory expropriated from Mexico and indigenous nations—the enlarged American interior. In the process, the new department was meant to enforce a clear distinction between foreign and domestic, but its operations betwixt and between constantly confounded such efforts. In this gray zone, Interior personnel oversaw matters related to the indigenous population, on the one hand, and land and natural resources, on the other. Both activities placed Interior on a collision course with the American military and capitalist interests. The department collaborated with and performed vital services for both, even if these relations took on ambivalent forms. First, Interior followed in the wake of the U.S. Army to function as a civilian salve to military might—the good cop to the bad cop. Interior's role allowed for U.S. relations with indigenous peoples to display the benevolent sheen of a civilizing mission rather than the violent stain of an unending war. Second, Interior consistently created conditions favorable to the capitalist development of land, helping advance the reach of white settlement and private industry. Relations with the extractive economy in particular were volatile, as

Interior sought both to promote and restrain investments through a variety of means related to surveying, parceling, codifying, and leasing. In navigating these tenuous relationships with brute force and blind profit, Interior helped to domesticate the midcontinent and the process of settler colonialism itself.

Such activities, in the eyes of commentators like Frederick Jackson Turner, stood as evidence of the close of the American frontier. Guided by the perception that Interior had completed the task it had been born to do, disposing of the expropriated and "public" domain, some called for the department's closure. Although abolishing the department was never seriously considered, such pressures compelled new strategies at the dawn of the twentieth century. Interior leaders pledged new allegiance to conservationism, a movement that despite its apparent separation from expansion more accurately resembled the flipside of the same coin. Reinforcing this point, Interior personnel became foot soldiers of U.S. overseas empire in the Philippines, Cuba, and Puerto Rico, recapitulating continental roles in far-flung contexts. The department born to incorporate expropriated lands ultimately continued to bear the imprint of that original calling, even as it adapted by pursuing new arenas of activity and impact. Thus, although Interior had changed a great deal in fifty years, from a fledgling circuit of clerks superintending facets of continental expansion to a centralized administration devoted to natural resource management, important continuities remained. Interior institutionally linked continental expansion, conservation, and overseas imperialism in U.S. history.

It is important to note, however, that the Interior Department's continued pursuit of frontiers was not a foregone conclusion, a point that becomes apparent when broadening the view, however superficially, to the larger settler colonial world. On July 1, 1874, the Canadian Department of the Interior was born. It had been made in the exact image of the American version to dispose of the dominion of land expropriated from First Nation and Metís peoples. Like the U.S. Interior Department, the Canadian version managed the extension of settlers and private interests in mining and timber through surveying, parceling, and leasing lands before embracing the conservation movement and tending to reclamation and national parks.[114] In short, the Canadian and U.S. Interior

Departments were analogs across borders. However, something quite different happened to the Canadian Interior Department. The government abolished it in 1936, decentralizing and redistributing its power across separate departments and the provincial governments of Alberta, Manitoba, and Saskatchewan. It is hard to imagine what demolishing an engine of governance once so central to nation building actually encompassed, but one visual available is this: it took 200 railway boxcars, full to the brim with files weighing roughly as much as 200 standard-issue army trucks, to reallocate the department's most essential documents to the three provincial governments.[115] In the case of Canada, settler colonial bureaucracy was not only domesticated. It was provincialized.

With this institutional counterpoint, we might ask whether buried with Canada's Interior Department was an important machinery of national expansion. Walter LaFeber once argued that at the apparent close of the frontier, the United States was confronted with a choice: "either radically readjust the political institutions to a nonexpanding society or find new areas for expansion."[116] Key moments of debate, like that captured in Pinchot's campaign to close offices of the department, as well as the comparisons with Canada, underline the extent to which the U.S. Interior Department's future was far from certain. In a series of contingent moments, U.S. leaders decided to redirect Interior to ever-widening horizons, including formal imperialism, rather than to reinvent or decentralize it. Instead, the nation displayed a deep attachment to settler colonial governance, precisely because institutions like the Interior Department did important ideological work to domesticate the nation's original empire. It is impossible to know what decentralizing these functions would have yielded, but one might wonder whether it could have changed the scale of U.S. government capacities to project power and assist capitalism beyond borders.

Such questions become all the more important when considering that Interior's involvement in formal imperialism would only grow over time, as we will see. Under President Franklin D. Roosevelt, the Interior Department became the home of the Division of Territories and Island Possessions, bringing many zones previously headed by the army and navy under civilian control. As global war loomed in the late 1930s, Interior's role managing formal imperialism became even more wedded to its role shaping U.S. mineral policy, as the United States lusted after materials needed for armament, many of which fell within territories like Alaska and the Philippines. In this way, the Interior Department ascended to a vaunted position at the core *and* on the peripheries of American power. The closing of the frontier, then, was anything but a closing. So long as the institution devoted to the work of the frontier persisted, new frontiers would systematically be sought, managed, and extracted.

CHAPTER TWO

New Jewels in the Crown
of American Empire

War clouds bring prosperity to producers of chromium. . . .
They have led to cynical reappraisals of the ultimate political
destiny of the Commonwealth.

Division of Territories and Island Possessions

O N A CHILLY DAY in Alaska in 1938, Ernest Gruening ascended a
mountain in a bucket. Gruening was visiting the operations at the
world-renowned Kennecott Copper mines as part of his second imperial
inspection of Alaska. The urbane East Coaster had recently been appointed the director of the new Division of Territories and Island Possessions, a branch of the U.S. Department of the Interior initiated by President Franklin D. Roosevelt to oversee territorial affairs in place of the
U.S. military. Using Kennecott's aerial tram system, and swinging "dangerously close" to the mountain, Gruening ascended 3,000 vertical feet
and 3.5 horizontal miles to the Bonanza mine. Once settled in the inner
chamber, he watched as the very last consignments of copper ore were
extracted from the mountain that had been, with the backing of Wall
Street financiers like the Guggenheims, among the most profitable in the
twentieth century.[1] The visit to the mines on this day left a lasting impres-
sion on Gruening, who would eventually make the arctic land his chosen
home, serving as its governor and first senator. He claimed that the territory of Alaska, like the Kennecott mines that had once been a pillar of its

economy, had been "gutted"—its prolific wealth of gold, silver, and copper withdrawn to line distant coffers. This unequal arrangement, in Gruening's view, represented the dark side of an otherwise benevolent American empire. It was this kind of exploitative arrangement that ensured that Alaska "was fief of the Department of the Interior, and its secretary was Lord of Alaska."[2]

Ernest Gruening's alpine adventure in Alaska teetered over a significant fault line in the history of U.S. global engagement. The world was shifting under his snowshoed feet. A global anti-imperialist movement increasingly challenged the international order underwritten by European colonization of the non-Western world. This critique drew greater moral force as the world braced for a war sparked by a different form of expansionism, that of fascist Germany and imperial Japan. Throughout these transformations, the United States sought to defuse the livewire of empire by distancing itself from activities most susceptible to charges of imperialism. In this effort, the Department of the Interior under the new and enterprising secretary, Harold L. Ickes, would play a formative role. As in the earlier era of continental expansion, American leaders aimed to offer a civilian corrective to former military rule in territorial affairs. They promoted the Interior Department from a supporting role in overseas imperialism to the lead, administering an intricate and far-flung imperial circuitry formerly controlled by the Departments of War and the Navy in the prelude to the Second World War, further evidence that the United States was hardly "isolationist," in thought or in practice, during these interwar decades.[3] With Franklin D. Roosevelt's creation of the Division of Territories and Island Possessions (DTIP) in 1934, Alaska, Hawai'i, the Virgin Islands, and Puerto Rico were brought under Interior's aegis, followed in due course by the guano islands, the Philippines, Guam, and Samoa. As the midcentury neared, Interior's empire would reach, in the words of one department circular, "from the Arctic Circle to Puerto Rico, from Maine to the South Pacific."[4]

Interior's involvements in territorial affairs increasingly intersected with its role in mineral affairs. Minerals were steadily becoming a cornerstone of industry and security, but they were also a thorny political issue. The department in the 1920s, for example, had headlined a disastrous spectacle in extraction, the Teapot Dome scandal, involving the leasing

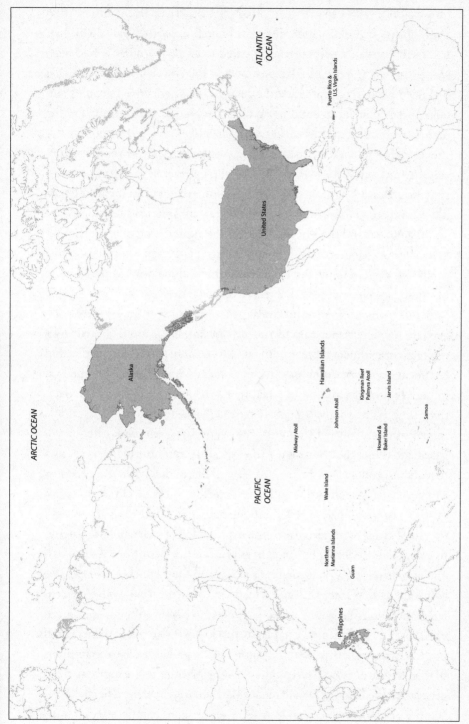

The far-flung jurisdiction of the Interior Department when it became the institutional home of the Division of Territories and Island Possessions in 1934.

of naval oil reserves to private industry. Ickes arrived in the direct aftermath of this scandal, which destroyed much departmental credibility. Ickes saw Interior's ignominy as one tied to its very origins; it had been set up "to be the 'exploiting' department of the Government," a task that had been necessary in westward expansion but had since become "suicidal."[5] Salvation lay in building on the conservation platform and forging natural resource expertise. Ickes was particularly fixated on cultivating a multiagency mineral technocracy and even went so far as to appoint himself the lead authority over regulating the petroleum industry. As wartime exigencies heightened desires for minerals for armament, officials like Ickes turned more and more to minerals in America's territories, including Alaska and the Philippines. Yet the exploitation of territories for raw materials had become highly politicized by the same anti-imperialist sentiment vaulted to the international stage by global war. Minerals were becoming a well-established object of imperial desire.

In this moment of powerful convergence, the Interior Department managed to exploit American territories for minerals amid global anti-imperialist sentiment by grounding its efforts more firmly in scientific and technical expertise. Whereas Interior officials had previously relied on imperial rationales rooted in racial hierarchy and discourses of civilization, they increasingly framed departmental activities as technocratic interventions. Toward this end, they mobilized the new category of "strategic minerals." Strategic minerals appeared utterly inert, yet as a discursive product they helped the United States downplay imperial lust by emphasizing technical neutrality. Interior officials held up strategic minerals to streamline and depoliticize activities closely associated with the worst kinds of imperialism—the exploitation of indigenous labor and raw materials for foreign profits. In short, Interior performed a set of balancing acts on par with Gruening's zip-line to the Kennecott mines. The adjustments that Interior leaders made in this transition would lay critical foundations for a new mode of American power in the world: modernization, or technical assistance to "backward" regions of the world. If imperial forerunners passed the baton of U.S. global reach to champions of modernization and development, as the broader historiography suggests, then the Interior Department stood squarely in the exchange lane.[6] Interior reframed American global power as technocratic interventions for a greater good—in this case, winning a war that posed a threat to whole world, territories included.

The Mineral Offensive

Minerals became a central hinge of the Interior Department in the first decade of the twentieth century, but they also exacerbated long-standing tensions in its design. As the United States experienced an upsurge of industrialization, many Americans debated how best to ensure reliable access to minerals—whether by the slower pace of conservation or the steady advance of privatization. Once again, Interior struggled to balance promoting and regulating extractive interests on the public domain. On the one hand, some Interior officials had been chastened by conservationist teachings and scientific findings that warned of resource scarcity. They tried to stay the mining claims being entered, slowing the process by which private industry unearthed minerals. For example, Otis Smith, a geologist who became the director of the Geological Survey, observed firsthand the problems of a property regime that fueled prodigal development of minerals like coal and oil on the public domain. In the 1910s and 1920s, he tried to withdraw public lands from private usage in places like the oil fields of California but with little success.[7] On the other hand, some in the department retained a commitment to opening public lands without hesitation to extractive capitalism. Such was the case with Albert B. Fall, the secretary of the interior appointed by President Warren G. Harding. Fall had been a New Mexico senator and a mining entrepreneur who in his political ascent became closely connected to leading oil moguls at a time when the oil industry itself was consolidating power on a national level. Fall made it clear upon his appointment that he would eschew conservation to support the steady operation of American corporations.[8]

At the same time, U.S. officials were also debating whether to prioritize domestic or foreign mineral reserves. High tariffs had bolstered the domestic minerals industry throughout the early twentieth century, as part of a broader trend of protectionism in the national economy. However, the onset of the First World War, which catalyzed notorious bottlenecks in key mineral supplies, challenged the previous faith in protectionism, or what critics later labeled economic nationalism. Many influential geologists and economists insisted that the uneven distribution of minerals in the world required national leaders to think beyond borders. The conservation debate, in this sense, was catapulted to the international stage. One such geologist, University of Wisconsin professor Charles Kenneth Leith, argued that the sporadic placement of minerals across the earth required international planning and the establishment of international trade agreements.[9] Already the American mining industry had been reaching into the wider world, especially oil companies like Standard Oil.[10] Exemplifying this international trend was Albert Fall who, as a senator, had been drawn into international politics through his interests in oil. His ties to the industry took him frequently to Mexico, site of the historic Tampico oil boom and ongoing American mining investments in the late 1910s. When the Mexican Revolution threatened the stability of firms' operation south of the border, for example, Fall sought to rally the administration of Woodrow Wilson to come to their defense by military action. Fall argued the Mexican government's radicalism would not only damage U.S. interests there but also bring sedition home in the form of a "Bolsheviki appeal to labor elements in the United States"—a melodramatic entreaty that, while not broadly influential, caught the attentions of U.S. officials like Secretary of State Robert Lansing and Interior Secretary Franklin K. Lane.[11]

These debates about the pace and place of resource extraction continued to unfold when the Teapot Dome scandal broke in 1922. Fall, then serving as Interior secretary, leased oil-rich land in Wyoming and California set aside as naval reserves to two private industrialists, Edward Doheny and Harry Sinclair. Doheny, who famously broke both legs falling down a mineshaft, was the head of Union Oil and an early promoter of Mexican oil developments that intersected with Fall's own interests in Mexico. Sinclair, the owner of Sinclair Refining Company, had gotten rich by capitalizing on Osage oil lands that also fell under Interior's jurisdiction in the astonishing period of corruption and guile leading up to a spate of Osage murders at the hands of whites in the early 1920s—a reminder that the department continued to play a dubious role in advancing extractive interests in indigenous lands.[12] Fall had opened the naval reserve near a quirky geological structure shaped like a teapot to noncompetitive bidding. Along the way, he received a personal gift of $100,000 in a black bag from Doheny, which investigators deemed an unequivocal bribe. Fall was found guilty of conspiracy, becoming the first cabinet member to be sent to jail. Doheny ended up being acquitted.[13] With its former leader behind bars, the Interior Department hit a new low. It had once again become a synonym for corruption.

As Interior faltered, the tensions between foreign and domestic mineral priorities, as well as spurring and slowing mineral extraction, continued unabated. Upon his election as president in 1928, Herbert Hoover ushered in an era of mineral protectionism, guiding U.S. policy toward

"His Little Tea Party," portraying Interior Secretary Albert Fall surrounded by little oil derricks in connection with the Teapot Dome scandal over opening naval reserves to private bid by Edward Doheny and Harry Sinclair. 1921. Printed with permission of the Rollin Kirby Estate, Prints and Photographs, Library of Congress.

domestic rather than foreign reserves. Ironically, Hoover, a Stanford-educated mining engineer, had made his fortune overseeing mineral operations that had taken him all over the globe. After training with the U.S. Geological Survey in 1896, Hoover moved to Western Australia and then China as an engineer for British and American firms there. He was for a time one of the best-known and best-paid mining engineers in the world.[14] Despite his own global intrigues, Hoover ran a campaign on the promise of tariffs, a promise he kept when signing the Smoot-Hawley Tariff Act in 1930, just as the effects of the Great Depression began to be felt. The protective tariffs accompanied intense coordination with the petroleum industry, what became the quintessential example of Hoover's associational state.[15] Yet some economists with a conservationist eye, like Erich Zimmerman, were challenging the wisdom of any policies, whether coordinated or laissez-faire, that hastened extraction of petroleum reserves in particular.[16] In the years after the Teapot Dome scandal, Interior leaders felt intense pressure to square the circle, protecting the domestic mining industry but doing so in a way that ensured a public interest in the long-term access to resources needed for war and peace.

Given Interior's ongoing balancing acts and recent public dishonor, few could have predicted the meteoric ascent in the department's future when newly elected President Franklin D. Roosevelt appointed Harold Ickes to be its secretary in 1932—few except perhaps Ickes himself. Ickes, a bullish politician from Chicago, had a penchant for the big picture, and the New Deal was one big and bold schematic. Leveraging public outrage over the recent Teapot Dome scandal, Ickes righteously vowed to cast aside "the criminality of an oil-besmeared Albert B. Fall" and to reform the "shame-stricken" department.[17] Building from the momentum of this crusade, Ickes would locate Interior at the core and peripheries of an expanding American state. Ickes began his offensive by positioning the department's expertise in natural resources and conservation as vital components of the New Deal push for economic growth. The Roosevelt administration sought to combat the effects of the Great Depression by implementing Keynesian economic theories calling for government intervention in the economy. The overarching goal of these interventions was to ensure full employment and full-scale production.[18] In keeping with this logic, Roosevelt pooled together a suite of programs designed to put people to work. He enlisted Ickes to administer what would become one of the New Deal's most recognizable platforms: the Public Works Administration (PWA). Although Ickes gladly wore this hat, his greater passion was in making conservation a departmental calling card. Conservation, as Ickes would repeatedly argue, extended far back in institutional memory and harmonized perfectly with the goals of the New Deal. It required rational planning of natural resource development with an eye to the broader needs of the national economy. In the spirit of these continuities, he would push, unsuccessfully, to rename Interior the "Department of Conservation."[19]

Because Ickes wanted the Interior Department to be the unquestioned center of the federal natural resource agenda, he fought to regain control over national forests, thus broadening the suite of resources under Interior's supervision. It had been a quarter century since Gifford Pinchot had successfully cleaved the Forest Service from the Interior Department, but Ickes was intent on resurrecting the long-buried dispute with the Department of Agriculture. Although the two departments shared responsibilities in directing projects for the Civilian Conservation Corps, forests remained a point of contention.[20] In the renewed conflict, the now seventy-one-year-old Pinchot remained a key player. Although Pinchot had a long-standing distrust of the Interior Department, he also liked Harold Ickes, a man he once described as "one of the most outstanding public servants of his time."[21] Pinchot temporarily threw his support behind a transfer of the Forest Service to an Interior Department overseen by Ickes, but the amity did not last long. Eventually, disillusioned with Interior's ongoing role in opening public lands to extraction, Pinchot broadcast his disapproval of Interior's control of national forests. He offered damning testimony to that effect: "I call to your attention the fact that, with the possible exception of the national parks, and I underline the word 'possible,' the Interior Department has never had control of a single publicly owned natural resource that it has not devastated, wasted and defiled."[22] Pinchot's condemnation contributed to the routing of yet another attempt on behalf of Interior to secure the premium program of the conservation agenda.

Interior's dwindling jurisdiction over biological resources faced another threatened "dispossession" in the realm of public lands. Since the embrace of conservation as a departmental platform, the Interior Department had placed greater emphasis on setting aside public lands for multiple uses, including livestock ranching. The Taylor Grazing Act of 1934 formalized this new arrangement in which public lands constituted an object of federal land management. It created a new arm under the Interior Department, the Grazing Service, to manage those lands. In the years after the legislation, Ickes fought with Secretary of Agriculture Henry Wallace for control of grazing lands and ultimately won the argument. Even so, Interior faced constant attempts to diminish its role. Western interests, for example, sought to localize control among ranchers. A continuation of a long-standing struggle tied to its history of managing continental expansion, Interior's domain diminished with the continued shrinking of public lands. By the 1940s, the reduction of the Grazing Service and the General Land Office—the long-struggling office that had disposed of land and resources in nineteenth-century expansion—would result in their merging as the Bureau of Land Management.[23] Such transformations would lead Ickes to complain, "Here again is a move . . . which might have the effect of dispossessing the Department of the Interior."[24] Ultimately, Ickes and his contemporaries missed the great irony in lamenting the dispossession of land from Interior, the agency that had been set up to superintend the dispossession of indigenous and foreign lands.

The failures to consolidate control over biological resources led Ickes to play to other strengths in mineral expertise. The Interior Department of the New Deal forged a powerful mineral technocracy headed by Walter C. Mendenhall of the Geological Survey and John Finch of the Bureau of Mines. The latter agency, which studied methods of producing, treating, and utilizing minerals, had been spawned from the Geological Survey's technical branch in 1910. However, the bureau had been reallocated to the Department of Commerce in 1925. In 1933, Ickes brought the Bureau of Mines back into the fold with the aim of broadening and tempering Interior's mineral resource repertoire. The result was that the two agencies came under the same official Interior Department letterhead for the first time in nearly a decade.[25] Throughout the New Deal, the sister agencies worked in tandem on a program of mineral resource conservation, producing countless maps, reports, and mineral statistics to aid private industry in their investments and eventually to support a nation-wide program focused on minerals desired for armament.[26]

Tightening the ties between Interior and minerals, Ickes appointed himself petroleum administrator in 1933. At a time when oil inched toward replacing coal as the primary national energy source, Ickes became the chief liaison between the federal government and the powerful petroleum industry.[27] He worked with a group of New Dealers under the mandates of the National Industrial Recovery Act to recommend and implement the Code of Fair Competition for the Petroleum Industry, known in the industry simply as "the Petroleum Code." Creating a Petroleum Administrative Board, Ickes attempted to set limits on oil production and interstate and foreign commerce as part of conservation. The petroleum industry in this same period was highly volatile. Oil operators of varying size struggled with the vicissitudes of supply and demand on domestic and global scales. Ultimately, major firms and some independent producers embraced the regulations on production, which disincentivized the initiation of new wells, for the greater stability they yielded.[28] But the Interior secretary's new and growing jurisdiction over petroleum could not help but conjure memories of earlier corruption. Ickes later claimed that the "spotty record of Interior" was ever in mind, prompting him to undertake extreme measures to oversee the activities of the different bureaus "lest one day it should rise to haunt me in the steam of another Teapot."[29] In 1935, the Supreme Court struck down the Petroleum Code on grounds that it was unconstitutional federal overreach, but Ickes's experiment with the petroleum industry was far from over.[30]

Leading up to and during the war, Ickes's role in shaping U.S. oil policy only grew at home *and* abroad. As the nation braced for global conflict, Ickes secured new titles as petroleum coordinator for defense and petroleum administrator for war.[31] Commenting on Ickes's growing menagerie of bureaucratic titles, Ernest Gruening would later explain to Tennessee Valley Authority administrator David Lilienthal, "[T]here is no part of the Government that [Ickes] doesn't want to get his hands on, and he is perfectly sure that he could run them all, and run them better than they are running now."[32] Rising to petroleum czar status in a time of international turmoil, Ickes increasingly eyed distant mineral and oil reserves. Where Albert Fall had played a part in clearing pathways for American oil investments in Mexico, Ickes took a lead role in spurring American oil investments in the Middle East, particularly around the Arabian-American Oil Company (Aramco) of Saudi Arabia, as will be considered later in greater depth.[33] What these transformations ultimately reveal is that during the New Deal, the Interior Department became a nucleus of U.S. mineral policy just as minerals were becoming increasingly central to national security and geopolitics. At the same time, Interior undertook a project that was drawing the department even further out into the world: territories and island possessions. If Ickes and his circle were becoming the brains behind American mineral policy, they were also becoming the heart of American empire.

Awakening from the Dream of Empire

In the second half of the nineteenth century, the United States aggregated territorial holdings that reached beyond the continental sweep of Manifest Destiny. Although the United States acquired the outlying territories of the guano islands beginning in 1856 and Alaska in 1867, the decisive shift of America's imperial paradigm hinged around U.S. involvements in the Spanish-American War in 1898, in which the American military secured U.S. rule over an even larger theatre in the Caribbean and Pacific. From the outset of U.S. overseas imperialism, the Interior Department helped undertake activities related to territorial management, including exploring natural resources and staffing territorial governors' offices. However, the Department of War and the Department of the Navy effectively ran the show. When American formal imperialism entered its autumn phase in the 1930s, the Interior Department became the central command for territorial affairs. With Executive Order No. 6726 of May 1934, Roosevelt created in the Interior Department the new Division of Territories and Island Possessions (DTIP). Unsurprisingly, U.S. military leaders were displeased, lodging heated complaints about the transfer on grounds that it diminished their stronghold and generally depleted the defense budget.[34] Unfazed by the criticism, Roosevelt transferred the reins of U.S. formal empire from a military to a civilian arm of the government and, in the process, signaled a gentler approach to U.S. power overseas.[35]

Such adjustments were crucial as critics around the globe rose to dispute the validity of imperialism. Within the United States, some American citizens had long raised objections to American empire on account of its moral reprehensibility, while others did on the racist grounds that imperialism would bring undesirable foreigners into American citizenship.[36] By the 1930s, a global anti-imperialist *and* antiracist movement was shaking the foundations of the global order, with figures like W. E. B. Du Bois, Mahatma Gandhi, and Ho Chi Minh joining and inspiring activist networks across the Atlantic World, British India, and Southeast Asia. Many sympathetic white Americans, including the noted historian Charles Beard, were joining the chorus of this transnational anticolonialism in varying degrees of radicalism.[37] Few did so as loudly or consistently as Ernest Gruening, a progressive reformer and journalist from New York who would oversee empire for the United States. Gruening would eventually secure a historical reputation as a devout anti-imperialist after famously casting one of two dissenting votes in the Senate debate over the Gulf of Tonkin Resolution that would initiate war with Vietnam.[38] His storied anti-imperialism built on a lifetime of passionate defenses of self-determination. In the 1910s and 1920s, while a journalist and managing editor, Gruening had railed against U.S. interventions in Haiti, the Dominican Republic, and Nicaragua and pushed for their independence. He also derided capitalist manipulations in Mexico, a nation from which he reported on the ground, blaming Albert Fall in his capacity as Interior secretary for rousing in the federal government a hard-line policy toward the new Mexican government that further impoverished the nation. Such experiences informed his desire to petition Roosevelt to be an advisor to the U.S. delegation at the Montevideo Conference that would give birth to the Good Neighbor Policy. There, he promoted a hemispheric solidarity predicated on self-determination.[39]

Gruening's anti-imperialism was perhaps most vividly captured in an article he wrote just months prior to agreeing to direct DTIP. Entitled "Our Era of 'Imperialism' Nears Its End," the multipage article, which appeared in *The Nation* and the *New York Times,* observed that the imperial ideology of Manifest Destiny was giving way to a new approach grounded in equal negotiations between nation-states.[40] Gruening detailed the history of America's imperial expansion and military and financial interventions, which had produced 125,000 square miles of territory and 200,000 square miles of nominally sovereign dependencies. Seeing cause for cheer, he insisted that the New Deal was rooting out this previous form of empire, "replacing the imperialism of the past generation." In Gruening's eyes, this transformation was the result of a changing international scene. Attempts to impose American political forms on others had failed. These failures, in turn, showed that imperialism was tantamount to self-damage. He argued that acquired territory "has often proved a *liability* rather than an asset."[41] Gruening maintained a belief in the supremacy of America's brand of democracy but also upheld that the sources of the best democracy emerged from local conditions, not from the contrivances of outsiders. Consequently, the new generation was "awakening from the dream of empire" and moving toward a new destiny of "peace and goodwill amid neighbors."[42] Imperialism, in other words, had become outmoded and out of step with the times.

It thus posed a bit of a quandary when just one month later President Roosevelt propositioned Gruening with an offer to direct the new division in Interior devoted to managing America's empire. When Roosevelt offered him the assignment, Gruening countered, "Well, a democracy shouldn't have any colonies." Roosevelt smiled and shrugged, acknowledging that he thought Gruening was right to point out this contradiction. He rather vaguely encouraged Gruening to see what might develop. Gruening took this to mean that he would be encouraged to use this role to diminish the "colonial status" of places under his jurisdiction.[43] The paradoxes Gruening faced, like those of the wider nation, would not be easy to resolve.

Ernest Gruening agreed to manage American empire in part because he, like many before him and since, believed it was exceptional. The worst kinds of imperialism, in his view, were those overseen by other nations and rooted in biological racism and raw material exploitation, two processes intimately interwoven. This becomes apparent when considering Gruening's account of his own path to anti-imperialist righteousness. The process began with a formative encounter while a Harvard medical student with Sir Arthur Conan Doyle's book *The Crime of the Congo,* an exposé of the vicious colonial administration of King Leopold of Belgium. King Leopold, in the name of European supremacy over African races, oversaw the systematic mutilation and murder of the Congolese people. Gruening was moved by the then-controversial book and horrified by how "the hands and feet of Congolese children were cut off" for insufficient yields of rubber. The extractive imperialists of the Congo, Doyle had argued, like the diamond hunters of Southern Africa, represented the malignant ends of European imperial lust.[44] Throughout his career, Gruening reasoned that imperialism built on racial terror was ultimately perverse.

Though unmentioned by Gruening, the United States also had a shameful record of racial ideologies, labor, and violence in its own empire. Racial hierarchy, as George F. Becker's earlier observations in the Philippines attest, was foundational to U.S. formal imperialism. Becker had joined the wide network of institutions and actors, including Theodore Roosevelt, espousing discourses that upheld white supremacy over the so-called barbarian or primitive races, legitimizing U.S. rule over races deemed unfit for self-governance.[45] The United States had made blood and phenotype the nuts and bolts of its imperial machine, much like the domestic counterpart of Jim Crow. Animated by this racial worldview, the U.S. imperial government under President William McKinley and President Theodore Roosevelt had been unquestionably gruesome. Army officer Leonard Wood, who had called for surveys of the minerals of Cuba, eventually oversaw "nation-building" efforts in the Philippines. As the Governor General of the Philippines, Wood launched a famously bloody campaign against the defecting Taosug Muslims in the Moro region on March 3, 1906, in which an estimated 1,000 men, women, and children were murdered. News of the massacre, accompanied by grisly photographs, reached the mainland and ignited a scandal. Roosevelt wrote to Wood, his former companion in the Rough Riders, not to scold him but rather to convey his congratulations.[46]

After becoming director of DTIP, Gruening exhibited discomfort with this legacy. A few years into his tenure, Gruening lectured his frequently dissatisfied boss, Harold Ickes, on the ways that America was regrettably "exploiting a colonial empire" in Alaska. The proof, Gruening insisted, was in American racism, or "the attitude of the white people *towards those of darker skin,* whom they lump under the label 'native' regardless of whether they are Eskimos, Indians, or Aleuts."[47] Guided by these convictions, Gruening eventually led a campaign against segregation practices that denied indigenous Alaskans access to private businesses across the territory.[48] Nevertheless, he would equivocate in his own commitment to racial equality. In Puerto Rico, Gruening dismissed the concerns of Puerto Rican nationalists in favor of the racist colonial government, a stance that made him one of the most hated figures in the territory. Overall, Gruening consistently demonstrated an elitism that bordered on disdain for other racial groups, yet he publicly offered that a societal belief in the inferiority of other races was a key ingredient for a most toxic recipe of empire.[49]

Try though he might to soften the image of American empire, Gruening faced growing criticisms from anticolonial sympathizers. These critics accused the United States of being as unjust an empire as others throughout the world. In Puerto Rico, the United States faced charges that it was, in Gruening's words, "holding an alien people in bondage."[50] The evil of bondage drew unavoidable ties between race and exploitation. At the same time, the American people vocalized a greater discontent with their nation's imperialism. With events during his reign like the murder of civilians marching in support of the nationalist cause led by Pedro Albizu Campos at Ponce, Puerto Rico, on Palm Sunday 1937, Gruening categorically failed to uphold the image of benevolent empire.[51] More and more, the American public was, as Ickes summarized, "basically sympathetic to stories of exploitation and oppression in the colonial area."[52] Such experiences revealed that as the United States claimed moral authority amid grassroots challenges to the racist and imperialist global order, the Interior Department would require new approaches in the enactment of imperialism.

Another arm of Interior's organizational chart seemed to provide a template for administrative alternatives: the Bureau of Indian Affairs, which was in the throes of a famous period of reform. After decades of policies and legal rulings shoring up forced assimilation that followed in the wake of the General Allotment Act, Interior leaders in the New Deal began pursuing a reformist agenda that touted self-determination and emphasized economic development. Ickes was a loud proponent of the Wheeler-Howard Act, or Indian Reorganization Act, which rolled back the tide of the earlier assimilationist model of an allotment system that left 90,000

Native Americans landless and destitute.[53] Ickes's sympathetic attitudes toward American Indians converged with his visible support of African Americans and other minorities to ensure his reputation as one of the most progressive members of Roosevelt's cabinet on the question of race.[54] Joining Ickes in such public displays of compassion across the color line was John Collier, the new commissioner of Indian affairs. Collier aimed to make amends for allotment's "train of evil consequences" through various reforms, which included restoring lands, providing economic opportunities (beginning with $10 million of revolving credit), and creating conditions by which indigenous peoples could have a role managing their affairs in dialogue with the federal government.[55] Moreover, the federal government withdrew indigenous lands from the public domain, providing greater protections against encroaching miners.[56] The new approach, which abandoned the language of racial superiority, nevertheless maintained a faith in essential differences between whites and indigenous peoples, as well as the inferiority of indigenous ways in terms of social, political, and economic development. Building on these assumptions, U.S. officials oriented indigenous affairs to the paradigm of technical assistance during the New Deal.[57] Such technocratic rather than civilizational missions would become the bread and butter of postwar aid programs.

Learning from activities at home and abroad, Interior leaders increasingly adopted policies of imperial management rooted in claims of technical expertise. They framed the department's role in territories as an advisory one oriented to similar uplift in economic development. DTIP personnel would provide neutral and scientific expertise in a variety of projects bent on spurring regional growth, efforts that in small ways prioritized the training of territorial subjects. For example, Ernest Gruening would lead relief and reconstruction efforts in Puerto Rico that aimed to offset local economic woes, framed as a problem of overpopulation and natural disasters such as hurricanes, by developing sugar, tobacco, and coffee industries, as well as by building schools and homes for workers in a region. Programs of social reform had been implemented earlier in the Philippines, but officials placed greater emphasis on the ways in which such undertakings were moving the territories toward self-help.[58] In Alaska, DTIP would also oversee equal efforts to catalyze economic development through infrastructural projects of road and rail construction, as well as the creation of small farming communities to encourage settlement. The Alaskan efforts led one DTIP official to describe the territory as "a great empire awaiting development."[59] The language chosen was prescient. It unknowingly signaled a national shift from methods of imperial rule to methods of what would later be called "development."

The transition from the former colonial approach overseen by the military to one overseen by Interior was far from seamless. Some military brass in Puerto Rico, like General William Tecumseh Sherman before them, were reticent to accept Interior's newfound authority and its new brand as the softer side of American empire. This was perhaps most evident in Gruening's stopover in Puerto Rico on his imperial tour in January 1936. At a ceremony in the Luquillo National Forest, the "only tropical rain forest under the American flag" (hardly the only rain forest under American empire, but the only one designated as a national reserve), U.S. officials like Gruening and Ickes joined Puerto Rican locals to formalize Interior's new leadership. After Ickes spoke about creating a national monument in the park, Colonel Otis R. Cole of the U.S. Army, the commanding officer of the entourage and prior administrator of island affairs, expressed sheer contempt for the change in leadership. In impromptu remarks slurred by apparent drunkenness, Cole put the problem colorfully: "I don't know a God-damn thing about the Department of the Interior, and you don't know a God-damn thing about the army." He continued, "I want to tell you that if you take away our base, we'll be back here with machine guns to put these people down!"[60]

A Vast Storehouse of Strategic Minerals

A global crucible of war powerfully if ambivalently welded together America's mineral and territorial affairs. The escalating conflict that led to the Japanese invasion of Pearl Harbor on December 7, 1941, solidified the perceived importance of both activities: territories' outlying geographies were vulnerable *and* strategic in the wartime cartography that linked the United States with Europe and Asia, and minerals' strength and fuel properties were vital to military arsenals. The two projects converged as the United States increasingly saw minerals within the territories as

Harold Ickes in Puerto Rico conducting an imperial inspection of troops. Although Interior was meant to offer a corrective to military rule, showing a softer side of American empire, the continuity between their modes of imperial management is apparent. 1936. International News Photographs, Prints and Photographs, Library of Congress.

being vital to conducting war. Accordingly, the Interior Department's appropriation jumped $21 million from 1941 to 1942, a direct effect of increased strategic mineral activities in Alaska and other territories.[61] The Interior Department had long been active in mineral exploration of territorial holdings like Puerto Rico, the Philippines, and Alaska. Geological work in Alaska, for example, had been under way since various gold discoveries in the 1880s, nearly two decades before George Becker and David T. Day arrived in the Pacific and Caribbean in 1899. Philip Smith, who would come to direct the Alaskan branch of the Geological Survey, had "mushed into the far interior" to Nome in search of gold, copper, and silver in the early 1920s.[62]

Although mineral exploration in the territories was not new, the threat of war radically altered the content and pace of extraction in the territories. The former era of resource exploitation, one that made gold, silver, and copper their kings, gave way to a new one fixated on the chromium,

Philip Smith, director of the Alaskan branch of the Geological Survey, outfitted for a geological reconnaissance of Alaska. 1928. *National Republic* magazine.

tin, and platinum used for implements of war. Yet intensifying extractive operations in places like Alaska and the Philippines posed a different kind of problem. Exploiting territories for raw materials drew volatile associations with an imperialism the United States sought to disavow, an exigency all the greater in the context of the ideological battle in the wartime propaganda effort. In this milieu, officials in the Interior Department and army and navy rallied around a banner of their own creation, "strategic minerals." Beginning in 1937, Interior and defense agencies offered up the category of strategic minerals to secure funds from Congress to put toward enhanced exploration and development of resources. The category encompassed a range of materials used in industry and defense, like manganese, chromium, tin, and molybdenum, all building blocks of

steel, as well as coal and oil needed for energy, among other key functions in industrial society.[63] Strategic minerals were legally defined in
the Strategic and Critical Materials Act in 1939, a product of the combined efforts of the Army and Navy Munitions Board, Interior officials,
and Congress. The act defined strategic minerals as resources "essential
to the needs of industry for the manufacture of supplies for the armed
forces and civilian population in time of a national emergency."[64] Thus,
rather than being linked by some chemical essence, these minerals were
linked by their importance to the war machine.

More than just helping to garner funds from Congress, the new and
technical category of strategic minerals also helped Interior officials maintain an appearance of disinterest and neutrality in exacting minerals
beyond the mainland. First, Interior officials like Harold Ickes and leaders
of the Bureau of Mines emphasized the "utilization" of the minerals. They
suggested strategic minerals were wanted not for their exchange values
but for their use values.[65] If exchange values—the abstracted value of commodities needed for their exchange in a market—were associated with
monetary greed, then use values—the instrumentality of a thing—appeared
anodyne by comparison. What mattered was not profit, but rather that
minerals found their way into "airplanes, machine guns, and tanks,"
which were necessary for a wider humanity to fight fascism.[66] Exchange
in a global market mattered to Interior officials insofar as dependence on
foreign trade for minerals might make the nation vulnerable in a military
context. The emphasis on utility thus helped Interior to circumvent the
troubling associations between minerals and imperial greed, and to forge
new associations as the material bulwark against national emergency.
Exigency, not the avarice of imperialist bogeymen like King Leopold,
underscored strategic mineral gambits.[67]

Officials went further than portraying strategic minerals as instruments;
they also portrayed them as agents, claiming that they *worked* for the
nation. Harold Ickes, for example, personified strategic minerals as soldiers in the war. He offered that if he had to "pin a medal on the one
element that . . . has made the most important single contribution to the
inevitable downfall of our enemy" it would "without hesitation" be natural
crude oil, as well as coal, iron ore, aluminum, manganese, and copper.[68]

Giving minerals a life of their own helped to cover over the labor, including indigenous labor, required to extract raw materials. In another visceral example of this trend, Ickes suggested that strategic minerals would "turn back the would-be enslavers of mankind."[69] Not only were minerals separate from coerced labor, they were its adversary. Such personification decontextualized minerals from extractive labor and even positioned minerals as agents liberating all of humanity. The commodity fetish, by which labor becomes abstracted into things with a social life of their own, thus found new and geopolitical life in the category of strategic minerals. Precisely how strategic minerals that won the war were harnessed, in places like the island of Cebu in the Philippines, remained concealed from view.

Such ways of imagining strategic minerals helped to obscure the paradox at the heart of their earliest definition: they were always already outside of the nation. Put differently, strategic and critical minerals were synonymous with minerals the U.S. *did not have* or had in short supply—minerals "essential to the common defense or industrial needs of the United States" that were otherwise "inadequate" in terms of "domestic" sources. This definition, in turn, placed emphasis on the mineral possibilities of zones outside the United States, beginning with those outlying zones belonging to the United States, the territories. The Strategic and Critical Materials Act under Section 7 commissioned Interior to lead mineral investigations, particularly of metallic ores, within American borders *and* its territories and island possessions. The act called for increasing territorial strategic efforts in "public and privately owned mineral deposits through core drilling, sampling, laboratory testing, trenching, and shaft sinking."[70] In short, strategic minerals marshaled significant government activities in the territories.

The passage of the Strategic and Critical Materials Act ultimately launched more—and more invasive—mineral explorations in the territories, furthering the nation's sense of entitlement to their resources. With additional funds for the Geological Survey work from the Department of War, geologists scoured Alaska, a region one-fifth the size of the United States. An estimated 300,000 square miles of land remained "entirely unsurveyed," or as Philip Smith characterized it, "virgin."[71] Gendered discourses prevailed in geological reconnaissance of the territories and, as we will see, in countless zones newly infiltrated by American operatives.

Surveying as an enterprise was in many ways a man's world, though some women, like Harriet Connor Brown and Martha Hallman, had helped compile reports in Cuba and maps of Alaska. *American* women's roles were nevertheless far removed from the actual sites of exploration and extraction. Their male colleagues in the field, meanwhile, frequently feminized land as virginal, untouched, or fertile, all common tropes of exploration in Western enlightenment modernity. This set of gendered associations, in keeping with the mandates of patriarchy, naturalized a kind of domination over the object of desire—in this case land and resources.[72]

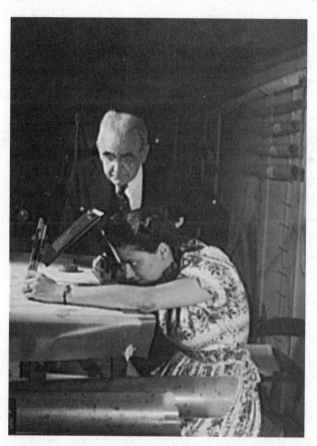

Philip Smith and engineering aide Martha Hallman use an oblique sketch master on a map of Alaska. Smith looks over Hallman and the contours of Alaska, which he described, like many Interior officials, in the gender metric of "virginity." 1943. Prints and Photographs, Library of Congress.

A snapshot of Interior's mineral activities in 1941 reveals the extent of its gaze over Alaskan reserves. The number of geological reconnaissance missions had at that point increased from *seven* three years before the Strategic and Critical Materials Act to *thirty-seven* three years after it.[73] Geologists in the field, for example, investigated tin used in alloys in the Lost River area of the western Seward Peninsula. They examined nickel used in stainless steel and welding rods in Yakobi Island west of Juneau. And they surveyed for chromite used in steel in Seldovia near the tip of the Kenai Peninsula, mercury used in thermostats and electrical tools in Sleitmut in the Kuskokwim Valley, tungsten used in electrical light and industrial cutting equipment in the Hyder district of southeast Alaska, and antimony used in battery grids and automobiles in the Kantishna district on the northern slopes of the Alaska Range.[74] Alaska in the strategic mineral era began producing 98 percent of "domestic" tin for the United States, as well as high proportions of its platinum and tungsten.[75] Throughout, the Interior Department publicly heralded Alaska as a storehouse for strategic mineral deposits. It was, in the words of one report, both a "treasure house of natural wealth" and a "strategic link in the armor of national defense."[76]

Having sized up Alaska for its minerals, Ickes courted private capital to bankroll their extraction. He extended a formal invitation to private capital to collaborate with government in developing the minerals of "our last frontier," his chosen slogan for Alaska. Ickes proposed joint ventures between government and corporations, or charters, that would support the advance of operations into the region—helping the nation to supplement minerals predominantly imported from Asia and Europe, while avoiding the trend of "draining [Alaska's] wealth to the pockets of absentee owners."[77] Despite such inducements, the department struggled to get corporations to invest. Some of the ores discovered, like tin in Alaska, were not nearly as high grade as other sources, such as Bolivian tin. The Reconstruction Finance Corporation had been providing assistance for mineral investments in lower-grade ores, but firms continued to be timid about projects "of considerable risk."[78] Since private cooperation seemed necessary to avoiding wartime bottlenecks, the Interior Department committed considerable resources to developing technological processes for making low-grade ores more profitable. Ultimately, during the war, the American government was bending over backwards to encourage extractive investments, though not always succeeding. A lesson was emerging that would have relevance in the postwar era: if government wanted certain corporations to spread into "virgin" zones when risks were anticipated and rewards were uncertain, it needed to create conditions that seriously reduced risk.

Elsewhere in the territories, U.S. officials aimed to cash in on the strategic minerals funds. In Puerto Rico, a colony with only a few known minerals, Governor William Leahy called for more surveys of the island. Working with Gruening of DTIP, Leahy shone a spotlight on Juana Diaz, a prolific mine that had produced manganese since its opening in 1915.[79] World War I stimulated production and carried through the 1930s, a period during which the mine yielded around 60,000 tons of ore.[80] By 1943, the Geological Survey returned to the region to conduct a preliminary reconnaissance of the manganese deposits. Also in the mix were two American companies, Bethlehem Steel and Freeport Sulphur, which were contemplating investment opportunities there with the help of the engineering and consulting firm Arthur D. Little.[81] Throughout, DTIP provided interested parties with reports and other information that might offer "a partial basis for stimulating interest in the development of the island."[82] As Teodoro Moscoso, a Puerto Rican industrialist, wrote, Ickes and the Interior Department had "been a champion for the intensive exploitations" of various mineral ores in service of the war effort.[83] The efforts were somewhat in vain. The final Geological Survey report revealed disappointing findings concerning the minerals of the island.[84]

Strategic minerals in the Philippines were more promising, but they also triggered tricky debates about American imperialism, including the fate of Philippine independence. Because of the island's vital supply of minerals used in the production of steel, some American officials and investors joined a chorus of voices calling for reneging on the Tydings-McDuffie Act of 1934, the U.S. commitment to grant independence if certain conditions of development were met. The American mining entrepreneur Courtney Whitney, of the Consolidated Mining Company in Luzon (who would later advise General Douglas MacArthur in the Philippines), predicted in late 1937 that natural resources "will have a profound influence upon the future sovereignty over the Philippines, when *and if,* the American flag is withdrawn"—citing reserves of chromium, used in the production of armor plates, airplanes, and guns, as evidence of the need for continued U.S. engagement there.[85] The value of strategic minerals in the Philippines made Whitney doubt whether the United States would follow through on its promise to relinquish control and grant independence. At the time Whitney wrote, only about 2,000 of the 500,000 tons of chrome ore America consumed came from mainland mines.[86] Meanwhile, the production of chromium in the Philippines jumped from 1,200 tons in 1935 to 70,000 tons in 1938—nearly 60 times more in just three years.[87] As one Interior report later summarized, this "magical increase" of chromium production revealed the "feverish haste with which a war-made world is now re-arming itself."[88] Chrome ore from the Philippines therefore had a potentially serious role to play in alleviating dependence on other nations. While U.S. sovereignty still reigned supreme, Whitney argued, the chrome ores should be brought within the physical borders of the United States to help prepare for the national emergency on the horizon.[89]

The prospect of a Japanese invasion of the archipelago added to the anxiety about U.S. mining operations there. Trade routes were much easier to Japan than to the United States. In 1940, Congress passed the Export Control Act to regulate the trade of commodities from the Philippines and authorized the United States to terminate the sale of strategic minerals from the Philippines to Japan. The restrictions posed a problem for American companies that had long been established there, like the copper firm Nielson and Company, which no longer could get products to American smelters or other nodes of the global market.[90] Immediately after Pearl Harbor, DTIP and War Department officials worried that these same resources fell in the path of Japanese expansionism. They secretly feared the loss of an estimated 150,000 tons of chrome ore in the Philippines to Japan.[91] These anxieties about the operations of American firms and mineral supplies in overseas territories reveal the extent to which U.S. imperialism in the region, bolstered by Geological Survey explorations that had helped guide private investments as early as 1899, was also bound with American capitalism.

When the Japanese did invade and occupy the Philippines in early 1942, U.S. officials closely monitored their movements around strategic minerals. Tellingly, they were kept informed of events on the ground by an American businessman with ties to the mining industry, Charles "Chick" Parsons, who had been in Manila since 1920 as secretary to General Leonard Wood. Working for the Luzon Stevedoring Company, he oversaw mining operations in chrome and manganese. Corresponding with the U.S. government in 1942, Parsons detailed conditions of the occupation, including the internment camps and American Red Cross stations. However, he offered an even more detailed assessment of the mining situation in the Philippines under Japanese control, explaining the Japanese forces' progress in shipping manganese ores from Busuanga and Siquijor, in transporting chrome from Acoje, and in extracting other base metals in the region. He reported on the state of the equipment and transport availability, making note of the destroyed piers and rails that factored into the mineral supply chain. He estimated that the Japanese forces had accessed a large amount of manganese—20,000 tons—at storage facilities in Cebu and Manila.[92]

In this context, DTIP officials came to share Courtney Whitney's prewar anxieties about the ultimate danger Philippine independence posed to American material interests. If reserves crucial to the production of steel proved essential to the United States or other powers, would they really liberate the territory? President Manuel Quezon of the Philippines, who vacillated in his own desire for independence, sought assurances from Ickes in this uncertain milieu that "the US government intended to give the Philippines their independence." Ickes, eager to bolster his position in a negotiation process that involved other factions of the American state, including the State Department, promised Quezon that he would use his strong standing with Congress to advocate on their behalf.[93] Nevertheless, DTIP reports in the ensuing years documented increasing skepticism about independence, especially as companies like Union Carbide and Consolidated Mining Company eyed profits in the mineral industry. "War clouds bring prosperity to producers of chromium," one such report noted, leading to "cynical reappraisals" of the "ultimate political destiny" of the Philippines.[94]

Although Interior was centrally involved in the debates about the Philippines, its jurisdiction there during the war years was unclear as part of an ongoing ambiguity of territories' status in relation to U.S. sovereignty.

Interior vied at times with the State Department in managing affairs of the archipelago. The State Department maintained a role in the Philippines working with the Commonwealth government that ran counter to Ickes's desire to consolidate control for his department. He argued that territorial and foreign affairs were "two entirely separate and unrelated functions," and that the State Department lacked the qualifications to oversee the situation in the Philippines. Great Britain's foreign offices, moreover, did not administer colonies. The State Department's involvement, he suggested, would damage U.S. foreign policy in other regions throughout the world, including South America, when the United States was trying to disavow that it had "greed for more territory."[95] Ickes's logic was rooted in deep-seated contradictions of empire. Territorial affairs were not as easily cleaved from foreign affairs as he supposed, and the involvement of the State Department surely bolstered claims that the United States was treating the archipelago on a parity with other diplomatic allies. Yet the State Department's involvement could raise concerns on the island over the people's status and rights as territorial subjects. Gray zones dominated in Interior's role in territorial affairs, which Ickes described as "quasi-diplomatic"—a fitting title in keeping with the logic that territories, like indigenous nations before them, were "foreign to the United States in a domestic sense."[96] Nevertheless, Ickes clung to the idea that whatever its liminal standing, Interior's mode of doing imperialism was more just than that of any other arm of the American state.

The fiction that Interior offered such a benevolent counterpoint to other kinds of imperialism was also difficult to sustain in Alaska. The department directed personnel in Alaska to abandon all projects that were not directly related to bolstering war materials in ways that shored up national rather than territorial interests. Building from modest yet impactful congressional and Strategic and Critical Materials Act funds of $114,000, geologists identified and unearthed greater proportions of strategic minerals.[97] The geologists, outfitted with tents provided by Abercrombie & Fitch, K-rations, jeeps, and other survey equipment, trekked across Alaska in search of mercury, antimony, tungsten, and molybdenite, while mapping prospects and taking core samples to mail back to laboratories in Washington, D.C.[98] In 1943, the mineral experts identified chromium at the Chrome Queen deposits at Red Mountain near the town of Seldovia in southern Alaska, which resulted in the mining of between 1,500 and 2,000 tons of the valuable ore (for comparison, five years earlier, the entire mainland United States had a total annual production of 2,000 tons).[99] Also that year, in the Kantishna district in Denali National Park in central Alaska, the Geological Survey helped facilitate the transfer of nearly 100 tons of antimony ore to U.S. procurement agencies for wartime stockpiling.[100] The stakes were high, and Philip Smith, the geologist in charge of the Alaskan branch, explained, "Not only are we individually on trial, but the whole profession of geology is on the spot to demonstrate that it can contribute significant data to the Nation at this time."[101]

While the efforts may have helped "the Nation," many Alaskans grew disillusioned with the way that Washington interfered in the territory for the benefit of those far removed from it. These tensions were evident in the wartime coal industry, as some profited and others did not. During the war years, coal production nearly doubled, from 238,000 tons in 1941 to an estimated 450,000 tons in 1942. Most of the tonnage came from the Eska Mine, Evans-Jones Mine, and Healy River Coal fields, the latter of which was licensed to private operators who led strip mining of reserves with an estimated 850 million tons of coal.[102] In the middle of these developments, Japanese forces invaded the Aleutian Islands and ignited a panic about the coal supply in the region the following winter of 1943. The problem was not so much one of resource exhaustion, but rather manpower shortages that created a huge deficit in both military and civilian sources of coal, forcing the government to ship coal from Seattle to Alaska.[103] Interior officials sought to solve the manpower deficit with measures that, if implemented, would cut against the labor protections put in place by the New Deal. First, they proposed making use of soldier labor, which exacerbated labor unrest because of wage differentials; soldiers earned a mere $2 per day and civilian miners earned nearly $10.[104] Officials next suggested "importing" civilian miners from the United States, calling for the relaxing of restrictions put in place by the War Manpower Commission.[105]

As another dubious solution, Interior officials enlisted indigenous laborers to mine coal in the northernmost Arctic slope. At the time, Ernest Gruening was leading operations not as the director of DTIP but as the new governor of Alaska. Gruening had been assigned to this post in late

1939 by Roosevelt at the urging of his longtime adversary, Harold Ickes. Ickes cited Gruening's alleged failings of leadership as reason for the move. It was an appointment that Gruening fought tooth and nail, unsuccessfully, to avoid exile in what Interior personnel labeled "the Siberia of the Department."[106] In February 1943, Governor Gruening wrote to Ickes about Alaska's deteriorating coal situation and offered a solution. Gruening suggested that Barrow, where "Natives outnumbered whites 20 to 1," would be an ideal spot for development.[107] Under the supervision of Bureau of Mines engineer Robert S. Sanford, a few dozen "Eskimos" served as coal miners. The task was arduous: long and cold winter nights meant the work had to be done by artificial light in subzero weather in a year that brought unusually high winds and drifting snow. Indigenous workers lived in tents or sod igloos. The supervisors begrudgingly paid a seventy-five cents per hour wage to keep men on the job—although they were still earning three-fourths the wage per day that white civilian miners earned. "It has been very difficult," wrote one Interior official, "to get help among the Natives for erecting the tractor shelters, building the sleds, and preparing for mining."[108] Despite such inimical conditions, indigenous workers eventually unearthed 1,000 tons of coal from the mineral beds at Barrow from 1943 to 1944.[109] Although this amount was insignificant to the broader machinery of war, it was important for offsetting shortages in a region that saw the redirection of valuable resources away from local contexts and toward the war effort. It marked one among many instances in which indigenous peoples became enfolded into adjunct labor regimes organized under wartime exigencies.[110]

In Alaska, it was hard to keep up the pretense that the presence of the federal government was not about exploitation designed to serve outsiders. Residents felt particular antipathy toward Ickes, who taxed transportation systems that brought in and sent out goods, withdrew lands from private citizens, and intensified mineral extraction. Many Alaskans took issue not with the extraction of resources per se but with how government determined, through its strategic mineral programs, the *type* of minerals extracted. For example, some gold mines were shut down, and some miners redirected to sourcing coal for war.[111] Territorial subjects cried out against the regulations imposed by Washington that meant extraction was tailored not necessarily to local interests but rather to national priorities.

Alaskans had a point. By 1942, the United States had exacted a mineral value of $800 million from the territory—the culmination of a spectacle of extractive desire that had left its traces in the cartography through landmarks like Copper River, Tin City, and Antimony Creek.[112] Yet the territory lacked infrastructure and economic development beyond the mining economy. The gashes in the earth and the reliance on racialized labor testified to the ways in which local resources were still being redirected to outsiders: both the Guggenheims *and* Uncle Sam. This was the arrangement that made, in Gruening's view, Alaska a "fief" and Ickes a "lord." Interior officials may have tried to position their imperial management as a departure from the domination of old, but minerals were canaries crying out through the emptiness of that noble rhetoric.

THE INTERIOR DEPARTMENT ASSUMED control of America's imperial circuitry in the twilight of imperialism. Emboldened by the global fight against encroaching Axis powers, anticolonial movements across the globe, as well as at home, were shaking the foundations of imperial governance the world over. If war helped to solidify the ignominy of exploitative imperialism, it also catalyzed a great desire for minerals that made up military arsenals—minerals that happened to exist in the territories of Alaska and the Philippines. At the intersection of territorial affairs and mineral affairs, the Interior Department, led by Harold Ickes, necessarily shifted tactics and discourses to uphold the image of American benevolence on the global stage. Officials consciously abandoned rationales grounded in racial hierarchies that had animated civilizing missions in American empire at the turn of the twentieth century and leaned into the language of scientific and technical assistance. The category of "strategic minerals" fit into this broader agenda, allowing officials to emphasize instrumentality over monetary value and mask the still-troubling arrangements of labor that sourced the materials falling under this new banner. Capitalist interests like the Bethlehem Steel Company, looking to invest in Puerto Rico, and the Luzon Stevedoring Company and Kennecott Copper Company, already established in the Philippines and Alaska, remained important to the process of Interior's expansive agenda as stakeholders. But the U.S. government also struggled to consistently court investment. Unlike the earlier era of imperialism, the government viewed its role helping to create conditions for profit as ancillary to securing material needed for arsenals. Throughout, strategic minerals helped to disguise the mechanisms by which minerals beyond the mainland United States were unleashed from local contexts by local laborers for the express benefit of outsiders.

The territories that factored into Interior's strategic mineral agenda, meanwhile, would have separate and important roles to play in the world. America followed through on its promise in the Tydings-McDuffie Act to grant independence to the Philippines should it meet certain conditions of development. In a speech entitled "The Philippines Comes of Age," Harold Ickes celebrated America's liberation of its former territory despite the predictions of many cynics.[113] He announced that the United States would be granting independence on July 4, 1946, and doing so with pride. Anticipating the developmentalist logic of the postwar era, Ickes compared the Philippines to a child going through different stages of growth under the benevolent tutelage of the United States. Through education and public health programs, the United States had been training the Philippines "to take its place in a community of nations."[114] The territory with the most strategic mineral potential of all, Alaska, would eventually be brought completely into the fold through formal statehood. In the postwar years, the Geological Survey oversaw in Alaska investigations in a strategic mineral that would usher in a new boom: oil.[115]

Even as America, Interior, and Ernest Gruening were extricating the nation from empire, other impulses were pushing them further outward. Namely, as Interior Department leaders attempted to prove institutional relevance in a changing world, the compulsion to leverage old skills in new contexts was increasing. Interior technicians ventured farther abroad, as mineral attachés and technicians in a new form of cooperation in Latin America, a crucial step on the path to America's formal entre into the "development age" of the postwar era. Personnel who cut their teeth on formal territories, like Robert Sanford of the Bureau of Mines, would venture into this international development arena. In 1949, Sanford traveled to Afghanistan and later became the first American technician to arrive in Nepal under the Point Four program, building upon two decades of experience in the Alaska territory.[116] Interior technicians like Sanford would oversee mining operations throughout the developing world in ways that, despite claims and intentions to provide neutral assistance, frequently perpetuated similar hidden violence. Interior's adaptations in the realms of territorial and mineral affairs reveal a desire on behalf of the American state to maintain key benefits of imperialism—raw materials newly branded as strategic minerals—without the burden of playing the imperialist villain.

CHAPTER THREE

The Treasure of the Western Hemisphere

I wonder at how little we knew then about our neighbors.

W. D. Johnston, Geological Survey

I N THE SPRING OF 1941, Eugene Callaghan, a U.S. Geological Survey man from Utah, found himself in Bolivia. Passing through the famed mining regions of Oruro and Potosí, he gathered intelligence on tin, an element that underwrote key alloys in a global war economy strapped for metal needed in tanks, planes, and arms. Callaghan acted with the full cooperation of the Bolivian government and was not alone in his international efforts. Dozens of his peers from the U.S. Department of the Interior were similarly trading domestic assignments for ones scattered throughout Latin America as part of the new State Department–run Interdepartmental Committee on Scientific and Cultural Cooperation, an entity designed to facilitate inter-American knowledge exchanges. Under its auspices, a network of Interior geologists hunted for minerals across the Western Hemisphere in anticipation of the nation's need to arm itself for war. Callaghan and his assistant, for their part, embedded themselves with local and foreign mining operators to gather detailed accounts of regional mining histories. They investigated the trails and roads linking mines to ports and studied the mining methods of indigenous laborers.[1]

During his sidewinding journey across Bolivia, Callaghan discerned mineral riches that reminded him of "the famous camps of the western United States."[2] In this unfamiliar land, he saw a slice of the American West, a region with which he was well acquainted. It was not so wholly strange, in this context, that a man without any experience abroad or diplomatic training should be enlisted on a mission of global significance.

With the onset of global war, the United States launched a cooperative program of strategic mineral procurement in the Western Hemisphere helmed by the U.S. Department of the Interior. The department's sister mineral agencies of the Geological Survey and the Bureau of Mines, already pursuing new strategic minerals in U.S. territories, stood ready to be conscripted into a project of geological reconnaissance in Latin America. The extension of American power in the politics, economics, and environments of Latin America was not particularly new. The United States had long overseen military occupations and interventions in Nicaragua, Panama, Guatemala, Haiti, the Dominican Republic, Cuba, and El Salvador, while profit-seeking institutions, like the United Fruit Company, Phelps Dodge Corporation, and Standard Oil similarly had extracted raw materials there for decades.[3] However, with the unveiling of the Good Neighbor policy in 1933, President Franklin D. Roosevelt had overtly reoriented U.S.-Latin American relations away from U.S.-led exploitation and toward a greater degree of reciprocity and self-determination. With this policy, Roosevelt publicly laid to rest the Monroe Doctrine, the 1823 policy affirming U.S. dominance in the hemisphere against competing European powers, and the Roosevelt Corollary of 1904, which extended this role to declare the nation an international police power. In contrast to these erstwhile pillars of American hemispheric action, the Good Neighbor policy preached—and, to some extent, delivered—nonintervention.[4]

The escalation of global war, however, elicited a different tune from American officials. Those planning for the nation's military preparedness in the event of a declaration of war increasingly eyed minerals in Latin America, a point that became evident at the Eighth American Scientific Congress in 1940. At this event, which was presided over by Secretary of State Cordell Hull, the germ of the idea for cooperative mineral programs was born. Amid the many scientific exchanges—including a paper by

Albert Einstein on theoretical physics—geologists participated in a dialogue about bolstering the mineral stronghold of the hemisphere. Charles Kenneth Leith, the most well-respected geologist in the United States who was not on the Geological Survey payroll, kicked off the debate with a speech entitled "Minerals and the Monroe Doctrine." Fending off encroaching fascism, he argued, required dusting off the recently maligned Monroe Doctrine to create "an impregnable bulwark" for the Western Hemisphere against the advance of aggressor nations. He thus called for the disinterment of both Latin American minerals and a U.S. policy of political and economic intervention that had been publicly laid to rest.[5]

This chapter offers new insight into how the United States secured the Latin American minerals it sought for the arsenal of democracy at war. Historians have revealed the careful negotiations required to bring materials out of foreign landscapes and into American manufacturing facilities in wartime, a process that required slackening protectionist attitudes and tariffs. However, they have largely confined their analyses to elite decision makers, economic planners, and allied industrialists, overlooking a more earthbound complex of procurement rooted in cooperation.[6] The cooperative mineral programs spearheaded by Interior technicians hastened the extraction of minerals like tin, manganese, chromium, and tungsten in Latin America by helping to confer much-needed information *and* legitimacy for the extension of U.S. power. Thus, even as Latin American nations challenged outside exploitation of their natural resources, cooperation became a means for officials to further American procurement initiatives without drawing charges that the United States was reverting to intervention.[7] Reciprocity and exchange of mineral knowledge could and would elicit support from Latin American governments. Cooperative mineral programs, in short, were the neighborly way to do extraction.

Throughout the new undertaking, conceptions about nature played an important role in rationalizing the involvement of the Interior Department and the United States more broadly in the American republics. On the one hand, conservation movements at home stoked the desire of leaders like Harold Ickes to partake in strategic mineral gambits in Latin America; foreign resources seemed a corrective to domestic resource scarcity.[8] On the other hand, for both participants at the Eighth American Scientific

Conference and Interior experts in the field, ideas about nature also provided important mooring for geological work across borders. It united the New World around a shared land mass and shared destiny of cultivating and utilizing land. In their new trappings, Interior personnel like Callaghan drew upon what they knew—strata, outcrops, bedrock, faults, and folds—for orientation in new environs. Thus, if mineral activities in U.S. formal territories illustrate shifting rationales for American empire, the mineral activities in Latin America help to reveal justifications emerging for other forms of U.S. technical intervention, including those in unequivocally foreign zones. Ultimately, these seemingly technical and apolitical efforts would contribute to a U.S. procurement agenda that unearthed Latin American minerals at exponentially higher rates than in prior history, an activity with serious economic and environmental consequences for participating communities. Wartime production merely whetted the appetite for what might follow in a peacetime economy. The result was that cooperative mineral programs continued in the postwar era as well—an era committed to the watchword of self-determination and the agenda of development.

Mountains of Bolivia and antimony mines at the epicenter of tin extraction. 1941. Papers of Eugene Callaghan, Manuscripts Division, Marriott Library, University of Utah.

Cooperation in the New World

For one week in May 1940, thousands of scientists and educators from nations across Western Hemisphere assembled in Washington, D.C. The Eighth American Scientific Congress aimed to spark research exchanges across national borders in furtherance of scientific knowledge, a cause of a common humanity. The meeting was convened by the Pan American Union, an international organization founded in 1890 that debated matters related to trade and law within the hemisphere and made policy recommendations. Since the Pan American Union's founding, its leaders had organized meetings in host cities such as Buenos Aires, Montevideo, Santiago, Rio de Janeiro, Lima, and Mexico City. This latest installment in Washington, D.C., coincided with the fiftieth anniversary of the 1890 founding. It convened scientists working in a variety of disciplines, including anthropology, biology, agriculture, public health, physical and chemical sciences, and education, among others.[9]

President Franklin D. Roosevelt opened the conference proceedings with a radio address on the supreme virtue in such scientific and cultural exchanges. Yet his comments were deeply colored by looming war. On the other side of the globe, the German army steamrolled through Western Europe, eliciting the surrender of three independent nations. Such horrors, Roosevelt offered in his address, were disheartening, but they also cast into high relief how the rest of the world abhorred "conquest and war and bloodshed" and instead believed "the hand of neighbor shall not be lifted against neighbor," an unmistakable reference to the special relations between the United States and Latin America. Roosevelt then transitioned to the undertaking at hand, the Eighth American Scientific Congress, contending that the Western Hemisphere, or what he carefully called the New World, was "no accident." The New World, he observed, was a project struck off by the very best adventurers and visionaries of an Old World that—despite being newly embroiled in war—had once privileged science and culture over the "crudities and barbarities of less civilized eras." The New World, Roosevelt argued, was the last refuge for open dialogue and reciprocal relations in the world.[10]

The tenets of openness and reciprocity had been building blocks of U.S.-Latin American relations since the New Deal. At a 1933 conference in Montevideo, Uruguay, President Roosevelt had unveiled the Good Neighbor policy, which marked an express departure from the U.S. domination of old that had been set out in the Monroe Doctrine and Theodore Roosevelt's refurbishment, the Roosevelt Corollary, designed to amplify America's policing power in the region. The incumbent president sought to reorient national policy in the Western Hemisphere in the years after decades of U.S. intervention in the Caribbean. The United States faced increasing pressure from peasants, workers, and elites in Latin America who had become increasingly disillusioned with the preponderance of American companies and military personnel in their nations. It was thus little wonder that the Roosevelt administration invited renowned anti-imperialists like Ernest Gruening to take part in the proceedings of the Montevideo conference; officials sought both a symbolic and substantive renovation of policy. In and through the negotiations at Montevideo, Roosevelt established a new paradigm rooted in nonintervention, withdrawal of U.S. military forces, and the revision of agreements that blatantly favored the United States. In this new context, the United States exhibited a greater tolerance of Latin American nations' independent desires and actions.[11]

Rather than drastically altering hemispheric dynamics, the Good Neighbor policy became a gentler means by which to further U.S. influence in the region.[12] U.S. multinational companies in the agricultural and mining industries continued to exert incredible economic power. In a vivid critique of this ongoing economic hegemony, the Mexican government famously nationalized the petroleum industry in 1938. American and Anglo companies had dominated Mexico's petroleum industry in the interwar period, a drama in which former Interior Secretary Albert B. Fall had played a key role. In a defiant display of nationalism years later, Mexican President Lázaro Cárdenas expropriated the petroleum industry, effectively dissolving American and other foreign ownership of oil companies and consolidating these holdings under the national Petróleos Mexicanos (Pemex).[13] The Mexican nationalization bedeviled U.S. policymakers in the decade that followed. As one Interior Department report on the nationalization condescendingly summarized in 1941, the expropriation had made high returns on mining "a thing of the past" and encouraged among Mexicans a complacency tied to the "free and easy life of merchant princes."[14] Ultimately, the nationalization exposed the failures of the Good Neighbor policy to restrict U.S. interference in Latin America, despite the policy's promise to serve as a safeguard against it.

Both enthusiasm for and criticism of the Good Neighbor policy therefore framed the Eighth American Scientific Congress. When the 300 scientists from Latin America joined 2,000 of their colleagues from the United States at the 1940 meeting, cracks had surfaced in the collegial façade of U.S.-Latin American relations. In a clear attempt to offset these tensions, the U.S. organizing committee turned the conference into a pageant of anti-imperialist commitment. Officials began by decrying German belligerence in its global ambitions and declaring respect for each nation's self-determination. Secretary of State Cordell Hull made this deference to sovereignty clear in his opening remarks. "Each of our nations has its own problems and its own preoccupations," he began, and each representative similarly maintained loyalty to his or her "own country" and its particular "needs and problems."[15] He effectively acknowledged the type of national interests that had animated unilateral action like the Mexican nationalization. The spectacle of anti-imperialism would end with a postconference trip by steamer to Yorktown, Virginia, which was meant to remind the participants of America's own birth in anticolonial struggle. There they visited the scene of the surrender of America's former colonial overlords, Great Britain, to the apotheosis of U.S. anti-imperialism, George Washington.[16]

Operating uneasily alongside this anti-imperialist pageantry was the continual recourse to the attendees' shared New World identity. Beginning with Roosevelt, U.S. officials addressing the attendees conveyed a symbolic commitment to "the destiny of the New World."[17] The New World cartography advanced in and through these citations was complex. It conjured the arrival of European colonizers in uncharted continents (indigenous populations were not part of the imaginary), a process that linked peoples to the north and south in the hemisphere. Undersecretary of State Sumner Welles celebrated the era in which "our forefathers were busy exploring this hemisphere, were clearing its forests and were breaking its virgin soil," all the while enabling the flow of ideas rooted in philosophy and science from the Old World. The New World, Welles implied, was the heir to this heroic effort of mastering the earth. The chosen representative of Latin American nations, Dr. Domingo F. Ramos of Cuba, echoed these sentiments. After citing a shared history as members of the New World, he called attention to the namesake of the hotel in which they gathered, the Mayflower, as a reminder of the brave Europeans who civilized their hemisphere.[18] The masters of ceremony thus emphasized the Western enlightenment rationality on which the sciences were based, as well as the systematic use of natural resources, while downplaying the history of imperialism to which it was also inextricably tied. To celebrate what united them was to celebrate imperialism.

Such contradictions did little to slow the proliferation of declarations of hemispheric amity. In speeches at the conference, leaders found an imaginative range of ways to reinforce this relationship. Roosevelt and Hull consistently referred to "the Americas," "American republics," and "sister republics," while Roosevelt in particular painted a portrait of a family under siege by a common enemy. He observed that "every single acre—every hectare—in all the Americas from the Arctic to the Antarctic" was closer to the attacks of aggressor nations in Europe than all wars of previous human history.[19] The trend toward the hemisphere was not the exclusive province of the United States. As Ramos summarized in his remarks as the representative of Latin America at the congress, "No more does the name 'America' mean 'North America,' nor does it mean 'Our America' of the Latin Americans." He added, "There is only one America, . . . which embraces all the continent from the Behring Strait to that of Magellan, or better still, from pole to pole."[20] Hemispheric cooperation in a global context of war had helped to meld an assortment of divided states into a greater whole, one naturalized by both Roosevelt and Ramos as continents spanning from pole to pole. As the authors of the Pan American Union bulletin summarized, "Science recognizes no frontiers."[21] The Eighth American Scientific Congress was a meditation on how blurring boundaries in the name of science might make a better world.

The geologists who assembled at the meeting offered one vision for how to bring about this better world: acquiring strategic minerals in Latin America. While the geological papers covered a variety of topics in theoretical geology, tectonics, and volcanology, the practical pursuit of mineral resources emerged as a key concern. In several sessions devoted to strategic minerals, luminaries in the field from across the United

States and Latin America shared the latest accounts of the progress of mineral development in each country. Representing the United States, Charles Kenneth Leith joined the renowned petroleum geologists Everette DeGolyer and James Terry Duce, as well as a team of U.S. Geological Survey scientists including Hugh D. Miser, Ernest Burchard, and Parker D. Trask, who would eventually conduct a key manganese investigation in Mexico as part of the cooperative mineral programs.[22] Dozens of experts representing nations to the south, including Venezuelan Minister of Public Works Pedro Ignacio Aguerrevere, Mexican chief of geophysics in the Geological Institute Luis Flores Covarrubias, and Brazilian director of the Geology and Mineral Division of the Ministry of Agriculture Glycon de Paiva Teixeira, also reported on the latest developments in the mining industries of their countries.[23]

The reality was that Interior Department geologists and mineral experts had been monitoring the situation in Europe and turning to Latin America as a potential solution since the mid-1930s. The Bureau of Mines initiated a Foreign Mineral Service Division in 1935 to gather information on minerals and mining methods across Europe. Its experts undertook posts in industrial areas in Great Britain, France, Belgium, and Germany. Acting as a liaison between Interior, the Foreign Service office of the State Department, and local governments, the mineral experts conducted an economic survey of the international flow of minerals. The efforts resulted in *Mineral Raw Materials* (1937), a publication recounting the production, distribution, and consumption of thirty-two major minerals from antimony to zinc, from Austria to South Africa.[24] In the late 1930s, the Bureau of Mines representative in Europe, Charles W. Wright, returned with some disturbing news. As hostilities were growing in Europe, German engineers in particular had pioneered new technologies and processes to offset limited national resources by optimizing lower-grade ores. Germany found particular success in the area of synthetic fuels, far outpacing the United States.[25] To avoid being embroiled in potential war, the Bureau of Mines foreign mineral division moved from an office in London to one in La Paz, Bolivia, in 1937. This move, the bureau's director explained, would serve as a "practical demonstration of the President's 'Good Neighbor' policy."[26] The goal was to "foster the mineral industries of these sister republics" and to "open new sources of supply" to America with a clear eye to activities in Europe.[27]

Mineral development was not the only Interior Department activity under way in Latin America prior to the Eighth American Scientific Congress. One month earlier, Interior Department personnel had traveled to Mexico City to participate in the first Inter-American Conference on Indian Life. Among the U.S. officials in attendance were Bureau of Indian Affairs commissioner John Collier and future Interior secretary Oscar L. Chapman.[28] They joined representatives from Canada, Mexico, and fifteen Latin American nations in a conversation about crafting a "hemisphere-wide Indian policy" on the grounds that problems faced by indigenous peoples, including the encroachment of whites on their lands, were "almost the same" across borders. The resulting seventy-three-page report covered a range of topics related to socioeconomic problems and proposed solutions for indigenous peoples, including agricultural development, industrialization, public health, and education. However, the report made no mention of minerals and mining. This was a conspicuous absence. Indigenous communities in places like Bolivia, Mexico, and Peru had long been at the center of storied mining economies and conflict. Moreover, President Cárdenas, who just two years earlier had nationalized the Mexican petroleum industry, offered the opening remarks for the event.[29] Minerals perhaps seemed too loaded a topic given the historic dispossessions done in service of raw material exploitation across the Western Hemisphere.

In summer 1940, as the German war machine blazed across Europe, the topic of raw materials in Latin America surfaced without apparent controversy in Leith's opening remarks at the Eighth American Scientific Congress. Leith, a sixty-six-year-old University of Wisconsin professor, had been a prodigious contributor to U.S. mineral policy throughout the twentieth century. In the interwar period, Leith engaged in the contentious debates in the mining industry about promoting foreign or domestic resources through trade or tariff. Leith believed in the importance of exchanging unevenly distributed minerals across national borders and loudly promoted internationalism in mineral policy leading up to the 1940s.[30] His remarks at the Eighth American Scientific Conference quickly became a reflection on the Monroe Doctrine, a policy that had similarly called for downplaying national borders within the hemisphere. He began by expounding the ways that minerals defined political power: they defined a nation's "capacity to make guns, ships, airplanes, and motors." Leith never once mentioned the word "strategic," or the category of "strategic minerals," even as he emphasized the same minerals understood to be building blocks of the implements of war. This omission suggests the label was more important to scientists working in government—those trying to garner funds for projects across borders—than to those scientists working in academia, albeit many (including Leith) consistently worked as adjuncts in the American state.[31] Defending the mineral stronghold, he continued, was tantamount to defending democracy itself. In the face of dictators bent on expansion, it was providential that "the Americas" had such natural mineral abundance. A threat to one nation's minerals in the hemisphere, Leith argued, "weakens by just so much the power of this region as a whole."[32]

Since the United States had distinguished itself as the most capable of converting mineral abundance into usable force, Leith maintained that it must lead. It should oversee "the development of raw material resources necessary for the defense of the Monroe Doctrine against outside aggression." It was therefore time, in Leith's view, to set aside the recent nationalist actions, like the Mexican expropriation, which compelled nations in Latin America to begin "closing the door" to "outside exploration and development," prohibiting the flow of resources across borders. Such impulses, he argued, needed to be set aside. To defend the hemisphere against encroaching forces would necessitate a return to developing the "resources of the Americas in their complementary relationships." What Leith called for, then, was for Latin American nations to open their doors to U.S. mineral enthusiasts who might harness the minerals of war. He did not clarify whether American direct investment or trade would define these relationships. What mattered, more than the means, was the end result: the exchange of minerals across borders would maintain the "cooperative peace of the Western Hemisphere."[33]

Following Leith's appeal, the participating geologists reached a broad consensus that an official program for inter-American mineral pursuits was needed. They ultimately adopted a resolution that aimed to determine the scope of natural resources in the Western Hemisphere.[34] As

director of the Geological Survey W. C. Mendenhall would later summarize, these conversations initiated a process by which the United
States developed a policy of resource exploration rooted in *cooperation*. Throughout the conference, American leaders had emphasized cooperation and mutual benefit—two deeply entrenched values that had
long been espoused by Latin American leaders.[35] In the invitation to
the attendees, for example, the State Department insisted that the United
States sought to promote "friendly cooperation" in the Western Hemisphere. In his opening radio address, Roosevelt also testified to the importance of "the spirit of cooperation" to advancing more peaceful relations.[36] The geologists built upon this call. "It was *natural*," Mendenhall
observed, "that the Geological Survey's initial move should be an evaluation of how the cooperative geological program could best serve in the
procurement of strategic minerals."[37] Mendenhall's claim that crossing
borders to procure minerals was natural harmonized with the broader
effort on behalf of U.S. officials to naturalize ties among the so-called
American republics of the New World. From the vantage point of officials and geologists, it was one big, happy hemisphere.

The proposed cooperative mineral agenda in Latin America ultimately
gained traction because it dovetailed with transformations already under
way to meet the material demands of war. The Roosevelt administration
had begun cobbling together ad hoc committees for this purpose in the
late 1930s and continued to do so leading up to America's formal entrance
into the war. The Army-Navy Munitions Board, central to the passage of
the Strategic and Critical Materials Act of 1939, was joined by new agencies like the War Resources Board and National Defense Advisory Commission, as well as the purchasing agencies of the U.S. Metals Reserve
Company and U.S. Purchasing Commission. Ickes, meanwhile, became
the petroleum coordinator for defense and later the petroleum administrator for war. These different entities would converge, at times fractiously,
to marshal the resources for defense buildup.[38] Within this broader bureaucratic ecology, the Interior Department provided personnel to procure minerals and promote inter-American relations, a task Ickes would
be all too happy to trot out as an example of the essential programming
overseen by the Interior Department. His department was proudly securing the materials needed for the "arsenal of democracy" at home and

abroad.[39] For the initial programs, Congress provided the seed money, $25,000, before quickly increasing the allocation to $150,000, a price tag offset with money from the newly formed Board of Economic Warfare.[40] The funds for cooperative mineral work in Latin America were a modest entry in the balance sheet of procurement, but they were small in part because government officials planned to rely on their allies in foreign nations and the private sector to finance much of the extractive enterprises. With the backing of funds from Uncle Sam, the Geological Survey was about to put boots on the bedrock.

Geological Reconnaissance

"I wonder," W. D. Johnston observed, "at how little we knew then about our neighbors." Johnston was looking back on the initial encounters between Interior geologists and locals in Latin American nations under the cooperative mineral programs of the 1940s.[41] When making this observation in 1952, he was serving as the director of the Geological Survey's foreign minerals division under the Point Four program of international development—a sage, de facto diplomat who had traveled the world over. Yet when he first arrived in Brazil's most lucrative mining region, Minas Gerais, in 1941, he was just one of many technicians doing strategic mineral work in a foreign land and feeling unprepared for the task. Their training had not been in the nuances of American foreign relations, the Portuguese or Spanish languages, or Latin America's many national cultures. Instead, the grounding for these geologists in their new environs came from the physical contours of the land itself. The geological formations they examined in Latin America were wrought by the same million-year processes of erosion and reaction as those in North America. The terrain, whether serpentine folds dotted with chrome or pegmatite beds suffused with mica and beryl, seemed to care little for political boundaries of national sovereignty, the comparatively new inventions of enlightenment modernity.

While U.S. decision makers emphasized an "American" political alliance, technicians in the field framed their international activity as a natural extension of their work with resource extraction in the American West. Looking on these foreign but familiar structures, Interior geologists drew upon institutional memory in prospecting the continental landscape. The technicians were not the first Geological Survey personnel to venture beyond borders (Clarence King, the first director of the Geological Survey, had overseen investigations in Mexico in the 1880s), but theirs was the first systematic effort to disseminate personnel to foreign nations.[42] The reports they would compile revealed an impulse to conflate home and abroad. Doing so helped the geologists to understand their work as being concerned with the natural world and divorced from the political world. Authors, for instance, frequently drew comparisons to landscapes back in the United States. The manganese beds of Haiti conjured those of Colorado, while the deposits near Durango and Guanajuato, Mexico, resembled those of the Black Range in New Mexico and Lander County, Nevada. Often, these conflations were rooted in hands-on experience. William T. Pecora, who would become the director of the Geological Survey in the 1960s, oversaw multiple mineral expeditions in Brazil. He observed in the nickel-rich region of Goaiz the likeness of Riddle, Oregon, the place he had prospected just a few years before.[43] The bibliographies cited in the reports overwhelmingly referred to Geological Survey work done throughout the western United States and Alaska. What else would they cite? Their repertoire of geological knowledge was inseparable from the decades of exploration of an expanse of territory that had once been expropriated from indigenous peoples and Mexico, a nation that, in the new geopolitical context, had become a target of cooperative mineral work.[44] For the transplanted geologists, those interpreters of earthly scripts, it seemed natural to collapse home and abroad into one entity, the Americas. Geology was the ultimate boundary eraser.

Under the new directive of the Interdepartmental Committee on Scientific and Cultural Cooperation, dozens of Interior geologists and mineral experts embarked on fact-finding missions in Latin America. These missions took many forms. The first involved geological reconnaissance on the ground. Agents set out to provide "prompt, reliable, first-hand information" of the terrain and, in so doing, lay foundations for long-term trade relations.[45] Geological Survey men (and it was all men) led teams of geologists in investigations of areas in their assigned countries. These teams coordinated with local officials and mine operators before undertaking their surveys, which targeted specific minerals or mineral types.

For instance, Thomas P. Thayer examined chromite in Cuba, while Eugene Callaghan examined tin in Bolivia. Over the course of three to six months, the geologists traveled to hundreds of deposits and existing mines, covering around one hundred acres with each assignment. Identifying ores of interest, they evaluated their grade, a metric denoting the concentration of the desired element. They determined, as one example, what percentage of a rock aggregate was usable manganese. All of this information shaped the geologists' opinions, conveyed in reports, as to whether the establishment of mining operations was warranted or not. The geologists would be amazed by the findings, writing in correspondence and reports about the potential of the "virgin ground" discovered.[46] As one technician observed of Cuba, "There are some real ore bodies in that country!"[47]

The reconnaissance frequently began with gathering details about the history of mining in the region. The geologists venturing abroad were walking into a region with centuries of overlapping imperial intentions. The indigenous inhabitants of Latin America had known and made use of minerals like tin, petroleum, and gold in the pre-Columbian era.[48] When the Interior geologists arrived, they were inundated by accounts of the transition from indigenous mining economies to those implemented during Spanish colonization. Local prospectors in Bolivia, for example, had recounted for Callaghan the colorful history of silver and tin mining in the famed Potosí Hill. According to the handed-down stories, an indigenous sheepherder named Diego Huellpe tracked his lost llama to that fateful hill. There, unearthly sounds emanating from the geological structure gave him a fright. Fighting through a superstitious fear of what time revealed to be mere churnings of sulfur and chloride, he discovered the silver vein that captivated the imaginations of countless Spanish adventurers and prompted their further invasion in the region.[49] The Spanish colonization that ensued, and that indeed featured prominently in most local mining histories, initiated a generations-long tradition of unrestrained exploitation of the region's copious material resources. It was a ritual of capital accumulation that relied on systems of coerced labor. The arrival of a new armada of European and American business interests in the nineteenth century constituted a variation on a theme, as the investors built more industrialized structures of extraction atop the already

dense scaffolding of competing European colonialisms and local indigenous mining cultures.[50] The Interior geologists and mineral experts constantly remarked on the persistence of these histories in the present
mining economy. They observed, for example, that "native" mining had
continued "with little change in mining method since the colonial period."[51] Such language suggested that the geologists also saw the journey
south as a form of time travel.

Interior geologists, hardly the first outsiders or U.S. citizens to arrive
in Latin America, relied on the help of existing mining outfits in their
search for subterranean treasures. Many of the American companies that
had been in the region for decades offered important information to the
Geological Survey teams upon arrival. For example, in Colombia, the
companies of Texas Petroleum, Richmond Petroleum, and the American
Metal Company provided to the Interior geologists useful background
on assorted minerals.[52] In a more speculative kind of venture, Interior
agents also turned to Standard Oil for consultations in the fledgling attempt to initiate oil operations in Cuba.[53] Local mining companies and
those owned or formerly owned by non-American outside investors also
opened their doors to the Interior geologists, offering crucial support and
information. Callaghan, for example, began his inquest into the tin deposits of Oruro by turning to the Compañia Minera de Oruro, a firm
owned by German tin baron Moritz Hochschild, for annual reports on
findings and earnings.[54] In Brazil, William Pecora acquired valuable
statistics from the mine operators, foremen, merchants, and export companies in place. These statistics, in turn, helped Pecora to summarize
production and calculate reserves for the final Geological Survey report
on mica.[55] Capitalists of different national origin saw in the cooperative
mineral programs an ally that might spur development in the region and
secure buyers in the form of U.S. procurement agencies. This, in turn,
meant steady profits. It was not an explicit aim of the cooperative programs to further the interests of *American* firms over others, but there
would be accusations that this is precisely what they did.

Alongside mineral reconnaissance, the geological diplomats also
reported extensively on the labor situation in each country. In the process, they drew problematic conclusions about the ability and *exploit-
ability* of the workers. Many field agents gathered census data and local

testimonies to summarize and evaluate the labor population at the ready, a taxonomy that mirrored George F. Becker's accounts of Filipino laborers in 1899. The report on the worker population in Colombia, for example, explained, "Coal-black Negroes predominate, but there also are mulattos, whites, and indigenous Indians."[56] In addition to this crude demography, the geologists' reports commented on "native mining," which came to be synonymous with the removal of minerals "by hand." Such methods, the reports observed, had continued without improvement for centuries.[57] Although the manual labor of this approach to mining was undoubtedly difficult and dangerous, it was also autonomous; the direct producers of the minerals determined the shape and purpose of their production. Interior geologists, as we shall see, continually pushed to introduce new technologies into the production process to correct the supposed ills of native mining by hand, which historically had met local and regional mineral needs.

The technicians complained about the inability or unwillingness of local workers to adapt to such methods. Phil Guild, for example, noted, with a little agitation, that when instituting new drilling operations in Cuba, it was necessary "to keep constant check on them, and give them instructions on how to run their machines."[58] The workers were not adopting the new methods with the desired speed. Guild's framing implied that workers could not be trusted to fulfill complicated tasks on their own for reasons of individual shortcomings rather than external factors, such as the imposition of foreign models explained in foreign languages. This bias mirrored the assumption by sociologists of Third World development that peasant classes had an irrational and unmotivated attitude toward the introduction of capitalist industrial processes into their regions.[59] Throughout, ideas about human superiority or inferiority were being routed through a seemingly neutral standard of technologic capability rather than the supposed biological difference that had been so central to cataloguing human differences—divided between civilized and primitive societies—in Becker's calculus at the turn of the twentieth century. These hierarchies of technical ability laid foundations for an ideology that would gain prominence in the Point Four program: "resource primitivism," which upheld that primitive people misunderstood and undervalued their own resources and needed constant supervision.

Callaghan made detailed and at times sensitive observations about local labor conditions in Bolivia. Much has been written of the dogged resistance among Bolivian tin workers to the introduction of capitalist modes of production in their communities. This resistance manifested in labor-union organizing in the mid-1940s, leading up to the expropriation of the tin industry in 1952, as well as in folklore that, as Michael Taussig has convincingly argued, used the figure of the devil to make sense of the violence imposed upon laborers by the transplant processes of commoditization.[60] Callaghan was therefore making an on-the-ground study of Bolivia at a decisive moment. In the region of Oruro, a hub of tin mining, Callaghan observed how indigenous women were central to the extraction of tin and antimony. He noted how these women broke up the ore with hammers and single jacks to free antimony-bearing material from the rock aggregate before sorting out the finer material by hand jigging. Through such procedures, they extracted 500 tons of antimony in four months.[61] Callaghan took numerous photos documenting their methods. Protected from the sun by tall hats and shawls, and settled on the ground, the women at the Tronchiri mine sorted out antimony on the *cancha,* or the flat surface. In similar attire, the women working in the Huanuni district walked along the tramway where the tin granules they screened by hand would be sent to mill. For these employees of the Bolivian Tin and Tungsten Mines Corporation, Callaghan reported, the daily ritual of work built toward the festival time in February. Then the local workers loaded the best ore mined, or *guia,* on a special train and presented it to the company for a ceremonious inspection.[62] Although Callaghan seemed to maintain some reverence for such local traditions, he was at other times repulsed by their inefficiency. Elsewhere he regretted how "only a small amount of tin has been produced by native contractors using primitive methods."[63] Callaghan, like most of his peers, looked with condescension on the laborers being enfolded into a production process that was humming along at a breakneck pace because of war.

While frequently dismissive of the workers' skill, Interior agents were also scouting for unskilled, cheap labor. Keeping mining cheap was an objective of the American geologists because it helped attract the investors who made it possible to get minerals out of the ground for the war effort; it also ensured that prices would be favorable when U.S. procurement agencies bought the material at the end of the production cycle. In Costa Rica, when Interior agents calculated the costs to develop the mining industry, labor emerged as an important question. The nation's skilled labor was already wrapped up in infrastructure projects like the Panama Canal Zone and the Pan-American Highway, but there were plenty of unskilled laborers on hand accustomed to receiving low wages (around 75 cents an hour, the price paid to indigenous Alaskans for mining coal in the Arctic slope).[64] The geologists assigned to Haiti were also explicit about the way that labor could be secured at minimal expense. "The low cost of labor in Haiti," the geologists observed, "makes it possible to mine ore cheaply by hand drilling and hand sorting."[65] This would be particularly true, they suggested, if open-pit mining operations could be instituted, as common laborers could "be procured in abundance at a rate of 30 cents (U.S. currency) a day."[66] Field agents like Parker D. Trask therefore paid careful attention to any shifting trends in the labor climate in their locales. Trask noted that in Mexico the cost of labor was the "most important single factor" in making manganese mining profitable for local

Bolivian women at the mine. Callaghan viewed these operations, and "native mining" practices, with admiration and condescension. 1941. Papers of Eugene Callaghan, Manuscripts Division, Marriott Library, University of Utah.

operators and reasonable for the U.S. government. If the wage scale rose, technicians would need to collaborate with local governments and investors to develop cheaper methods for extracting ores.[67] Controlling the cost of extractive labor was as important to the cooperative mineral programs as shaping its organization.

The geologists ultimately pooled the resulting intelligence into voluminous reports. In the span of just four years, they produced forty entries, around one hundred pages each.[68] Upon completion, the reports were sent to the war agencies, such as the War Production Board and the Board of Economic Warfare.[69] In keeping with the protocols of cooperation, officials also provided reports "to citizens of the countries in which the deposits are situated," a passive phrasing that signaled a tenuous relationship between locals and those minerals and subtly undercut local ownership. Nevertheless, they disseminated (frequently bilingual) maps to their partners.[70] There were exceptions to this dogma of openness. The reports of Eugene Callaghan in Bolivia, for example, were designated confidential and were never published for the broader public. Discoveries in the tin capital of the world appeared to the American state to be too valuable to the war effort to disseminate more broadly.[71] The remaining reports, the cumulative efforts of dozens of geologists and collaborators over the span of several months, ultimately worked to aid both in state-led procurement and in private investment. Even the realization that reserves were not worthy of development was valuable information for potential investors. As one report on the minerals of Colombia summarized, the team's discovery of uneconomic deposits worked "to save others the time-consuming task of tracking them down, examining them, and appraising them."[72]

Meanwhile, from their offices in nearby American embassies, the Bureau of Mines experts who worked as mineral attachés compiled and disseminated economic data and coordinated with geologists on the ground to establish a thorough mineral intelligence base. For example, Wright worked with Geological Survey technicians in Brazil to assess six samples from nickel deposits, and Callaghan made use of Wright's reports on the minerals of Bolivia.[73] Consolidating information about mineral flows across the globe became increasingly difficult as the United States entered the war. Nations began censoring mineral information, prompting the Bureau of Mines to pursue new channels of gathering information "badly needed," including obtaining statistics on a confidential basis from sources in non-enemy countries and filling in gaps with the testimonies of German émigrés to the United States.[74] In mining regions or American embassies throughout Latin America, Interior agents helped to acquire the information about minerals necessary to hasten their flow to the United States.

Ultimately, the strategic mineral programs in Latin America consti-tuted the underbelly of the Interior Department's renowned conservation programs at home. In 1942, a low point in the Allies' efforts to stem Axis infiltration across the globe, Secretary of the Interior Harold Ickes blamed America's failure to implement a meaningful conservation program for minerals in the years before. This former mineral profligacy, Ickes argued, was the reason for the current uncertainty about national brawn in war-time. For years, he claimed, the United States had "deluded" itself with the belief that it was self-sufficient and its resources were inexhaustible. Yet a "painful hangover" resulted from this misguided notion. "We woke up to find out that we did not have enough steel to do the job." Ickes con-tinued, "[W]e did not have enough aluminum; we were short of power; we lacked magnesium; our sources of manganese were too far away to do us much good . . . and the chaos of war tied our petroleum service into knots."[75] For Ickes, the United States had run its economy on "fat" and "went merrily on [its] way, using only the best, and therefore the most profitable," while "'had-not' nations turned to secondary ores and low-grade minerals and, by sweat and effort, learned how to use them."[76] While the United States sat idly, the comparatively resource-poor Ger-many and Japan toiled over methods to get the most out of lower grades, developing lean and hard-bodied war machines, much to the wonderment of American technicians.[77] For Ickes, catching up required a combination of conservationism at home and unencumbered extraction elsewhere. In short, the Interior Department's strategy for supplying the minerals needed to win the war increasingly required securing resources from Latin America. In the process, materials would be unearthed in Latin American in ways that hardly conformed to conservationist principles of the department.

Holes in the Ground

The year 1943 was like Christmas morning for Brazilian mine operators in the mica business. Backed by funds from the United States, a bundle of extractive toys arrived in Minas Gerais in the form of bulldozers, tractors, scrapers, air compressors, jackhammers, hoists, pumps, mine tracks, and mine cars. The high-tech gifts were meant to spur the production of mica, a mineral crucial to electrical switchboards, on which the logistics of war relied. Before the arrival of U.S. technical advisors, all mica mining in Minas Gerais was developed on a "primitive basis" without geological surveys or advanced technologies.[78] However, after receiving technical aid in the form of Interior geologists like William T. Pecora, as well as subsidies from the U.S. Purchasing Commission, Brazilian mine operators acquired gleaming new means of production.[79] This "earth-moving equipment" bolstered the haulage, ventilation, and overall efficiency of underground mining. But it also enabled new open-pit mining operations on a grand scale that would unearth the ore at an astonishing rate—approximately 2.5 million cubic meters in the span of a year.[80] The recent construction of mine-access roads linking to the federal Rio-Baía highway, in turn, brought the increased tonnage of mica to the processing shops and ports of Rio de Janeiro.[81] Such renovations of mining technology and infrastructure ultimately helped establish a pipeline for strategic minerals to the United States.

U.S. Geological Survey technicians in Latin America realized quickly that to upend the earth for minerals, other renovations of society were needed. Careful not to cast judgment on the elites and officials hosting them as part of this neighborly cooperation, Interior experts offered subtle critiques of the existing practices for utilizing landscapes. Infrastructure and technology became watchwords for making normative claims about the societies in which U.S. officials were embedded. The U.S. geologists, for example, suggested that the introduction of certain infrastructures and technologies would counter the ruggedness and inaccessibility of the terrain, which had prevented these nations from using the mineral base beyond local requirements and from generating surpluses for trade. The nation that did not have adequate accommodations did not produce minerals on a scale that allowed for their greater integration into the global market, the clear measure of an advanced society. A lack of market integration was the real malady, of which lacking infrastructure was a symptom and improved infrastructure a potential cure. A familiar refrain emerged in reports to the effect that production would increase with the "opening and improving roads and by introducing efficient mining and milling equipment."[82] The desire to extract strategic minerals for war, put differently, bolstered a desire to remake the infrastructure of Latin American nations more broadly. Such projects, in turn, became the central hinge of policy in postwar development.

The problems of infrastructure, in the eyes of the geologists, were manifold. First, the nations lacked adequate road, rail, and water transportation systems. In Haiti, the lucrative manganese deposit of Morne Macaque was an uneasy distance from existing roads and sea ports. In order to bring trucks in and out of the site, a new road would need to be built at an estimated cost of $15,000.[83] Across the Latin American republics, access to water needed for mining and sorting processes could be seriously limited, while, on the flipside, wet seasons could make bad roads insurmountable. Such was the case in Costa Rica, where rainy months made heavy hauling "impossible."[84] The experts working in cooperative mineral programs observed the problems and recommended technical transformations. Their reports, which circulated to U.S. agencies providing aid, to companies looking to invest, and to local governments, constantly called for further economic renovations to turn abundant reserves into worthwhile investments. In some cases, these suggestions materialized in actual projects. The iron deposits of Mato Grasso in Brazil, for example, laid dormant until road repairs requested by American geologists opened them up to shipping routes. The United States would eventually purchase 17,225 tons of ore from the newly accessible region.[85]

Interior agents also sought to modernize the means of production, as in the case of the Brazilian mica industry. A broad network of Interior employees, some in the field and some in Washington, D.C., worked with companies on the ground to distribute technologies like cableways, mine machineries, and haulage tunnels that sped extraction—in most cases paid for by the operators themselves. Geological Survey employees at home, for example, knew the day that the high-speed drill arrived and was first put to use in Cuba, as well as how the magnetometer was working in delimiting boundaries of exploration.[86] These implements were actually subsidized by participating companies, not the U.S. government. Such arrangements seemed to allow the U.S. government to maintain the appearance of neutral broker in the region. It further preempted spiraling requests for funds from the U.S. government through cooperative programs. Thayer explained to the Cuban Foreign Service representative that drilling was at the expense of the companies, and that the Geological Survey itself was purely operating on a consulting basis. He explained, in simple terms, "[T]he Geological Survey had no funds, equipment, or organization to drill deposits for individuals in Cuba at Government expense."[87]

The relationship between the U.S. government and American mining firms was both intimate and rife with conflict. The chrome situation in Cuba revealed these volatile relations. The Interior geologists like Thayer worked closely with the American-owned Bethlehem Steel corporation, which oversaw chromite operations in the Camaguey district and iron ore mining in the province of Oriente in Cuba.[88] A powerhouse steel producer, Bethlehem Steel had owned iron mining properties in Cuba since the early 1900s, consolidating more control over the island's iron mines after purchasing the Pennsylvania Steel Company in 1917, as the United States entered the First World War. In collaborating with the government to meet wartime demands, Bethlehem's leaders learned an important lesson: corporations alone could not provide the capital necessary and therefore had to rely on the government for financing. With assistance from the government, production could meet increased demands and generate sizeable profits. By the outset of the Second World War, the company also had iron properties across Latin America, including in the province of Coquimbo in Chile, and in the state of Bolivar in Venezuela—a mineral base they estimated to encompass 118 million tons of ore.[89] At the same time, Geological Survey personnel served as a gatekeeper between mine operators in Latin America and U.S. purchasing agencies. Companies like the American-owned Bethlehem Steel and Cuban-owned Moa Company vied for contracts for the sale of their war materiel. Thayer worried that the Cuban operators might levy a "charge of discrimination" against the Geological Survey for favoring companies of American origin.[90] Another geologist, Herbert Hawkes, explained to Bethlehem Steel's representative the importance of maintaining the appearance of neutrality in their interactions. "Comments already have been made," Hawkes argued, "to the effect that the Survey is playing favorites with Bethlehem." He added that such perceptions, even if "not altogether justified" could "work to the detriment of all parties concerned." Hawkes sought to avoid "any justification for damaging gossip—damaging to the interests of both the Survey and Bethlehem."[91]

However, if the U.S. government attracted charges of favoritism toward Bethlehem Steel, it also drew accusations of meddling in the company's affairs. Bethlehem personnel were also frustrated with the pains the Geological Survey took to instill certain methods of extraction in Cuba.[92] After meetings in New York and Washington, D.C., in 1942, Geological Survey employees arranged to have the Gulf Research and Development Company introduce a gravimeter, a new technology for extracting ores, to Bethlehem operators. Despite federal attempts to get Bethlehem to adopt new methods, the mine operators resisted. As result, Interior employees like Thayer complained that the latest products pioneered by government research were "a little too visionary for a hard-headed mining company."[93] Such commentary betrayed the racial assumptions that clouded the technicians' perceptions: whereas indigenous miners who refused to adopt such technologies were "primitive," American mining operators who resisted were instead "hard-headed." After much back-and-forth over the issue, Bethlehem Steel eventually embraced the technology. Thayer later argued that the resulting yields of chromite ore should have been "credited entirely to the gravity work."[94] The government geologist, in short, took credit for part of the extractive success.

Despite the at times vexed relations between the U.S. government, U.S. companies, and local interests, the production of strategic minerals in the handful of years of cooperative mineral programs rose at an astonishing rate. Several participating nations yielded an output of ore in the years between 1941 and 1945 that was exponentially greater than the total tonnage of the entire history of mining in these regions. The premiere mine of Argentina, for example, produced 65 percent more wolframite (a source of tungsten) than in all the years on record before U.S. geologists arrived.[95]

The release of manganese from the strata in Cuba was even more impressive. In the seventy years before U.S. strategic mineral work, Cuba had yielded a total output of 1.2 million tons of ores. In the year of 1941 alone, it produced 225,000 tons—nearly 20 percent of the total from several decades of production.[96] Although it is difficult to quantify the Interior Department's contribution to these efforts, many geologists on the ground were certain that their efforts were vital to the fabulous increase in production. Thayer, who worked on chrome ores in Cuba at a time when Cuba produced more than half of the chrome needed to fill U.S. requirements, ultimately claimed credit for the increase. Their work in the region, he later summarized, "has paid off handsomely."[97]

The Minas Gerais region of Brazil, meanwhile, earned its reputation for being the epicenter of U.S.-Latin American mineral trade with the help of cooperative mineral programs and the U.S. procurement apparatus. It produced 7,200 metric tons of sheet mica, 114,000 tons of kaolin, 6.5 tons of gemstone minerals, 530 tons of beryl, and 110 tons of tantalite and columbite at an estimated value of $25 million.[98] Arguably the most pronounced developments in mining in Brazil centered around the mineral at the heart of electronics—mica. Although mica had been extracted in the region since 1900, production spiked precipitously in the years after 1940. In just five years under cooperative mineral programs, Brazil yielded 300 times the amount of mica that had been produced over the previous four decades.[99] Between 1941 and 1943, Brazilian companies sold sheet mica to the U.S. Purchasing Commission amounting to $9.2 million. Upwards of 14,000 metric tons of mine-crude mica was recovered in 1944.[100] From the perspective of the geologists providing technical assistance as part of the scientific exchange programs overseen by the State Department, this increase, automatically assumed to be both desirable and necessary, was the result of "the application of modern mining techniques" and the "fortuitous discovery" of more deposits, in which they had been integrally involved.[101]

Yet strategic mineral booms in Latin America were followed by busts, creating economic uncertainty and wreaking ecological havoc in the region. On the one hand, the singular fixation on minerals prevented the development of multifaceted economies to offset fluctuations in global markets around narrow commodities. The end of the wartime economy, for example, shifted the market and chastened buyers. In Mexico, the U.S. Metals Reserve Company, one of the consortium of procurement agencies working to meet wartime requirements, ceased buying manganese ore in the summer of 1945. The close of war brought with it an opening of trade routes that could lead to higher-grade ores than those that Mexico could provide.[102] Thus, although manganese production in the nation had more than doubled from 35,000 tons in 1942 to 80,500 tons in 1943, production was cut in half in 1944 and continued to drop years later.[103] On the other hand, orienting economies to mineral extraction both diminished biodiversity and unleashed toxic chemicals and tailings into the air, watersheds, and food systems, a set of problems that would become a catalyst for environmental activism. Deforestation plagued Brazil after the war years, a result of the massive excavation projects for strategic resources.[104] Speaking to these economic and ecological shortcomings, one Brazilian official in 1942 derided the U.S. mineral agenda in Latin America as "the same old mentality of exploiting raw materials, which leaves us with holes in the ground and no industries."[105] U.S. agents, meanwhile, were well aware that the intensification of extraction would

Mica sheets extracted in Minas Gerais, Brazil. Mica formed the basis of electronics and communications for the war effort. 1944. U.S. Geological Survey Bulletin.

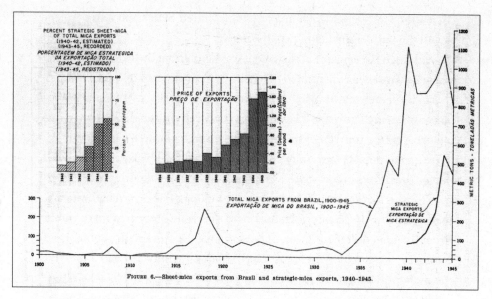

FIGURE 6.—Sheet-mica exports from Brazil and strategic-mica exports, 1940–1945.

Graph of mica production showing exponential growth of output during the war years. 1944. U.S. Geological Survey Bulletin.

exhaust known reserves. Pecora, for example, readily acknowledged that the ratcheting up of mica production in Brazil had "seriously depleted" local minerals.[106] However, Pecora, like others, maintained a casual attitude about such impacts, steadfast in his belief that Latin American minerals were an absolute necessity to the war machine.

Concern over such damage had been papered over by the hemispheric gloss of the moment. As American and Interior officials condemned Germany and Japan for raw material expansionism, they spearheaded the extension of the U.S. mineral stronghold into Latin America. The simultaneous derision and disavowal of exploitation was readily apparent in Harold Ickes's article "Hitler Reaches for the World's Oil." In the piece, Ickes in his capacity as petroleum administrator for war explained that petroleum reserves outside the United States, which were "vastly greater" than those within it, fell "within striking distance" of the enemy. Germany, being "oil-hungry" and aided by an expansionist Japan, had squeezed the oil potential of the Eastern Hemisphere. Ickes thus urged that the United States must keep South America and its "enormous potentialities . . . out of the hands of the Axis at all costs."[107] Ickes mirrored the language of Roosevelt and the other participants in the Eighth American

Scientific Congress, which imagined the United States and Latin America in the path of unwieldy expansionism.

Although the sense of besiegement was acutely felt by Ickes and others, the narrative they constructed of material expansionism by Germany and Japan ultimately naturalized America's own material expansionism. The accompanying figure for Ickes's article captured this tendency by vividly coloring in the portrait of the hemisphere and its minerals under attack. The image depicts Germany and Japan as two oil-black octopi (Italy, a lesser threat, was represented as a baby octopus) extending their tentacles toward oil derricks dotted around the globe. The only remaining targets reside in the Western Hemisphere. Such imagery was inseparable from the famed depictions of oil tycoon John D. Rockefeller and corporations more generally as monstrosities radiating outward and animated by monopolistic greed. Repurposed for this critique of Axis mania, the wide-reaching beasts close in on the otherwise tranquil Americas, united in their verdant green hue and hydrocarbon plenty—the New World. The United States, despite its strategic mineral work across the exact expanse of mineral-rich land, appears not as a creature of avarice but rather as another potential victim.[108] The Monroe Doctrine—the belief that the threat of European expansion required the extension of U.S. power across the hemisphere—was alive and well between the tentacles of the Axis powers.

Although the political rhetoric of mineral vulnerability helped erase the projection of U.S. power across Latin America, the framework of cooperation had been working to effect the same ends. With the entrance of U.S. agents in Latin America through cooperative mineral programs, control of mineral production was slowly and subtly being wrested from local producers. Not only did the U.S. government garner a heightened awareness of the mineral potential of the region, with a thorough knowledge of the most lucrative mines, but it also helped contour the shape of development, which, for all its championing of the free market, unfolded in an effectively closed system of trade that began and ended with the United States. Despite a universal move toward hemispheric unity in both the image and the debates surrounding the minerals of "the Americas," the activities such imaginaries called forth helped to ensure an uneven process by which U.S. procurement agendas devoured local landscapes.

THE WAR FOR OIL. Who controls the greater share of the world's oil controls the world, hence every major Axis drive today is directed toward which lands whose aggregate reserves will far outlast those of the United States

"Hitler reaches for world's oil," a map featured in Harold Ickes's August 1942 *Collier's* article showcasing the national panic over German and Japanese expansionism for oil sources, including those in the Western Hemisphere. The threat justified resuscitating the Monroe Doctrine and spearheading hemispheric cooperation to extract strategic minerals. Papers of Harold Ickes, Library of Congress.

Cooperative mineral programs effectively covered over the exploitation, the extraction of resources by and for outsiders. In this way, the efforts of the Interior Department to release minerals from the terrain in Latin America came to be a kind of liberation geology—an unearthing process done to turn back would-be conquerors.

MINERALS AND THE MONROE DOCTRINE, as Leith had hoped, did become part of American strategies for winning the war. The Eighth American Scientific Congress of 1940 provided a ready, Pan-American audience for this argument, as well as a space in which a cooperative mineral program could be debated and developed. The Interior Department, already venturing into far-flung areas through its management of territorial affairs, once again provided personnel for the infiltration of an extracontinental arena of activity, one to which American and multinational companies were increasingly moving. Although Interior geologists and mineral experts were not the first American agents in the field, or the most well-funded in the broader machinery of strategic mineral procurement, they completed reconnaissance of minerals vital to U.S. armament throughout Latin America. Their role was significant. In addition to the ground-truth their reports provided, the technicians helped to legitimize the extractive operations that were intensifying across a region otherwise challenging intervention and nationalizing extractive industries in turn. The framework of cooperation under which they leveraged their skills harmonized with local calls for more mutualism and reciprocity, as promised in the Good Neighbor policy. The contradictions inherent in the cooperative mineral programs—of protection against fascist expansion through acceptance of U.S. expansion, of intervention in a policy of nonintervention, and of exploitation in cooperation—faded into the backdrop as officials across the hemisphere brought the New World into the forefront of the wartime cartography. For the unlikely diplomats from the Interior Department, geology itself helped to naturalize this collapse of political borders in service of a greater earthly unity.

The experiences of Interior geologists and mineral experts in Latin America would, like those in the western United States before it, shore up similar operations in new contexts. The cooperative mineral programs in Latin America were ultimately so effective, or perceived to be so effective, that numerous officials wished to continue the work after the war. Thayer would clearly articulate this desire while still embedded in Cuba. The "fundamental question" for Interior and other agencies, he explained, was "whether to limit our program to specific deposit work, which is all that is needed for the war effort now," or to take on a long-range approach like that in the United States. He observed that the long-range option had attracted some "unfavorable notice" from local operators and workers. Thayer, for his part, was interested in pursuing "broader lines" in the mineral agenda but did not want to aggravate local critics.[109] The state procurement apparatus appeared to agree with the desirability of pursuing broader lines and demonstrated less trepidation about being unpopular. Geological Survey director W. C. Mendenhall, for example, saw in reconnaissance in the wartime emergency an enduring value with relevance to the postwar economy.[110] U.S. officials ultimately decided to continue the mineral work done under the Interdepartmental Committee on Scientific and Cultural Cooperation in new forms. As W. D. Johnston summarized, after V-J Day, leaders in the agenda began to "reorient our program to, what we then thought to be, the future needs of peace."[111]

Within a few years, the Point Four program of assistance to developing nations provided an ideal framework to support them. In this transition period, numerous Interior geologists and mineral experts would get new assignments that cast them even further into the world—to Africa, Asia, and the Middle East.[112] While W. D. Johnston would direct the entire division of the Geological Survey overseeing this international apparatus, other alumni of the cooperative programs became embedded in new nations. Parker D. Trask left the manganese deposits of wartime Mexico for a postwar tour of Egypt that circled from Cairo and the Suez Canal to Mt. Sinai in search of manganese, gold, silver, and copper.[113] With even more immediate consequences, Thomas Thayer, who had worked so diligently to secure Cuban chromite, ventured to Liberia to prospect iron ore in the Bomi Hills region, collaborating with Liberian President William Tubman and propelling the investments of American mining companies.[114] These veterans of the Latin American cooperative mineral programs thus formed an important if overlooked segment of the first wave of U.S. technicians dispersing across nations participating in a new form of technical assistance to the world: international development. In this sense, minerals, those sticky symbols of imperialist exploitation, provided critical foundations for an American project that officials would sell as the very opposite of imperialism.

CHAPTER FOUR

Unearthing Development

The old imperialism—exploitation ~~of native labor~~ for ~~foreign~~ profit—
has ~~been rejected by the world~~ no place in our plans.

Early draft of Harry S. Truman's 1949 inaugural address

WHEN WILLIAM E. WARNE prepared to leave his Washington, D.C.,
desk job in 1951 to direct the country mission of the U.S. Point
Four program in Iran, he admitted that his new assignment was a bit
strange. Warne had been an assistant secretary of the Department of the
Interior, with an expertise ranging from indigenous affairs to water reclamation. He claimed that his work, like that of his colleagues in the Interior Department, was "as distinct as the name implies from that done
by the State Department abroad." Despite the apparent jurisdictional disconnect, by the time he arrived in Tehran, he was one of hundreds of
Interior personnel dispersed across the globe as part of Point Four, President Harry S. Truman's policy to send scientific and technical assistance
to "backward" countries. Warne and his fellow Interior internationals
joked that they would have to launch a new arm under Interior called
"the Office of the Exterior."[1] However, as explanation for their global
portfolio, Warne offered that they were to do what they did "expertly"
at home; they were "to apply techniques proved valuable in the Indian

Service to encourage isolated peoples to adopt modern methods in their work . . . [and] to utilize their resources to their own best possible advantage."[2]

So it was that Warne headed the Point Four offices in Tehran when Mohammed Mosaddeq, the popularly elected premier who had nationalized the Iranian petroleum industry, scaled a wall in his pajamas to seek refuge there in February 1953. That night, Mosaddeq's complex, which adjoined the Point Four offices, had been engulfed in a riot. Warne had not only worked close to Mosaddeq, but also worked closely with him in projects associated with international development like pest control, livestock raising, and malaria prevention. Throughout these interactions, however, Warne fixated on oil. "Perhaps in the Interior Department," Warne observed, "we were more than usually aware of the potential importance of Iranian oil in the war situation."[3] In Warne's assessment, Mosaddeq's move to expropriate oil operations dominated by British and American interests marked both an act of "fanatical nationalism" and a tremendous failure to understand oil's value, inflicting undue economic harm on the nation. After the August 1953 coup to oust Mosaddeq—secretly backed by the United States and its Central Intelligence Agency—Warne expressed relief. With the obstinate ruler out of the way, Warne could focus on doing his job: helping to implement new geological surveys and to organize the new petroleum industry, effectively opening a vital resource frontier in Iran.

At the genesis of America's international development mission, the Interior Department spearheaded a quest for minerals across participating nations in the Third World. During his January 20, 1949, inaugural address, Truman outlined a decidely hopeful vision for providing technical and scientific "know-how" to the "backward" areas of the world. The resulting Point Four program sent thousands of U.S. technicians abroad to work under the State Department's new Technical Cooperation Administration (TCA).[4] Strategic mineral pursuits are not often associated with the agenda of international development. Historians of postwar modernization and development have instead emphasized the agricultural, public health, educational, and infrastructure projects that overtly aimed to bring about social improvement, debating, in the process, the relative importance of top-down or bottom-up approaches to renovating societies in the image of American modernity.[5] Falling explicitly beyond the bounds of these ethical commitments were mineral projects overseen by the Interior Department. Strategic mineral agendas were a significant—if outlying—feature of the TCA and the later U.S. Agency for International Development. Although decision makers acknowledged that such mineral programs failed to yield social improvement in participating nations—an effect of the capital-intensive nature of extraction—they insisted on their continuation at the hands of Interior mineral experts.[6] Interior's mineral programs thus bring together two rich strands of scholarship that view American global action in the postwar era somewhat differently: the history of Cold War resource scrambles framed as "hard" power and the history of international development framed as "soft" power.[7] Interior's strategic mineral work fell in a murky middle zone, and this is why Interior has appeared to be so marginal to both processes.

Interior technicians completed crucial spadework both for American strategic interests and for the spread of American and multinational firms overseas in the postwar era. With an explicit mandate to further corporate interests overseas, Interior agents undertook elaborate protocols to identify, evaluate, and unearth minerals desired for both national security *and* economic profit, while easing the process of making investments overseas by revising mining laws and providing on-the-ground consultations. Interior officials, working with the permission of foreign governments seeking desired aid dollars, ultimately helped curtail the risks for companies in their overseas investments.[8] The global integration of markets thus took shape not just through public–private collaborations in the abstract arena of finance and trade but also in the material arena of earthbound interventions into the landscape.[9] Consequently, the mineral programs brought together Cold War strategy and postwar economic globalization.

American officials justified their extractive ambitions by repurposing long-standing ideas about nature. They offered that resources were global and thus belonging to all (resource globalism) and that resources were dangerously misunderstood and undervalued by people across the globe (resource primitivism). Resource globalism built on the internationalism of geologists and officials like Charles Kenneth Leith, but downplayed

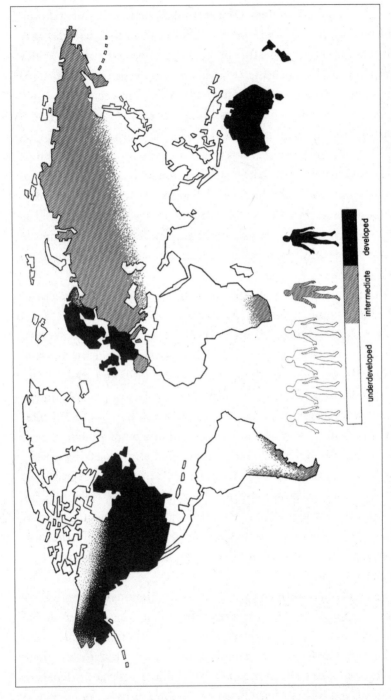

Map showing a spectrum from "underdeveloped" to "developed" nations. Underdeveloped nations are carefully coded as white, while political foes from recent and ongoing wars are labeled "intermediate" (as are some allies in the Southern Hemisphere with European settler legacies). 1949. United States Department of State.

rather than highlighted the importance of national borders.[10] Resource primitivism revived the age-old colonial logic that insisted "primitive" people failed to value and tend land properly and should therefore be dispossessed of it. In keeping with the technocratic impulse to categorize and parse, these resource ideologies localized claims within the more finite container of "natural resources." Both resource globalism and resource primitivism allowed their champions a means to downplay national borders and conflate foreign and domestic, both of which lent legibility to the Interior Department's further extension beyond U.S. formal sovereignty. Moreover, they converged in an important and culturally vibrant tool of the development effort: mineral films like *The Evolution of the Oil Industry*, co-produced by the Interior Department and mining companies such as the Sinclair Refining Company. When Warne initiated mineral projects in Iran immediately following the Mosaddeq coup, for example, he wrote directly to Washington requesting twenty of the mineral films, insisting that they were "most urgently needed."[11] In the ideologies of resource globalism and resource primitivism, Interior's contradictory role pursuing minerals beyond borders seemed not only natural but also righteous.

A Mineral Agenda in International Development

In the postwar era, the Interior Department's mineral experts began forecasting resource depletion. A powerful combination of national economic growth and national security demands had chipped away at existing domestic reserves in the years immediately following World War II. On the one hand, military armament had taken its toll on domestic and territorial resources. As Secretary of the Interior Julius Krug, who filled the gaping hole at the head of the Interior bureaucracy left by his predecessor Harold Ickes, explained in early 1949, "Two great wars and profligate waste have eaten into our natural resources."[12] With the escalation of Cold War animosities between the United States and the Soviet Union, the demand for minerals such as cobalt, tungsten, and chromium, which were used in manufacturing facilities to shape and cut plates for planes, as well as the uranium at the heart of the production of nuclear weapons, only increased.[13] On the other hand, the nation was steadily becoming a "consumers' republic," in which American consumers demanded objects underwritten by finite resources, such as automobiles, washing machines, electric irons, mechanical refrigerators, stoves, toasters, vacuum cleaners, electric fans, and televisions. Steel and iron for metallic frames, copper for electric wiring, and petroleum for plastics and (most significantly) fuel formed the backbone of a surging standard of living tied directly to postwar consumption. The nation, scholars have shown, became powerfully dependent on and oriented to hydrocarbons and petroleum in particular.[14] In this sense, the military-industrial complex and the culture of abundance converged to intensify federal anxieties about America's mineral solvency.

Faced with swelling mineral consumption, Interior leaders bashed heads with other federal officials in offering solutions. With the passage of the Strategic and Critical Materials Stockpiling Act of 1946, the Interior Department advocated for a lead role in the Munitions Board that had historically been overseen by the army and navy, a project that yielded more than a little acrimony between the civilian and military agencies. The act, which built on the earlier Strategic and Critical Materials Act of 1939, granted the executive branch greater license to determine production needs and stockpiling initiatives. As the pie of executive authority grew, Interior leaders leveraged its natural resource expertise for a larger slice. Interior had motives for doing so in the face of postwar criticisms, playing out in Senate Appropriations Committee meetings, that it was a taxpayer burden. The Departments of War and the Navy, meanwhile, wanted to bolster their own authority in mineral policy to ensure that security determined stockpiling quotas, rather than economic interests that civilian agencies like Interior were sure to represent. Throughout these debates, the Interior Department mineral expert Elmer Pehrson went toe-to-toe with the Joint Chiefs of Staff on matters of stockpiling goals. Where the Joint Chiefs advocated a smaller stockpile tailored to narrow strategic interests, Pehrson pushed for a larger stockpile to provide money to corporate allies abroad while also strengthening the domestic minerals industry for civilian uses. Interior ultimately won the argument, drawing on congressional support tied to the mining industry, and the secretaries of War, the Navy, *and* Interior jointly would lead stockpiling efforts under the Munitions Board.[15]

From this expanded platform, Interior officials frequently made projections that stoked public fears of mineral depletion. Director of the U.S. Bureau of Mines James Boyd circulated charts to Congress and other government branches that sensationalized resource scarcity. The chart "Road to Depletion" visualized the course of depletion for vital commodities, estimating domestic tungsten, mercury, chromium, and manganese to run out by the mid-1950s; lead by the 1960s; zinc and copper by the 1970s; and iron ore, coal, and bauxite by the 1980s.[16] The projections were wrong, it turned out, but compelling. This was especially true when paired with synopses of American consumption. The chart "Our Share of the World's Wealth," for example, visualized how feverish was the national appetite. It showed that despite comprising only 7 percent of the world's population, the United States used 50 percent of its minerals and 70 percent of its oil—all in the peacetime operation of industry.[17]

One solution Interior officials offered to the resource depletion they feared was using the Marshall Plan for European recovery to acquire minerals. In June 1947, George Marshall had urged that the economic integration of Germany would satisfy security and economic needs of both Western Europe and the United States. The discussion of such a program's viability and desirability rippled through the U.S. government.[18] In response to this proposed plan, Krug and the Interior Department were tasked with compiling an intergovernmental report to assess whether domestic resource capacities were such that the United States might reasonably provide foreign aid for European recovery. The resulting report, *National Resources and Foreign Aid* (1947), concluded that the United States, though stretched materially, could and should participate in the effort outlined in the Marshall Plan. Krug cautioned, however, that the United States could not "long underwrite the material deficits of other nations."[19] Drawing upon this report, a subcommittee on economic foreign policy, instructively titled the Strategic Minerals and U.S. Stockpiles in Return for Aid Under the European Recovery Program, convened on October 10, 1947, to debate the merits of using the Marshall Plan to procure minerals. The Interior representative on the committee, Daniel Goldy, later explained the overriding hesitation to do so. Although making procurement an "avowed objective" would "assist in selling the program to the American public," Goldy explained, it could also appear to foreign audiences that the United States intended to "interfere" in their economies "in furtherance of our military aims."[20] Thus, American officials decided that extracting European minerals in return for aid was morally inadvisable. As the United States fashioned an image of global leadership, such manipulative ends in foreign assistance would be a blemish.

When the debates about the would-be Point Four program began, the same ethical inhibitions about mineral procurement in aid carried forward, at least initially. This was evident, firstly, in the way that President Truman introduced the Point Four program in his inaugural address by insisting, "The old imperialism—exploitation for profit—has no place in our plans."[21] This new policy of aid to underdeveloped countries, in other words, would not be the continuation of imperial pursuits of base material interest. From the outset, however, the Point Four idea raised heated debates about whether a program of assistance to the underdeveloped world could or should advance U.S. material interests. The original Point Four vision aimed to give the United States a positive objective to curry favor with potential allies in the free world against the Cold War foe of the Soviet Union. However, advisors in the Truman administration such as Walter Salant and David Lloyd suspected, correctly, that conservative critics would protest the extension of U.S. aid dollars across the globe on grounds that it was a New Deal welfare state run amok. A perceived antidote to such criticisms was to emphasize the way in which the policy could work for the American economy and the businesses at its heart.[22] Although Truman's advisors largely concluded that such a policy should help to spur trade between nations and create conditions favorable to the operations of American capitalism abroad, they did not suggest that the policy would specifically aid strategic mineral pursuits, likely out of a fear that doing so would raise alarm bells.

Foreign minerals posed an ongoing public relations liability, especially in the context of decolonization. Minerals had become ready symbols of imperialist exploitation and, through expropriations that followed the Mexican one in 1938, anti-imperialist defiance. Boyd in his capacity as Bureau of Mines director would acknowledge this murky history and U.S. complicity therein. "The empire of Cecil Rhodes was built on gold and diamonds," Boyd explained, and "the colonies he founded are important producers of copper, lead, zinc, vanadium, cobalt, chrome, gold, and coal." Rhodes, the De Beers mineral magnate, who drew upon racialized labor across southern Africa to unearth his fortune, had famously claimed, "Expansion is everything," and "I would annex the planets if I could."[23] Since the United States depended on the products of that regrettable "empire," Boyd continued, "we are accepting, though reluctantly, an increasing responsibility for it."[24] Mineral gambits, put differently, conjured images of the old imperialism that Truman would claim had no place in American foreign policy, in part because anti-imperialist fervor was a nuisance. Early versions of the Point Four speech made clear that such associations between racialized labor and exploitation in empire had become liabilities to be avoided. In drafts of Truman's speech one week before the inaugural address, the notorious line had a slightly (and tellingly) different phrasing: "The old imperialism—exploitation *of native labor* for *foreign* profit—has *been rejected by the world.*" This phrasing conjured images of a coercive and extractive rule predicated on racialized labor. The earlier phrasing also acknowledged that such actions had been "rejected by the world."[25] The Truman administration, in short, had positioned Point Four in contrast to a racialized form of material exploitation that was too controversial to name.

When the Point Four program launched in 1950, and Interior geologists joined other technicians under its banner to work on dam construction, water resources, and minerals programs, there was no *coordinated* effort to expand U.S. mineral interests overseas. However, the onset of the Korean War in the summer of 1950, in which U.S. armed forces intervened to establish and police a border between communist North Korea and the U.S.-backed South Korean regime, changed everything. The federal government would decide to use Point Four to secure minerals. The process began with the Defense Production Act of 1950, which reshuffled the agencies devoted to resource planning. A long list of agencies and committees were generated, including the Interior-run Defense Materials Procurement Agency and Petroleum Administration for Defense and the interagency National Resources Security Board that brought together personnel from the Interior Department, State Department, and the Departments of War and the Navy, newly merged in the Department of Defense. Alongside these federal groups, the act initiated the President's Materials Policy Commission (PMPC), an ad hoc panel of experts that would assess the resource situation, headed by William S. Paley of CBS.[26] If resources were perceived to be scarce, there was no shortage of resource *advisory boards* at the dawn of an attritional Korean War—or of differing priorities, whether civilian or military, therein. Yet there was also synergy and an overarching commitment to bolstering America's resources.[27] Within this broader ecology, the civilian- and industry-led PMPC worked to compile a report drawing upon the advice of numerous government agencies and industrial representatives that ultimately forecasted American domestic shortages in minerals at the heart of the communications, transportation, commercial, defense, and agricultural industries.[28] The report, like Boyd's earlier charts, predicted major shortages of major raw materials by the 1970s. These findings, moreover, would be hugely influential in shaping public opinion and catalyzing renewed interest in foreign minerals.[29]

One of the key recommendations the Paley Commission leaders offered based on this perception of depletion was that the Point Four program would be an ideal venue for furthering U.S. mineral interests. These suggestions, in turn, would lessen concerns about the negative appearance of pursuing minerals under the rubric of assistance. On May 10, 1951, Paley wrote to Point Four's first director, Henry G. Bennett, about the possibilities of wedding the pursuit of strategic minerals and the Point Four program. Bennett replied with great enthusiasm, agreeing with Paley that mineral gambits carried out in foreign aid would smooth their operation. Bennett offered that Point Four could "gain access to many countries and areas which would not be receptive to a program identified *solely* with exploiting their resources for the express benefit of the U.S."[30] He added that Point Four technicians might operate beyond the kind of international reproach that had befallen other companies or imperial governments in their quest for foreign raw materials. In short, Bennett and Paley explicitly aimed to use Point Four as a Trojan horse for American strategic mineral interests in underdeveloped nations. Where Goldy had earlier worried about how procuring minerals through the Marshall Plan could *ignite* charges of exploitation, Paley and Bennett celebrated how the Point Four program could *defuse* charges of exploitation.

Another member of the Paley commission was instrumental to this marriage of interests: Charles Kenneth Leith, the credentialed geologist who had called for the resurrection of the Monroe Doctrine in wartime hemispheric affairs. Leith and the Paley Commission pointed to these earlier undertakings in their reports calling for strategic mineral work in Point Four, citing the successes of the Interior Department's Geological Survey and the Bureau of Mines in Latin America as evidence of the need for more programs.[31] During one PMPC meeting in December 1951, the now seventy-seven-year-old Leith advocated making "mineral development . . . the spearhead of the Point IV program."[32] Building on earlier arguments that insisted minerals across the hemisphere belonged to all the hemisphere, Leith insisted that minerals across the world belonged to all the world. Given the expanded network facilitated by the launch of the Point Four program, the Latin America model could go global.[33]

Though Leith had long been an internationalist, in the Point Four era he increasingly advanced a vision that downplayed the borders at the heart of internationalism. Instead, he outlined the contours of a new, if related, ideology of intervention: resource globalism. In the process, Leith made greater recourse to nature, which he juxtaposed to its supposed opposite, politics.[34] He disavowed national sovereignty and political agendas in a resource agenda that crossed borders, precisely because borders got in the way of solving border-crossing problems. In 1951 PMPC talks, for example, Leith urged that minerals represented a "world problem" rather than a "political problem." He complained of the recent rise of "restricted nationalism" across the globe, a reference both to the recent nationalization of the Iranian petroleum industry and to decolonization movements that sought protections for their resources from outside exploitation. These movements had been emboldened by new global commitments to national sovereignty and self-determination, exemplified by the founding of the United Nations in 1945. Operating in this new postwar and post-self-determination paradigm, Leith posited not an overtly *political* solution to the mineral problem, which might ring of manipulation, but an ostensibly *apolitical* one, which downplayed partisan interests. Leith argued that restricted nationalism was preventing the easy flow of "world minerals."[35] Drawing on his training as a geologist, Leith insisted that minerals were embedded in the earth as part of *nature*—a nature indifferent to political sovereignty.

The PMPC decisively adopted Leith's resource globalism in its influential and broadly disseminated report *Resources for Freedom* (1952). The cover illustration featured on each of the five volumes vividly captured this vision. It depicted a globe filled not with distinct continents, let alone the markers of national boundaries, but rather oil derricks, atomic energy facilities, hydroelectric dams, lumber operations, refineries, and mines.[36] In this rendering of the globe, natural resources dominate, while national sovereignty falls from view. Only gridlines of longitude and latitude remain—manmade markers that rather than dividing peoples into nations, divided nature into units awaiting utilization. The grid mirrored the logic of parceling that had been central to Interior's role incorporating and metabolizing land and resources in settler colonial expansion. In this

Resources for Freedom cover featuring a globe filled not with continents or nation-states but with resources—coal, oil, uranium, timber, and water—awaiting use. 1952. President's Materials Policy Commission.

new and decidedly global era, nature helped decision makers scrub the world clean of the same meddlesome political borders that had been sanctified in postwar multilateral institutions.

Resource globalism unsurprisingly had eager champions in the Interior Department, which was just turning one hundred years old. After Truman unveiled the Point Four vision, Secretary Krug argued in 1949 that minerals "do not really belong to any one corporation or to any one Nation; they belong to all mankind."[37] Krug further argued that Point Four would ensure "the protection and wise use of man's common heritage of natural wealth, wherever it may be."[38] Such invocations of a common heritage were becoming commonplace in the postwar era as a justification for intervention, as Melani McAlister has convincingly argued.[39] What was distinct about the widely invoked ideology of resource globalism, however, was the centrality of understandings of earthly nature to the argument. This is most evident in the speech given by Interior Assistant Secretary Vernon Northrop on United Nations Day. "Natural resources—land, water, and minerals—know no national boundaries," Northrop argued. "Like earth, of which they are a part, they are global."[40] Ultimately, Interior officials' recourse to resource globalism had the effect of deterritorializing the American interior, projecting it onto a global screen like that in the *Resources for Freedom* logo.

The PMPC's desire to extract minerals through Point Four, though framed centrally as a national security concern, was bound up with the push to spread American capitalism overseas. The authors of the Point Four vision in the Truman administration had anticipated the pushback they would face from the business sector. Although many businessmen, especially financiers, had lent their support to New Deal policies that encouraged trade liberalization, many leaders of extractive industries remained particularly hostile to them on grounds that they supported workers' rights to organize and initiated progressive tax structures. Regardless of their relative warmth to such policies, most businessmen saw in the Point Four program an attempt to extend the New Deal on a global scale.[41] The PMPC, itself an ad hoc agency comprised of members of industry, reached out to the leaders of the nation's largest extractive firms. They hoped private industrialists would take on a collaborating role for extractive agendas in Point Four, which in turn would bolster U.S.

strategic mineral procurement. Despite the fact that many American firms had undertaken overseas investments, many remained concerned about the volatility of foreign governments, currency fluctuations, pro-labor sentiment, and the nagging threat of expropriation like in the Mexican and Iranian nationalizations of oil. These firms preferred avoiding the risk of foreign investment by maintaining emphasis on domestic production.[42] Industrialists would tolerate Point Four, however, if the program expressly mitigated those risks. Wall Street financier Winthrop Aldrich made this clear. "The more closely a foreign country reaches the point where it is on a parity of risk with, say, the State of Massachusetts," Aldrich explained, "the more apt American private capital is to make an investment in that country."[43] Businessmen would endorse a Point Four that advanced capitalist interests abroad by making foreign spaces comparable with domestic ones.

To convince extractive firms that Point Four would make the world safe for investment, the commission offered that the U.S. government would create conditions favorable to American capitalism overseas. The commission outlined numerous ways in which government could serve industry abroad, helping to secure special tax allowances, protections from currency fluctuation and expropriation risks, and assistance in negotiating agreements with foreign governments for entrance into their mineral reserves. American mining companies, when surveyed by the PMPC in June and July 1951 on such measures, resoundingly supported the idea.[44] In so doing, companies like Alcoa, DuPont, and the National Lead Company also endorsed the ensuing expansion of government power. Even as many of these companies' representatives articulated free market views, they overwhelmingly concluded that government assistance and intervention in the economy—so long as it also meant low-risk capitalist expansion abroad—was a good thing.[45] Of equal importance, PMPC leaders and Bennett, director of Point Four, also outlined ways in which technicians on the ground would both locate minerals of interest for companies and work to modify local mining laws in order to smooth processes of extraction.[46] Ultimately, the convergence of the PMPC, the Point Four program, and private industry in this moment revealed that strategic interests in minerals for armament and private interests in minerals for profits were deeply and messily entangled.

Interior technicians would be the agents sent to secure these overlapping and at times conflicting interests in extraction in the Third World. When the PMPC looked for foot soldiers for this errand, the Interior Department was the clear repository of such expertise with its unparalleled technocracy for geologic investigation and mineral development in the sister agencies of the Geological Survey and the Bureau of Mines, both of which had already disseminating technicians abroad as part of Point Four agreements. What the PMPC did in the post-Korean War context was lend greater continuity within and resources to Interior's mineral programs in Point Four. They recommended that the meager Point Four budgets for Interior's Geological Survey and Bureau of Mines work be tripled from $1.3 million to $4 million in September 1951. Congress ultimately approved these increases one year later on grounds that the funds would help to marshal resources needed by the United States. In the five years that followed, the projects grew accordingly.[47] The growth of these programs helped shore up both the creation of Geological Survey and Bureau of Mines foreign operating divisions and the creation in the Interior Department of a Division of International Activities that collaborated directly with the United Nations.[48]

As Interior personnel ventured further and further abroad, they invoked not only resource globalism but also resource primitivism, a set of ideas that had underscored Interior's historic and ongoing management of indigenous peoples, land, and resources. Scholars have shown that primitivism, the simultaneous attraction to and disdain for peoples deemed to be trapped in prehistoric time and thus antimodern, became a key way the United States and European nations justified their imperialist endeavors. Primitivism was often, though not always, framed in the language of benevolence.[49] In the Point Four era, Interior officials refurbished these primitivist assumptions in ways more suited to an era of self-determination. They claimed that what differentiated human groups on a spectrum of modernity was the uses toward which they put their mineral resources. Thus, minerals became a yardstick that measured a civilization's superiority or inferiority. Resource primitivism added technocratic valences to an age-old imperialist rationale calling for intervention on grounds that certain peoples misused nature and thus should be dispossessed of it. Interior officials who had collaborated with PMPC members on the Point Four strategy had summarized this worldview most concisely when they explained that "primitive areas of the world" exhibited a "lack of appreciation of the value and vital role of certain minerals" to society.[50]

Many bureaucrats who had been tapped to lead country missions similarly framed their experiences in the logic of resource primitivism. Such was the case with Point Four's director of Near East operations, E. Reesman ("Sy") Fryer, a former Interior man. Fryer warned country mission directors that they would face tasks similar to tribes and resources of the American West.[51] Leaders like Warne and Fryer likened the conditions of poor resource management in foreign countries to that on Native American reservations. Such comparisons helped to explain why so many Bureau of Indian Affairs (BIA) officials led country missions in places like Libya, Brazil, Peru, Ecuador, Indonesia, and the Philippines.[52] Interior's apparatus for managing indigenous peoples and resources, such advocates of resource primitivism offered, was an ideal model for technical assistance in the Point Four program. Officials also began viewing this relationship in reverse—seeing the foreign in the putatively if incompletely domestic. One Interior Department pamphlet even described the BIA as a "Grassroots Point IV Program" within U.S. borders. Officials drew such comparisons at a time when the Interior Department and Congress began seriously attacking indigenous sovereignty, as Chapter 7 will consider.[53] Resource ideologies not only aided Interior and other American officials in justifying their involvements overseas; they also became an instrument of the international development apparatus itself, one designed to convey those messages in 35 millimeter and Technicolor.

Resource Ideologies on the March

By the early 1950s, the Interior Department had amassed a library of hundreds of mineral films, sponsored by private industry, that sought to sell a vision of American extractive supremacy to people inside and outside the nation. In this sense, the public and private sectors joined forces not only in the project of capitalist expansion in the world but also in the realm of cultural production in support of those ends.[54] The Interior Department had been producing such films with industry since the 1920s for a wide array of domestic audiences in school and civic settings. The 35-millimeter educational films were designed to educate the public on minerals and the "essential role they play in the national economy."[55] However, Interior officials began to see possibilities in extending the films' reach from domestic audiences to those overseas. In the Point Four era, Interior officials decided to utilize these films as indoctrination tools, hoping they would ease the implementation of U.S. supervision over mining projects in Point Four countries—if not winning hearts and minds, then training hands to work.[56] At the program's height in 1956, the motion pictures circulated to 66 million people at home and abroad.[57] Although the films ostensibly depicted neutral geological, mining, and refining processes for major commodities, they also frequently stitched together discursive worldviews that insisted minerals were global and that Native Americans and members of the developing world were united in their inadequacies of resource management. These films ultimately reveal, in richly textured and Technicolor sequences, the extent to which resource globalism and resource primitivism saturated the Interior Department, as well as the faith Interior leaders had in those ideologies to help carry their work into the world.

Some films situated minerals in a world historical perspective. Such was the case with *The Evolution of the Oil Industry* (1951), co-produced by the Interior Department and the Sinclair Refining Company. The film opens with a long-haired and bare-chested man plowing the ground. The narration announces, "From the dawn of history mankind has revealed an unconquerable urge to improve his lot"—a persistent desire to reduce drudgery and move "beyond the horizons of his limited domain." The voiceover explains that throughout this continual struggle, mankind was "unprepared to see the potential servant" in that subterranean hydrocarbon treasure: oil. A brief montage recounts prior misguided uses of petroleum with re-enactments of its utilization across time and space— by the Babylonians for ceremonial torches, by Chinese for "primitive" energy facilities, and by Native Americans for skin lubricant. In the latter vignette, two scantily clad and feather-adorned American Indian men, or rather white men dressed as Indians, rub petroleum on each other. These droll scenes build momentum to the climactic staging of the first mechanized drilling of oil in 1859 in Titusville, Pennsylvania. It was the industrialists of America, the film reminds us, who first realized oil's rightful purpose in fueling entire societies.[58] The Phelps Dodge Corporation film *A Story of Copper* (1953) constructed a similar global architecture onscreen. Traveling "back into the dimly lit past" of the Stone Age, the film showcases the uses of copper by cavemen and ancient Egyptians, who invented bronze, a copper and tin alloy. These achievements build to the Industrial Revolution in the United States. America, the voiceover explains, extended copper's uses "to ever broadening horizons."[59] Interior mineral films framed in antiquity underscored this material point: minerals belonged to all mankind, as they always had "from the dawn of history" and were necessary, according to *The Evolution of the Oil Industry*, for the welfare of the nation and the world—the rationality, in short, of resource globalism.

If some films relied on a world historical framework to legitimate intervention, then others relied on the frontier myth of the American West to instill a similar lesson. This genre of the Interior Department film library—"state" films like *Arizona and Its Natural Resources* (1955), as well as those on Oklahoma, Texas, and Idaho—trafficked more in the mode of resource primitivism. The West's troubled past—and indeed the Interior Department's troubled past—with the violent conquest of indigenous peoples and Mexico, was both emblazoned on the screen and cheerfully disavowed as a necessary sacrifice to the forward motion of mineral-backed industrialization.[60] A touchstone in this series, *Arizona and Its Natural Resources* exalted the progress of industry while acknowledging, in part, the history of conquest that paved the way to the modern state of mobility and convenience. The film begins with the Spanish *conquistadores* in their misguided quest for treasure in the land that would become Arizona. In the film, an armor-clad conquistador stands atop a vast desert plain and surveys the golden horizon. The accompanying narration explains that this barren yet beautiful land was first home "to the people of remote Indian civilizations." The figure onscreen, we are told, is the sixteenth-century Spanish conquistador, that "hunter of gold," who sought a mythic paradise of plenty: the seven cities of Cibola. The camera cuts to his perspective, in which a glimmering castle materializes at a distance before fading into oblivion, a mere mirage playing upon the light. This quixotic conquistador never suspected the "true and tremendous wealth" that lay beneath his feet, the voiceover proclaims, and "like the Indian before him, he saw only the burning deserts of the south . . . seemingly without purpose, without promise."

Ignorant of the value of minerals, indigenous peoples and the more recently arrived Spaniards both underappreciated the land itself and inadvertently impeded their own freedom from drudgery. The unappreciative Spaniards claimed the territory that eventually became Mexico, but the film holds that this unjust act was made right by the absorption of that territory into the United States. The film links the Spanish colonizers directly to Mexico, a fixture of the "underdeveloped" world in contemporary political discourse. The narration exalts the transition between imperial occupiers as one "from an uninspiring past to an awe-inspiring future." A new people were destined to inherit this resource-laden earth, as the montage reveals: white homesteaders in covered wagons. Briskly, a dissolve introduces modern-day Arizona, rife with cities, trains, and copper smelters. Over triumphant fanfare the narrator declares, "Today modern man with his imagination and ingenuity has explored and developed the hidden wealth of Arizona, that tremendous treasure that neither early Indian nor conquistador even dreamed existed."[61]

The production notes for *Arizona and Its Natural Resources* reveal that this message of resource primitivism, and by extension those in other films in the series, was most consciously crafted by the Interior Department. Interior's head of the motion pictures division, Allan Sherman, wrote to the filmmaker of the importance of contrasting the conquistadores of old with the industrialists of today. This narrative, according to Sherman, would convey that Arizona "is a land rich in natural resources and blessed with potential greatness—*unrealized*, however, until modern man applied his daring, imagination, ingenuity, and better equipment and knowledge."[62] Sherman's commentary on the imprudent conquistadores, who in the film come to stand in for Mexico, matches Interior's argument made to PMPC that "primitive areas of the world" demonstrated a "lack of appreciation of the value and vital role of certain minerals."[63] The film, like the resource primitivism belying foreign policy, upheld the supremacy of U.S. mineral expertise and the implied need to spread that expertise beyond their otherwise limited horizons.

In the early 1950s, Interior technicians began to disseminate the films to Point Four countries in an explicit attempt to assist with their various mineral programs. Although part of the work of the visual media was to overcome language barriers, Interior personnel also contended that the distribution of films abroad would ease the migration of their technical training apparatus, or as one technician put it, to help carry their "activities to the other side of the world."[64] Interior leaders assumed and claimed that films, and the ideas they conveyed, had a role to play in making its presence abroad palatable and, in so doing, believed in the power of resource ideologies to generate local consent to transformations led by outsiders. When Cuban miners threatened strikes in 1954, for example, Interior screened its films in cities like Havana, Santiago, and Matahambre. At each showing, hundreds of miners, industrialists, and geologists gathered to watch films, including *The Evolution of the Oil Industry*.[65] Upon viewing these films in Havana, Pedro E. Muñiz, the mining chief for BANFAIC, el Banco Fomento de Fomento Agricola y Industrial de Cuba, lauded the films as "an excellent medium of dissemination and instruction" and expressed both gratitude for "this important technical contribution" and interest in "receiving more, similar films."[66] Muñiz, an industrial leader, worked closely with the U.S. government. His praise suggests that the films did play a part in smoothing the processes of U.S.-supervised extraction, though this rosy portrait warrants further scrutiny. For example, William Warne, who had requested mineral films for Iran, recounted an instance when some villager threw a rock at one of the "motion-picture wagons."[67] The mineral films, like those from the broader Point Four propaganda wing, were by no means uniformly received. Nevertheless, by 1955, twenty-five titles from the Interior's Bureau of Mines film library, including *The Evolution of the Oil Industry* and *Arizona and Its Natural Resources,* were in circulation in almost every country to receive aid in mineral resources.[68] While the films undoubtedly did less to pacify local dissent than bureaucrats believed, many nevertheless kept the faith that the films were important in softening the ground for mineral projects in their local contexts. The motion pictures became one tool among many to further transplant American influence and capitalist interests in mineral reserves across borders.

Spadework of Extractive Capitalism

By the mid-1950s, W. D. Johnston had seen enough mineral programs across Latin America, Africa, and Asia to know the pattern of diminishing returns that faced foreign countries who accepted their assistance. Johnston had been overseeing Interior's mineral programs in Third World countries for more than a decade. Once a field agent of the Latin American cooperative mineral programs, he was now the director of the Geological Survey's foreign geology branch. At this point, he had to acknowledge that mineral programs did not provide long-term benefit to local communities, thereby making it so that those countries would no longer require outside assistance. Johnston's growing awareness of the mineral programs' shortcomings created a problem. The State Department–run Technical Cooperation Administration (TCA) mandated that all technical assistance programs meet the criterion of bringing about social improvement. Yet as Johnston knew, the extraction of minerals on an industrial scale required outside investors and funds, and this initiated a cycle in which materials and profits were extracted from local landscapes and sent abroad. As a result, participating countries maintained rather than outgrew reliance on foreign assistance, in direct violation of the stated credo of development.[69]

Despite these known shortcomings, Interior leaders insisted on the vital importance of proceeding with the extractive agenda. Johnston and the director of the Bureau of Mines foreign branch, Louis Turnbull, outlined three critical functions that Interior's mineral programs performed. First, the mineral programs provided critical information to the United States on strategic minerals. Second, they influenced local opinions in host countries in ways favorable to extractive operations. Third, they generated reports on which private interests could base their investment decisions.[70] Despite concerns about the way the mineral agenda deviated from the credo of technical cooperation, the State Department officials ultimately concluded that "their long-run and overall importance to major U.S. strategic interests makes their continuation desirable."[71] In short, strategic interest and economic globalization converged, with the added bonus of greater local consent to extraction.

After PMPC and Point Four administrators forged an alliance in 1951, Interior technicians unearthed minerals with U.S. interests ever in mind. Although the TCA under Truman had a procurement agenda, these strategic priorities became even more pointed when President Dwight Eisenhower and his administration took the reins of technical assistance in 1953. The resulting Mutual Security Administration heightened the imperative of bolstering "security" through aid.[72] With this changing of the guard, tension emerged among Interior personnel between those who supported their department's Defense Materials Procurement Agency (DMPA), a proponent of no-holds-barred strategic mineral acquisition, and those who supported the TCA's closer adherence to the Point Four ideals of promoting long-term benefits in local contexts. In correspondence between an Interior official in Washington and a technician in the field, they discussed the rumors of a power shift in favor of the procurement more tailored to U.S. "self-interested" strategic mineral agendas than to the agenda devoted to "helping worthy allies with underdeveloped territory to help themselves." The official concluded, "We are hoping for some sort of a middle-ground solution," one that would "not destroy the faith that is being built up through genuine technical cooperation" but would also "permit maximum advantage to the U.S. as a result of technical assistance programs."[73] The resulting middle ground was nonetheless one that shored up America's strategic and economic position. For example, in Brazil and Cuba, they searched for manganese, which was crucial to the production of steel, while in Peru and Mexico they sought lead used in automobiles. In the Philippines, they targeted copper that linked the communications industry, while in Thailand and Nepal they prioritized columbite, tungsten, and cobalt, all metals used in the manufacture of planes. They scoured the mountains of Afghanistan for chrome, used in steel and industrial cutting machines.[74]

At this point, it is important to address the scale and significance of U.S. mineral programs. They were, on some level, a small fraction of the overall activities in international development. Prior to the Korean War, they constituted only 1 percent of the overall budget, though this increased with the appeal by the PMPC for additional congressional funds.[75] However, the modesty of this budgetary entry seems less astonishing when considering that minerals in the national economy of the

United States, one of the largest mineral producers in the world, had also consistently weighed in at around 1 to 2 percent of the gross domestic product.[76] The modest allocation also must be understood in relation to the fact that much of the process relied on attracting outside investors to front some costs for capital-intensive operations in return for the benefit of saving on the costs of difficult exploration and entering into zones made more amenable to their presence. The greatest significance of the mineral work stemmed from the fact that, as in countless expansionist enterprises over the previous century, the Interior Department was helping to spearhead exploitation while trying to appear like it was not being exploitative. Its paradoxical impulses harmonized with a variety of public and private agendas, inconspicuously furthering both American state power and capitalist development. On the ground, these grander strategies were hardly visible or at the forefront of concerns. Instead, Interior technicians relied on their "know-how," a legacy of expansionism that had come to appear as inert as dirt from the ground. Embedded in their respective Point Four nations, Interior technicians undertook a constellation of extractive procedures. They initiated geological surveys, oversaw lab testing, supervised mine construction, revised mining codes, and consulted with private industry. In no country did these processes take identical shape, an effect of the different political, economic, cultural, and geologic features of a particular region. Nevertheless, the broader pattern of extractive know-how and interventions maintained a consistent shape across time and space.

The mineral efforts began, as Interior's activity nearly always did, with an exploration of the terrain. Interior personnel from the Geological Survey trekked across the physical landscape for a period of several weeks to several months. In the course of their surveys, they crossed vast distances, identifying geological formations. Through their mapping and photography, the geologists made outcroppings dating back to, say, the Precambrian Era into legible objects of modernity. The travelogues of Geological Survey men (and it was all men in the field through Point Four) on assignment in Peru offers one window on these undertakings. Over the course of one year, the geologists George Ericksen, Frank Simons, and Richard Lewis explored minerals of "strategic importance," including lead, iron, tungsten, copper, and zinc.[77] In March 1953, outfitted with burros and mapping equipment, the U.S. geologists led Peruvian trainees on a survey expedition in the central regions of the nation. Their expedition was cut short by bad weather, resulting in only nine days in the field. In the ensuing months, they fared better, successfully examining deposits and mapping existing mines across the Atacocha District. They faced transportation difficulties through La Union region in June, before turning to more fruitful reconnaissance of tungsten deposits of the Pasto Bueno and Mundo Nuevo districts.[78]

The geological field trips entailed the usual difficulties of a whimsical nature. As in Peru, teams of geologists ran afoul of poor weather and patchy roads, which at times forced them to cancel or repeat a field trip. Interior geologists who took to the skies for aerial surveys, increasingly used in the Point Four program, faced other challenges: cloud cover in higher elevations could obstruct visuals. The geologist Joseph Harrington, who worked on both the Colombian and Egyptian missions, remarked on these complexities. Identifying worthwhile deposits, he explained, could take between 200 and 300 field studies. Their efforts thus frequently amounted to "countless frustrating chases."[79] In the Philippines, five decades after George F. Becker conducted surveys from a gunboat following the Spanish-American War and four years after the Philippines' independence, Ronald K. Sorem and four members of the Philippines Bureau of Mines (established by the U.S. government during the imperial period) surveyed a 400-square-kilometer region on south-central Siquijor for manganese in 1950. They evaluated forty manganese mines and prospects just in the month of January alone. The following month, Sorem repeated the process on Busuanga Island, the largest producer of manganese in the Philippines at the time.[80] In all participating Point Four countries, geologists met with exasperating obstacles. Nevertheless, as Harrington cheerily observed after outlining all the disappointments, one quality discovery was more than enough reward for their labors.[81]

What was ultimately so significant about Interior's ritual of hit-and-miss surveying was that it spared representatives of private industry countless misses. The reports they produced, which could amount to hundreds of pages of painstakingly detailed information about rocks, ultimately trickled back not only to local governments but also to the U.S.

government and mining companies. When compiled in one bibliography, the citations of Geological Survey work from cooperative mineral programs of the 1940s to the international development work through the 1960s sprawled across fifty-five pages. Technical assistance work in Mexico alone generated 105 geological reports.[82] With these thick reports in hand, representatives of U.S.-based companies could make informed decisions about overseas investments. For example, in Liberia the work of an Interior geologist was crucial to attracting the interest of the midwestern company Republic Steel. Thomas P. Thayer, who had overseen chromite extraction in Cuba during World War II, produced a report on iron ore that captured the enterprising imagination of New York businessman Lansdell K. Christie.[83] Christie, in turn, secured concessions from the struggling Liberian Mining Company. Republic Steel ultimately purchased those concessions and in 1951 initiated production on its first venture overseas. In their immediate retelling of this history, Republic Steel representatives wrote out the role of the U.S. government entirely. They told *Fortune* magazine that the reserve was "the best open-hearth ore we have ever found."[84] Yet Republic Steel did not do the finding. Rather, Interior geologists, Point Four administrators, and, by extension, U.S. taxpayer dollars, had shouldered that burden.

Interior mineral experts—and by extension American companies—knew not only the location of reserves to the exact coordinate but also their quality to the nearest decimal. Technicians from the Bureau of Mines tested mineral samples, which could weigh as much as 4,000 pounds (roughly the weight of a full-size vehicle), using a variety of analytics. Mineral experts in India discovered a source of lignite, a substance used in synthetic fuels, and immediately tested its grade through carbonization and hydrogenation processes.[85] Other minerals, such as manganese and copper, underwent different experiments for evaluation, including gravity, froth flotation, and acid tests.[86] Most often, U.S. technicians sent the samples aboard cargo ships to facilities in Denver, Salt Lake City, Pittsburgh, and College Park. However, Interior experts also oversaw the construction of mineral research labs in host countries like Egypt, Israel, and Nepal. In Cuba, the resulting laboratory reportedly tested 200 mineral samples per day.[87] Determining high or low grade further aided investment decisions. While stationed in Mexico in 1954, for example, geologist Frank Noe assisted the National Lead Company with lab analysis. The company's staff had located materials with possible fissionable qualities—a sign of uranium—in the Oaxaca region of Mexico. To determine the uranium potential of the material, Noe sent the samples to the Atomic Energy Commission for testing.[88] Thus, through the surveying and lab testing of minerals, Interior technicians could say with confidence how many tons of ore (e.g., 120,000) averaging what mineral concentration (e.g., 1.35 percent copper) rested in a corner of a nation (e.g., the Mahad Dahab mine in the Hejaz region of Saudi Arabia).[89]

The whole point was to take minerals out of the ground and swiftly. Interior agents helped organize local mining operations in ways that sped the recovery of minerals. They introduced new methods of drilling and transportation that required the use of ever more sophisticated technologies. In the Philippines and Columbia, Bureau of Mines technicians equipped miners with underground lighting, tramming systems, and pneumatic picks, as well as high-tech coal washeries and handling plants to treat the coal.[90] In the process, foreign countries frequently had to purchase expensive and highly specialized equipment from the United States, which quickened the pace of extraction in ways that, beyond meeting local needs, would require nations to trade their minerals on a global market.[91] In Afghanistan, the Interior mineral expert overseeing coal production lamented that the miners' methods "were extremely primitive" until U.S. technologies intervened to make supply outpace demand, allowing for the nation to advertise coal for sale on the market for the "first time in history."[92] The reorganization of mining industries therefore generated momentum that propelled the integration of commodity markets.

These markets, however, were hardly predicated on equal relationships. Because the United States prioritized the agendas of procurement and overseas investment over local needs, Point Four mineral programs often constrained foreign nations' economic growth. In some cases, Interior experts created conditions in which participating nations were operating in closed rather than "free" markets. After extracting beryl (a light mineral used in various alloys and in nuclear weapons) in Afghanistan's Dora Sorcar region, Interior agents arranged for the U.S. government and its allied Beryllium Company of America to purchase all the beryl—all in an attempt to prevent the other major buyer of beryl, the Soviet Union, from accessing the material.[93] At other times, U.S. technicians inadvertently saddled some Point Four nations with a newly minted but quickly devalued commodity by prioritizing U.S. needs. Reaping the benefits from mineral development, particularly on single commodities, depended on ever-shifting world supplies. As host nations took measures to develop minerals and create infrastructure to support the new industry, they became vulnerable to the vicissitudes of the market. Such was the case in manganese extraction in Jordan. In the summer of 1952, a U.S. mineral engineer evaluated a high-grade manganese deposit in the Wadi Dana region. To accommodate the manganese project, the government of Jordan worked with a local company to finance the new roads necessary for shipping the notoriously onerous commodity.[94] But Jordan's infrastructural projects designed to spur manganese production were in vain. When the Point Four bureaucrats in charge of economic development attempted to sell Jordan's manganese to the Electro-Manganese Corporation in East Orange, New Jersey, and Union Carbide in 1954, the ore was deemed too low in quality, in part because the world market had become oversupplied from America's ongoing contrivances to access it across borders.[95]

In initiating these transformations, Interior technicians met with resistance in the form of local labor movements. In Cuba, workers complained of occurrences of manganese poisoning, a neurological disorder resembling Parkinson's disease that causes tremors, spasms, and mood changes. The public health crisis among miners galvanized what Interior administrators deemed troublesome labor organizing. Alan Probert, the Bureau of Mines foreign operations head, lamented, "Radical labor elements usually seize upon matters of this sort for a campaign."[96] Labor unrest also emerged in Point Four mineral programs in Chile in 1955, leading one Interior technician to quip, "Remember that John L. Lewis had the miners out of the coal pits on strike in the middle of the war"—referring to the Congress of Industrial Organizations' co-founder.[97] From his position at the head of Point Four foreign geology work, Johnston, looked on these labor skirmishes and other challenges to extraction internal and external to the TCA as a nuisance. He observed that bureaucratic "wheels will turn slowly and many little people stand ready with their monkey wrenches in hand."[98]

From the embassies, Interior personnel used their influence to alter mining codes in ways that were favorable to mineral exploration and foreign investment. In 1952, the TCA leadership, who would eventually exhibit ambivalence about mineral objectives in technical assistance, explicitly endorsed the alteration of mining and corporation laws to the Point Four agenda. Juridical reform was of "long-range importance" to the program, they claimed, for its ability to help spread American capital abroad.[99] Accordingly, Interior agents worked with local governments of Liberia, Colombia, and Afghanistan to revise mining laws, while Turkey, Lebanon, and Costa Rica also adopted new mining codes.[100] An exemplary case of these alterations unfolded in Egypt. Alan Probert worked from his desk in Washington, D.C., to change Egyptian mineral laws that restrained exploration with a circuitous process for entering patents, prohibited foreign companies from making investments, and allowed the government confiscation of property through expropriation, a long-held fear among U.S. officials and mining investors alike.[101] After a meeting with Egypt's director of fuel affairs, Mahmud Abu Zeid, Probert boasted that he "could convince the government on the law needed!"[102] The mining codes were in fact revised in keeping with Probert's wishes. Although Egyptian capitalists also had a stake in these transformations, Probert's influence is well documented. His contact Zeid was a central author of key proposals to change mining policies, and the *Egyptian Gazette* credited Point Four officials with guiding the alterations.[103] The new laws, moreover, opened concessions once again to foreign companies. These revisions ultimately assisted Standard Vacuum (Chevron), Anglo-Egyptian (Royal Dutch Shell), Continental Oil Company (Conoco), and Mobil in their Egyptian investments.[104]

The Point Four program also made Interior personnel into consultants for private industry. Probert and Johnston both worked from their desks in the Department of the Interior building to facilitate contacts between American companies and foreign governments, as they did with the Billman Coal Company and Reynolds Metals Company on Colombian coal and Saudi Arabian bauxite, respectively.[105] On the ground in local scenes, Interior geologists also functioned as liaisons for private industry. The U.S. geologist Richard Bogue, for example, had been asked by Saudi officials to help interest American investors in iron deposits. Bogue

Interior overseeing drilling operations in Egypt. Officials worked to alter mining codes to allow for the freer extraction of resources by foreign firms. 1954. Records of U.S. Foreign Assistance Agencies, 1948–1961, National Archives and Records Administration.

accordingly led a representative of Bethlehem Steel to investigate the deposits in Saudi Arabia, which were deemed unworthy of immediate development.[106] Similarly, following the 1953 Egyptian mining code revisions, Interior technicians met with representatives of numerous mining companies that were seeking to break into the international field. These included Continental Ore Company, Magnet Cove Barium Corporation, Sun Oil Company, Freeport Sulphur Company, and Texas Gulf Sulfur Company.[107] For American companies looking to invest overseas, the Interior Department was once again at the ready with the know-how needed to open up new frontiers.

ONE DECADE AFTER THE IRANIAN REVOLUTION OF 1979, William E. Warne reflected on his earlier experience in directing Point Four in Iran. Claiming that he knew nothing of the CIA's role in the Mosaddeq overthrow, Warne recalled that after the coup the U.S. government sent Howard Page of the Standard Oil Company and Undersecretary of State

Herbert Hoover, Jr., to meet with Warne and the new government in Iran, headed by interim leader Fazlollah Zhahedi. That fall of 1954, seven months after Warne requested "most urgently needed" Interior films like *The Evolution of the Oil Industry*, the three Americans worked with the new government to unleash the flow of Iranian oil. Warne said of this interaction, "We in *Point IV showed them* how to organize a national oil company. We set up the organization plan that they finally adopted."[108] Though Warne exaggerated his role in the multinational effort to establish what became British Petroleum, he nevertheless spotlighted a long-overlooked apparatus constructed in the postwar era to accomplish similar material goals in a quieter way. Warne, for instance, not only guided *petroleum* extraction in Iran but also initiated the usual geological reconnaissance, sending experts to examine Iranian coal, copper, iron, and lead deposits. Interior technicians across the globe furthered U.S. mineral interests as part of a standard operating procedure of extraction. Most often, a clandestine coup was not necessary.[109]

Interior's mineral programs in Point Four furthered American interests in terms of national security and overseas investments. On the one hand, Interior technicians identified reserves of strategic minerals across the globe. Once minerals were out of the ground, participating nations needed to do something with the materials. For some strategic minerals, like beryl in Afghanistan, the United States arranged exclusive trade agreements that shored up American armament in keeping with stated Cold War national security objectives. On the other hand, Interior personnel also implemented capitalist modes of production across the landscapes of the Third World. Their renovations of the terrain made the prospects for American and multinational investments overseas all the better and more low-risk. American and multinational companies, whether they decided to invest or not, reaped the benefits of having an expanded network of agents in the field without the burden of financing them; American taxpayers footed the bill. In this sense, the overlapping goals to further American geopolitical and economic aims through Point Four mineral programs were realized.

Interior's mineral work abated at the end of the 1950s, as the Point Four vision lost momentum in the second term of the Eisenhower administration before being reorganized under the Kennedy administration as the

U.S. Agency for International Development. The mineral panics that had opened the decade began to subside—temporarily, it would turn out—as reports surfaced affirming that supply comfortably outpaced demand, a partial effect of state and corporate efforts to expand access to minerals across the so-called backward areas of the world. Third World nationalist movements of the late 1950s and 1960s, meanwhile, would prove a further stumbling block to Interior's global engagements, as foreign leaders doubled down on commitments to protect minerals using international forums like the United Nations.[110] These heightened forms of resistance ultimately helped compel the Interior Department to venture into a different offshore zone closer to home and underwater: the mineral-rich continental shelf.

CHAPTER FIVE

The Bounty of the Seas

[W]e were fortunate, we hit it lucky, the government, the people
did in having our lease sale off Louisiana, right in the middle of the
Middle East crisis . . . American industry is looking homeward.

Stewart Udall

I N JANUARY 1946, Harold Ickes was celebrating more than the usual
promise that comes with ringing in a new year. He was also giddy at
the opening of one of America's "new frontiers." Just three months before, President Harry S. Truman had, at Ickes's urging, claimed the right
to all mineral resources discovered in the continental shelf. Ickes, the out-
going secretary of the interior, could not help but revel in the sheer magnitude of the annexation. The continental shelf encompassed 760,000
square miles of submerged lands contiguous with the United States
coastline; it was one-fifth the size of the nation and nearly as large as
the Louisiana Purchase (as Ickes was sure to point out). The continental shelf's oil potential was insufficiently known but estimated to be
beyond compare. Much to Ickes's bewilderment, however, the American public seemed not to take notice of the epic transformation inherent in the incorporation of the continental shelf into the national
framework. Looking to the past provided Ickes some consolation, as it
promised that time would reveal its real significance. "History," he explained, "will probably record that the assertion by the United States of

jurisdiction over the resources of these areas was one of the Nation's significant expansions."[1]

In the pursuit of minerals in the 1950s and 1960s, the U.S. government, led by the Interior Department, turned more and more to the continental shelf that had so captivated Ickes. The oceans had long underscored geopolitical power. They both connected and separated nations, chafing against the seemingly clear political borders that defined them. International law had determined that oceans constituted a shared heritage as an arena of trade, resources, and migration, open to all and the territory of none.[2] While historians have acknowledged the importance of the oceans to enabling American expansionism, they have largely overlooked how the United States' entrance into the continental shelf was itself an expansion of historical significance, as Harold Ickes argued. It was a radical redrawing of territorial sovereignty that fell almost immediately from view.[3] This oversight is a partial effect of the lack of serious attention to the role of minerals in shaping twentieth-century U.S. policies relating to the seas. Those who have considered mineral development on the continental shelf, meanwhile, have frequently elided the role of the American state in the process, emphasizing instead the business pioneers who moved offshore in pursuit of profits, seemingly on their own.[4] Though companies themselves played a major role, the government—at both the state and federal levels—ultimately authorized and oversaw this activity. The eventual executive order of 1945 enlarged the scope of that activity and brought much of it under federal jurisdiction. In this way, the incorporation of the continental shelf vastly extended American state and corporate power into the world; that this world was underwater should not distract from the expansionist mandate that drove it.

In the move offshore, the Interior Department navigated three interrelated contradictions of significance to America's shifting political, economic, and environmental priorities on a global stage. The first contradiction was that the extension of national sovereignty threatened to cut against the new postwar international order. With the enclosure of the continental shelf in a zone that had been considered a shared heritage, Interior officials worked to avoid the appearance of a national land grab. The reality was that the continental shelf expansion closely resembled the nation's nineteenth-century continental expansion in a variety of ways, from the strategies mobilized to the controversies—over state and federal power, foreign and domestic boundaries—raised. Balancing over the fault line between enclosure and commons became even more challenging in the 1960s, as Interior leaders aimed to develop the deep ocean floor, the region *beyond* national limits that remained an international zone. As justification, Interior officials made recourse, as they often did, to the global good, framing the agenda as one that invited international cooperation.[5] Second, Interior officials positioned the move offshore as an alternative to the move overseas, but the two enterprises were in reality deeply connected. With rising Third World nationalism in the 1960s, for example, the United States viewed the continental shelf as a reliable energy solution that was closer to home. However, the Interior Department simultaneously played a role in the offshore territory *and* overseas, guided by the faith that oil in particular must be secured in both places. Stewart Udall, the long-serving Interior secretary in the Kennedy and Johnson administrations, is one figure who spanned these realms of activity. Like the sprawling department he headed, Udall simultaneously oversaw resource management in far-flung regions across the globe, including Latin America, Africa, and the Middle East, and submerged lands.

Finally, the Interior Department spearheaded economic development of the continental shelf in ways that undermined its mandate to ensure environmental protection. The Interior Department's storied role in the conservation of natural resources had, by the 1960s, morphed into a role defining and defending "the environment."[6] Despite the apparent environmentalism of the department and its leader, Interior became a key driver in a frenzied offshore oil bonanza that yielded the largest environmental disaster the nation had yet to experience, the Santa Barbara oil spill. The spill helped to catapult environmental concern into mainstream debates and cast doubt over Interior's abilities in environmental management, leading to the creation of a rival bureaucracy: the Environmental Protection Agency.[7] The reality was that the incommensurability of the Interior Department's roles in environmental management and economic development constantly plagued the department in the twentieth century. Throughout, Interior consistently justified its extractive mandate by pointing to the same environment those actions helped to defile. Udall, for example, positioned Interior's activities in pursuing resources in foreign nations and the seas as utterly natural and necessary—Interior's studious management of the environment required it to examine the whole earthly "web of life" or "commons."[8] Through such discursive maneuvers, Interior's ubiquity across the globe in this era appeared as natural as the ecological interconnections newly understood to fan out over the earth.

Continental Shelf Expansion

The annexation of the continental shelf in 1945 had resulted from anxieties tied to wartime oil shortages. Total war greatly depleted America's base of mineral resources. In the fight against the Axis powers, the United States and the Allies expended 6 billion barrels of oil, one-third of known oil reserves at the time, just as petroleum was on its way to overtaking coal as the favored source of energy.[9] Those planning for America's natural resources, like the petroleum administrator for war, Harold Ickes, were thus intently focused on opening up pathways to new sources of oil. Although Latin America had been one target, Ickes like many other officials zeroed his focus on the oil fields of the Middle East. Ickes made calculated plays to extend federal control over the Arabian-American Oil Company (Aramco) with the creation of the government-run Petroleum Reserves Corporation. He further pushed the U.S. government to finance the building of the Trans-Arabian pipeline in Saudi Arabia. These projects ultimately outpaced Ickes's own sprawling ambitions. The negotiations over the Petroleum Reserves Corporation ultimately fell through because the threat of an Axis advance in the Middle East subsided in late 1943, a development that undercut both the United States' promise to offer Saudi Arabia protection and collective fears about oil shortages.[10]

These failed negotiations intensified Ickes's desire to extend U.S. jurisdiction over the continental shelf. Oil firms like Gulf Oil, Texaco, and Shell had been prospecting and operating in the submerged lands off the coast of Louisiana since the 1910s and 1920s, an activity that fell under the authority of coastal states rather than the federal government. New discoveries in 1937 promised an impressive supply just in time for global armament for war, as experts estimated that the Gulf of Mexico held as much as 22 billion barrels of petroleum.[11] In the context of these developments, Franklin D. Roosevelt had written to Ickes to develop a strategy for optimizing the federal government's jurisdiction and use of the submerged lands.[12] The two went back and forth on the issue, which was frequently placed on the back burner over the next few years. In June 1943, Ickes raised the submerged lands question with Roosevelt again, underlining the importance of the continental shelf as a national storehouse of mineral wealth. He urged Roosevelt to broaden the reach of U.S. jurisdiction offshore from the existing three-mile mandate (a legacy of the eighteenth century that represented the distance a cannon shot fired from land could reach into the sea) to as much as 150 miles.[13] Despite the obvious legal and political difficulties that could arise in the international arena, Ickes saw in this bold gesture the unparalleled opportunity to lay the groundwork "for availing ourselves fully of the riches in this submerged land" in both ongoing war and future peace. Roosevelt replied in perfect harmony, offering that extending the three-mile limit amounted to "common sense" in the context of budding international demand for oil.[14]

However, Roosevelt and Ickes's continental shelf agenda quickly became a contentious one within the federal government. The push to extend sovereign claims over a zone that had long been considered international posed challenging questions for U.S. foreign policy. Secretary of State Cordell Hull, for example, expressed deep concern over any attempt, so close to the fight against Nazi and Japanese expansionism, to assert national sovereignty over a region maintained as a shared resource by international law. In his position, Hull had long toiled to avoid the "Niagara of war." He used trade liberalization as a bulwark against the economic nationalism that was increasingly understood to precipitate military belligerence.[15] Thus, at the Eighth American Scientific Congress two years earlier, Hull had promoted the exchange of resources and ideas across borders as a foundation for armistice.[16] He therefore struggled to embrace a policy that seemed to mark a territorial enclosure in a zone that had long been understood to be a global gateway. He feared monopolizing the resources of the shelf would damage U.S. relations with the wider world.[17]

Despite these hesitations, State Department officials eventually began testing the waters of international opinion on the shelf issue. They put feelers out to coastal nations, all likely to be directly impacted by the precedents set by the United States' annexation of the continental shelf. Many nations across the globe, especially those with submerged lands, stood to gain from the extension of sovereign borders beyond the traditional three-mile limit. These included Venezuela and the Soviet Union, which had already been venturing into offshore drilling in Lake Maracaibo and the Caspian Sea, respectively.[18] The State Department further approached nations like Great Britain, Canada, Cuba, Denmark, Portugal, and Mexico—a combination of trade partners, wartime allies, and border states primed for potential disputes over boundaries between extended territorial planes. To the surprise of Hull, the governments of these nations offered resounding support.[19] The litmus test revealed that the American enclosure of the shelf lands would not elicit a deeply negative reaction. With such hopeful indications, the State Department offered support for the agenda.

After years of debate, which exasperated the otherwise energetic Ickes, the proclamation he imagined came to fruition. On September 28, 1945, newly installed president Harry Truman made two declarations concerning the mineral resources of the continental shelf and the fisheries of the high seas over it. In the official decree, Truman began by outlining the long-range need for sources of petroleum and other minerals. He reasoned in the proclamation that because of new technologies in resource exploration and extraction, it was now "practicable" for the United States to make use of the "subsoil and seabed of the continental shelf by the contiguous nation," which he described as an "extension of the land-mass of the coastal nation" that "naturally" belonged to it. This phrasing emphasized the natural quality of the relationship between submerged lands and those above sea level—what Roosevelt had earlier described as "common sense." Truman's second proclamation added to this jurisdiction the remainder of the high seas over that seabed except in the case of navigation, which would remain free to other states.[20] The proclamation thus laid a foundation and generated the driving force for the nation's systematic leap, by executive fiat, into the subsoil under the seas.

The debates over expansion into the continental shelf conjured earlier debates over expansion into the continental West and the Interior Department's role therein. First, Truman's proclamation prompted a showdown between federal authority and states' rights that strikingly resembled the nineteenth-century contest over transferring supervision of "domestic" affairs from states to the federal government. In the continental shelf debate, proponents of state control, including the governments of Louisiana, Texas, and California, argued that they had been effectively leasing the shelf since the 1920s based on authority stemming from earlier charters. Federal regulations, they claimed, would slow the process. In contrast, those favoring federal control, including the Interior Department and allies in the Departments of Justice and Defense, insisted that federal government was best positioned to oversee leasing in conformity with the national interest. The new Interior secretary Julius A. Krug, for example, argued that experts in federal government, unlike the laissez-faire state governments, could "protect" the continental shelf as "a national asset vital to the security of the Nation." He added, "It would be the height of folly to let this rich heritage be used up on the same basis that has wasted so many of our exhausted assets."[21] With this claim, Krug portrayed the Interior Department, however unconsciously, as a funhouse mirror image of its nineteenth-century self. In the nineteenth century, the department had nearly been disassembled for its permissive leasing of the public domain; in the twentieth century, the department claimed to be the only one capable of overseeing the judicious leasing of the underwater public domain.[22] These continuities and discontinuities with Interior's earlier history notwithstanding, the federal government ultimately won the argument. Supreme Court rulings in California and Texas determined federal oversight was necessary on grounds of the continental shelf's importance to national security and *international* affairs.[23]

Consequently, as the Interior Department secured the lead role in managing the continental shelf, linkages between Interior's past and present continued to proliferate in unexpected ways. First, Interior, the arm of the government inaugurated to oversee "domestic" affairs (via foreign expansion), secured authority over the submerged territory on grounds of its "international" significance. Interior officials in this instance did not disavow or question their international role. Its part in a project of global significance seemed apparent. The department would once again take a lead role in surveying and parceling that uncharted land for American and private interests. As one Interior report summarized, the department was up to the task because of "decades of experience" with land use problems of a similar nature.[24] The Geological Survey, for example, explored and mapped 20 million acres of underwater territory in the mid-1950s. Its agents, through trial and error, established fixed markers on dry land to register the positions of specific coordinates for later sale.[25] Interior's Bureau of Land Management, the office that subsumed the General Land Office, oversaw the auction of leases for drilling. Interior thus continued to balance its contradictory role in promoting and regulating extractive capitalism. Although department leaders had effectively positioned it as the center of conservationism, they still promoted privatization and extractive capitalism in particular. Interior leaders were tasked with "unlocking" the vast resources of the shelf, "a treasure valued in the billions of dollars."[26] Within the first few years of transactions, the bureau supervised approximately 400 leases in the waters off Louisiana and Texas. By 1957, $252 million in revenue had been generated and turned over to the Treasury Department.[27] Although many oil companies initially feared the transfer of leasing authority to the federal government, they quickly celebrated how the new system actually streamlined efforts to enter bids and secure tracts for drilling on the continental shelf.[28]

The move to the continental shelf was never as natural as promoters like Ickes and Truman suggested. This is especially evident in the ongoing debates over how to define the continental shelf at home and abroad. In 1946, Ickes and Truman had described the continental shelf as the natural zone that gently sloped off the shore of continents up to a depth of 100 fathoms, or 600 feet. This was the measurement that allowed Ickes to claim an expanse of 750,000 square miles to the United States' name.[29] However, these boundaries had no legal backbone. In 1953, Congress passed the Outer Continental Shelf Act, which clarified the zone's jurisdictional boundaries. The legislation upheld a horizontal rather than a vertical limit. It maintained that submerged lands between three and ten and a half miles from national borders were the purview of the nation, while those within the three-mile limit fell within the purview of coastal states, such as Texas and Louisiana. Though national in scope, the Outer Continental Shelf Act aimed to set a precedent in international law concerning the orderly development of resources in the ocean floor without trespassing on the national sovereignty of others.[30]

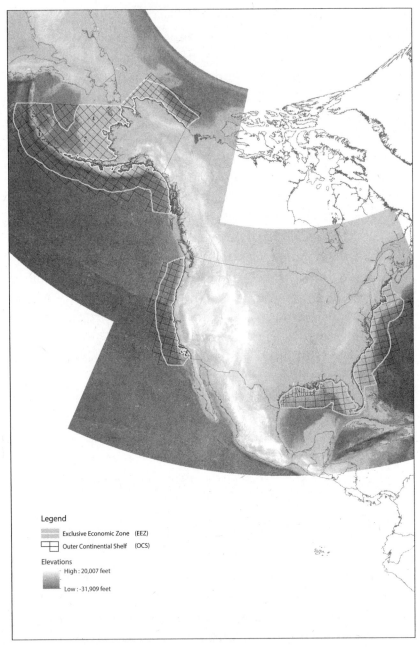

Map of the continental shelf showing competing political borders: the curving line of internationally recognized borders (Exclusive Economic Zone) and the grid unilaterally demarcated by the United States (Outer Continental Shelf). The elevation map reveals that the naturally occurring shelf does not correspond to the political borders, despite much political rhetoric claiming it was "natural."

As debates over the scope of the shelf seeped into the international arena, they aggravated long-standing fissures between national sovereignty and international law. After decades of negotiations, the United States ultimately forged a unilateral path and flouted the final international regime. Between 1956 and 1982, three formative United Nations Conferences on the Law of the Sea convened to establish the law defining exclusive economic zones (EEZ), which would consist of submerged lands to a 200-meter depth, or 200 nautical miles distance from land, whatever limit was reached first. Although the United States had been pivotal to these negotiations and set important precedents for the final rulings, it never ratified this agreement.[31] The U.S. government protested because of an article that allowed for an international legal regime to govern the extraction of minerals *beyond* the continental shelf in the deep ocean floor, a point to which we will return. In defining its distinct outer continental shelf (OCS), the United States largely conformed to the international standards, but it also deviated from them. The United States' submerged territory was ever so slightly larger than the international zone, encompassing roughly 850,000 square miles, but not so much larger as to cause serious offense.[32] Moreover, American officials mapped the OCS as a vast plane of parcels that the Interior Department had surveyed and codified. Thus, whereas the eventual international zone came to resemble organic curving lines, the American zone came to resemble a grid. The OCS grid instantiated the long-standing impulse to view nonhuman nature as resource awaiting utilization rather than a system participating in and shaped by human interactions. Interior perpetuated this utilitarian worldview even as it took on a role promoting ecological systems on a global scale.

A World of Nature and Politics

Stewart Udall envisioned a world of borderless nature held in common, but he also worked as an operative in a world of national divisions. Appointed by President John F. Kennedy, Udall, a politician from Arizona of Mormon faith, brought a down-to-earth and plainspoken charm to the Interior Department, building on the prestige and power that Ickes had fought tooth and nail to secure. Under Udall's new brand of leadership,

Interior assumed a lead role in environmental stewardship, an outgrowth of the department's time-honored conservationism.[33] Throughout his tenure, Udall increasingly brought environmentalism to the core of departmental activity, coalescing three prominent yet disparate streams of environmental thought: the utilitarian, aesthetic, and systemic. He championed at various points the more traditional wise use of natural resources, the metaphysical benefits of scenic nature, and the importance of protecting interdependent ecological systems from industrial and population growth.[34] Udall also tapped into neo-Malthusian fears that population growth was spiraling out of control and whittling away at vital resources, a vision that would eventually gain broad cultural articulation in Paul and Anne Ehrlich's best seller *The Population Bomb* (1968).[35] In 1963, Udall wrote *The Quiet Crisis,* a book that, like Rachel Carson's game changer of the year before, *Silent Spring,* helped propel a conversation about deleterious human impacts on the invaluable yet vulnerable environment. Solidifying his status as an environmental steward, Udall helped promote the Wilderness Act (1964) and fought to expand the National Park Service during his reign.[36]

Less known about Udall's lauded environmental management, however, is the extent to which he framed it in relation to the global context. Also lost in historical assessments was his central role in furthering U.S. mineral and oil interests, deeply global in orientation, in ways that frequently cut against the environmental well-being he so loudly championed. For many, the notion that Udall should have a global agenda of significance might seem odd. The Kennedy administration, for example, had early played up his supposed amateurism in the realm of foreign affairs. Udall made a gaffe in a press conference, conflating India and Pakistan in his remarks, and Kennedy ran interference with the press by joking, "That's why I appointed him Secretary of the *In*terior."[37] Such comments obscured a great deal. The truth was that Udall could scarcely avoid cultivating a global vision and repertoire, an effect of the entire expansionist trajectory of the department he helmed. In addition to overseeing affairs with semi-sovereign indigenous nations, Udall superintended a network of U.S. territories that spanned the globe. To travel around them, as he did in 1962, required covering 25,000 miles of ground and ocean. During this landmark tour, Udall inspected American Samoa,

Guam, and the Trust Territory of the Pacific Islands, a constellation of 2,000 islands, which had been administered by Interior since falling under the trusteeship of the United Nations in 1947. The Micronesian and Polynesian inhabitants of the trust territories had recently been unknowingly subjected to radioactive isotopes in the United States' testing of atomic weapons at Bikini Atoll.[38] With this history looming, Udall's errand was to salve America's image as the benevolent caretaker of the islands on a global stage. He unveiled a plan to improve social, political, and economic conditions on the islands. Although these territories offered little in the way of mineral potential, Udall saw exciting horizons in fishing and tourism industries; he was enchanted with the island amusements, including costumed dancers and floral ornaments.[39] However, he and Interior officials remained skeptical and anxious about territorial affairs. They conveyed concern about rising nationalism and economic stagnation in those regions, noting condescendingly that the islands remained "extremely primitive socially and culturally."[40]

Udall's rotation through the territorial circuit prepared him well for his ensuing migrations throughout Latin America, Africa, the Middle East, and even the Soviet Union. Three months after his trip to the territories, for example, Udall met with Premier Nikita Khrushchev to tour and discuss the hydroelectric power facilities of the Soviet Union—only to unknowingly to become a courier for intelligence that sparked the Cuban Missile Crisis. Udall met Khrushchev at his villa in Petsunda, Georgia. Sitting by the pool, the two covered far more ground, ideological and material, than dam building. Udall began the conversation by comparing his humble upbringing in Arizona to that of the archetypal peasant of Soviet society. He continued the comparisons between the United States and Soviet Union by citing their shared natural resource abundance, including American rivers and Soviet coal and petroleum. Udall even championed the shared "pioneering spirit" of the people working in energy development in both nations. Udall's attempts at flattery were met with brisk rejoinders from Khrushchev, who admitted to certain similarities before claiming the superior strength of the Soviet Union in relation to America's fading power and "impotence." Udall countered these visions with a positive portrait of American power rooted in the Democratic Party, and Kennedy in particular, which had become champions within the

Udall, wearing a floral necklace, visits with two Samoan women during an inspection of the territories. 1962. Papers of Stewart Udall, Special Collections, University of Arizona.

capitalist system of the working class in ways that would be unrecognizable to Karl Marx himself. Khrushchev acknowledged some differences across party lines and commended Kennedy's force of personality, reminiscent of Franklin D. Roosevelt. But his comments turned to a potential war that could destroy entire cities and countries in an hour, hinting to Udall of the military buildup in Cuba: "It's been a long time since you could spank us like a little boy—now we can swat your ass." The Soviet Union, Khrushchev confided, responded when Fidel Castro requested aid in its defense—defense, he observed, against the kind of colonialism that the United States itself overthrew in its struggle for independence. Having provided this implicit warning, Khrushchev concluded the meeting by underlining the importance of keeping this meeting off the record, instructing Udall to "tell the press we talked about electric power plants."[41] In so doing, the Soviet premier articulated something that Interior officials understood very well—that natural resources provided easy cover for calculated political moves.

The cloak-and-dagger meeting with Khrushchev notwithstanding, most of Udall's diplomatic tours were in Third World nations. Udall at times traveled abroad as a cabinet-level representative of the U.S. govern-ment, demonstrating support for new presidents like Leon Valencia in Colombia, Jomo Kenyatta in newly independent Kenya, and Raul Leoni in Venezuela, but his international missions were most often in support of Interior's ongoing programs in natural resource development abroad.[42] In the fall of 1965, for example, Udall undertook a trip to South America that was kicked off by the Inter-American Conference on the Conser-vation of Renewable Natural Resources in the Western Hemisphere in Mar del Plata, Argentina. There, Udall had commemorated the strong ties between the "sister republics" of the hemisphere initiated in Franklin D. Roosevelt's Good Neighbor policy. Udall claimed that policy had also birthed conservation programs for soil, wildlife, rivers, forests, and land. His list of advancements in natural resources from this policy omitted the cooperative mineral programs that had played the original starring role.[43]

During his trips across Third World nations, Udall championed a va-riety of natural resource agendas. In South America, Udall built on pre-vious and ongoing projects in the region, including those related to soil conservation and combatting deforestation. He extolled the virtues of wildlife preservation in Africa and desalination of brackish water in the Middle East. In all regions, Udall promoted the creation of national parks—an agenda in which Udall led by doing, undertaking numerous kayaking, hiking, and mountain climbing trips through the national parks of the nation and the world. Pointing to the United States' own Yellow-stone National Park, which he claimed launched a "world park move-ment," Udall encouraged government officials abroad to take up the call to preserve landscapes for their scenic wonders.[44] This platform of nature tourism harmonized with programming Udall oversaw back in the United States and its territories. In Latin America, for example, he broad-ened the popular National Park Service slogan from the early twentieth century, "See America First," to include neighbors in the Western Hemi-sphere: "See *the Americas* First."[45] Udall similarly promoted national park creation in Tanzania and Kenya during a trip to East Africa, in which he climbed Mount Kilimanjaro (and helped carry an injured member of the party back down the mountain for medical treatment, a feat of heroism the magazine feature on the excursion was sure to recount).[46] Collaboration with the United States, Udall argued, would spur economic development rooted in tourism and the aesthetic wonders of regional land-scapes the world over.

The outward orientation of the department both inspired and required Udall to portray the environment as global in scope. Building on the arguments Interior officials had long made about the uneven distribution of minerals, water, and other resources in the world, he called for cooperation and interdependence across national borders. However, unlike his predecessors, he acknowledged the role of the United States and other industrialized nations in catalyzing the plunder of land and resources that in turn damaged vital forests and soils. Udall also departed from the earlier strategies by making ecological arguments for American presence in foreign countries. The United States, despite follies of the past, had developed a multifaceted scientific approach to managing ecological systems. In his speech at the Inter-American Conference in Mar del Plata, he argued that mankind was a part of "the web of life"—a web that he claimed had reached as far as the polar bears of the Arctic, which would become a favored symbol of environmental concern. Pollution was wreaking its havoc on these vital relations. Citing comparative studies of resource problems in Africa, Japan, and the Soviet Union, Udall insisted that nations must strive for an "ideal ecological cycle" that seeks to protect rivers, skies, land, and wildlife.[47] The field of ecology had already begun to portray facets of nature as participants in an interconnected world system, a claim that influenced the secretary of the interior, but ecological thinking also provided important explanations for his presence in nations throughout the Third World.[48] The web of life required the mobility of environmental experts across it.

The idea of an earthly commons also provided an ideal framing to rationalize the continued operations of American power in the world. The commons would get its most famous articulation in Garrett Hardin's 1968 *Science* article "The Tragedy of the Commons," which argued that shared facets of the natural world were vulnerable because of collective indifference and thus should be privatized to incentivize good custodianship.[49] Years before this seminal publication, Udall was making a similar argument all over the world, if offering different, more international solutions (in public). At the conference on conservation in Argentina, Udall urged collaboration in solving "common problems." Just days later in Santiago,

Udall addresses an audience in Santiago, Chile, during his tour tied to the Inter-American Conference on the Conservation of Renewable Natural Resources. 1965. Papers of Stewart Udall, Special Collections, University of Arizona.

he encouraged attempts on behalf of the United States and Latin American nations "to manage and use wisely our natural resources and those which we share in common—the poles, the oceans, the atmosphere and outer space."[50] During an earlier trip to Africa, Udall claimed that "common management" over "resources owned in common" would bring about world order.[51] In short, Udall constructed a vision of a world filled with common features of nature. These common features, which would soon and famously be labeled "the commons," required collective action rather than political division. Within this broader worldview, the oceans were a particularly useful feature of the commons with which to make claims for action beyond borders. For example, in an address before an international audience gathered in Seattle for the First World Conference on Parks, Udall offered, "The air that we breathe is common air, the seas at our borders are common seas."[52] Oceans' metaphorical power, like that of the atmosphere, was tied to boundlessness. Political borders eroded under their watery force. For Udall, oceans justified international reach in talking points overseas.

For all the portrayals of global harmony, Udall's travels also consistently dovetailed with mineral development, increasingly understood as a fulcrum of political manipulation and a catalyst of environmental degradation. At the outset of the Cold War, the United States and Soviet Union had initiated an assault on resources in Third World nations. The United States had also intervened in those nations to ensure American access to resources deemed strategic, going so far as to oust leaders who challenged outside exploitation. Some of the most overt and sinister examples included U.S. complicity in the 1953 overthrow of Mohammed Mosaddeq in Iran to support U.S. oil interests, the 1954 coup deposing Jacobo Árbenz in Guatemala to protect the United Fruit Company's investments, and the 1961 assassination of Patrice Lumumba to clear the way to extensive minerals of the Katanga province in the Democratic Republic of the Congo.[53] Such interventions helped to prompt the tenacious spread of more aggressive nationalist movements. In 1962, seven years after the Bandung Conference brought together twenty-nine formerly colonized nations from Africa, Asia, and the Middle East, some Third World leaders turned to the United Nations to help protect natural resources from outside exploitation. There, they advanced a resolution that "asserted permanent national sovereignty over natural resources" in their nations.[54]

Mineral industries were also becoming more closely associated with ecological damage. Preservationist and conservationist thinkers like John Muir and organizations like the Sierra Club had long decried mining for its destruction of aesthetic wonders of "wilderness." Some of the mining industry's contributions to pollution, from the materials it used to by-products it unleashed, had been well established. The Interior Department, for example, had been designated to deal with pollution and oil spills since the Oil Pollution Act of 1924. By the 1960s, however, such threats were being identified and named in more public forums. Carson's *Silent Spring* had placed a spotlight on the dangers that various toxins, from chemical pesticides to radioactive uranium, posed to nonhuman nature and public health. Moreover, in 1965, the U.S. President's Science Advisory Committee issued a report warning that humans were, through the burning of fossil fuels, emitting carbon dioxide into the atmosphere at alarming rates. This accumulation was on course to alter the composition of the earth's atmosphere.[55] More citizens and scientists were pointing to mining as a key environmental offender.

Udall championed this same mining industry at home and abroad, even while underlining the importance of protecting the environment. At home, Udall was pivotal in shifting the American Southwest from a power grid tied to hydroelectric dams—a renovation of landscape that disrupted fisheries, watersheds, and terrestrial ecologies—to a power grid reliant on the strip mining of coal on the Navajo reservation, a process that contaminated streams, air, land, and bodies. Udall undoubtedly valued natural wonders and lamented pollution, but he consistently prioritized strengthening ties with extractive industries during his tenure, seemingly without a sense of their points of incommensurability.[56] Abroad, Udall publicly lauded conservation and privately met with officials to discuss growing mining economies, tour mining facilities, and visit Geological Survey operatives in the field. In Chile, for example, Udall met with Eduardo Simián, the minister of mines, on October 23, 1965, to assess the new copper legislation in the nation. Simián debriefed Udall on the latest "mineral picture," emphasizing the famed nitrate production, crucial to fertilizers and industrial agriculture, which was poised to meet the usual projections. Iron ore and natural gas production would be up, Simián noted, but petroleum production was expected to drop. Udall listened with interest before offering to supply Interior technicians to assist in exploration and mineral development programs. Simián made no response, yet Udall assumed that he registered and requited the offer.[57] While on his tour promoting national parks in Africa, a region that did not have many Interior technicians under international development agreements because of the recent or lingering presence of European colonial administrations, he received similar reports from officials on the production of minerals.[58]

In February 1967, Udall undertook a two-week tour of Kuwait, Iran, Jordan, and Saudi Arabia that dramatized the contradiction between the global sheen of environmental management and the unilateral thrust of U.S. mineral interests. Udall's ostensible purpose in the Middle East was to discuss the latest developments in desalination, a technical undertaking that promised to alleviate the region's water shortages and bolster agricultural industries in places like Jordan. However, his trip coincided with a moment of intersecting crises in the region: the ongoing struggle between Israel and Palestine following the creation of the state of Israel and a tug-of-war between Egypt and Saudi Arabia that was playing out through the civil war in Yemen. American ties to longtime ally and oil supplier Saudi Arabia persisted but were veering into greater uncertainty.

Udall's sojourn in the region during such a volatile time dredged up questions among American and foreign press corps. Before the trip, one American reporter had asked what he aimed to do in Saudi Arabia. Udall responded that he would touch base with ongoing Interior Department programs: "We have had geological survey teams looking for water and minerals in that country."[59] When asked a follow-up question about the significance of these travels, he responded that there was no significance. He merely had received invitations to a region he had never visited despite the continued presence of his Interior Department.[60] Even more pointedly, Arab news media raised red flags about his presence in Saudi Arabia. Days into Udall's visit, Radio Voice of the Arabs broadcast an incendiary report that cast doubt on his purpose. The report claimed that the Saudi establishment, increasingly coming under fire for being a pawn of imperialist forces and oil monopolies, "wants people to forget about reason and logic and believe that the Secretary has come to Saudi Arabia to discuss desalination." The report countered that the Arabian people were "too smart to be taken in by such patent lies."[61] The broadcast referred to recent developments that challenged Saudi Arabia's stronghold in the region. Just weeks before, nationalist commandos bombed oil installations near Dammam, leading the Saudi government and Aramco to increase security.[62] The exposé on Secretary Udall in Arab media accused him of being in the Middle East on an intelligence mission designed to affirm ties to King Faisal and to stabilize the oil situation.

In reality, Udall was in Saudi Arabia to do precisely what Arab media charged. On orders from Secretary of State Dean Rusk and President Lyndon B. Johnson, he undertook a mission of fact finding, bridge building, and stabilization. Landing in Jidda on February 4, Udall offered a statement that commemorated U.S.-Saudi relations, citing their exceptional collaboration over the years, which included Interior mineral programs. "It has been a source of pride and pleasure," Udall announced, "that my own department, the Department of the Interior, has participated in some of these joint ventures." He then recounted a partial history of the Geological Survey's search for minerals in Saudi Arabia, claiming, inaccurately, that this mission had been active since 1963 when such activities had, in reality, been initiated in the early 1950s.[63] The next day, Udall visited the U.S. Geological Survey offices in Jidda. Interior's ongoing involvements in mineral programs under the international development regime thus provided a scaffolding over which Udall's trip to Saudi Arabia could take shape. After meeting with Interior personnel at the station, he then visited contacts in the oil industry. He boarded an aircraft to inspect the Gawar oil field from the sky before heading to a luncheon hosted by Thomas Barger, the president of Aramco, the company that former secretary Harold Ickes had long eyed as a would-be prize of U.S. oil policy. Udall then toured Aramco installations and participated in a conference at its headquarters.[64]

Udall also met with King Faisal Ibn Abdul Aziz as part of this errand. After a private meeting with King Faisal on February 6, Udall wrote directly to President Johnson to report on the deteriorating situation. Faisal had confided in Udall that he was highly distressed over the conflict in Yemen, which he feared would spread to Saudi Arabia after the exit of British forces. He implored the United States to assist in deescalating the crises in the region, expressing dismay that the United States had "not shown much interest" in Saudi Arabia while throwing support behind Egyptian leader Gamal Abdel Nasser, who, in Faisal's view, was entering into his own Vietnam with involvement in the Yemen civil war.[65] Udall also offered lengthier observations to Rusk about the state of affairs in the Middle East. Udall claimed that he walked away from the discussions with a great optimism about the future of the region. The new generation of leaders, he urged, were forward thinking. "Even Faisal, the old camel raider, is exhibiting democratic instincts," Udall observed, "and the Shah's 'white revolution' in Iran is solidly impressive."[66]

Although tone-deaf in his appraisal of the stability of a region on the brink of the Arab-Israeli War, Udall was clear-eyed about certain issues, especially the oil situation. He observed a problem in the way the oil companies like Aramco failed to embed themselves in local communities. He admonished them for building up huge walls around their compounds and separating themselves from the "natives." He urged them to hire well-educated locals to become top executives to smooth over relations between them. Citing his close ties to the American oil industry, he claimed, "I intend to talk to the right leaders of the oil industry about this."[67] On an earlier trip to Africa, Udall had similarly contemplated the importance of uplifting local laborers to management as a tool of pacification. In Uganda, Udall visited the Kilembe Copper Mines near Queen Elizabeth National Park. The representative from the Ministry of Commerce explained how the mining industry suffered because Africans were not in scientific and technical positions. An ongoing legacy of British colonialism, most leadership positions in the mining industry remained with outsiders, while less than 10 percent of Africans employed, a proportion that the minister called "pitifully small," were even trained in natural resource management.[68] Udall agreed that this was a troubling arrangement. It was inequitable, and the resulting discontent was bad for busi-

Udall visits with King Faisal Ibn Abdul Aziz about the oil situation in Egypt in February 1967, months before the Arab-Israeli war. Papers of Stewart Udall, Special Collections, University of Arizona.

ness. Traveling across the Third World thus affirmed for Udall the importance of technical assistance: training "natives" in management would make them more amenable to the presence of foreign companies.

Despite being in the Middle East to smooth over the oil situation, Udall dismissed the charges of Arab news media by pointing to environmental management. He mobilized a self-effacing rhetoric that played upon the assumptions that the mundane work of the Interior Department and the "naturalness" of natural resources stood as proof positive that his purposes were disinterested and apolitical. In remarks that directly responded to the accusations of Arab media, Udall implored his audience not to give them any credence. "But really I am an *innocent* Minister of the Interior who should be called Minister of Natural Resources," he argued, "and this has been the mission which I am on."[69] With this statement, Udall made two significant and interrelated claims. First, he addressed implicit comparisons between the Department of the Interior in the United States, which managed natural resources, and Ministries of the Interior in the rest of the world, which oversaw matters of law, security, and espionage. These different trajectories, though left unsaid by Udall, stemmed from America's distinct bureaucratic development tied to settler colonialism. Secondly, Udall pointed to nature to downplay politics. His concern with natural resources stood, in his argument, as evidence of his innocence. In making this claim, Udall reenacted a script used by numerous Interior officials in their global ventures. Natural resources, to paraphrase an Interior official from an earlier era, were like the earth from which they came. They knew no national borders. They had little to do with the politics of the world. This self-effacing rhetoric attempted to deflect claims that such projects were in service of securing U.S. access to raw materials long associated with exploitation.

Ultimately, Udall's circumnavigations taught valuable lessons about operating in a world contoured by politics and nature. It was becoming increasingly difficult to insist upon the innocence and neutrality of U.S. action around natural resources in the Third World. Environmental management, what Udall positioned as an "innocent" activity, appeared to some critics as a façade that covered over oppressive power structures.[70] With growing resistance abroad, including attacks on oil installations, alternate arenas of activity became desirable. Arenas that were *unpeopled* had an even greater appeal. For Interior officials, the oceans and the continental shelf, degree by degree, became a way to avoid the hazards encountered in Third World nations. This did not mean that the U.S. government and allied corporations relinquished holdings overseas. One Interior Department report on the global mineral situation, for example, suggested that the politicization of extraction across the globe necessitated both expanding mineral activity in the oceans *and* revitalizing mineral assistance programs in the U.S. Agency for International Development that had reorganized the Point Four program. International development, in other words, would remain an important means to clear pathways to foreign minerals for the United States. In this transitional moment, the push into the continental shelf and developing nations would fall under the same banner: a means to access minerals "beyond the territorial limits of the United States."[71]

Tragedy in the Commons

In the mid-1960s, two decades after Ickes admonished the American public for overlooking the continental shelf, the nation was starting to take notice. Offshore drilling activities, and the revenues they generated, increased dramatically. The number of new oil wells, for example, doubled from 500 in 1961 to 1,100 in 1967.[72] As explanation for why the continental shelf was having its moment, Udall pointed to the events surrounding his recent journey to the Middle East. The crises mounting overseas, he argued before the American press corps, dissuaded American companies from investing. Volatility in the region posed too great a risk. Consequently, American industrialists were, in Udall's words, "looking homeward" to the continental shelf contiguous with the United States as part of the goal to achieve self-sufficiency and national security.[73] "The nation," he proclaimed, "is beginning to realize what a tremendous national resource we do have in our continental shelves."[74]

For Interior, taking advantage of offshore bounty required improved methods of exploration. The U.S. Geological Survey had struggled to keep pace with the petroleum industry technologically, as operators moved to tap deposits in unmapped zones. To bridge this gap, the Geological Survey opened an Office of Marine Geology and Hydrology in

Menlo Park, California, in 1965. The scientists gathered in this facility worked to map submerged lands off the Atlantic coast from Maine to Florida and the Pacific coast and Alaska. In Alaska, the crown jewel of Interior's wartime strategic mineral work in the territories, the new branch surveyed for old prizes—gold, tin, platinum, and petroleum—this time below sea level.[75] By the end of the decade, the effort to map the continental shelf had expanded to the Gulf and Caribbean region, as well as oceanic islands. Offshore exploration, in this way, traced part of the perimeter of U.S. formal imperialism.[76] The Johnson administration estimated that it would require twenty years of research before the offshore geology was mapped to the extent needed to identify areas of mineral potential.[77] Nevertheless, officials saw enough value in the continental shelf to undertake long-range planning.

Interior also helped pioneer new technologies for offshore extraction. The oil industry had adapted onshore technologies to marine environments with relative ease, though greater depths required different drills, seals, and fixed installations. Mining for metals in the ocean floor, however, was a great deal more difficult than drilling for oil. Marine minerals, including prized manganese nodules, required even more invasive processes to unearth from watery depths. As early as 1952 in the report *Resources for Freedom,* the Paley Commission had suggested the importance of deep sea resources for meeting the challenges of resource scarcity. In the 1960s and 1970s, U.S. officials maintained the faith that these nodules, rich in nickel, copper, cobalt, and manganese metals, would supplement those available from conventional sources, including those imported from overseas.[78] They brought with them greater risks for less obvious rewards. To mitigate some of these difficulties, the Bureau of Mines founded a Marine Mineral Mining Technology Center in Tiburon, California. There, technicians spearheaded research in undersea mining.[79] In the submerged lands off California, the bureau took core samples in search of metals like chromium and titanium. Its research vessel was named the *Virginia City,* a reference to the storied boomtown from the era of Interior's earliest involvements in the American West.[80]

Interior did not work in isolation or without conflict. In the fall of 1965, the Johnson administration launched an Interagency Committee on Oceanography, which brought together Interior personnel and representatives of private industries invested in marine resources, falling along broad lines of minerals and fishing. The group aimed to determine how best to make use of the vast resources of the seas and what government's proper role should be therein. Internal fissures beleaguered the group, most notably along the interests of fishing and mining. Mining operations often cut against commercial fishing. Some fisheries owners, for example, sought a moratorium on petroleum exploration off the coast of New England on grounds that it threatened marine life and thus commercial fishing.[81] Different agencies within Interior, including the Geological Survey and the Fish and Wildlife Service, struggled to balance multiple uses of the zone. Representatives of private industry, meanwhile, argued that there should be minimal government involvement, but they wanted government agencies to continue conducting geological investigations and disseminating information on the environmental conditions that might impact operations on or under the sea.[82] Toward this end, members of the interagency committee pushed Congress to allocate funds for one year of ocean exploration to various Interior bureaus amounting to $4.5 million, with $2 million for the Geological Survey, $1 million for the Bureau of Mines, and $1.5 million for the Bureau of Commercial Fisheries.[83] Private industry, in short, wanted less government regulation, not less government involvement.

The following year, another, more extensive interagency apparatus for administering activities in the continental shelf emerged that similarly promoted capitalist activity. Congress passed the Marine Resources and Engineering Development Act of 1966, which marshaled significant bureaucratic power to develop a long-range national program to accelerate the development of marine resources.[84] Udall joined the administrator of the National Aeronautics and Space Administration (NASA), James Webb, and other cabinet members and advisors, on the resulting Marine Sciences Commission. One contingent of Republican representatives, disgusted with the begetting of more and more bureaucracy, nicknamed the sprawling marine agency "the wet NASA."[85] The belief that the government should work to clear pathways for industry to underwater investments quickly became a guiding light for the commission's bureaucratic efforts. Udall and Interior offered up plans to coordinate programs in ways that would promote getting the information needed for "the encouragement of private industrial activity and sound investment in offshore venture."[86]

Throughout, American leaders hoped to capitalize on the lead in ocean technologies to reap benefits of the deep ocean floor, a legal gray zone beyond the continental shelf. International law had been ambiguous on the permissible activities in the deep ocean floor, which had previously been inaccessible for technological reasons.[87] What would it mean to mine the deep ocean floor, a commons belonging to all and existing outside national sovereignty? The international legal regime had not addressed this possibility, in large part because the prospect had been such a fanciful one in the decades before. However, by late 1967, the scenario was less a wonder ripped from the pages of a Jules Verne novel than an experiment in adapting and recombining existing technologies. The Interior Department collaborated, seemingly amicably, with the military and private industry to bring mining the deep ocean floor within reach. Working at the Bureau of Mines' new facilities in Tiburon, Interior experts joined those from the U.S. Navy to develop a new submersible vessel, *Sealab II*, as well as a vacuum that would raise seabed minerals to the surface.[88] Private firms like Lockheed Missiles & Space Company were also actively involved. Lockheed, for example, funded research on a deep-sea core sampler, a rare reversal of the usual arrangement by which research funds *from* government went *to* private industry.[89] The collaborators eventually broke tremendous barriers. For example, Interior sent four scientists to inhabit the deep ocean floor for sixty days while monitoring the marine environment and geology. These Interior "aquanauts," submerged near the Virgin Islands, gave Jacques Cousteau and his popular program *The Undersea World* a run for their money, setting a world record for the longest time any humans had lived on the deep ocean floor.[90] The Interior Department was pushing the threshold of the seemingly fathomless ocean.

Throughout, the United States was attempting to shape laws to support mining activities in the deep sea. Interior officials formed a committee to advise on policies on mineral resources of the deep ocean floor, contemplating what domestic and international laws would maximize economic benefit to the nation. They sought to get out in front of the international legal regime being shaped by the Intergovernmental

Oceanographic Commission and the U.N. General Assembly. Those multilateral entities had met in Paris that October to study issues relating to the deep ocean minerals. Keeping a watchful eye on these international developments, Interior leaders made recommendations for the outer limits of the continental shelf.[91] They ultimately hoped to make recommendations "as to what boundary, or alternative boundaries, appear to be in the best interests of the United States."[92] The international community did not heed Interior's recommendations. Instead, the matter of deep sea minerals became the point of contention that prevented the United States from ratifying the U.N. Conference on the Law of the Seas in 1982. The United States wanted all mining activities in the deep sea to be allowed to all with the capability to capitalize on it. Developing nations represented in the meetings, however, recognized that such permissive laws would give industrialized nations, with their superior technologies, an incredible advantage. Some of these nations, joined by the Soviet Union, thus pushed for international mandates that permitted activities with an agreement for technology transfer—sharing information about how to mine at such depths. The United States refused to accept these terms.[93]

If the United States at times eschewed international cooperation, it had also made international cooperation a key component of its ocean strategy. Amid the initial debates over deep sea mining, the Johnson administration proposed an International Decade of Ocean Exploration for the 1970s. In this "historic and unprecedented adventure," Johnson claimed, the international community would collaborate and pool together information to provide a more synthetic understanding of the resources of the seas.[94] As the early proposals made clear, international cooperation in the decade would "bring closer the day when the people of the world can exploit new sources of minerals and fossil fuels."[95] Although framed as a desire to help developing countries by tapping into new sources of food and other resources (and the country of Malta had indeed brought this suggestion to the U.N. in 1968), the International Decade also promised considerable profit. Officials privately estimated that the exploitation of ocean resources might yield $300 million.[96] A large portion of these potential revenues would come from minerals. In order for this dream to come to fruition, the international community would need to offer geological information pertaining to the continental shelf regions of each nation and contribute funds toward efforts at mapping, coring, and drilling the deep ocean floor.[97] That the call to share information about seabed minerals coincided with avowed attempts of the United States to use its lead in technology to further unilateral goals underlines the clear limitations of America's cooperative rhetoric.

The rosy future of oil and mining operations in the oceans was then powerfully cast into doubt with the *Torrey Canyon* oil spill of 1967. In late May, the tanker SS *Torrey Canyon*—linked to Union Oil, the same company behind the Santa Barbara oil spill—ran aground near the coast of Cornwall, precipitating the world's first catastrophic oil spill. The ensuing 30 million gallons of unleashed oil wreaked havoc on the marine resources and beaches of England and France. The United States had earlier experienced oil spills on a much smaller scale. Along the coast of Virginia, for example, a tanker transporting crude oil up the York River lost over 31,500 gallons, leaving its mark on ten miles of river ecosystem. Months later, Cape Cod experienced a similar fate on a larger scale of thirty miles when oil from an unknown source seeped along the coastlines. Regardless of the events that initiated oil pollution, whether from tanker, pipelines, or offshore installations, the impacts on local economies and ecologies were substantive: defiling scenic wonders, killing marine life and numerous species, and adding unknown toxins to the food chain.[98] The combination of smaller scale crises at home and the vivid spectacle of the *Torrey Canyon* disaster jolted the Johnson administration to attention.

The Interior Department was the federal arm designated to organize responses to oil spills. After the *Torrey Canyon* spill, Johnson tasked Udall and the Interior Department with developing "multi-agency contingency plans" to deal with oil emergencies in the seas.[99] In response, Udall urged Johnson to take seriously the possibility that offshore areas in the United States were just as vulnerable unless immediate precautions were taken.[100] Udall eventually oversaw a study to examine the prevention of and response to oil pollution. Although the inquiry began with concerns related to transport vessels like SS *Torrey Canyon*, the resulting report assessed the dangers of the entire oil supply chain from extraction to disposal. Regarding extraction, operators had not had serious incidents in the decade of offshore drilling in the Gulf of Mexico, though some Interior geologists were wary of the potential impacts of seismic activity or the wear and tear of infrastructure on steady oil operations in the marine ecosystems. Concerns over offshore drilling were ultimately subordinated to concerns over transport—or exporting and importing oil on tankers without incident.[101]

Johnson and Udall pushed ahead with parceling and leasing the continental shelf for the nation's economic development despite known environmental risks. In 1967, Johnson instructed Udall to prioritize securing additional revenues from offshore leasing.[102] Although Interior leaders had continued selling leases through the 1960s, legal disputes with state governments seeking control of shelf activities forestalled the comprehensive opening of federal submerged lands to bidding until 1968.[103] At that time, some within Interior, including Assistant Secretary Stanley Cain, pushed for a one-year moratorium on drilling to allow the Interior Department time to debate the merits of different boundaries for ecological sanctuaries and other regulations.[104] Undeterred, Udall oversaw the largest offshore leasing bonanza in the nation's history. The process unconsciously mirrored the earlier era of continental expansion, as parcels adjacent to key arenas of westward settlement, including petroleum-rich California, Texas, and Alaska, were opened to the bids of oil operators. The Interior Department, state governments, and local businesses all speculated that the resulting offshore industry would provide a boon to economic development in the form of employment opportunities, federal revenues, and private profits.[105]

The mother lode of lease sales revolved, fatefully, around the submerged lands in the Santa Barbara Channel. The parcels were nestled within the crescent of fifty-seven miles of California shoreline marked by rolling hills and framed by the Santa Ynez mountains. The picturesque beaches were a lifeline of the extensive tourism industry in the area. When Udall initiated the sale of leases adjacent to this scenic wonder, locals expressed concerns about hazards to the environment, as well as potential eyesores posed by drilling rigs. Although oil had long been drilled in these tidelands, beginning in the mid-1890s and carrying through the California State Lands Act of 1938, never had they been beyond the three-mile limit or on such a colossal scale.[106] By 1968, the rights to drill 540,000 acres of submerged land were up for grabs. The oil companies flocked to the lease sale. By the close of bidding, the department had generated $700 million in revenue for the U.S. government, breaking the record.[107] A few months later, in New Orleans, the Interior Department held another auction for oil leases in the waters adjacent to Texas.[108] In the course of such sales over one year, the United States generated nearly $1.5 billion in royalties—more revenue, in Udall's words, than "in the entire history of the Continental Shelf."[109] In celebrating these feats before the press corps, Udall emphasized the benefits to America's national security and self-sufficiency with relation to oil, not on what those revenues would mean, in keeping with the promises of the Great Society, for the American people more broadly construed.

The joy over the offshore bonanza was quickly extinguished when a blowout at an installation six miles off the coast of Santa Barbara catalyzed an unprecedented oil spill. On January 28, 1969, just one week after the inauguration of President Richard Nixon and the conclusion of Udall's term as secretary, Platform A-21, operated by Union Oil, sprang a leak. The Union Oil Company had joined Texaco, Gulf, and Mobil in entering a bid on Parcel 241, which shared a border with the designated ecological sanctuary. The resulting bid of over $61 million set an all-time record.[110] Within a month of the sale, the Geological Survey had approved five oil wells. The fourth well, A-21, was drilled to a depth of 3,479 feet. On January 28, as the drill retracted, oil began leaking, releasing between 12,600 and 21,000 gallons daily until the pipe was sealed on February 7. New leaks sullied waters through early March.[111] Almost one year to the day after the sale of the continental shelf leases, the channel was contaminated with what one expert later estimated to be 3.2 million gallons of oil.[112]

The well-documented damage became a media spectacle galvanizing environmental concern. Within a few days, the winds and waves had brought the plume of oil to the Santa Barbara beaches, destroying numerous plant species in the tidal regions and blackening the coasts. The Federal Water Pollution Control Administration under the Interior Department revealed that thousands of birds were killed. Ninety percent of the 1,500 blackened fowl brought to rescue centers died.[113] On nearby San Miguel Island, an entire population of seals and sea lions were killed. In June 1969, *Life* magazine featured a spread with numerous photos detailing the extensive damage to marine ecosystems that was so affecting and widely read that Interior officials went on an offensive, denying

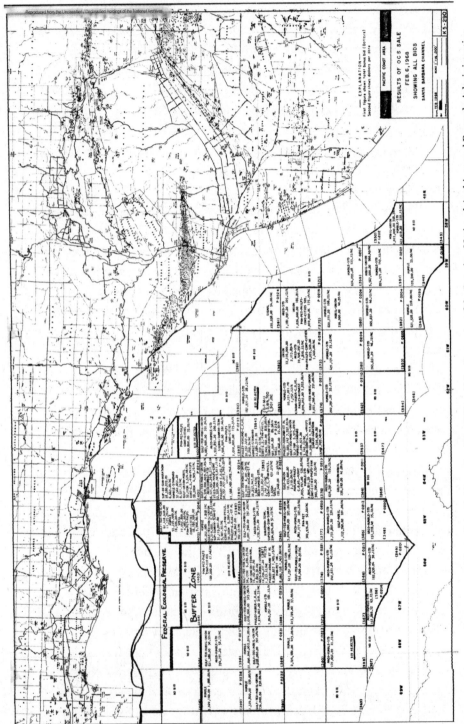

Leases in the Santa Barbara Channel. 1968. Records of the Office of the Secretary of the Interior, National Archives and Records Administration.

(temporarily) that oil was the cause of widespread death among the seal population.[114] This was only the start of the troubles. In an attempt to clean the channel, the interagency cleanup teams used chemical dispersants like polycomplex A-11, known to be lethal to many fish species, and the Standard Oil–patented Corexit, known to have long-term adverse biological effects. Corexit would eventually prove, when mixed with crude oil, to be five times as toxic for marine life. Even as the Santa Barbara cleanup teams deployed the chemical dispersants in the channel, experts agreed that such treatments were "still very primitive."[115]

In the wake of the disaster, both the oil companies and the Interior Department drew charges of negligence. Ronald Reagan, then governor of California, admonished the oil industry, insisting it take a lead role in the

Oil spill at the Union Oil installation on Parcel 241 in the Santa Barbara Channel, leased by Udall and the Interior Department. The spill released 3.2 million gallons of oil into the channel, wreaking havoc on marine ecosystems and drawing mainstream environmental concern. 1969. Records of the Office of the Secretary of the Interior, National Archives and Records Administration.

cleanup.[116] Lawsuit after lawsuit followed. A group of 10,000 property owners from Santa Barbara and Ventura County filed a class action suit against the oil companies and the Interior Department for damages amounting to $1.3 billion—almost the value of the entire leasing bonanza of 1968.[117] Property owners called Interior negligent for allowing drilling to take place without adequate investigations, standards, or safeguards, and for failing to properly supervise activities.[118] After the blowout, the new Secretary of the Interior Walter J. Hickel initiated a moratorium on drilling operations and revised the regulations governing offshore drilling to place oil operators in "absolute liability" for any resulting oil pollution. This drew further accusations by representatives of the oil industry, who claimed Interior's mandate that companies cease drilling on their legally purchased leases and its revision of regulations on the fly to be unlawful. As some oil representatives who filed suit against Interior pointed out, Interior officials *knew*, as the companies did, all the risks attendant to exploration in the shelf when they accepted bids for its leasing. They *knew* that the Santa Barbara Channel posed a particularly dangerous set of conditions because of the documented seismic activities of its faults. They *knew* that operators could not guarantee that blowouts would be avoided.[119]

Ultimately, Interior's failure to balance economic development and environmental protection threw a wrench into its expansionist trajectory. The spill precipitated what Hickel called "the most intensive review in the Department of the Interior's 120-year history"—a larger investigation than in the wake of the Teapot Dome scandal.[120] More significantly, the Santa Barbara oil spill helped to prompt legislation that would cut into Interior's authority in environmental management: the National Environmental Policy Act of 1969. The legislation created a new arm of the government to act as a safeguard for the environment, the Environmental Protection Agency, a move that met with much protest by Interior Department leadership.[121] Looking back on the offshore lease bonanza and the recent disaster, former Interior secretary Stewart Udall was "sickened" by the damage. He took full responsibility for it, as permitting operations in the Santa Barbara Channel was his decision. Across the mineral technocracy of the Interior Department, Udall reflected, there had been broad consensus that oil drilling posed no serious threat to the environment;

they had never even seriously entertained the idea of tighter regulations over wells in the continental shelf. Yet Udall recalled the SS *Torrey Canyon* just two years before, which had taught that a spill of this magnitude could yield catastrophe for marine ecosystems that would linger for an unknown, and possibly indefinite, amount of time.[122] In this way, the Santa Barbara oil spill seemed to dispel the fantasy that the move off-shore, unpeopled though it was, could issue forth without serious social repercussions. It became the Interior secretary's personal tragedy of the commons.

IN THE DECADES after the second world war, the American state and allied corporations ventured offshore and underwater in pursuit of a new mineral frontier to rival the continental West of the nineteenth century. The move into the continental shelf, a first step in a broader journey to access the bounty of the seas, was thus a significant expansion. Officials tried to position it as a natural entity and natural extension of U.S. power, but it was highly political and much contested. Although the extension of U.S. sovereignty over the continental shelf initially threatened to disturb a postwar international order rooted in a belief that the oceans were a shared heritage, Harold Ickes and the Interior Department helped to position enclosures of submerged lands as beneficial to the nation and the world. Offshore drilling eventually seemed a corrective to dependence on foreign nations for oil, but the activities were deeply interconnected. As the nation moved both underwater *and* overseas, the Interior Department represented an institutional bridge. Around the world, for example, Udall continued departmental efforts in resource management across borders. As evidence of the importance of such activities, he pointed to environmental ideas, including ecological systems and natural features held, like the oceans, in common. Ultimately, such arguments were wearing thin, as Udall saw firsthand. Critics in Saudi Arabia, for example, appeared unconvinced that natural resources had nothing to do with politics.

Directing extractive operations "homeward," the nation proceeded full steam ahead on a mineral agenda in the seas. Drilling on the continental shelf grew exponentially in the 1960s. Yet developing the shelf pushed the nation to other murky and international zones, including the deep ocean floor. America's desire to capitalize on its lead in ocean mining technologies ultimately prevented it from ratifying the international agreements on the Law of the Seas. For all its recourse to international cooperation and global commons, the United States pursued narrow unilateral interests. A similar dynamic was at play in the realm of economic development and environmental risk. Even as Udall and the Interior Department garnered a reputation for environmentalism, they continually pushed for extractive developments of known danger to ecological systems. The impossibility of this balancing act became painfully apparent in the wake of the Santa Barbara oil spill. The Interior Department's failures to regulate the offshore oil industry created a scandal and challenged the legitimacy of the department's environmental management.

However, at the same time, Interior's contradictory project to ensure capitalist development and ecological well-being would drift into other global commons, including the seemingly far-out realm of outer space. In the context of space exploration, the challenges posed by conflicting imperatives continued to plague the department. A new project that was pitched as a benefit to the world—the earth resource satellite that became Landsat—would disproportionately benefit the few, the world's richest oil companies. The firms' move into new frontiers of investment catalyzed activities with troubling effects on the social and material landscapes of Third World Nations.

CHAPTER SIX

Prospecting the Final Frontier

I would annex the planets if I could.

Cecil Rhodes

O N APRIL 6, 1967, Stewart Udall was touting the latest achievements of the U.S. Interior Department in Houston, Texas. Before
a meeting of oceanographers, Udall waxed poetic about outer space and
the department's collaborations with the National Aeronautics and Space
Administration (NASA) in the journey beyond the planet. He had earlier spent his day touring the Johnson Space Center, NASA's hub of
innovation, symbolically affirming the agencies' ties: Interior geologists
and mineral experts were conducting research on celestial bodies, a step
on the path to landing a man on the moon. Making sense of the department's seemingly far-out programming, Udall drew upon an appropriately
geological metaphor tied to one of his favorite pastimes: mountain
climbing. Outer space was just another mountain to conquer. Once at the
summit, Udall explained, the look skyward shifted inevitably back to the
earth, providing a perspective that revealed new "details, patterns, and
relationships" that were impossible to view from the ground. A similar
process was at play in the Interior Department. Its work in the heavens
renewed attention to the earth in the form of a satellite agenda designed

to view Earth's resources. From the vantage point of space, he argued, the whole earth could be mapped and its resources managed for the better-ment of all—especially Third World nations. Udall was also excited about how the satellites would illuminate mineral-rich lands. He pre-dicted, "If we don't find the pot of gold at the end of the rainbow, then we may someday spot it *from* the rainbow." Satellites, he hoped, could provide such a view, "literally prospecting from the sky."[1]

In the 1960s, the United States jumped into outer space, and with it went the Department of the Interior. The seemingly provincial depart-ment had by that time circled the globe under the auspices of international development and reached into the ocean floor. As countless Interior of-ficials had done in the previous decades, the next generation of leaders looked for new arenas in which to leverage its hard-earned natural and mineral resource expertise. For a department born of and for America's westward expansionism and in a constant push to prove its relevance, President John F. Kennedy's buoyant promise that space exploration would open a "new frontier" for the American nation resonated deeply.[2] As Udall put it, the Interior Department, with knowledge "sharpened by more than a century of resource investigations," was ideally suited to the task of breaking new barriers.[3] After first joining with NASA in 1961 to work on the problem of lunar geology, crucial to the much-lauded Apollo project, the Interior Department began investigating possibilities in ac-cessing extraterrestrial minerals, seemingly infinite and increasingly within reach. Unlocking the mineral potential of outer space seemed one way for American officials to justify the pricey space bureaucracy at a time when long-standing rationales, including Cold War competition with the Soviet Union, were growing tired. Following a call to emphasize the practical benefits of space to American taxpayers, Interior techni-cians turned attentions back to the earth, reenacting Udall's parable of the mountain climber. Interior became a prime mover in the earth re-source satellite agenda that gave birth to the Landsat satellite. Landsat is less renowned than manned space flight and other satellite programs, from the communications satellite that connected the global village to the military reconnaissance satellites that heightened the Cold War. Despite a reputation for falling far short of its designers' dreams to improve land use across the world, Landsat has recently drawn historical attention for its role in environmental management across the world and in more recent efforts tracking patterns related to climate change.[4]

An exploration of how the United States' mineral aspirations shaped and were facilitated by the Landsat agenda challenges this legacy, both its seeming insignificance and its unequivocal environmentalism. Landsat emerged as American and Interior officials in the 1960s, joined by decision makers like the father of modernization himself, Walt W. Rostow, sought to bring the mineral-rich interiors of the Third World into global circulation. The satellite bridged two imperatives in Interior's ongoing mineral programs in developing nations: the Cold War push for strategic materials and the postwar drive for economic integration. As Interior technicians continued projects in places like Minas Gerais, Brazil, under the new U.S. Agency for International Development (USAID), they desired inventive ways to circumvent physical and political resistance to extractive operations. First, Interior personnel continued to struggle with rugged terrain and inadequate infrastructure in their harried quest for comprehensive knowledge of the region's minerals. Second, Third World leaders increasingly fought to protect their minerals from outsiders as part of a broader resource sovereignty movement in decolonization. A satellite of geological reconnaissance seemed an ideal solution to both problems because it could float freely across borders, a result of international space laws allowing the orbit of peaceful space-based objects. Officials wanted Landsat to become a vehicle—and space a new and resistance-free pathway—to convey the United States further into Latin America, Africa, and Asia.[5] Landsat was in this sense a dramatic continuation of the department's century-long pursuit of new frontiers, a project newly fitted to the gleaming tomorrowland of the Space Age.

Before and after Landsat's launch in 1972, American and Interior officials insisted the satellite would be a global and environmental good. It would improve conditions in poorer countries of the world, they argued, through USAID programs devoted to natural resource development. Interior leaders further argued that doing so would act as a safeguard for the environment, an object of widespread concern thanks to transnational movements that increasingly viewed the earth as an interconnected system, in which air, water, and ozone crossed rather than conformed to national borders. Udall, bringing these arguments together, insisted that the celestial view would reveal "the 'oneness' of our total environment" on the path toward "improving the human condition all over our globe."[6] However, the global and environmental promise that helped legitimize the satellite was not sustained for two major reasons. First, the satellite's designers made choices that ensured its predominant usage by the oil and mining industry rather than poor people in developing nations. With the help of Landsat programs in USAID, for example, Chevron discovered a vast petroleum reserve in Sudan in 1977, initiating a "black gold" rush there. Second, American officials used Landsat to galvanize the extraction of resources in unindustrialized nations on grounds that those nations, unlike the United States, did not need to conserve their resources like oil. As in earlier eras, this new wave of American environmental management justified American border crossings to access resources elsewhere in a partial effort to conserve resources at home.[7] Interior's skyward journey ultimately intensified U.S. capacities to know and exploit the earth, a process that, despite claims to promote a global and environmental good, ensured an unequal distribution of economic benefits and environmental woes.

Climbing the Mountain

The space race captured the popular imagination in the 1960s, as the United States and Soviet Union pushed known limits to human innovation and experience. As part of the brinkmanship in ingenuity, NASA oversaw a program designed to land men on the moon, Apollo. Yet the goal required a knowledge of uncharted regions and lunar geology, and this knowledge was the purview of the Interior Department. NASA enlisted Interior's Geological Survey in 1961 to investigate these remote geological conditions. It subsequently inaugurated a new branch of Astrogeology for the extraterrestrial mission. Beyond assessing geology in advance of the lunar landing, NASA and Interior officials had also determined that astronauts like Virgil "Gus" Grissom, Gordon Cooper, and Jim Lovell needed to appraise geology in their alien surroundings. This meant they needed to be trained in geology. The agencies therefore designed classroom lectures and organized field trips to landscapes across the American West that "simulated lunar conditions," places like the

Grand Canyon and the Navajo reservations that had been long-standing targets of Interior activity, so astronauts might learn to recognize, map, and describe geological formations.[8] Years before walking on the moon, and under the supervision of the Interior Department, Neil Armstrong became an amateur geologist.

Interior geologists also contributed to studies of lunar geology through the Surveyor program, a series of unmanned vehicles designed to soft-land on the moon. Developed by NASA technicians in the Jet Propulsion Laboratory (JPL) of the California Institute of Technology, with the help of the Astrogeology branch, the Surveyor vehicles sought to collect scientific data of the lunar terrain to transmit back to earth.[9] The name "Surveyor" highlighted a shared agenda between the program and the Geological Survey: geological reconnaissance, the procedures to know the contours and material composition of a given terrain.[10] In addition to taking images of the moon, Surveyor vehicles performed physical experimentations with lunar minerals in the field that mirrored Geological Survey techniques back on Earth. Through remote-control mechanisms, the vehicles dug trenches and excavated lunar soil that was tested using alpha scattering devices. From these investigations, NASA and the Geological Survey learned that the moon's surface had elements of magnesium, aluminum, sulfur, iron, cobalt, and nickel, among others.[11] They also cultivated a set of techniques in remotely accessing geological information that became vital to the later satellites.

Building on these advances in lunar geology, officials began promoting the mineral potential of space. Extraterrestrial minerals, they hoped, could offset growing critiques of NASA. Although space exploration had long been justified on grounds of an urgent geopolitical contest between the United States and the Soviet Union following the launch of Sputnik in 1957, some American citizens by the mid-1960s seemed less convinced by the rationale, especially in relation to a NASA budget entry of nearly $5 billion a year.[12] The most pointed and publicized of these attacks came from Barry Goldwater, the senator from Arizona and Republican candidate in the 1964 presidential election. Goldwater consistently lambasted NASA in the election cycle for its price tag. "We are spending entirely too much money on the manned moon program," he lamented.[13] For Goldwater, only a space program oriented to *military* preparedness was worth continuing. President Johnson and the space bureaucracy countered by emphasizing *civilian* and "practical uses of space," taking pains to enumerate NASA's many contributions in weather preparedness, navigation, mapmaking, and international cooperation.[14] At the same time, the Johnson administration and the space bureaucracy began touting extraterrestrial minerals—seemingly boundless and, equally helpful, inoffensive. Celestial bodies were not populated, after all. In April 1964, a deputy administrator of NASA, Hugh Dryden, told the readership of the *New York Times,* "Geologically, we have no reason to doubt that the moon and the nearby planets, being solid bodies, may be rich in rare mineral resources, possibly offering economic returns far outweighing the costs of exploration."[15]

It was in this context that Interior began research on how to mine the moon in 1965. The idea seemed stolen from the science fiction of the day. That same year the novel *Dune* staged a strikingly parallel scenario: a distant planet served as a mining colony for an intergalactic society. The novel was written by Frank Herbert, a journalist with abiding ties to the Interior Department; he had worked closely with Interior on the Continental Shelf Lands Act as a Senate staffer and lobbied his friend and Secretary of the Interior Douglas McKay (unsuccessfully) for an appointment in American Samoa under the Office of the Territories. Herbert was thus well acquainted with America's extractive and imperial legacies when crafting *Dune,* a fable of ecological and societal devastations resulting from a collective attachment to minerals that eventually secured Herbert's place as a leading voice of the mainstream environmental movement.[16] Where Herbert was deeply critical of the desire for extraterrestrial minerals on grounds that it distracted from the need to rethink limits and priorities on Earth, American officials were upbeat. Despite the seemingly fanciful elements of extraterrestrial mining, Interior officials grounded the venture in a long lineage of pursuits—and Interior Department pursuits—of new frontiers. "Lunar mining," as the circular announcing the undertaking observed, was "an inevitable extension of man's effort to adapt to widening frontiers."[17] Interior's Bureau of Mines took the lead on this attempt to open "the first extraterrestrial mine," overseeing experimentation in techniques from blasting and conventional drilling to the running of conveyor belts amid the extremes of a simulated lunar environment. The scientists estimated that acetylene, a potential fuel source, could be trapped in lunar rocks.[18] Interior and NASA officials ultimately believed this experimentation served a long-range project to use space resources as a launch point for further space exploration.[19] Although officials publicly celebrated extraterrestrial resources, they knew that it was not a viable option for economic development; if mining in zero-gravity environments was difficult, shipping the products back to earth would be highly uneconomic.[20] The lunar mining research was perhaps never meant to be a revolution in the American mining economy, but it served as a public relations nugget for an American public in the throes of space fantasies like that depicted (and problematized) in *Dune*—fantasies that built on something the Interior Department knew well: ever-widening frontiers.

Such cornucopian fantasies of space, or the belief in its limitless bounty, unfolded alongside the institution of international laws prohibiting territorial claims to the moon and other celestial bodies. As the Soviets and the United States inched closer to a lunar landing in the mid-1960s, some legal minds raised questions about what this new arena of activity would

Bureau of Mines promotional material showing a scientist looking "very much like an astronaut" in testing a plasma torch for applications in mining the moon. Records of the Bureau of Mines, National Archives and Records Administration.

mean for sovereignty.[21] One international lawyer likened the journey into space to the opening of the Oklahoma territory in 1889, asking, "Can nations avoid an outer space stampede?"[22] To prevent a stampede going against their favor, with terms defined by the Soviets, Johnson's national security and international affairs advisers sought to draft rules and do so in a way advantageous to the United States.[23] The team's suggestions materialized almost point for point in the Outer Space Treaty adopted by the United Nations, including the Soviet Union, in 1967. The treaty held that celestial bodies were "not subject to national appropriation by claim of sovereignty, by means of use or occupation, or by any other means."[24] The treaty remained silent on legal parameters for natural resource exploitation therein. The result was that the only reference to "use" of materials in the treaty implied that it was valid insofar as it did not simultaneously advance national sovereignty. Anyone with the technological capability to appropriate material could do so; none could be denied access on grounds that it fell under competing sovereign protections. Such was the logic that had framed Interior's and the United States' position on the deep ocean floor as well, a vision that eventually was challenged by the Group of 77 at the United Nations. In the treaty, technological capability was tantamount to sovereignty, even if it would be several decades before extraterrestrial mining ambitions inched meaningfully toward realization.

If the potential to harness resources in space was distant, then the potential to harness resources on Earth using the vantage point of space was much more immediate. In this sense, the exploration of extraterrestrial geology was ultimately most important for inspiring a reflexive set of questions about the earth. Geologists in NASA and the Interior Department began to imagine the limit-altering possibilities for geological exploration in the prospect from outer space. One eager new employee of the Johnson Space Center, Peter Badgley, a Princeton-trained geologist who had worked at the Colorado School of Mines, was central to this process. Badgley did not work for the Interior Department, but he had collaborated with Interior and the Army Corps of Engineers beginning in 1964, early in the process of designing technologies that could use space to view Earth's resources.[25] Several precedents had laid a foundation for such a technology. The well-established practice of aerial photography had already lifted geological prospecting from the ground, while other space programs, including the TIROS weather satellite, Gemini manned orbiting vehicles, and top-secret reconnaissance satellites like CORONA, had also galvanized interest among scientists in surveilling the earth.[26] Badgley and his team of scientists began researching how recombining technological features from these programs, as well as multispectral scanners that identified mineralized zones from a distance, might produce a technology ideally suited to resource exploration. Tapping into the broader political debates surrounding NASA, Badgley shrewdly positioned the satellites-in-the-making as an economic boon for the NASA program, one that could justify its increasingly politicized budget. The group sketched an outline for technologies in "remote sensing," the technical term for gathering data based on various stimuli from a distance, that might invigorate land use on Earth.[27] For advice in this venture, NASA and Badgley turned to the natural resource experts in the Department of the Interior.

Interior Department leadership jumped at the satellite agenda for its potential to further natural resource development on a global scale. The historic and ongoing experiences of Interior personnel in mineral programs across the Third World were vital to sparking institutional interest in earth resource satellites. This is perhaps most evident in the fact that the newly appointed director of the Geological Survey, William T. Pecora, a man who had his start as a career geologist working in U.S. wartime mineral programs in Brazil and Colombia, was the chief advocate of the idea. By the time Pecora became the director of the Geological Survey in the 1960s, Interior geologists had been exploring and developing minerals in Third World nations for decades.[28] Working under USAID, the new agency that subsumed the Point Four program, Interior geologists and mineral experts retained important positions surveying for minerals and serving as mineral attachés.[29] However, these regions remained difficult to access because of harsh terrain and failing infrastructure. Geologists in places like Brazil's Minas Gerais, where Pecora had conducted influential investigations of mica, were experimenting with new methods for detecting untapped minerals. They ultimately began crafting a blueprint for a "geological laboratory" in space, which they hoped would "lead to important new finds in unmapped areas of Asia, Africa, and South America."[30] In short, they were imagining exactly the type of space technology that NASA geologists were conjuring back in Houston, placing particular emphasis on how it would assist with U.S. mineral programs in Third World nations.

Secretary Udall agreed with Pecora about the value of outer space to mineral development, seeing it as a means to further departmental collaborations with industry in extraction. When Pecora recommended that the Interior Department embrace the satellite agenda, taking "our proper lead role," Udall threw the full force of the institution behind it.[31] Udall immediately registered the benefits of the satellite to natural resource planning that might curtail the negative effects of population and industrial growth, but he also was ever the champion of extractive interests and deeply utilitarian. He consistently claimed that chief among the satellite's many rewards would be its ability to reveal geological structures of "economic significance."[32] The value he perceived in the satellite to the mining economy became evident in an October 1965 exchange between Udall and Dean McGee, the president of the Kerr-McGee Corporation, at the time the largest uranium producer in the world. McGee, an old acquaintance of Lyndon Johnson, wrote the White House to register concern about a "diminishing rate of discovery" of minerals across North America and to seek government support in developing technologies that could make the land into "virgin prospecting ground again." Udall replied by celebrating the long-standing efforts of the Interior Department to pioneer technologies to push mineral limits. Magnetometers used in submarines during World War II, for example, had become a standard prospecting tool of the mineral industry. "The jump into space," Udall offered, would add "a new dimension" to this story. Udall then informed McGee of the departmental efforts to use the vantage point of space for mineral exploration.[33] According to Udall, outer space created possibilities to intensify mineral detection and extraction on Earth. Private industry was not a meaningful player in the satellite's design phase, but its desires and interests were ever in mind.

The desire to advance extractive capitalism with the satellite dovetailed with the push to secure America's mineral stronghold in a Cold War context. Adding significantly to the allure of the satellites in the Johnson administration, for example, Walt W. Rostow, Johnson's special national security advisor, called for creative approaches to accessing Third World resources in his report "The Frontiers of South America," written in his capacity as the chairman of the State Department's Policy Planning Council. Although Rostow was most interested in advancing "underdeveloped" societies through modernizing policies, a point well documented by historians, he also sought to renovate "underdeveloped" landscapes through innovative mineral programs. He linked both agendas to America's Cold War strategy for defeating the Soviet Union. His report observed that the "rugged terrain" of that continent had prevented crucial knowledge of its geology and made finding "the real potential of the interior . . . a slow-moving project."[34] Rostow suggested that *satellites* could expedite accessing "the interior," which clearly represented to him a cache of mineral wealth, by circumventing such troubles on the ground; they could clear the way to geological mapping, mineral exploration, and "other constructive purposes."[35] In the process, the satellite would make South America into usable terrain—an appeal that harmonized with oil magnate Dean McGee's call to make the land "virgin" once again.

Yet Rostow and U.S. geologists faced more than the challenges posed by rock and strata, even if those were easier ones to discuss openly. Adding to the difficulty of access were Third World leaders who called for recognition of their natural resource sovereignty. Having already appealed to the United Nations in 1962 to outline clear legal mandates upholding the right to protection from exploitation of resources by outsiders, foreign governments also seized 128 petroleum and mining investments across the globe in the 1960s and 1970s.[36] The trend of hardening sovereignty was vividly symbolized in the rise of the Organization of Petroleum Exporting Countries (OPEC), founded by Saudi Arabian Abdullah Tariki and Venezuelan Juan Pablo Pérez Alfonzo, which promised to challenge Western hegemony over the global economy. While some national governments, like Shah Mohammad Reza Pahlavi's administration in Iran, were aligning with U.S. and European interests in resource extraction, others were building barriers against them.[37] Thus, although officials like Rostow spoke in the language of *physical* obstructions to minerals, *political* ones, in this tumultuous moment, were just as troublesome. These political problems, in turn, made a satellite that could reduce one aspect of risk in foreign investment—the risk of exploration—more appealing. In the face of increasingly risky overseas operations in nations armed with better tools to protect their minerals, the U.S. government and private industry sought better tools as well.

In the summer of 1966, geopolitical and extractive ambitions were aligning. NASA, Interior, and Cold War modernizers thought many problems might be solved with one technology: it was a win-win-win. On August 25, 1966, the Interior Department and NASA hosted a meeting at the Geological Survey headquarters to discuss Rostow's proposal to use a satellite in identifying resources in Latin America. Representatives from other agencies, including USAID and the Department of Agriculture, also attended. Interior personnel predictably supported the global initiative, while some NASA officials, including the Johnson Space Center director Leonard Jaffe, registered a degree of skepticism. It would not be the first point of interagency contention in the struggle to shape the satellite and its eventual use. Representing one dissenting view at NASA, Jaffe disapproved on somewhat condescending grounds, believing those in developing nations would not be able to make use of such "exotic" technologies.[38] Jaffe, like many NASA officials, was less invested in linking space to international development. He believed that the satellite's chief value would be in new resource development in industrialized nations, not in poorer nations that had been such a preoccupation of Interior leaders and Walt Rostow.

However, most criticisms of the global reach of the earth resource satellite agenda stemmed from fears of a potential diplomatic crisis. Civilian satellites crossed borders freely under the Open Skies agreements, international accords allowing for the peaceful use of space-based objects, that followed after the launch of Sputnik. Security advisors predicted that opening a discussion of an earth resource satellite would ring of exploitation. Charles E. Johnson of the National Security Council (NSC) feared, justly, that the new technologies would agitate the Soviet Union. Rostow, well versed in Cold War defense exigencies from his coinciding role overseeing strategy for the Vietnam War, had outlined a similar concern in his report. "A major political problem," he acknowledged, "may be the attitude of South American and other countries toward a method of exploration which the Communists will probably label 'spying.'"[39] U.S. officials were deeply afraid of eliciting accusations of espionage, especially because they feared this might draw attention to the coinciding overflight of reconnaissance satellites, the secretive and legally murky technology that had become a feature of America's Cold War strategy. Reconnaissance satellites were under the separate jurisdiction of the Department of Defense and drew authorization from undisclosed executive orders.[40] Interior's civilian activities had long been positioned as a corrective to military might, causing historic and ongoing tension between the two arms of government. In the space race, earth resource satellites thus threatened to disturb the tenuous balance between avowed civilian and undisclosed military satellites by triggering alarms about the legitimacy of space-based objects' flow across borders in general. The existence of satellites under one department's jurisdiction created anxiety about exposure or blowback in the other's realm. Relations between Interior and the Department of Defense thus remained fractious, if ultimately serving similar ends—the extension of U.S. power across the world. Earth resource satellite promoters, in short, faced acute pressure to ensure that they presented the earth resource satellites to the international community in an exceedingly delicate and indisputably benevolent fashion.

It thus created a temporary crisis when Udall preemptively announced the earth resource satellite agenda without the approval of other federal agencies or the Johnson administration. Udall and Pecora had grown tired of waiting to proceed with a technology of such obvious benefit to the nation and the world. On September 21, 1966, Udall issued a press release announcing Project EROS, the Earth Resources Observation Satellite, which he claimed would allow the department to oversee natural resource planning and to "improve the quality of our environment" for the benefit of all humanity. Yet if the press release emphasized these global and environmental benefits, it also made clear that mineral extraction was a key priority. It reveled in the satellite's "ability to 'see' more easily beneath the water and forest or soil cover"—in other words, its ability to discern minerals that formed the earth's crust.[41] Pecora, whom Udall named head of Project EROS, later celebrated the ways in which the satellite would allow the United States to "aggressively and imaginatively press the search" for the "*world's* undeveloped resources."[42] Udall was nearly fired for his brazen move, done to advance an agenda of unknown consequences for U.S. foreign relations. Charles E. Johnson of the National Security

Council was enraged by Udall's power play, indicating in correspondence that neither the White House nor NASA was ready to move on the "improbably named" EROS—a commentary on Interior's clumsy attempt to symbolically align its own agenda, named after the winged god of sexual desire, with the prestige programming of Apollo or Mercury.[43] However, the cat was out of the proverbial bag, and the other agencies necessarily threw support behind the initiative or risk appearing like they had been trying to keep it under wraps.[44]

With the satellite agenda out in public, officials focused energies on building international consent in the proving ground of international development. To cultivate "a new climate of international legitimacy" for the satellites, the U.S. government created pilot programs for the remote-sensing agenda in Brazil and Mexico under USAID agreements.[45] In November 1966, NASA worked with the State Department and the Interior Department to test the feasibility of relaying data acquired from aircraft and satellites to ground stations built in Brazil and Mexico and back

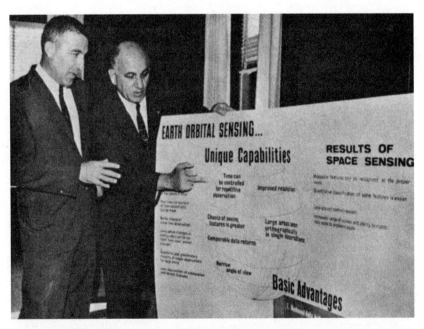

Udall and Geological Survey director William Pecora discuss the Earth Resources Observation Satellites. 1966. National Security Files of Charles E. Johnson, Lyndon Baines Johnson Library.

to the United States for further analysis. While experimenting with this technological base, U.S. personnel trained locals in the techniques of remote sensing, which would be utilized with the eventual satellites.[46] Udall and Pecora, for their part at the periphery of the international project, made recommendations for remote-sensing features in the Mexico-Brazil agreements, requesting a combination of infrared and ultraviolet sensors and radar that could produce images of one hundred square miles, anticipating many of the capacities of the eventual satellite.[47] These early experiments seemed to generate much international goodwill toward the potential launch of the satellite. They further won over Johnson of the NSC, who had earlier dismissed EROS as an ill-conceived Interior Department power play. After the Brazil and Mexico test runs, he declared, "[T]he potential usefulness of the earth resources survey program is worldwide in scope."[48]

Satellite promoters needed not only to win the hearts and minds of international audiences but also to win budget lines from other arms of the federal government. Officials sought to charm the stone-faced Bureau of the Budget and a typically divided Congress. The arguments that sustained the satellite agenda along bipartisan lines were ultimately rooted in its alleged benefits to capitalist development. The Johnson administration, in the final year of its tenure, worked to position EROS as a "tangible, indeed exciting" example of NASA producing practical benefits to American citizens.[49] Many shared in this vision across party lines in Congress. One Republican senator from Kansas, Frank Carlson, declared in 1968 that "the potential benefits from earth resources observation satellites alone would justify the cost of the entire U.S. space program," offering a tremendous boon to geologists and farmers.[50] The push to secure funding for the satellite carried through to the administration of Richard Nixon. At this stage, another Republican, Senator Karl E. Mundt, played a key role in keeping the EROS program alive and ultimately securing the final approval for funding in 1970. By no coincidence, the bill called for the creation of a data center to be run by the Interior Department, located in Sioux Falls in Mundt's home state of South Dakota.[51] At home, the winning argument for the satellite was not global and environmental good, but rather the promise of unilateral economic gain.

In promoting the satellite agenda abroad, officials downplayed America's own economic gain. Instead, they took a page from Udall's playbook of sublimation, even after his term ended in January 1969. Udall had earlier observed that although there might be a "political stir" about the satellite's boundary crossing, people needed to remember that the view from space was not "a covetous assessment" of the planet, but rather an "inquisitive, anxious, loving look at the planet we call home."[52] When newly elected President Richard Nixon faced the U.N. General Assembly in September 1969, two months after the landing of Apollo 11 and with a backdrop of an escalating war in Vietnam that was further unraveling America's claims to moral leadership, he adopted the same rhetorical strategy. Nixon urged that the earth resource satellite agenda would be a global and environmental good. It would locate fish in oceans, minerals on land, and crop patterns across seasons—all for the benefit of "the world community."[53] The United Nations assembly conveyed support for this vision. The U.N. secretariat, for example, issued statements that the satellite would have wide-reaching benefits, while individual nations such as Ghana, Brazil, Egypt, and Thailand offered warm endorsements.[54]

Yet some were predictably unconvinced by the universalizing bromides being put forward. The Soviet Union protested the satellite on grounds that for all these claims of global goodwill, it subverted national sovereignty. Soviet officials argued that countries had a "sovereign right to 'dispose' of resources and to 'dispose' of information relating to their resources."[55] Put differently, the Soviets claimed that acquiring knowledge of a nation's resources without permission was as much a violation of sovereignty as acquiring the actual resources without permission. In so doing, the Soviet official identified a key threat to sovereignty in an earth resource satellite agenda that pushed established limits of human activity. Satellites may not have unearthed resources themselves, but they did uncouple information needed to unearth minerals from its former, more terrestrial constraints. Whereas Interior geologists previously operated within bounds of territories to access this information—for example, leading teams across the landscape in a ground survey or fueling or registering an airplane within national borders for an aerial survey—they could now access vast quantities of information without ever setting foot or landing gear on the ground. Despite making this incisive observation about how the move to space altered the relationship between information and material, the Soviet Union remained in the minority opinion. The earth resource satellite, which would quickly be rebranded "Landsat," was a "go" for launch.

Over the Rainbow

After garnering support at home and abroad, the first Landsat satellite rode a rocket into the upper atmosphere in 1972. When Stewart Udall had earlier hoped that the view from the mountaintop would reveal patterns previously unseen, he understood that these patterns would include many ecological features but would also lend themselves especially well to estimating the resources *beneath* the earth's surface.[56] The government officials who took the torch from Udall after his time in office shared in this knowledge. In the pivotal design phase, they made technological decisions that ensured the satellites' primary usage for mineral development. This was especially true of the sensors that would be featured on the orbiting vehicles. NASA officials promoted the use of multispectral scanners, a process using reflective mirrors to scan a scene, which revealed information about the earth by capturing different light patterns reflected from earthly formations. Interior officials pushed for more rudimentary vidicon television cameras, akin to photography on Earth, skeptical of a less tried-and-true means of visualizing the earth. Striking a compromise between the aspiration of NASA and the pragmatism of Interior, both sensors were featured on the first satellite, the product of the combined labors of General Electric, Hughes Aircraft, and RCA, the companies that secured the coveted government contracts. Throughout the debate over the imaging system, designers generally agreed upon the desired prospect and resolution: the sensors captured frames of approximately one hundred square nautical miles. The resolution of the resulting images fell somewhere between weather satellites' coarse representations of wide-ranging cloud cover and reconnaissance satellites' fine-grain portraits of small-scale structures.[57]

It was the focus and framing of the Landsat sensors that bore the most telling mark of the mineral dreams that had inspired the whole program. This is because the resulting canvas was ideal for mineral prospecting.

In the field of practical geology, the closer one was to the ground, the more difficult it could be to see geological structures that foretold resource potential, including domes, anticlines, and wrench faults, all of which extend dozens of miles. Aerial photographs did not capture a wide enough canvas, and thus were needed in far greater number to reveal patterns of interest. However, the vantage point from space, like that of the mountaintop, revealed new patterns, much like pointillism in art or, as one observer at the time noted, the paintings of Jackson Pollock.[58] In the process, small-scale facets of the human and natural environment—shrubs, houses, trees, wildlife, farms, streams, and people—blurred and blended, while the large-scale folds and furrows of geology came into focus. The resulting patterns became hieroglyphs that revealed, to the trained eye, subterranean secrets.[59] Put plainly, in the prospect from Landsat, "x" marked the spot for the proverbial pot of gold. Although the resulting images allowed trained users to discern many things, including melting ice, crop cycles, and deforestation, the satellite's most obvious and immediate utility was in revealing geological patterns.[60] It pointed the way to minerals.

In the process, the sweeping view from space radically cut down on the labor required to map and to know the earth. As Udall had explained at the Johnson Space Center in 1967, space photography could visualize in "just one pass" and a "single glance" a sweeping mosaic of land patterns. He claimed then that the satellites would produce in their eighteen-day orbits the same amount of information that aerial surveys could in the span of twenty years.[61] Although he overestimated the efficiency and reliability of the imagery, he accurately conveyed the way the satellite would help streamline and deterritorialize exploration. Previously the U.S. government had to rely on a patchwork of hundreds of ground and aerial surveys to discern the mineral potential of a region. Even surveys by plane had been tethered to airport hangers and fueling stations within national borders. With the satellite, suspended in the low gravity conditions of the upper atmosphere, the U.S. government now had a totalizing, satellite's-eye view without the burden of engaging with local environments, infrastructures, and protocols.[62] In the process, the images, mirroring the satellite's own indifference to sovereignty, omitted political borders entirely.

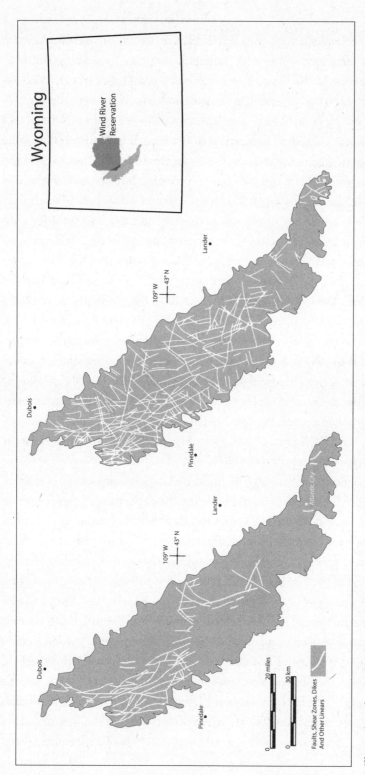

Illustration of a 1973 NASA schematic comparing geological knowledge of fault lines and other petroleum indicators before Landsat (left) and after Landsat (right) in Wyoming, including Wind River Reservation.

If the technological features lent themselves to extractive ends, the management structure prioritized unilateral interests by making the U.S. government, via the Interior Department, a gatekeeper of that information. Yet some had offered less unilateral alternatives along the way, including giving control to private industry or to the United Nations and World Bank. Udall had mentioned in his speech in Houston that some had suggested bringing the satellite under the U.N., an effort to calm the potential political stir about its border crossing. Multilateral control was not an idea he seriously entertained, nor would many U.S. officials who anticipated taxpayers would rail against subsidizing a technology controlled by a body increasingly perceived to be ineffective. Instead, control of the satellite remained with NASA and control of the data center fell under the Interior Department, even as data centers would later be built in some developing nations.[63] The EROS Data Center in Sioux Falls, run by the Geological Survey, became a clearinghouse of Landsat images. Interior thus supervised thousands of transactions to grant interested parties access to information. A variety of clients, including state agencies, private industries, and foreign nations, turned to the Geological Survey for Landsat data, called "scenes." By completing a standard order form, these clients could access geological information for a fee around $200.[64] In 1976, the EROS Data Center earned $2.3 million in revenues from the sale of approximately 300,000 scenes.[65]

Throughout these debates, the Interior Department jockeyed for a central role in the Landsat venture by citing the department's growing environmental responsibilities. During and after the Udall era, Interior leaders advocating for Landsat invoked different types of environmentalism, from wise use to environmental protectionism, as evidence of its legitimacy. Udall had made a habit of celebrating environment as the global commons, a system of shared responsibility and benefit. Invoking and elevating the rhetoric of Interior officials since the midcentury, Udall claimed that natural resources were "a heritage of all mankind," which in turn "transcend provincial boundaries." If natural resources transcended boundaries, then so too must environmental management. This was his central argument for Landsat in the late 1960s, one that Interior officials of the 1970s would recapitulate when promoting it in the first decade of its usage.[66] Such claims built upon the new purchase of environmentalism.

Many environmental reformers called for transnational approaches to combating ecological degradation, a point evident in the rise of movements like Save the Whales, *The Whole Earth Catalog*, and Greenpeace.[67] These transformations—vividly symbolized by another example of space photography, *Earthrise*—helped to shore up Landsat's planetary environmentalism, or the claim that the view from space would discern precisely this bigger picture to solve the border-crossing problems of Planet Earth. These arguments laid a foundation for the satellite's eventual legacy as an environmental custodian, in spite of its leading role in promoting extractive activities known to spur the worst kind of environmental degradation, a problem of which the public was increasingly aware following the Santa Barbara oil spill and the environmental activism it helped inspire.

Landsat's planetary reach touched ground through the arena of international development. U.S. officials working on Landsat quickly turned their attentions to foreign nations and USAID, which became part of the process for greasing the wheels of geological reconnaissance across borders. Under formal agreements, USAID adopted remote sensing as part of its programming. Its technicians, building upon the Geological Survey's existing cooperative programs abroad, trained locals in remote-sensing techniques on site, while foreign nationals also traveled to the EROS Data Center in Sioux Falls for training backed by American funds.[68] USAID had wanted to develop ground stations in host countries in order to palliate "strong nationalist tendencies in many developing nations."[69] In Brazil, India, Argentina, and South Africa, technicians helped construct ground stations at a cost of approximately $6 million.[70] Throughout, U.S. officials claimed that information about resources would help alleviate poverty in developing nations. Like the pilot programs in Brazil and Mexico in the 1960s, USAID remote-sensing programs helped create a "climate of international legitimacy" for the satellite. By 1975 a reported 120 countries, both part of and separate from USAID, purchased 50,000 Landsat images to assist with resource development.[71] Many officials and scientists throughout the Third World eagerly embraced the Landsat agenda and the USAID dollars that accompanied it. The satellite training programs provided opportunities for citizens to undertake trades related to science and engineering, and scientists from places like India would become participants in an international community of academics studying remote sensing.[72]

However, there was a problem. Some critics at the time observed that the benefits of these programs were not being distributed to the people. Rather, these satellites advanced the interests of Third World elites who generally offered their support to the U.S. government and allied corporations, oil and mining firms in particular. Some of the biggest champions of the agenda were governments under the firm hand of dictators who colluded with U.S. modernizers backing their repressive regimes in return for compliance with their increasingly neoliberal policies, including Ferdinand Marcos in the Philippines, General Suharto in Indonesia, Jean-Bédel Bokassa in Central African Republic, Shah Mohammad Reza Pahlavi in Iran, and Augusto Pinochet in Chile. It did not help

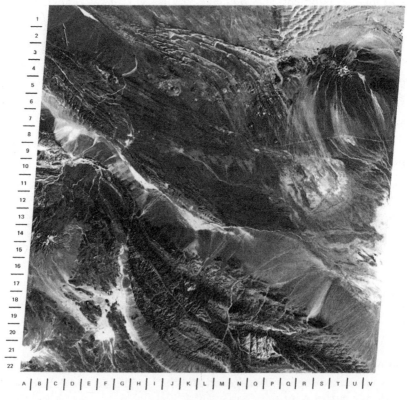

Landsat image of copper fields in Pakistan. 1972. National Aeronautics and Space Administration.

matters that minerals were themselves such an emphasis. Geological investigation programs more than doubled the next most represented USAID programs, ground water and agriculture.[73] These mineral priorities, for example, became a point of contention in Bolivia. In keeping with Rostow's original vision, Landsat helped identify new mineral frontiers in South America, especially through the Altiplano region that fans out across Bolivia, Peru, Chile, and Argentina.[74] One of the major discoveries enabled by $10,000-worth of Landsat images was lithium, a commodity newly valued for its use in nuclear manufacturing facilities, in the Salar de Uyuni salt flat of Bolivia.[75] Lithium discoveries helped attract million-dollar investments from U.S. firms for infrastructure projects to open mining districts to ports and became the basis of the more recent "lithium triangle" tied to smart technologies.[76] While these developments were celebrated by some, other Bolivians worried that a familiar pattern was unfolding. A country long exploited for its mineral reserves, Bolivia struggled to develop other resources, including vegetation, water, and soil. "If Bolivia wants to approach true development," one Bolivian scientist argued, "*all* of its resources must be known."[77]

Even so, mining programs in USAID proliferated. The government of the Philippines under Ferdinand Marcos, infamous for his ruthlessness and corruption, was particularly supportive of Landsat. Immediately after the launch of the earth resource satellite in 1972, Filipino officials and trainees collaborated with U.S. officials in the remote sensing of two regions, the Baguio Mineral District, site of ongoing gold and copper mining, and Mindoro Island, whose name derived from the Spanish phrase *mina de oro*, goldmine. Although the mineral potential of these regions was already established in earlier imperial contexts, the satellite filled in important gaps of information about faults and lineaments, providing a "precise and complete geological map of the island which can be utilized for development planning of the island's mineral resources."[78] In the Central African Republic, meanwhile, the Geological Survey oversaw projects in search of gold, platinum, and diamonds at the invitation of Jean-Bédel Bokassa, the controversial dictator who had just crowned himself emperor in a lavish (and appropriately gilded and diamond-encrusted) ceremony.[79] General Suharto in Indonesia was similarly cooperative with the USAID apparatus, famously taking kickbacks from aid programs and restricting rights of citizens while the United States and the World Bank held Indonesia up as a model of effective economic development.[80] His government allowed U.S. Geological Survey technician William Carter to explore for reserves of nickel in the southern portion of Gag Island in Indonesia. Carter worked alongside a representative of the U.S. Steel Company, which was eager to expand its portfolio in Indonesia, in which it had already invested. Investments, however, had been curtailed by the difficulties of mapping mineral reserves in areas of dense, tropical vegetation.[81]

Private industry and, to be more precise, the world's largest oil and mining firms, therefore did have a key role in the Landsat mineral agenda, even if those involvements are harder to trace. By the mid-1970s, nonrenewable resource firms claimed to represent half of the entire field of Landsat users (according to NASA, they constituted closer to one-third of overall users). The firms repeatedly cited this statistic in their lobbying efforts through the nonprofit they formed, the Geosat Committee. The companies behind the Geosat Committee amounted to one hundred and included Chevron, Exxon, Conoco, Shell Oil, Mobil Oil, Phillips Petroleum, ARCO, Texas Gulf, Phelps Dodge Corporation, Bethlehem Steel, and National Lead Company, to name just a few.[82] Chevron had by 1975 allocated $100,000 per year on Landsat images. For comparison, in 1975, the Geological Survey reported total sales of Landsat data to be $909,000.[83] Research offices of Exxon and Gulf similarly relied on the data to help locate areas worthy of further investigation and to predict which reserves would be high producers.[84] For a time, Landsat data was considered an extremely effective predictive tool in mineral prospecting. One geological consultant working for the Classic Mining Corporation, for example, had developed metrics using the images that could almost guarantee which reserves would produce oil—all ten wells that he recommended in Wyoming became lucrative producers.[85] Such successes led one mining executive to call Landsat "the most important development since the invention of the magnetometer in the 1940s," a resounding compliment that harkened back to Udall's earlier correspondence with the Kerr-McGee executive, in which he anticipated precisely this outcome.[86]

Mining and oil companies found the greatest value of Landsat to be in curtailing the risks of foreign investment. With Landsat, companies could better fix one key variable of the risk calculation: exploration. Utilizing the publicly funded technological infrastructure, a system that no single corporation could have taken on in isolation, private companies like Conoco and Chevron could make surer investment decisions. As one Landsat report summarized, the data was so valuable because it made it "possible for the petroleum and mining companies to make preliminary assessments . . . before entering into negotiations or making payments for *foreign concessions.*"[87] Locating sure-fire mineral reserves was one way to bolster foreign investments, even though the threat of expropriation and other complications on the ground lingered. With the remote-sensing technology, the American state, and by extension American tax-payers, shouldered part of the risk of exploratory efforts that aided private industry in mining enterprises beyond borders.[88] The full extent of extractive firms' success abroad is unclear. From the beginning, and citing proprietary reasons, firms refused to disclose the uses toward which they put the data and where they focused their attentions, purchasing Landsat images through blinds. Corporate representatives undertook such measures as a means to keep their objectives off the public record, ostensibly to keep a competitive edge over other firms. Clearly, corporate strategists understood that information about resources was a vital resource of its own worth protecting. One Landsat consultant estimated in 1978 that oil companies had made $1 billion from discoveries guided by Landsat data home and abroad.[89] The profits derived from Landsat, like the satellite itself, remain out of view.

What does become visible in the archive, however, are fleeting moments in which extractive corporations collaborated with the American state to use Landsat data in the so-called energy crises. To powerful effect, the oil embargo of 1973 restricted Western nations' access to oil in Arab states for their part in supporting Israel in the new Arab-Israeli War, or the Yom Kippur War. The Nixon administration had continued to support Israel in the wake of its seizure of Egyptian territory in 1967, just months after Udall had visited the Middle East and reported his optimism about regional stability to President Johnson and Secretary of State Dean Rusk. Despite many attempts on behalf of Arab nations, the Soviet Union, and the United Nations to elicit a compromise, Nixon maintained a firm line against Palestine and intensified aid to the Israeli military. Arab members of OPEC decided to act, removing oil from the market at a time when the United States was worried over its newly perceived shortages after decades of being a leading exporter of oil. The maneuver catalyzed what commentators then and since labeled a "crisis" and "oil shock" rather than the effect of deeply entrenched and long-standing energy problems in the global system.[90] The U.S. government responded by doubling down on an array of alternate energy sources, including off-shore drilling and nuclear power.[91]

As Landsat also became a strategy for dealing with the energy crisis, the geopolitical objectives, capitalist desires, and environmental hedging came to a head. U.S. officials aimed to initiate extractive operations in non-OPEC nations participating in USAID. As part of this agenda, the U.S. government collaborated with Chevron to locate oil in Sudan in 1977. The United States had only recently renewed diplomatic relations with Sudan, which severed ties after the Arab-Israeli War and forged alliances with the Soviet Union. USAID was crucial to repairing relations, putting forth a $10 million assistance program for agricultural development. Along with U.S. government officials, as the *New York Times* reported, came the "brief-case toting American businessman."[92] Such was the case with Chevron. Using Landsat data in cooperation with USAID, Chevron leaders discovered a vast expanse of petroleum-rich land in southern Sudan. In 1977, Chevron drilled the nation's first onshore well, extracting 500 barrels per day. Two ensuing wells produced 7,900 and 3,900 barrels per day, helping generate widespread interest in the oil fields of Sudan.[93] As Charles K. Paul of the Bureau of Science and Technology said of the Sudanese reserves, U.S. technicians were "sitting on a 'black gold' mine over there."[94] In the ensuing years, the oil industry became a central hinge of national unrest between Khartoum and southern Sudan leading up to the Second Sudanese Civil War, which saw political repression, widespread famine, and scorched-earth campaigns.[95] The use of Landsat to spur extraction in Sudan fell far short of the promises to improve conditions in developing nations—to yield global and environmental good.

Landsat's role in the energy crisis challenged its promoters' claim that environmentalism, or at least environmentalism across borders, was at the project's heart. Charles K. Paul, who headed geological remote-sensing operations in USAID in the late 1970s, claimed that Landsat helped the United States map out a strategy for how to "deal politically with developing countries with potentially rich petroleum reserves" and what to expect in terms of potential imports down the road.[96] Some officials made more explicit how these activities would support U.S. energy objectives. R. A. Summers of the Department of Energy, the department that subsumed key Interior Department functions with its founding in 1977, coauthored a paper explaining the interagency agenda to use Landsat to accelerate the exploration of uranium, oil, and gas in "undeveloped or difficult-access regions of the world"—what they called, much like McGee and countless Interior officials before him, "virgin areas."[97] The authors made clear that the agenda would conserve resources at home by exploiting resources in Third World nations. "The conservation ethic has *little relevance* to developing countries," the report claimed. "The developing world," in contrast to industrialized nations, "needs to *speed up* exploration and development of its own conventional energy sources."[98] Landsat, as this report made clear, would even the score, pushing less-industrialized nations to shoulder the environmental burdens of global energy production that they had previously shirked. Conservation was a privilege reserved for industrialized nations, the nations that had exhausted resources and polluted ecosystems at home and abroad.

The disconnect between rhetoric and reality in the Landsat agenda drew criticism in developing nations. At the Twelfth International Symposium on Remote Sensing of Environment in Manila in April 1978, Ferdinand Marcos conveyed this ambivalence. On the one hand, he celebrated how the satellite invited humans to see Earth as "one contiguous physical entity" rather than an assemblage of political "divisions and boundaries"—a vision that harmonized impeccably with Udall's earlier one. On the other hand, he also acknowledged how some Third World leaders viewed "unrestricted satellite surveillance and the consequent dissemination of data about their countries as an invasion of national privacy." Landsat marked for some an "infringement on their own sovereign slice of earth."[99] Such criticisms underlined how the universalizing agenda ultimately facilitated border crossings that undermined sovereignty. Building on these conclusions, the Group of 77, which promoted collective economic interests of Third World nations in the United Nations, added that the satellite's disregard for national sovereignty created structures of inequality between industrialized nations, which became "sensing" states, and poorer nations, which became "sensed" states—a new take on the "have" and "have not" formulation of uneven development.[100] The group's delegates from Brazil, Argentina, Mexico, and India therefore demanded that nations give prior consent to being sensed, but the United States retained the right both to view resources across borders and to distribute the resulting information without consent of the nations under surveillance.[101] Information about resources, like resources themselves, was an important feature of national sovereignty—one that was becoming harder to protect.

Mounting a resistance to this far-out structure was thus exceedingly difficult, both politically and physically. To begin with, few beyond government elites and technicians in Third World nations would have been aware of the Landsat agenda. Those who, like the Group of 77, did raise objections to the "sensing" and "sensed" states dynamic through official political channels like the UN had little success.[102] These political limitations were matched with physical ones. Landsat was quite literally out of reach. It was hard to throw a wrench in the system, a challenge Timothy Mitchell has seen at play in the transition from the grounded coal-based economy to the diffuse petroleum-based economy.[103] With Landsat, in the absence of having ballistics weapon systems to down the satellite, nations could not extricate themselves from the view. The result was that many, including an array of well-meaning scientists and unscrupulous dictators, embraced the technology. Some critics at the time, however, told news reporters that USAID nations adopting the Landsat program often did so to protect their minerals "from the rapacious West" and that they had effectively been "forced" to "rush headlong into the deeper waters of remote sensing."[104] It was perhaps appropriate that these ambivalent developments coincided with the emergence of the intellectual tradition of postcolonialism, which brought the totalizing gaze of Western enlightenment modernity into the bull's-eye of its critique. Postcolonial thinkers like Edward Said, though not critiquing Landsat directly, nevertheless provided a language for challenging the production and distribution of knowledge of non-Western cultures and landscapes.[105]

The difficulty that Third World leaders faced in resisting the agenda was precisely the point. Landsat was meant to provide a resistance-free pathway to mineral reserves across the world. It was meant, first and foremost, to aid in U.S. Cold War geopolitics and the globalization of extractive capitalism. In the process, U.S. officials ensured an uneven distribution of both the economic benefits and environmental tolls of extraction. Perhaps this realization is what led Joe Morgan, an Interior geologist working in remote sensing in USAID who had attended the meeting in Manila, to vocalize extreme disillusionment with the Landsat agenda. Nearly one decade into the satellite effort in international development, Morgan remarked, "[W]e should all quit kidding ourselves about benefits to the poor by having improved information regarding resources."[106] Morgan's conclusion that the satellite program was not benefitting USAID nations was clear even if the justification for his assessment was not. He might have been acknowledging that these technologies worked, in the longer term, to further poor nations' dependence on American management and to enter them into a losing bidding war with private industry for information about their own resources. All Landsat users were equal, yes. But some Landsat users were more equal than others.

THE JOURNEY INTO SPACE and its promise to open up new material horizons beyond the planet ultimately had a boomerang effect, bolstering U.S. capacities to further infiltrate elusive interiors on Earth. The Interior Department's century of efforts to open up new frontiers had not only prepared it well for this unusual task, but also called forth the unusual task in the first place. Interior mineral experts embedded in the international development apparatus joined with NASA geologists and high-level Cold War modernizers in a chorus of satellite boosterism. The satellite, in their view, would circumvent physical and political resistance on Earth on the path to minerals in service of both U.S. Cold War ascendance and U.S. global economic hegemony. The American state and allied corporations thus stood to gain much from the endeavor, which seemed to offer both practical and economic benefits. While such unilateral benefits helped secure bipartisan support for the satellite agenda at home, officials instead emphasized the global and environmental benefits in promoting its usage abroad, especially within USAID. Nations participating in USAID embraced the agenda with varying degrees of enthusiasm and ambivalence. Ultimately, what began in a look skyward ended in places like the oil fields of Sudan. Thus, despite Landsat boosters' claims that viewing the world from space would benefit humanity and the natural world, the satellite became a tool to further capitalist exploitation. The U.S. government, private industrialists, and Third World elites experienced economic gains, while the supposed targets of development, the world's poor, were left with the environmental impacts and few of the financial rewards. The view from the rainbow may have inspired dreams of global and environmental harmony, but in the first decade, it yielded only the prosaic pot of gold for a handful of elites.

The heyday of Landsat mineral pursuits in the 1970s lost speed in the 1980s. Facing continued budgetary criticism, as well as the charge that American taxpayers had unfairly shouldered the cost of mineral exploration for private companies, the administrations of Jimmy Carter and Ronald Reagan reorganized Landsat management. A gradual and ultimately temporary process of commercialization ensued, in which the satellite was brought under control of the private sector.[107] By the 1990s, the humbled Landsat program, saved from extinction by Congressional intervention, came once again under the control of the U.S. government through the National Oceanographic and Atmospheric Administration (NOAA), NASA, and Interior's Geological Survey.[108] In this new phase, Landsat became a platform for mapping key environmental issues, including deforestation in the Amazon basin in Brazil and tracking patterns related to climate change, marking the culmination of an equivocal environmental legacy.[109] So it was that the extractive and global ambitions of American decision makers underwriting the earth resource satellite agenda were themselves overwritten.

The same forces buoying Landsat's appeal, the so-called crises of energy in the 1970s, rejuvenated attention on the mineral-rich lands belonging to American Indians nominally within U.S. borders. The United States began seeing "wealth" in the supposed wastelands where American Indians had been relocated or allowed to stay through Interior Department policies designed to bring interior that which had been exterior. Yet the stories of Landsat and the recolonization of indigenous lands were deeply entangled. The same border-crossing machine that initiated a black gold rush in Sudan also illuminated subterranean treasures on indigenous reservations. For example, the Geological Survey promotional material showcasing Landsat's potential to increase prospectors' view of faults and domes actually portrayed a large swath of the Wind River reservation in Wyoming. The Eastern Shoshone people living on that satellite grid would face increased pressures to lease their lands to global energy companies like Exxon. Yet a grassroots indigenous movement would rise to challenge the infiltration of these and other indigenous lands for resources led by the Interior Department. To do so, one pan-tribal coalition would turn to an even wider world and a group that had seemingly found ways to intervene in such processes, OPEC. The coalition called itself "the Indian OPEC."

CHAPTER SEVEN

The Wealth of the Wastelands

Standing alone, they were vulnerable to exploitation by energy
companies with the help of . . . the Old Interior Department.

Peter MacDonald, Navajo Tribal Chairman

I N 1977, Navajo tribal chairman Peter MacDonald related an unusual
encounter for the *Christian Science Monitor* in the style of an Indian
joke. Several years before, MacDonald recalled, a tribal medicine man had
watched Apollo astronauts test a moon buggy in the dunes of the reservation. After learning the astronauts' purpose there, the medicine man
explained through a translator that his ancestors "had come from the
moon, riding down on its rays." The astronauts were amused and offered
to take a recorded message from this elder to the moon. Accepting,
the man greeted his distant cousins and then warned them of these
"suspicious-looking white men, especially if they tried to get lunar mineral rights."[1] MacDonald presented this tongue-in-cheek anecdote in an
article that reported on indigenous efforts to combat exploitation of their
minerals like coal, uranium, and oil in the energy crisis. These efforts
included forming coalitions across Native American nations *and* the
world. MacDonald, for example, chaired a pan-tribal coalition that forged
ties with the infamous Organization of Petroleum Exporting Countries
(OPEC) and self-labeled as "the Indian OPEC." As justification for these

controversial transnational strategies, MacDonald pointed to the story of the medicine man, which crystallized for him how material exploitation had linked events previously understood to be separate. The history of this expansionism, in his estimation, went from the reservation, to OPEC nations, to the moon, and back.

The U.S. Department of the Interior had in many ways undertaken the seemingly absurd trajectory that MacDonald offered up in his anecdote. With the intensification of national strife in the global crises of energy in the 1970s, the Interior Department joined American officials and energy firms alike in turning attentions to the energy-rich indigenous reservations of the American West. In an irony that would escape few of the contemporary commentators, the seeming wastelands to which many Native Americans had been relocated or allowed to stay in the nineteenth century—a spatial arrangement overseen by the Interior Department itself—were revealed by the Geological Survey to cover approximately half of the nation's uranium, one-third of its low-sulfur strippable coal, and a decent percentage of its oil shale and natural gas.[2] As one Houston-based investor would remark of the indigenous land base, "It's the last untapped, virgin, energy-rich land left in this country."[3] With national appetites whetted for untapped energy, the Interior Department's global mineral project came home to roost.

Here we will shift perspective from the Interior Department to an indigenous coalition that confronted it head on, the Council of Energy Resource Tribes (CERT), chaired by Peter MacDonald. Both CERT and MacDonald have deeply divided legacies in the history of the indigenous sovereignty movement of the 1970s. CERT advanced a pro-energy development agenda that detractors argued flouted traditional ways while creating new power structures along lines of "have" and "have not" tribes. MacDonald, known for his signature pin-striped suits and limousine, drew charges of self-promotion, guile, and corruption—the latter culminating in a jail sentence in the next decade.[4] Despite their controversial status, MacDonald and CERT staged two significant interventions in Interior's attempt to bring minerals into the national fold. First, CERT directly challenged the claim that the Interior Department was a just and judicious manager of natural resources by placing a spotlight on its long history of mismanagement of the resources of its wards, Native Americans.

The coalition argued, unswervingly and effectively, that the Interior Department's agenda had been mired in negligence and cupidity, supporting ongoing processes of colonial dispossession. To MacDonald, the invasion of indigenous lands by mining and oil interests had always been facilitated by "the Old Interior Department."[5] These indigenous-led challenges to the Interior Department accompanied national criticism of its ineptitude in managing the energy crisis, which would lead to the founding of yet another competing agency, the Department of Energy.

Second, by offering up the label of "the Indian OPEC," the coalition made a powerful argument for the deep connections between U.S. continental expansion and overseas intervention. Although CERT leaders like MacDonald did not identify nor seek to expose the Interior Department's actual hand in extractive enterprises across the world, they insisted that the fates of indigenous and developing nations were intertwined through a shared history of mineral exploitation. In the Indian OPEC imaginary, minerals formed the basis for a remapping of affiliation anchored not in geography, culture, or race, but in a genealogy of mineral exploitation.[6] Whereas critics at the time and historians since have examined U.S. energy policies with Native Americans and with foreign nations along bifurcated lines, the Indian OPEC insisted on their deeper connection. Attention to these connections, in turn, provides a more comprehensive account of America's pursuit of energy resources in the formative decade of the 1970s.[7] Thus, although the collision of the Indian OPEC and the Interior Department unfolded overtly within the borders of home, it was deeply entangled with the wider world. Their convergence in this moment represented the culmination of a global struggle—a struggle over the power to twist and shape the material world—fought over the original battlefield, indigenous lands of the continental West.

Shifting perspective to this indigenous coalition reveals how the extension of American power beyond U.S. formal sovereignty operated always in dialogue and never in isolation. An analysis of CERT and the imaginary it constructed through the Indian OPEC labeling allows for a more granular—if incomplete—analysis of select actors and institutions beyond the American state and private industry that shaped and were shaped by extractive agendas. CERT is no stand-in for the wider indigenous sovereignty movement, let alone the movements of Third World nationalism and environmentalism that also negotiated the terms of extraction's unfolding, but it does stand as further evidence of the halting, fractious, and contingent nature of Interior's sprawling trajectory. The history of the Indian OPEC ultimately provides a prism through which to view the many forces, including social movements, geopolitics, and privatization, that sapped Interior of much power in the 1980s—a decline vividly symbolized by the appointment by Ronald Reagan of the staunchly antigovernment Secretary of the Interior James G. Watt. What stood ready to take Interior's place in leading America's extractive agendas was private industry and an entity that the department had long trailed and supplanted, the U.S. military.

A New Cartography of Energy

The Council of Energy Resource Tribes emerged from a crisis of energy and a quirk of geology. Neither of these was as straightforwardly natural as they first appeared, and both involved the subtle hand of the Interior Department. In the early 1970s, a confluence of geological restraints, economic decline, and U.S. foreign policy mishaps fomented a perceived shortage of energy. Although a broader set of mineral resources had been central to the U.S. government's concerns in the postwar era, by the 1970s, those that fell under the banner of "energy," including oil, coal, gas, and uranium, had become a key locus of attention for the U.S. government and much of the world.[8] The Interior Department had played a consistent role since the New Deal in planning for national access to those resources. In 1970, Interior officials and oil producers began declaring the geological limits of domestic oil supplies, predicting that the U.S. was reaching peak production. Based on surveys of known and prospective reserves, they concluded that the supply of oil would never surpass the benchmark output of that year, particularly in the face of consistently rising oil demand. This problem was apparently compounded by the general trend toward "stagflation," the potent combination of price inflation and economic stagnation.[9] After the Nixon administration removed import tariffs that cushioned U.S. independent oil producers from cheap foreign oil in the spring of 1973, foreign oil imports nearly doubled to 6 million barrels per day.[10]

Global events exacerbated these transformations in domestic production. The ongoing Vietnam War posed its own form of material drain, but also seriously undercut the credibility of the United States in its attempts to put forth an image of benevolence in Third World nations where it had sought access to minerals of interest.[11] These tensions came to a head with the Arab-Israeli War in early October 1973, when Arab members of OPEC decided to retaliate against Nixon's ongoing support of Israel. Formed by Abdullah Tariki of Saudi Arabia and Juan Pablo Pérez Alfonzo of Venezuela in the early 1960s, OPEC worked to combat long-standing European and American intervention in petroleum-rich nations and Western hegemony in the world economy—a hegemony the Interior Department helped construct through USAID.[12] In the aftermath of the Yom Kippur War, Arab members of OPEC withdrew important sources of Middle East oil from the market.[13] Gas prices doubled and eventually tripled. News media captured the resultant chaos with a dizzying array of images of tangled lines of automobiles orbiting gas pumps. The vivid spectacle neatly heralded the decline of the American Century, a period in which the United States had dominated world oil production, boasted the world's strongest economy, and exerted influence in Third World politics through a variety of means—war in Korea, coups, assassinations, and aid dollars—on its path to geopolitical and economic supremacy. However, with the deteriorating situation in Vietnam and the so-called energy crisis, the United States looked out on a very different horizon.[14]

As policymakers and private producers grappled with the real and imagined energy shortages, a variety of solutions—foreign and domestic—were brought to the table. This, in turn, resuscitated a long-standing debate between the Interior Department and the extractive industry over whether U.S. policy should emphasize the development of foreign or domestic resources. In one vision of how to solve the energy crisis, the United States continued to trust the potential of foreign oil sources despite the recent protests emanating from Arab oil producers. This time, policymakers widened their gaze beyond oil's accepted postwar "center of gravity," as the petroleum geologist Everette DeGolyer once put it, in the Middle East, outlining plans to invest in other foreign sources of oil (including Norway) and under the sea (especially the Gulf of Mexico).[15] An alternate vision emphasized domestic sources of unconventional energy resources, notably nuclear energy and low-sulfur strippable coal, which had the added political benefit of lower emissions in a moment of growing national concern over air pollution. Such energy resources were especially prevalent in western states such as Colorado, New Mexico, and Arizona. Throughout these debates, tensions between the government and the divided private mining sector escalated, as each jockeyed for the role as savior of the American consumer in the journey out of energy price hikes.[16]

The debate was complicated by the fact that a disproportionate amount of so-called domestic resources lay within Native American reservations— only partly understood to be domestic. Numerous news reports at the time delighted in the irony that wastelands to which indigenous people had been allocated turned out to be awash in mineral wealth. As one newspaper article remarked at the time, the Indians had been placed on this land precisely because "nobody cared about such things in Sherman's day."[17] However, what appeared to some commentators as unforeseen advantage was the mixed legacy of systemic disadvantage. The earlier era of settler colonialism, from the military might of General William T. Sherman to the civilian efforts of the Interior Department, had produced the political cartography underscoring this newly minted geological bonanza. That earlier process had facilitated the relocation of some nations onto designated reservations or the return of some nations to ancestral lands of diminished size—all on grounds that those lands were wastelands, or what MacDonald called "a pittance, the worst, least desirable, most remote, barren, unwanted, forsaken land around."[18] U.S. Indian policy had overwhelmingly served interests of white settlers and private industries since the nineteenth century. Although the Indian Reorganization Act of 1934 had yielded greater self-determination for indigenous peoples and established a system of mineral leasing to prevent outright land dispossession, the following decades brought numerous political campaigns to dissolve indigenous sovereignty and land holdings. The termination era of the 1950s was one of many flashpoints in U.S. history when the tides had turned violently against indigenous sovereignty. Leaders in Congress and Interior, including Secretaries Oscar Chapman and Douglas McKay, advocated for greatly constraining tribal power, in some cases transferring civil and criminal jurisdiction from tribes to states. The House Concurrent Resolution 108 sought to abrogate existing treaties and forcibly integrate American Indians into American society, relocating them off the reservation and into low-paying jobs in urban centers, while also seizing a significant portion of land from terminated tribes, such as the Klamath nation in the timber-rich Pacific Northwest. Termination policies cleared the way to their greater assimilation into society but yielded terrors in the form of unemployment, dilapidated housing, and rampant alcoholism.[19]

These termination policies met with the resistance of indigenous activists who, like the later CERT activists, increasingly framed their struggle in a global context. Specifically, activists like renowned intellectual D'Arcy McNickle, an enrolled member of the Flathead reservation, argued that Native Americans deserved fairer deals from the U.S. government—deals like those given to foreign governments under the Point Four program. McNickle, cofounder of the National Congress of American Indians (NCAI), drew a direct line between the experiences of foreign people abroad and indigenous people within U.S. borders. NCAI joined with the Association of American Indian Affairs (AAIA), a rights organization run by non-Indians, to petition for a Point Four program for Native Americans. Ironically, the Interior Department had earlier insisted that the Bureau of Indian Affairs (BIA) *was* a Point Four for Indians. However, from the perspective of indigenous nations whose rights were besieged by termination policies, foreign governments appeared to have more rights to self-determination than tribes. McNickle maintained that the United States would have no ideological legs to stand on when offering social improvement to developing countries if it maintained its commitment to termination policies and the havoc they wreaked on economies of reservations.[20]

Despite the transnational strategies of postwar indigenous activists, the abrogation of tribal sovereignty ensued and helped to open indigenous lands to extraction in the postwar energy boom of the Atomic West. At the dawn of the atomic era and the Cold War brinkmanship between the United States and the Soviet Union, the Geological Survey uncovered vast uranium reserves in Navajo, Hopi, and Laguna Pueblo lands of the American West. The BIA worked closely with private firms and the U.S. Atomic Energy Commission (AEC) to encourage tribal councils, the entities created by Interior to negotiate and approve government policies, to open indigenous lands to mineral leases.[21] In the early 1950s, for example, the BIA and AEC helped the Kerr-McGee Corporation to secure leases for uranium deposits on the Navajo reservation to be mined by Navajo workers at $1.60 per hour wages in poorly ventilated facilities.[22] The Anaconda Mining Company, later the Atlantic Richfield Company (ARCO), similarly acquired nearly 5,000 acres of uranium-rich land in the Laguna Pueblo reservation with federal help. The resulting uranium mines were, for a time, the largest in the world and later became epicenters of a scandalous public health crisis stemming from local exposure to cancer-causing radiation.[23]

Although indigenous leaders frequently negotiated these terms, they were at what is best described as an extreme disadvantage. Many members of the tribal council were illiterate and unfamiliar with the technical jargon of the contracts.[24] The resulting leases in uranium and other energy resources like oil, gas, and coal, mediated by the BIA, were starkly unequal. For example, the Peabody Coal Company secured leases for strippable coal on the Northern Cheyenne reservation of Wyoming in 1966 at a rate of 12 cents an acre, while lands of similar known potential were receiving $16 an acre. Such leases also locked indigenous nations to fixed royalties in perpetuity.[25] Experts two decades later estimated that fixed royalties in oil and gas sales valued at $341 million were producing less than $50 million for American Indians leasing land to companies.[26] Throughout, many indigenous farmers and sheep herders lamented the way in which their peoples' traditional economies disintegrated as result of the introduction of extractive enterprises, wresting local control over the modes of production and altering landscapes beyond recognition.[27] The social and environmental consequences of extraction mounted for indigenous peoples.

These dynamics were clearly at play in the controversy surrounding coal development at Black Mesa. In the mid-1960s, Interior's Geological Survey offered astonishing estimates of the coal potential—an estimated 4 billion tons—of the Black Mesa region, which encompassed a contested zone of shared use between the Navajo and Hopi nations in Arizona that would soon be divided by the Navajo-Hopi Land Settlement Act of 1974.[28] Backed with this geological information, the Bureau of Indian Affairs helped negotiate a 65,000-acre lease between the Peabody Coal Company and the tribal governments. Secretary of the Interior Stewart Udall had looked on these lease negotiations with pride in what he saw as "a first rate job of community building and community planning."[29] Yet the negotiations yielded inequitable terms, which allowed Peabody free range to extract coal, use ground water, and transport slurry without reprimand for the pollution and dislocation their enormous strip-mining operations caused. These operations, which would power the metropolitan centers of the American Southwest, hit the sheep-herding inhabitants of the region acutely, interfering with their livelihoods and contaminating their landscapes. Adding to the injury, the indigenous nations received royalties that, rather than reflecting increased market value for coal, remained at fixed rates in the ensuing decades. The Navajo, for example, were locked into royalties at 15 cents a ton even as the price of coal rose to $18 a ton.[30] The Black Mesa developments prompted indigenous and environmental activism as well as highly publicized conflict between Hopi and Navajo nations over land.[31]

Native American activism of the 1960s and 1970s won greater protections of tribal sovereignty and the land and resources it encompassed. Pan-tribal indigenous activism associated with the Red Power and the American Indian Movement (AIM) fought for legislation that made self-determination a watchword of federal Indian policy once again. Alongside legal challenges to diminished tribal jurisdiction, indigenous activists staged vivid media spectacles like the violent standoff of AIM activists against federal agents at the Wounded Knee reservation in South Dakota, fish-ins in the Pacific Northwest, and pan-tribal occupation of Alcatraz Island. Eventually, many non-Indian Americans demonstrated their support for the indigenous sovereignty movement, including the actor Marlon Brando, who enlisted Apache activist Sacheen Littlefeather to refuse his Academy Award to raise awareness about indigenous rights.[32] Thus, when news circulated that reservations overlay critical and coveted energy resources, Native Americans were achieving—or appearing to achieve—a surer footing in a plane of negotiating power. However, by the 1970s, the Interior Department and other arms of the federal government aided corporations in securing substantial energy leases on indigenous lands through territorial expansion, tax benefits, and import tariffs.[33] Although the apparent gains of indigenous activists led commentators to celebrate their great good fortune, the reality was that the struggle was just about to be ratcheted up.

The Birth of the Indian OPEC

In 1975, a group of Indian nations with mineral-rich lands founded a new organization, the Council of Energy Resource Tribes (CERT), and staged a dramatic intervention in the extractive ambitions of the Interior Department and corporate allies. The charter members, which included Northern Cheyenne, Navajo, Blackfeet, Laguna Pueblo, Fort Peck, and Jicarilla Apache, had all been subject to the misdealing of the Interior Department in entering into mineral leases with private energy companies. As CERT chairman Peter MacDonald summarized the situation, Native Americans "were vulnerable to exploitation by energy companies with the help of the Old BIA and the Old Interior Department."[34] CERT members thus adopted the attitude that if energy development was here to stay, then they wanted to promote greater economic, environmental, and social justice within it.[35] Doing so, CERT claimed, required limiting the Interior Department's role in stewarding their land and resources. Building on successes of the indigenous sovereignty movement, they developed a legal strategy to take Interior to court over the faulty agreements it authorized. One year earlier, a group of Crow activists forced the Interior Secretary Rogers Morton to rule against the validity of Westmoreland Company uranium leases sponsored by the BIA. Interior Department leadership feared that these rulings would set dangerous precedents and unravel important energy resource development in reservations of the American West. As the Crow continued to file lawsuits against American Metal Climax Company (AMAX), Gulf Oil, and Peabody Coal, one BIA official urged the Department of Justice to use "every procedural and technical device in the lawyer's arsenal to avoid a decision on the merits of the case."[36]

CERT also challenged the Interior Department with a savvy public relations campaign. The organization named Interior as their main antagonist in the growing news coverage of their colorful movement.[37] Hundreds of reports circulated describing a profound sense of disgust at the department's manipulation surrounding indigenous resources. As one

Laguna Pueblo leader Floyd Correa addresses an audience at the Council of Energy Resource Tribes annual meeting in Phoenix. Peter MacDonald sits nearest Correa on the right. 1979. Files of the Indian Rights Association, Historical Society of Pennsylvania.

article summarized, "The same Interior Department which is supposed to be the Indian's protector through the BIA is the Indian's antagonist through . . . other units," which were "aiding and abetting the energy companies."[38] CERT's activism exposed how Interior's natural resource management in indigenous lands frequently served the imperatives of global energy firms, ushering in a new era of exploitation characterized not by colonization through settlement and privatization but rather by extraction through leasing.

At stake in these debates was the self-same technical expertise that had become so central to the Interior Department's involvements across ever-shifting zones of influence. MacDonald understood that Native Americans had been swindled so often through asymmetries in information about resources in their landscapes. "Tribal governments lack knowledge of minerals and resources they possess," he argued, "[and] they come to the bargaining table with fragmented, inaccurate and outdated information" that puts well-informed corporations at an advantage.[39] Just as Soviet and Third World leaders critical of Landsat were concluding that the unequal distribution of resource knowledge posed a threat to sovereignty, Indian leaders were seeing a similar problem. To enact their goals of stabilizing reservation economies and protecting local environments, CERT thus determined that they needed to wrest the monopoly in technical expertise over natural resources from the Interior Department, cultivating their own expertise in energy development. MacDonald pushed for federal funds to open and staff an office devoted to this purpose—a group of geologists, chemists, hydrologists, and other specialists that could conduct work previously overseen by Interior's mineral agencies.[40]

It was in the context of this fight for technical expertise that CERT made a bold appeal to OPEC. Framing their struggle as global in reach and forging connections with the much-maligned OPEC secured the coalition a national reputation, and a divisive one at that. The controversy began as CERT leadership sought to take advantage of the fact that there was no monopoly on outrage felt toward U.S. state and corporate exploitation of resources. Nations across the globe had suffered an eerily similar geologic fate, and some, like those that formed OPEC, had even gone so far as to organize an international cartel to resist continual mineral exploitation. In the summer of 1977, MacDonald made contact with several undisclosed representatives of OPEC on grounds that they desired "technical assistance" with managing their energy resources.[41] With incredible if unacknowledged irony, CERT sought technical assistance from the same OPEC nations that had once been targets of the United States' and the Interior Department's own regime of technical assistance. In July, CERT hosted a series of meetings with OPEC representatives in Washington, D.C. For a variety of reasons, including a broader commitment to aiding decolonizing peoples and genuine sympathy for CERT's plight, OPEC members offered limited assistance to CERT.[42]

CERT even began calling itself the "Indian OPEC," strengthening symbolic ties between the two organizations and between American settler colonialism and the energy crisis. By 1977, the coalition was branding their endeavor the "Indian OPEC," "domestic OPEC," and "Native American OPEC."[43] CERT drew the contours of this transnational imaginary in mainstream media outlets from metropolitan newspapers to national magazines. MacDonald, the public face of CERT, who was considered at the time to be the most powerful American Indian in the United

States, explained, "There is only one parallel to the choice we face. The conditions of poverty and resource exploitation that prompted the formation of OPEC."[44] MacDonald elaborated that energy companies had slighted OPEC nations with comparable "bad leases and one-sided operations" in mineral development.[45] MacDonald insisted that resources linked OPEC and CERT in a "common situation."[46] He called OPEC "an analogue," or a kindred consortium, and indicated that CERT meant to take a cue from its concerted efforts to leverage resources for cultural and national survival.[47] In constructing this history, MacDonald placed a searing spotlight on a structure of global extractive capitalism, which left certain nations glutted and others gutted—even if his solutions to those problems would draw criticism for embracing rather than challenging capitalist development. MacDonald's strategic claims melded what had previously been conceived to be two starkly different things: America's settler colonial legacy and its foreign policy crises in the present.

MacDonald was not the first to draw a material connection between the plight of Native Americans and OPEC. Abdullah Tariki, the Saudi Arabian architect of OPEC, had framed the coalition's lineage in the history of U.S. dispossession of Native American lands. After founding OPEC in the 1960s, he explained, "We are the sons of the Indians of Manhattan. We want to change the deal."[48] Tariki's statement referred to the apocryphal sale of the island of Manhattan by the native inhabitants to Dutch traders for a laughable sum paid in trinkets. Native Americans, too, had been cheated of their land and resources. Tariki's likening of OPEC with Native Americans furthered the organization's aim to align itself with the decolonizing world. In press statements, OPEC leaders described themselves as being "full members of the Third World" and "a pioneering group of developing countries." In the fight against exploitation, OPEC claimed to share an interest and purpose with the postcolonial world. The organization was for a time one pivotal link between pan-Africanists and pan-Arabists of the Global South, like Gamal Abdel Nasser of Egypt, Julius Nyerere of Tanzania, and Sekou Touré of Guinea.[49] In keeping with this broader trend to further the struggle against colonialist exploitation, Tariki pointed to indigenous peoples of America. From these symbolic ancestors, Tariki's statement suggested, the OPEC nations had received an inheritance of duplicitous deals. Changing the deal, he seemed to suggest, would rewrite the supposed conclusion to the grand narrative of colonization.

Although OPEC would eventually break ties with CERT because of the negative media attention their alliance inspired, just two years later, CERT hired Ahmed Kooros, Iran's OPEC representative and head of finance and oil, as their economist. Kooros had counseled the repressive Iranian dictator Shah Mohammad Reza Pahlavi, and was one of the few members of that administration to be carried over after revolutionaries in Iran put the Islamist religious figure Ayatollah Khomeini in power. Reports estimated that Kooros was the "No. 2 man in Iran's oil industry" and one of the top five energy experts in the world.[50] Kooros also helped orchestrate the 1971 raising of oil prices by Persian Gulf oil-exporting countries in the Tehran agreement. While Kooros had a hand in this earlier altercation, he was not in reality central to the forces that led to the energy crisis. Iran did not join the boycott instituted by the Arab member states of OPEC, and the Shah, whom Kooros closely advised, had been a consistent ally to the United States, helping curtail the boycott's impact. Nevertheless, his hailing from the Middle East drew quick if inaccurate associations with national energy strife.[51]

Upon joining CERT in August 1979, Kooros (like MacDonald) cited a shared history of mineral exploitation as justification. The Iranian oil expert claimed that members of OPEC viewed their common mineral situation as the basis of affiliation, noting that American Indians were in "a position comparable" to OPEC in the 1960s.[52] He pointed to similar levels of underdevelopment that were exacerbated by a failure to grasp the significance of "a commodity that is non-renewable."[53] For Kooros, American Indians, like OPEC before them, believed that these highly coveted commodities offered the only avenue to economic improvement. Thus, they demanded a fairer return for those resources.[54] In the Indian OPEC, the connections outlined by Tariki at the birth of OPEC had found a new canvas on which to be drawn. Neither CERT nor its interlocutors across the globe identified the Interior Department specifically as their common antagonist, but they did cite processes in which it had been complicit. MacDonald even highlighted the role of the international development apparatus in facilitating resource exploitation: "richer nations receive back in foreign trade about 20 times what they pour out in aid" all while "they depend upon the poorer nations for critical minerals and natural re-sources."[55] In this sense, transnational alliances were a powerful if indi-rect critique of the global Interior.

The overtures to OPEC would elicit diverse responses that conveyed a popular discomfort with the claim that settler colonialism, believed to be in the past, and the crises of U.S. foreign policy, starkly immediate and present, were two sides of the same coin. The Carter administration and the Interior Department maintained a circumspect view of the OPEC al-liance, confident that OPEC would not in reality risk its negotiating po-sition with the U.S. government by forging ties with Native Americans. As one White House official observed, CERT had not sought any funds for energy development or advice for setting up a cartel within U.S. borders, a feat that he offered "would be impossible in any case."[56] The Interior Department likewise had not taken the Indian OPEC gesture too seriously. One Interior undersecretary even registered amusement, allegedly telling MacDonald in response to news about the OPEC meetings, "We're not the State Department. Go ahead and do it."[57] This comment belied the deeply entrenched but ultimately hollow assump-tion that Interior was not engaged with international affairs. Interior of-ficials in the BIA, meanwhile, advised the Carter administration that the meetings with OPEC the previous summer were purely technical—on matters of pricing and resource availability.[58] Nevertheless, Interior offi-cials claimed that the "OPEC ploy" was something "we don't like."[59]

Yet many Americans were not so nonchalant about the Indian OPEC imaginary. Whereas the Carter administration remained largely dispas-sionate in response to the Indian OPEC, the conservative response drew upon an affective reservoir of animosity directed at racial minorities per-ceived to be getting ahead at the expense of white citizens whether through affirmative action policies or, in the case of Native Americans, the treaty-conferred status as semi-sovereign. This white grievance and the resulting backlash against minorities, as scholars have shown, helped to catapult the rise of conservatism in the 1970s.[60] Because Native Americans, unlike African Americans and other targets of the conservative backlash, sought separation as well as some inclusionary rights, many critics chastised them for wanting it both ways: benefits of American citizenship and ben-efits of foreignness. For example, in September 1977, Kevin P. Phillips, the author of the Republican Party's "southern strategy" to win the White House, wrote an opinion piece on the indigenous sovereignty movement in the *Arizona Republic* that accused CERT of ushering in a foreign invasion on American soil. Phillips condemned their supposed "mutual-aid pact" with OPEC and its Middle East nations, as well as the apparent casualness with which the American public was handling these audacious tribal actions to bolster sovereignty. Pointing to the news that CERT hosted three meetings with OPEC, Phillips insisted that such opportunistic and separatist endeavors "deserve serious counter-measures." He suggested restricting sovereignty, eliminating reservations, and prosecuting CERT for the illicit conduct of U.S. diplomacy. He ended the editorial with a battle cry rooted in the imagery of American continental expansion: "It's time to call out the legislative cavalry!"[61]

One nationally syndicated Pat Oliphant political cartoon registered similar outrage at the prospect of collusion between Indians and OPEC. The cartoon, which ran with Phillips's piece, conflated energy-rich Indians and OPEC Arab energy sheiks (and OPEC often was conflated with its Arab member nations).[62] The scene portrayed a vast desert accentuated by plateaus, an amorphous landscape blending Monument Valley and the Middle East. In front of a sign that reads "Indian Oil Lands, Keep Off," a Native American, arms folded and weighted down by plush feathers, stands big nose to big nose with a dark-eyed and mustachioed Arab, wearing a dark robe labeled "OPEC" and leading an entourage of sheiks. Throughout the energy crisis, such racialized depictions of Arabs had become commonplace.[63] The aesthetic similarities of the Native American and Arab figures depicted in the cartoon thus harnessed the emotional intensity of discourses of American victimization in the global energy crisis. The Native American, channeling threadbare stereotypes of childlike simplicity, asks "How?" The Arab enthusiastically responds, "Easy!" In the cartoon's frame, two mice-sized white men scamper toward the corner with the battle cry, "The Cavalry! The Cavalry!"[64]

If Native Americans were separate from other minorities, they were also similar in the drains they purportedly posed to the American taxpayer (assumed to be white). Whereas African Americans had the misfortune to be stereotyped as welfare drains in a domestic context, Native Americans with energy resources were portrayed simultaneously as welfare drains *and* rich oil sheiks—in a domestic and foreign context.[65] The editors of the *Denver Post* suggested that OPEC's influence over the tribes might lead them to jeopardize national security, allowing Colonel Muammar Gaddafi of Libya, for example, to "ship Russian missiles to the reservation to guarantee the tribe's 'integrity.'" The editors quipped that due to liberal pro-Indian attitudes, American consumers were expected to "pony up cheerfully so the noose of escalating energy prices can be tightened around our necks."[66] These bodily analogies resonated with the prevalent narrative that OPEC cut off the nation's energy artery and strangled consumers.[67]

Fueled by these animosities, conservatives pushed forward anti-Indian legislation that harmonized with the broader backlash against minorities. The Interstate Congress for Equal Rights and Responsibility (ICERR), chief among these movements, was founded on the principle that liberal attitudes toward Native Americans were imperiling white Americans. The ICERR pamphlet entitled "Are We Giving Back America to the Indians?" captured the group's sense of besiegement in the face of such apparent privileges.[68] Activists like ICERR founder and state-chapter leader from Seattle, Washington, Howard Grey, looked on land disputes surrounding the indigenous sovereignty movement as illegitimate claims rooted in an irrelevant and bygone past. As Grey told the *New York Times,* "I get sick and tired of these tribal leaders saying you took our land away," insisting no living person perpetuated that historic violence of a supposedly distant past.[69] Republican representatives, responding in part to these grassroots conservative movements, proposed anti-Indian legislation before Congress, H.R. 9054, to abrogate all existing treaties and terminate reservations, unraveling, in effect, the gains of civil rights era.[70] The bill did not gain serious traction or come close to passing, but it signaled the extent to which efforts of Native Americans to protect their land and resources concerned many Americans who had long relied on the ability to access them at will.

Native Americans, meanwhile, remained seriously divided over the issue of mineral development. The tribal energy debate exacerbated the long-standing question of whether Native Americans should prioritize traditional economies, like those rooted in sheep-herding, or those predicated on capitalist development, like energy resource extraction, to ensure cultural survival—assuming no other middle ground existed. The problem was at least as old as colonial encounter itself, as the centuries of history since had exhibited a panoply of strategies mobilized, including accommodation, alliance, defiance, hybridization, contest, and refusal, in the face of the consistent if contingent advance of federal and private interests. The same difference of opinion was evident in the energy debate of the 1970s. Indigenous commentators at times summarized this contest as "pro-tradition" Indians versus "pro-development" Indians. Some critics who loosely fell in the tradition camp viewed the OPEC template as feeding the larger system of European and capitalist exploitation, while those supporting development argued that processes were under way and a greater control over its terms was the ideal toward which to strive. Ultimately, the debates around indigenous energy development resembled the competing visions, desires, and interests of people across the globe that faced the arrival of the American state in pursuit of minerals. There was dissension and fracture, complicity and critique, and greatest of all, ambivalence. The debates conveyed the diversity of opinions, the creativity of resistance, and the limitations to accommodation that underscored resistance to mineral development across the world.[71]

Much of the debate within the indigenous community about CERT and its activism hinged on the way it would create structures in which indigenous tribes with energy resources became the new power brokers, much as OPEC had become in the Third World. In a 1980 interview with Kooros, Mike Meyers, an editor of the indigenous newspaper *Akwesasne Notes*, asked about the moral stakes of energy development for Indians. Throughout the interview, Meyers claimed that Kooros and other OPEC leadership were indifferent to the "cost of exploitation in human terms" that followed rapid development in decolonizing countries. Meyers pointed to the turmoil in Iran after oil development tore through the nation and led to the emergence of an "oppressive power clique." Kooros said that he had warned the Shah's regime of the dangers of rapid development but was ignored. At present, however, Kooros insisted he did not have that responsibility. Meyers concluded the interview by asking whether Kooros felt he was "carrying out a neo-colonial role" in promoting energy development as a non-Indian. Kooros replied that he did not. "No matter what I do, or say," he lamented, "I'm seen as the oppressor!"[72] Peter

MacDonald, meanwhile, became a divisive figure in Native American politics. Russell Means, the cofounder of the American Indian Movement who had been central to the standoff with U.S. government officials at Wounded Knee II, would refer to the CERT chairman as "Peter Mac-Dollar" and write him off as an "apple"—red on the outside, white on the inside.[73]

OPEC had faced similar criticism that it was separated from the people it purported to represent. OPEC straddled an uncomfortable line between membership in the developing world and membership in the industrialized world. Despite its carefully cultivated ties with developing nations, OPEC drew fire for being indifferent to the suffering of their peers while assuming the tactics of the oppressor. The Tanzanian minister of Commerce, for example, accused OPEC in 1975 of having "turned their backs on developing countries" while President Mobutu of Zaire threatened to restore relations with Israel, an outcome the Arab members of OPEC had long labored against.[74] The animosity stemmed from OPEC's maintenance of high oil prices toward developing countries forced to import oil from OPEC. Although OPEC sought to pacify this discontent by providing its own form of aid, as well as by inviting laborers from Pakistan, India, and the Philippines to participate in work in OPEC nations, many Third World governments increasingly asked whether these concessions were sufficient. The reality, these leaders recognized, was that OPEC pursued its conflicting interests and was cut off from the broader postcolonial movement.[75]

Other indigenous criticisms called attention to the troubling interplay between Third World nations and Native American reservations in the context of environmentally degrading activities and related public health crises. Winona LaDuke, an Anishinaabe antinuclear activist who helped bring the 1979 uranium spill at the United Nuclear facilities on the Navajo reservation that July to the forefront of news media, criticized the OPEC association while offering support to CERT.[76] She argued that nationalization of mining industries across the globe, as well as the increasing instability of mining economies in South Africa, Namibia, and Australia, led U.S. companies to return to the "safe" climates posed by reservations. The United States adapted to the foreclosure of mining in one zone by intensifying its efforts in others. Such factors, she urged, made coalitions like CERT "more important than ever" to stem the tide of extractive interests that had been dissuaded from making or continuing overseas investments. The stakes of these unwanted attentions were high. As the antinuclear movement made known, accidents and radiation-induced cancers from working in the uranium mines had already claimed thousands of indigenous lives. Navajo uranium miners, for example, contracted stomach, lung, prostate, and other cancers at a rate between fifty to eighty times higher than the national average, a legacy that continues to enact its bodily violence on the population through congenital diseases.[77] LaDuke and others called attention to these radiation-related illnesses, hazardous tailings ponds, and factory malfunctions—all of which unfolded without adequate government regulation. LaDuke was sympathetic to the tolls members of the developing world paid for their resources, but because exploitation would either be directed at reservations or abroad, she appeared skeptical of the ability to forge a meaningful alliance.[78]

Perhaps the most obvious and widespread critique of CERT's tactics, however, concerned the environmental consequences of energy development. The organization's activism did in part run contrary to popular assumptions that Native Americans were superior environmental stewards. The famed Keep America Beautiful campaign of 1975, with its portrayal of an Indian crying at the sight of the polluted landscape, had helped to mainstream this long-standing stereotype that equated indigenous peoples with nature.[79] Running against centuries of stereotypes, a group of American Indians dedicated to energy development struck a discordant note for many, drawing the ire of an array of critics who assumed indigenous activism would conform to expectations rooted in ecological Indianness. One *Newsweek* article, for example, condescendingly noted that Native Americans, supposedly unaccustomed to the wiles of capitalism, might rush into development and "deplete precious resources too quickly."[80] Other reports played upon the apparent contradiction between indigenous energy development and indigenous respect for Mother Earth. In this spirit, CERT was accused of throwing environmental caution to the wind. Yet CERT also played into the popular associations between Native Americans and nature to make the argument that it was an organization with superior environmental authority. Leaders like

MacDonald offered that because of their "traditional religious orientation to the land—their Mother Earth—they can be trusted to enact environmental standards of their own that will be more than sufficient."[81]
CERT frequently cited its commitment to environmental protection.
Much of its activism fought for the guarantee that mineral leases have
clauses requiring environmental impact statements.[82]

Ultimately, despite such criticisms, CERT accomplished many of their
stated goals in creating alternative sources of expertise and eliciting fairer
deals from energy development. CERT received $200,000 in 1977 to fund
the opening of a Washington, D.C., office, hired non-Indian Ed Gabriel
as executive director, and secured $2 million in 1978 for its first-year op-
erating budget.[83] With these successes, the organization was able to shore
up its technical expertise in natural resource management, securing "technical assistance" on over seventy energy projects that ranged from feasibility studies and surveys to environmental protection.[84] As the election
year of 1980 approached, the Carter administration promised $24 million
to CERT if elected, in part to court indigenous votes in key western
states.[85] In the process, CERT also achieved fairer terms in mineral development. In some cases, as with negotiations concerning Laguna Pueblo
uranium mining and Northern Cheyenne coal leases, CERT placed
enough pressure on the Interior Department to redraw the terms of mineral leases.[86] In others, like the Navajo's dealings with Consolidated Coal
Company and Mobil Oil Corporation, Interior ruled in favor of corporations.[87] In all cases, CERT had supported the actual extraction of
minerals, just on more equitable terms. By 1980, CERT had engineered
several major mining enterprises in reservations across the West: coal
and uranium mines on the Navajo reservation, uranium mines on the
Laguna Pueblo and Spokane reservations, copper mines on the Papago
reservation, and a coal mine on the Hopi reservation, all done in conjunction with private mining companies.[88] For a time, the organization that
had called itself the Indian OPEC used its political, media, and environmental savvy to offset some of the deplorable inequalities built into their
reservation economies as a legacy of a U.S. extractive expansion that
would continue to arrive at their doorstep.

In the process, many of the members of CERT eventually aligned with
the solutions offered by presidential hopeful Ronald Reagan. While

courting CERT as part of an indigenous electorate that represented an increasingly powerful segment of western voters, Reagan promised something that many American Indians desired: a decrease in the meddling of government in indigenous affairs. Reagan sent a personal message to Peter MacDonald, a fellow Republican who celebrated Richard Nixon's deeply personal advocacy of indigenous rights, in advance of the CERT annual meeting in Washington, D.C., in 1980. Representatives from the Carter administration and top brass in the global energy sector would also turn out for the event in an attempt to secure the endorsement of the increasingly powerful organization. For too long, Reagan wrote, Native Americans had been ignored despite the hard work and sacrifice of organizations like CERT. Moving forward, Reagan insisted that "primary" among his concerns was the "improved future of the American Indian." He thus sought a CERT-Reagan "partnership."[89] Although Reagan spoke in broad and vague terms, his representative at the meetings, Senator Pete Domenici of New Mexico, spelled out the platform more clearly. "CERT's answer is also Governor Reagan's," Domenici said, "freedom and dignity based on self-reliance." He insisted the federal funds provided by the Carter administration were the equivalent of the "beads, blankets and mirrors the first settlers used to purchase Manhattan"—drawing on the same comparison that Tariki had in likening OPEC nations to indigenous nations. Domenici ultimately argued that the Republicans could do more to help secure the energy markets that would yield $1 trillion in fuel sources on tribal reservations.[90] The argument was consistent with the claims of the Reagan administration that the Great Society had failed to do what only downsizing government and deregulating capitalism would: alleviate poverty. What was needed to help conditions in indigenous reservations, they argued, was constraining government middlemen like those in the Department of the Interior.

A Fragmenting Interior

When Cecil Andrus, a former governor from Idaho, was chosen to be secretary of the interior by Jimmy Carter in 1976, he received a letter of congratulation from Stewart Udall. Udall had the luxury, and distinct political challenge, of serving nine years in his cabinet post, an unusually lengthy tenure in Interior surpassed only by the relentless Harold Ickes and his thirteen-year assignment. Udall offered Andrus some words of wisdom. Alongside the encouragement to show direct engagement with the regions under his influence through outdoor adventures and trips, showing a "public love affair with the land," Udall urged Andrus to be mindful of Interior's shifting bureaucratic power. As a steward of "one-fourth of [the] nation's land," Udall argued, it was vital to lead the "fight to protect and *expand* what is left of our natural estate."[91] Udall portrayed the "national estate," a rebranding of the public domain, as an entity under constant threat. Events of the 1970s created for Udall a set of anxieties that mirrored those of the Interior Department at the close of the nineteenth century. Times were changing. At the moment, Congress was debating a proposal by former president Richard Nixon to restrict the department's energy functions, and Udall argued that such revamping might open up new opportunities. He thus encouraged Andrus to take on a few key battles to keep the department on track. First, in a throwback to an almost century-long struggle, he urged Andrus to "fight like a tiger" to transfer the Forest Service back to Interior.[92]

However, Udall also advised that two key matters remained unresolved for the Interior Department in this transition: environmental protection and energy development. Udall was uniquely positioned to understand the tenuous juggling act in these central tasks of the department. His actions leading up to the Santa Barbara oil spill precipitated the creation of the Environmental Protection Agency in 1970, redirecting important environmental regulatory capacities away from Interior. The proposal to alter the federal approach to energy development, however, raised equally important questions for Interior. In the new energy terrain wrought of the withdrawal of some Middle Eastern oil, government officials doubted the ability of existing institutions, Interior included, to manage and coordinate national energy policy. This marked a serious reversal from World War II, when Interior Secretary Harold Ickes and his department had been entrusted with securing petroleum in times of national crisis.[93] Prior to the events of 1973–1974, the Interior Department under Nixon had guided a U.S. energy policy that was increasingly turning to unconventional fuel sources, including its offshore jurisdiction in the continental shelf. In the months prior to the embargo, Nixon planned a reorganization of federal bureaucracy to address the increasingly complex nature of the nation's energy network that included the proposed Department of Energy and Natural Resources, a petition that was ultimately unsuccessful.[94] When Udall wrote Andrus two years later, he insisted that Interior should help define the relationships between and among these agencies, clinging to key facets of the department's institutional power, like the Geological Survey, and its role in environmental management.[95]

In the wake of the energy price hike, the U.S. government underwent further regeneration, giving birth to agencies to rival an Interior Department in the national hot seat. Nixon announced the creation of a new Federal Energy Administration (FEA), which was launched under the administration of Gerald Ford. In 1977, Interior lost considerably more power with the creation of the cabinet-level arm to subsume duties of the FEA, the Department of Energy.[96] The creation of the Department of Energy signaled a growing sense that the Interior Department could not secure the nation's energy supply. Moreover, the move effectively split the Interior Department's mineral technocracy, a cornerstone of its twentieth-century power, in half. Its capacities became divided between "non-energy" and "energy" minerals. Much of Interior's energy bureaucracy migrated over to the new agency. In talks leading up to the bill creating the new department, Andrus, President Carter, and soon-to-be secretary of energy Jim Schlesinger negotiated the new terms of jurisdiction. They concluded that the Interior Department would retain its general leasing functions of public, indigenous, and offshore lands and resources, while the Department of Energy would develop regulations for such leasing by shaping competition clauses, alternative bidding systems, mandatory rates of production, and due diligence regulations.[97] Those Bureau of Mines personnel working on research and development of coal mining, surface mining, and coal preparation migrated to Energy, while those overseeing health, safety, and environmental control remained with Interior. This shift ultimately laid the groundwork for the eventual dissolution of the Bureau of Mines. The bureau, a once-influential branch of the department with enough of a monopoly on geological expertise to catalyze national fears of resource depletion, was abolished in 1996.[98]

The division in Interior's mineral technocracy compelled the new leadership to forge alliances with the rival Energy Department and emphasize other departmental functions in land use. Interior continued to perform much of its technical data–collecting functions, but reported its findings to the Department of Energy. The Department of Energy overtook the control of production rates relying on, but also double-checking, the work of Interior's Geological Survey. The two cabinet-level agencies became mutual watchdogs.[99] Amid these transformations, Andrus expounded on the importance of collaboration between the two departments and the broader federal government to not only improve "our ability to deal with energy problems, but to consider as well how best to assure use and conservation of all our natural resources in the public interest." As Interior's hold over mineral resource policy lessened, its leader emphasized a more wide-ranging commitment to promoting "multiple use" and environmental protection on public lands.[100]

With the election of Ronald Reagan in 1980, the reshuffling in the Interior Department became even more pronounced. Alongside his claim to save the nation from foreign policy debacles like those of the Iran hostage crisis, Reagan had made antigovernment rhetoric a centerpiece of his campaign, by which he largely meant defunding and reducing government capacities to regulate corporate activities.[101] Following his election, Reagan began an offensive against the struggling Interior Department. He commissioned a conservative think tank, the Heritage Foundation, to outline a plan for revamping the Interior Department's federal mandate. By the calculations of the Heritage Foundation, Interior had squandered its authority as natural resource manager by indulging in "regulatory excess." For example, the report accused Interior's Office of Surface Mining, which placed limits on extractive firms, of being "environmental zealots" and urged demoting strip-mining rules to mere guidelines. The Geological Survey, the think tank concluded, had seriously plateaued in its mineral mapping efforts and needed to intensify exploration. It ultimately concluded that Interior needed to revive its "mineral advocacy" role, opening more lands to mining and decreasing regulatory controls.[102]

Although the Interior Department had long promoted extractive capitalism, it also performed a consistent if contradictory role in regulating it. The new Reagan administration saw a value only in Interior's promotional qualities and worked to defang its regulatory capacities. Few things crystallized Reagan's intent to use Interior to exclusively promote rather than gently regulate capitalism more than his appointment of James G. Watt to be the secretary of the interior. Watt, an attorney from Colorado, who made a name for himself fighting against the Interior Department's restrictions on natural resource development, would become the most controversial figure to hold the post since the indicted felon Albert B. Fall. His brazen actions to shore up capitalist development with disregard for political, social, and environmental impact caused widespread public outrage, leading to his resignation just two short years after stepping into the office.[103] Yet his crusade to destroy the Interior Department from within would leave an indelible mark on the institution and, most devastatingly, the Native Americans under its trusteeship. As in that earlier era at the denouement of continental expansion, Watt sought a dramatic reversal—if not the absolute closing of the Interior Department, then the diminishment of its capabilities beyond recognition. This was a posture that CERT itself had championed, though on different terms. Whereas Watt wanted an end to social services, CERT wanted an end to guileful negotiations over indigenous energy development.

Watt, meanwhile, supported federal attempts to grease the wheels for energy firms in accessing tribal resources. He saw the government's environmental regulations and trustee status as an impediment to business and the utilization of natural resources. He therefore sought to dismantle the Interior Department's capacities in both arenas. In the realm of environment, he maintained a "remorselessly instrumental attitude toward the natural world," chasing profits by opening public lands to private development while shouting down opponents as environmental extremists, an impulsive modus operandi that even commentators lukewarm on environmental issues perceived as a danger to society.[104] Mineral interests were particularly close to his heart. Like the Heritage Foundation, with which he had close ties, he viewed Interior's regulations as a scourge on the mining industry that had suffered "every abuse of government."[105] Watt held particular ire towards those courts and institutions—the BIA included—that protected tribal lands and sovereignty in the face of energy developers. As an attorney, Watt had even written an amicus brief challenging the Jicarilla Apache tribe's right to tax energy companies on its lands.[106] In general, Watt publicly blamed Native Americans' destitution on their own cultural deficiencies. He aimed to gut the BIA, which increasingly employed American Indians, on grounds that it encouraged idleness and communalism that was, he rationalized, the seedbed of their poverty. Watt drew a firestorm of criticism for an interview in which he claimed, "If you want an example of the failure of socialism, don't go to Russia, come to America and go to the Indian reservations."[107] With offhand comments like these, Watt quickly became a liability and was dismissed from the Reagan cabinet in November 1983.

Even so, the effects of deregulation and defunding in the Interior Department were immediate. Reagan's defunding of the BIA and other civilian programs resulted in the loss of the vestiges of a social safety net for indigenous peoples. Housing and Urban Development (HUD) and the Comprehensive Employment and Training Act (CETA) provided crucial programs and jobs on reservations.[108] Their closure had a devastating effect on many tribal economies. In the course of one year with Reagan's new policies in place, Navajo per capita income dropped from $2,200 to $1,700, while unemployment reached 72 percent in comparison to the already abysmal 50 percent the previous year. Native American tribes were vulnerable, regardless of whether or not they had natural resources as insurance policies. As the *New Republic* reported in a cover feature, "Reagan on the Warpath," Indians driven by disillusionment with the federal government and outside pressures to lessen dependence attached themselves to corporations and the national economy. This attachment, author Hazel Hertzberg noted, yielded abjection when the economy was not booming. "The tribe is like a remote company town," she observed, "stranded when the company moves"—a claim that harkened to earlier boom and bust cycles of the American West and Interior's later operations in Latin America.[109] Reagan's plan for tribes in service of U.S. economic prosperity effectively diminished government services provided by the BIA and promoted private solutions, such as those offered by global energy firms. It was a domestic policy that, like the War on Drugs, exacerbated inequities and left the nation's poor and vulnerable populations to fend for themselves.[110]

As Reagan slashed budgets for civilian agencies, he drastically expanded funds for defense agencies. In the early 1980s, the Reagan administration directed lavish funds to support military modernization, all on grounds that the United States needed to defeat the "evil empire," as Reagan had, in the language of evangelical absolutism, dubbed the Soviet Union. He pitted good against evil. America's new war of moral attrition, an apex in its ongoing Cold War battle against communism, overflowed into many fronts, including a series of shadow wars in Nicaragua, Angola, and Afghanistan. The defense dollars mushroomed from $136 billion in 1980 to $244 billion in 1985, even as the deficit surpassed $200 billion.[111] The Reagan administration directed the deficit spending to the production and dissemination of an imaginative range of ballistics and weaponry. It was the largest defense buildup in history, the opulence of which was gaudily encapsulated in the Strategic Defense Initiative, or "Star Wars," the space-based system meant to destroy enemy missiles.[112] Defense agencies would become the preferred federal agents not only of America's fight against global communism but also of America's quest to secure mineral investments overseas, as we shall see.

Within U.S. borders, Peter MacDonald regretted his endorsement of Reaganomics almost immediately. Just one year after the CERT meeting in Washington, D.C., which had occasioned Reagan's solicitation of support, MacDonald gave a decidedly dissatisfied keynote address. He began by acknowledging that the year before, most of CERT's number were unified in their desire to "try an experiment: that less government rather than more would help the economy and help the nation"—the Reagan way. Despite an understanding that the elimination of government funds and services would be a difficult pill to swallow, MacDonald explained, the tribes did not anticipate the great extent to which tribal conditions would deteriorate. "We were prepared for short-term hardship," he reflected, but not for the tremendous failures of the private sector and its punishing economic realities. MacDonald began to face his own political troubles on the Navajo reservation as challengers like Peterson Zah secured a base of Navajo supporters moving into tribal council elections. MacDonald thus back-peddled, conveying his growing doubts about Reagan's faith in the free market to serve as an arbiter of justice. Nevertheless, he continued to describe himself as an "ally" of the Reagan administration. MacDonald instead chastised corporations, which lacked scruples in gambling for profit at the expense of those in need, like poverty-stricken American Indians.

Symbolizing further troubles for MacDonald, CERT closed their offices in Washington, D.C., in 1983. In the ensuing years, CERT continued its activism but did so in decidedly less public forms. MacDonald, too, descended from power and faced public charges of corruption on the Navajo reservation, leading to his eventual imprisonment.[113] News reportage of the time, and many historians since, attributed the group's decline to its Indian OPEC labeling and perceived ties to OPEC, which alienated consumers and became "an albatross," especially in the aftermath of the Iran hostage crisis.[114] Although CERT did lessen its recourse to OPEC and did shrink institutionally in the early 1980s, the foreign association was not the primary agent of its decline. Rather, the coalition weakened only *after* its robust embrace by the ascendant Reagan administration and allied energy companies. Reagan's policies tethered tribes' well-being to economic development, including royalties from extraction. Chained to the vicissitudes of narrow commodity markets, energy-rich tribes were sunk by a downward turn in the global energy market in 1981 that lowered gas prices and made Reagan appear to be the savior of the energy crisis.[115] Without government programs for poverty alleviation and job creation, many indigenous peoples were left with little to no safety net to offset the economic despair. As the Cold War entered its final decade, CERT, like developing countries pressed into service of barrier-free capitalist activity through the American state and its corporate allies, was enveloped by the unpredictable machinery of global capitalism.[116]

IN THE RISE AND FALL OF CERT, one discerns the convergence of forces bringing about the Interior Department's own decline. Interior had been created to bring expropriated lands into the fold, making them ready for capitalist utilization of natural resources and settlement of white Americans. This history irrevocably conditioned Interior's skill set, taken into new arenas of activity throughout the twentieth century—including to many of the nations that would eventually form OPEC. These involvements were part of a broader system of U.S. intervention that underscored the decision of Arab members of OPEC to cut off Western access to key oil sources. This same history also conditioned the wealth of the seeming wastelands, as the Interior Department and other arms of the federal government had allocated indigenous peoples to the lands, ancestral or adopted, that would eventually be billed as solutions to the energy crisis. As a new wave of capitalist development set in, indigenous social movements like the Indian OPEC staged a notable intervention by calling attention to Interior's legacy of negligence or outright chicanery and framing the problem in a global context, drawing comparisons between their plight and that of members of the Third World and OPEC specifically. In defense of their mineral rights, indigenous peoples stood in solidarity with OPEC, and even with the would-be inhabitants of the moon.

Interior wavered in the face of such indigenous movements. CERT and other American Indian organizations worked through the political and legal systems to constrain the department's capacities to advance private interests, at times at the expense of indigenous peoples' well-being. Such grassroots challenges to Interior's exploitative methods joined other challenges, including critics who questioned its ability to oversee environmental protection on the one hand and economic development on the other. The disillusionment following the Santa Barbara oil spill and the fallout from the energy crisis seemed to testify to Interior's wider failure in managing natural resources for the nation. New federal entities like the Environmental Protection Agency and the Department of Energy subsumed important functions previously overseen by Interior. As a final blow, the Ronald Reagan administration further undercut Interior's technocracy by slashing government spending on civilian agencies, offering private solutions to problems of indigenous and resource management, and deputizing the staunchly antigovernment James G. Watt to subvert Interior from within. Equally significant, Reagan redirected federal funds toward defense agencies, which would become the chosen institutional arm for American global power in many realms, including minerals, in the ensuing decades. The loss of funds paired with the self-destructive fury of Watt may not have brought the closing of the Interior Department, but it did seriously slow the momentum of the department's century-long expansionist project. Interior's inability to balance promoting and regulating capitalism, in the end, led to the fragmenting of its institutional power. It was an appropriate denouement to the Interior Department's global ambitions, for the barriers created by indigenous sovereignty had set the initial agenda: to bring interior that which stood obstinately exterior.

Epilogue

I n 2004, the U.S. Geological Survey of the Department of the Interior arrived in a war-torn Afghanistan. In the wake of America's War on Terror, these geologists and mineral experts searched for "untapped" deposits, especially those that might be rich in copper, iron, bauxite, and most of all, lithium and rare-earth elements. The latter materials had become highly coveted as part of a new "green" technology boom linked to smartphones and hybrid cars. As a result, the value of minerals in Afghanistan was estimated to be an astonishing $1 trillion.[1] Both the Geological Survey and news commentators framed these civilian-led exploratory surveys as a totally new kind of undertaking. The U.S. geologists, for example, claimed to cobble together their mineral reconnaissance from the traces of resource surveys left behind by the former Soviet Union, which began a military occupation in Afghanistan in the late Cold War.[2] However, such narratives deflected attention from sustained American and Interior Department involvements in the region. In reality, the mineral surveys in Afghanistan marked a return to form. Interior technicians had begun searching for strategic minerals in Afghanistan in the earliest days of international development. In the 1950s, for example, U.S. geologists uncovered chromite in the Logar province. In the 2000s, more than a half-century later, a new group of geologists would, without apparent irony, tout "discoveries" of chromite in the same province.[3] In the earlier period, the geologists had described the methods of mining as "extremely primitive," while in the later period, the chief Interior geologist in Afghanistan was similarly dismissive of the existing mining industry: "They've had some small artisanal mines," but the scale of mineral potential "will require more than just a gold pan."[4] Unbeknownst to the new generation of Interior geologists, institutional history was repeating itself.

This misremembering was one of countless erasures of the Interior Department's expansive unfolding from U.S. settler colonialism to U.S. Cold War hegemony. Most often, the omission was based in the largely unquestioned assumption that such outward projections were contradictory—if not impossible altogether. The Geological Survey's amnesia in post-9/11 Afghanistan drew upon this age-old tradition but also stemmed from more recent transformations. The former Soviet occupation had played its part in the disruption, but the Interior Department had also been caught in the crosscurrents of an indigenous movement that publicly thrashed it for centuries of deception and guile, a federal restructuring that gutted its mineral technocracy, and a presidential administration that eradicated government regulatory functions in service of barrier-free capitalism. Other changes unfolding on a global scale also impacted the department. For example, a shift in international development from government-led interventions to market-based solutions, including the ascendance of microfinance as the favored model of uplift, meant that federal funding for foreign assistance agencies dried up. Interior's role in international development also diminished.[5] In and through these transformations, the Interior Department's twentieth-century fight for bureaucratic power through expansionism came to a quiet, almost imperceptible halt. The department retreated from its global outposts, at least in part.

Standing in its place at the Cold War's end was a swelling defense industry. As the federal military spending initiated under Reagan grew in the ensuing decades with the Persian Gulf War and War on Terror, the U.S. military was armed and ready to secure U.S. mineral interests across the world. In Nigeria, the fifth largest oil exporter to America, U.S. armed forces mediated between the repressive Nigerian government and extractive giants like Shell Oil. The administration of Bill Clinton, for example, fed aid dollars to the Nigerian army, while George W. Bush, continuing these military training operations, committed 200 special operations forces to spearhead the nation's further militarization.[6] In ways that drew more attention and news cycles, American troops in 2003 steamrolled through Iraq to topple the dictatorship of Saddam Hussein, an agenda backed by false claims of reliable intelligence showing weapons of mass destruction that has since drawn accusations of "blood for oil."[7] The invasion of Iraq, both Bush administrations claimed, was good routing evil. If the Interior Department had consistently allowed the nation to frame expansion as a benevolent civilizing mission—countering military with civilian approaches, hard with soft power—then hawkish political leaders had, by the close of the twentieth century, managed to reframe military force as morally just. In this sense, the sweeping trajectory by which the United States pursued material ends under the benevolent guise of civilian power had reached an apparent end, in part because military intervention had become "humanitarian" intervention.[8] The Interior Department, as the Afghanistan surveys made clear, would still have an important role to play and an occasion for which to dust off its unparalleled know-how of expansion. But it would not be needed to soften hard power.

Alongside ongoing ties to U.S. military operations, Interior has continued its ambivalent role promoting and regulating a boundary-crossing extractive capitalism, struggling to balance economic development and environmental well-being. Interior authorized leases and drilling activities in indigenous lands, national parks, and the continental shelf, at times with catastrophic effects. In 2010, the *Deepwater Horizon* oil spill in the Gulf of Mexico revealed the perils of Interior's support of private profits over the public good. An explosion at one of the drilling installations run by BP, the company the Interior official William Warne had helped establish in Iran, ignited the largest spill in U.S. history, eclipsing the earlier disaster off the coast of Santa Barbara. The Interior Department's Minerals Management Service had not adequately regulated the BP facilities, an effect of being understaffed and cultivating trusting relations with the private sector.[9] The event was another perceived blight on the American public and transnational environments. Authorizing extractive activities like offshore drilling, strip mining, pipeline construction, and fracking, the Interior Department has contributed to the same environmental degradation it has purported to combat in the form of toxic tailings,

air pollution, and rising temperatures—interwoven legacies of the an-
thropogenic change of the planet's climate. These changes, in turn,
have disproportionately affected marginalized groups under the department's charge, including indigenous peoples in the path of energy pipeline developers and territorial subjects, like those in the Marshall Islands,
whose lands become engulfed by rising sea levels.[10]

Despite these contributions to climate-based deprivations, Interior has
retained the environmental badge it had studiously displayed since the
embrace of conservationism at the turn of the twentieth century. In the
decades since Harold Ickes and Stewart Udall gifted Interior its folksier
conservationist and environmental luster, the department has become
more closely associated with safeguarding wildlife and national parks—
"America's best idea"—than with the promotion of extractive capitalism.
Such associations hold despite policies promoting mining that cut against
the well-being of both.[11] The claim to environmental stewardship, which
had been at times sincere and at times a veneer covering over Interior's
more dubious extractive investments, powerfully shapes the public image
of the contemporary bureaucracy. This point is readily apparent when
surveying the Interior Department's social media presence: a catalog of
photographs of scenic vistas and majestic creatures from America's national parks, frequently tagged with the highly naturalized descriptor,
"no filter."[12] Interior's personnel and its province have come to appear as
unassuming and insular as those featured in the effervescent television
series *Parks and Recreation,* a fictionalized portrayal of the day-to-day
workings of one of its most local branches. Although the Interior Department continues to occupy the two city blocks of prime Washington,
D.C., real estate secured by Harold Ickes, it appears as innocuous as the
love of a public park.

Looking at the Interior Department's annual reports today, one might
conclude that its global investments, if meaningfully detailed at all, represent the fringes of a much wider mandate—a mandate that is otherwise
confined to the home. The department's undertakings overseas do con-
stitute a modest proportion of its overall dealings, much as they did even
at the zenith of its global portfolio after the mid-twentieth century. However, this book has endeavored to show that the extreme outer limits of
Interior's expansionism are significant not only in and of themselves, but

also for their testament to how Interior's mandate *within* U.S. borders continues to encompass the workings of settler colonialism, a process that, far from being settled, is ongoing. The outer limits reveal in the seemingly obvious domesticity of the department's authority, from public and submerged lands to indigenous and territorial affairs, an obstinate foreignness that never was and never could be fully vanquished, precisely because the projection of the United States over the continent was just that—a historical projection, not an uncontested, natural occurrence. Interior's original expansionism, put differently, was never complete, not so long as indigenous and other foreign peoples and nonhuman facets of the environment resisted, adapted, hybridized, and refused in the face of the sustained efforts to bring them interior. In this sense, the Interior Department can help us to see that the boundaries of home never settled—that U.S. global reach aims tenaciously inward as well as outward.

In the final accounting, it becomes clear that the U.S. Department of the Interior has haunted every meaningful threshold of U.S. expansionism. What appears at first as a paradox of American power reveals itself instead to be a key animating condition. The Interior Department had always been "exterior," working between military and civilian power and public and private interests to domesticate the continent and, in the process, to disavow America's original empire. In the twentieth century, the Interior Department pursued ever-widening frontiers following the north star of minerals. Interior's journey of regeneration through expansion, in turn, cleared pathways to capitalist extraction in indigenous lands, formal territories, foreign nations, submerged lands, and outer space—a wide-reaching trajectory that was both enabled and disguised by contradictions. By drawing and blurring boundaries between domestic and foreign, benevolence and exploitation, and nature and politics, the most overtly insular arm of the American state was able to remain perpetually at large and out of sight, extending the reach of American and capitalist institutions into landscapes across the planet. Acknowledging these contradictions of American power, past and present, might be a step on the path to relinquishing the violent and unsustainable pursuit of a global interior.

Notes

Introduction

1. Remarks by the Honorable Stewart L. Udall on Feb. 10, 1967, Folder: Feb. 2-12, 1967 Trip to Middle East (Plans, Corres., Itinerary), box 136, Secretary of the Interior Files, Stewart L. Udall Papers, Special Collections, University of Arizona Library, Tucson, AZ. Emphasis added.

2. Paul Kramer frames the career of American empire less by policing definitions of what empire is than by emphasizing what it does: as a starting point, imperial powers initiate asymmetries through constructions of hierarchy, discipline, dispossession, extraction, and exploitation. See "Power and Connection: Imperial Histories of the United States in the World," *American Historical Review* 116, no. 5 (December 2011): 1348-1391. Scholars have pinpointed the drivers of empire in both economic interests bent on raw materials, labor, and markets, as well as ideological convictions rooted in race, gender, and nation. On the material drives of American empire, especially the pursuit of markets, see William Appleman Williams, *The Tragedy of American Diplomacy* (New York: W. W. Norton, 1972); Walter LaFeber, *The New Empire: An Interpretation of American Expansion, 1860-1898* (Ithaca: Cornell University Press, 1963), 2; Lloyd C. Gardner, *Imperial America: American Foreign Policy since 1898* (New York: Harcourt Brace Jovanovich, 1976). On the ideological dynamos of U.S. imperial and foreign policy, see Amy Kaplan, *The Anarchy of Empire in the Making of U.S. Culture* (Cambridge: Harvard University Press, 2002); Matthew Frye Jacobson, *Barbarian Virtues: The United States Encounters Foreign Peoples at Home and Abroad, 1876-1917* (New Haven: Yale University Press, 2000); Amy Kaplan and Donald Pease, eds., *Cultures of U.S. Imperialism* (Durham: Duke University Press, 1993); Mary Renda, *Taking Haiti: Military Occupation and the Culture of U.S. Imperialism, 1915-1940* (Chapel Hill: University of North Carolina Press, 2001); Melani McAlister, *Epic Encounters: Culture, Media, and U.S. Interests in the Middle East, 1945-2000* (Berkeley: University of California

Press, 2005); Christina Klein, *Cold War Orientalism: Asia in the Middlebrow Imagination, 1945–1961* (Berkeley: University of California Press, 2002).

3. On American exceptionalism, see Amy Kaplan, "Left Alone with America," *Cultures of U.S. Imperialism,* ed. Amy Kaplan and Donald Pease (Durham: Duke University Press, 1994); Thomas Bender, "The American Way of Empire," *World Policy Journal* (Spring 2006). The transnational turn in history has also called for analyses that de-center the nation-state and push against trends to treat the United States as exceptional. See Ian Tyrrell, "Reflections on the Transnational Turn in United States History: Theory and Practice," *Journal of Global History* 3 (November 2009): 453–474.

4. Vernon Northrop, "Interior Role in International Activities," Remarks on United Nations Day, Oct. 24, 1952, Folder: Oct. 1952, box 6721, Publicity (080), RG 70, National Archives and Records Administration, College Park, MD (hereafter shortened to NARA).

5. Definitions of "the interior" that linked it to "domestic" and "home" as opposites of "foreign" are evident in congressional debates that gave life to the department. See Department of the Interior bill, 30th Cong., 2nd Sess., *Congressional Globe* 676 and 672 (March 3, 1849): S: 545. However, as scholars have incisively shown, the opposite of foreign was also domestic in the space of the household, hearth, and home. See Amy Kaplan, *The Anarchy of Empire.*

6. Despite its universalizing tendencies and limitations, including obscuring power on the ground, settler colonialism—expropriation on a vast geographic scale—is an analytic that allows for thinking about patterns of systemic dispossession and earth-moving, as well as continuities between other imperial projects. See the roundtable Brian DeLay, Alexandra Harmon, and Paul C. Rosier, "Forum: American Indians and the History of U.S. Foreign Relations," *Diplomatic History* 39, no. 5 (November 2015): 927–966; Frederick E. Hoxie, "Retrieving the Red Continent: Settler Colonialism and the History of American Indians in the US," *Ethnic and Racial Studies* 31, no. 6 (2008): 1153–1167; Pekka Hämäläinen, *The Comanche Empire* (New Haven: Yale University Press, 2008). Indigenous studies scholarship rooted in political theory denaturalizes U.S. sovereignty over the continent by emphasizing the illegality of the expropriation that ignited American rule of law. See Jodi Byrd, *The Transit of Empire: Indigenous Critiques of Colonialism* (Minneapolis: University of Minnesota Press, 2011).

7. A classic study on Interior's conservationism is Samuel P. Hays, *Conservation and the Gospel of Efficiency: The Progressive Conservation Movement, 1890–1920* (Cambridge: Harvard University Press, 1959).

8. Important work on the role of minerals in U.S. foreign policy nonetheless positions them as straightforward objects of rational interest that magnetically drew the United States into far corners of the world. See Daniel Yergin, *The Prize: The Epic Quest for Oil, Money & Power* (New York: Free Press, 2008); Tyler Priest, *Global Gambits: Big Steel and the U.S. Quest for Manganese* (New York: Praeger, 2003); David Painter, *Oil and the American Century* (Baltimore: Johns Hopkins University Press, 1986); Stephen D. Krasner, *Defending the National Interest: Raw Materials Investments and U.S. Foreign Policy* (Princeton: Princeton University Press, 1978); Mi-

chael T. Klare, *Resource Wars: The New Landscape of Global Conflict* (New York: Metropolitan Books, 2001); Alfred Eckes, *The United States and the Global Struggle for Minerals* (Austin: University of Texas Press, 1979). On the percentage of the GDP, which vacillated between 0.9 and 3.8 percent of the national economy with a mean of 1.9 percent (compared to a mean of 2.6 percent for agriculture and 19.9 percent for manufacturing) since statistics were taken in 1947, see "Gross-Domestic-Product-(GDP)-by-Industry," U.S. Bureau of Economic Analysis, Department of Commerce, https://www.bea.gov/industry/gdpbyind_data.htm.

9. On the myth of the frontier, see Richard Slotkin, *Regeneration through Violence: The Mythology of the American Frontier, 1600–1860* (Norman: University of Oklahoma Press, 2000); Slotkin, *Gunfighter Nation: The Myth of the Frontier in Twentieth-Century America* (Norman: University of Oklahoma Press, 1998). On the material bounty that came with identifying new frontiers and the new markets they would open, see Williams, *The Tragedy of American Diplomacy.*

10. The term signals a terrestrial metabolization that operated within formally established borders and corresponds in useful ways to Michel Foucault's concept of "interiorization," a process by which individuals incorporate norms, and become subjects, through their increased visibility to different institutions. Unlike Americanization, which targeted peoples, interiorization targeted the earth. See Michel Foucault, *Power/Knowledge: Selected Interviews and Other Writings 1972–1977,* trans. Colin Gordon, Leo Marshall, John Mepham, and Kate Soper, ed. Collin Gordon (New York: Pantheon Books, 1980), 154.

11. On "hard" power, see Melvyn P. Leffler, *A Preponderance of Power: National Security, the Truman Administration, and the Cold War* (Palo Alto: Stanford University Press, 1992); Stephen Kinzer, *Overthrow: America's Century of Regime Change from Hawaii to Iraq* (New York: Times Books, 2006); Odd Arne Westad, *The Global Cold War: Third World Interventions and the Making of Our Times* (New York: Cambridge University Press, 2007); Catherine Lutz, *The Bases of Empire: The Global Struggle against U.S. Military Posts* (New York: New York University Press, 2009). On "soft" power, see Emily S. Rosenberg, *Financial Missionaries to the World: The Politics and Culture of Dollar Diplomacy* (Cambridge: Harvard University Press, 1999); Elizabeth Borgwardt, *A New Deal for the World: America's Vision for Human Rights* (Cambridge: Belknap Press of Harvard University Press, 2005). American involvements in international development, historians have shown, were just as important to the furtherance of its geopolitical objectives in the Third World as warfare and political coups. See David Ekbladh, *Great American Mission: Modernization and the Construction of an American World Order* (Princeton: Princeton University Press, 2010); Nick Cullather, *The Hungry World: America's Cold War Battle Against Poverty in Asia* (Cambridge: Harvard University Press, 2010); Daniel Immerwahr, *Thinking Small: The United States and the Lure of Community Development* (Cambridge: Harvard University Press, 2015); Edward Miller, *Misalliance: Ngo Dinh Diem, the United States, and the Fate of South Vietnam* (Cambridge: Harvard University Press, 2013); Nils Gilman, *Mandarins of the Future: Modernization Theory in Cold War America* (Baltimore: Johns Hopkins University Press, 2003).

12. On environment as an object of international relations, see Ian Tyrrell, *Crisis of the Wasteful Nation: Conservation and Empire in Teddy Roosevelt's America* (Chicago: University of Chicago Press, 2015); Thomas Robertson, *The Malthusian Moment: Global Population Growth and the Birth of American Environmentalism* (New Brunswick: Rutgers University Press, 2012); Stephen Macekura, *Of Limits and Growth: The Rise of Global Sustainable Development in the Twentieth Century* (New York: Cambridge University Press, 2015); Erika Marie Bsumek, David Kinkela, and Mark A. Lawrence, eds., *Nation-States and the Global Environment: New Approaches to International Environmental History* (New York: Oxford University Press, 2013); Kurkpatrick Dorsey, *Whales and Nations: Environmental Diplomacy on the High Seas* (Seattle: University of Washington Press, 2013); David Kinkela, *DDT and the American Century: Global Health, Environmental Politics, and the Pesticide that Changed the World* (Chapel Hill: University of North Carolina Press, 2011). Environmental historians who have considered the global scale include Donald Worster, *Shrinking the Earth: The Rise and Decline of American Abundance* (New York: Oxford University Press, 2015); J. R. McNeill, *The Great Acceleration: An Environmental History of the Anthropocene since 1945* (Cambridge: Harvard University Press, 2015); Jessica B. Teisch, *Engineering Nature: Water, Development, and the Global Spread of American Environmental Expertise* (Chapel Hill: University of North Carolina Press, 2011). On environmental conditions and consequences in international relations, see Timothy Mitchell, *Rule of Experts: Egypt, Techno-Politics, Modernity* (Berkeley: University of California Press, 2001); David Biggs, *Quagmire: Nation-Building and Nature in the Mekong Delta* (Seattle: University of Washington Press, 2011); Kate Brown, *Plutopia: Nuclear Families, Atomic Cities, and the Great Soviet and American Plutonium Disasters* (New York: Oxford University Press, 2013). Other historians have begun to examine the role of nongovernmental organizations in globalizing environmental concern. See Frank Zelko, *Make It a Green Peace! The Rise of Countercultural Environmentalism* (New York: Oxford University Press, 2013). For a synthesis of environmental history and its recent move to the global, see Paul Sutter, "The World with Us: The State of American Environmental History," *Journal of American History* (June 2013): 94–119.

13. See Hays, *Conservation and the Gospel of Efficiency;* Brian Balogh, "Scientific Forestry and the Roots of the Modern American State: Gifford Pinchot's Path to Progressive Reform," *Environmental History* 7, no. 2 (2002): 198–225; Bruce J. Schulman, "Governing Nature, Nurturing Government: Resource Management and the Development of the American State, 1900–1912," *Journal of Policy History* 17, no. 4 (2005): 375–403; Adam Rome, "What Really Matters in History?: Environmental Perspectives on Modern America," *Environmental History* 7 (April 2002): 304. In an important departure from this domestic trend, Tyrrell has revealed how conservationist thought emerged in a global context and in service of empire building in *Crisis of the Wasteful Nation,* but does not analyze how settler colonialism underscored its codification in American governance.

14. Historians spanning subfields have told important parts of the story of Interior's environmental management but have largely overlooked its global trajectory. They have portrayed Interior as an internally directed arm of the federal government

without continuity of purpose. Scholars have affirmed this sense of disunity by parsing and narrowing in on the workings of its many bureaus, including the Bureau of Indian Affairs, Bureau of Reclamation, Geological Survey, Bureau of Land Management, and National Park Service. See Frederick Hoxie, *A Final Promise: The Campaign to Assimilate the Indians, 1880–1920* (Lincoln: University of Nebraska Press, 2001); Karl Jacoby, *Crimes Against Nature: Squatters, Poachers, Thieves, and the Hidden History of American Conservation* (Berkeley: University of California Press, 2001); Karen Merrill, *Public Lands and Political Meaning: Ranchers, the Government, and the Property between Them* (Berkeley: University of California Press, 2002); Mark David Spence, *Dispossessing Wilderness: Indian Removal and the Making of the National Parks* (New York: Oxford University Press, 1999); Donald Worster, *A River Running West: The Life of John Wesley Powell* (Oxford: Oxford University Press, 2001); William H. Goetzmann, *Exploration and Empire: The Explorer and the Scientist in the Winning of the American West* (New York: Knopf, 1966). Richard White has done the most to shed light on the multipronged efforts of the Interior Department to facilitate expansion, but he similarly emphasizes the domesticity of the department and the bureaus at the bottom of its organizational chart. See Richard White, *"It's Your Misfortune and None of My Own": A History of the American West* (Norman: University of Oklahoma Press, 1991), 132–135.

15. Northrop, "Interior Role in International Activities."

16. For just one example of scholarship troubling the politics-nature binary, see William Cronon, *Uncommon Ground: Rethinking the Human Place in Nature* (New York: W. W. Norton, 1996).

17. For a careful accounting of the work spanning the histories of American capitalism and the United States and the world, see Paul A. Kramer, "Embedding Capital: Political-Economic History, the United States, and the World," *Journal of the Gilded Age and Progressive Era* 15 (2016): 331–362. Scholars who show collusions between U.S. officials and financiers and economic planners in service of global market integration include Greta Krippner, *Capitalizing on Crisis: The Political Origins of the Rise of Finance* (Cambridge: Harvard University Press, 2011); Emily S. Rosenberg, *Financial Missionaries to the World: The Politics and Culture of Dollar Diplomacy* (Cambridge: Harvard University Press, 1999); Michael D. Hogan, *The Marshall Plan: America, Britain, and the Reconstruction of Western Europe, 1947–1952* (Cambridge: University of Cambridge Press, 1987); Victoria De Grazia, *Irresistible Empire: America's Advance through Twentieth-Century Europe* (Cambridge: Belknap Press of Harvard University Press, 2005); Michael E. Latham, ed., *Staging Growth: Modernization, Development, and the Global Cold War* (Amherst: University of Massachusetts Press, 2003); Amanda Kay McVety, *Enlightened Aid: U.S. Development as Foreign Policy in Ethiopia* (New York: Oxford University Press, 2012).

18. To separate public and private interests is to challenge, to an extent, classic Marxist interpretations of imperialism that view governments as instruments of capital. See Vladimir Ilyich Lenin, *Imperialism, the Highest Stage of Capitalism* (New York: Penguin, 2010); Rosa Luxemburg, *The Accumulation of Capital*, trans. Agnes Schwarzschild (1913; London: Routledge, 1951). Historians, especially in a U.S. context, have exposed the deep interdependence of the government and private industry that

belied their apparent antagonism. See Richard White, *Railroaded: The Transcontinentals and the Making of Modern America* (New York: W. W. Norton, 2011); William Novak, "The Myth of the 'Weak' American State," *American Historical Review* 113 (June 2008): 752–772; Gary Gerstle, "A State Both Strong and Weak," *American Historical Review* 115 (June 2010): 779–785; Jennifer Klein, *For All these Rights: Business, Labor, and the Shaping of America's Public-Private Welfare State* (Princeton: Princeton University Press, 2006); Allen Brinkley, *The End of Reform: New Deal Liberalism in Recession and War* (New York: Alfred A. Knopf, 1995). On neoliberal policies and free-market ideologies, see Kim Phillips-Fein, *Invisible Hands: The Businessmen's Crusade against the New Deal* (New York: W. W. Norton, 2009); Bethany Moreton, *To Serve God and Wal-Mart: The Making of Christian Free Enterprise* (Cambridge: Harvard University Press, 2009); Michel Foucault, *The Birth of Biopolitics: Lectures at the Collège de France, 1978–79*, trans. Graham Burchell, ed. Michel Senellart (New York: Palgrave MacMillan, 2008); Wendy Brown, "Neoliberalism and the End of Liberal Democracy," *Theory and Event* 7, no. 1 (2003). This analysis places these collusions and the asymmetries they produced historically in an imperial frame.

19. On the uneven distribution of economic tolls and environmental degradation, or "slow violence," see Rob Nixon, *Slow Violence and the Environmentalism of the Poor* (Cambridge: Harvard University Press, 2011). On sacrifice zones, racialized labor, and contaminated bodies, see Traci Brynne Voyles, *Wastelanding: Legacies of Uranium Mining in Navajo Country* (Minneapolis: University of Minnesota Press, 2015); Gabrielle Hecht, *Being Nuclear: Africans and the Global Uranium Trade* (Cambridge: MIT Press, 2012). On debt crises, see Macekura, *Of Limits and Growth*; Paul Adler, "'The Basis of a New Internationalism?': The Institute for Policy Studies and North-South Politics from the NIEO to Neoliberalism," *Diplomatic History* 41, no. 4 (Sept. 2017): 665–693. On global warming, see Joshua P. Howe, *Behind the Curve: Science and the Politics of Global Warming* (Seattle: University of Washington Press, 2014). On the general pattern of uneven development, see David Harvey, *The Spaces of Global Capitalism: Towards a Theory of Uneven Geographical Development* (London: Verso Press, 2006).

20. Key works on agency include William H. Sewell, Jr., *Logics of History: Social Theory and Social Transformation* (Chicago: University of Chicago Press, 2005); Mary Douglas, *How Institutions Think, Frank W. Abrams Lectures* (Syracuse: Syracuse University Press, 1986). Institutions are not individuals and do not have minds of their own. Nor are members unthinking drones of the institution. Yet certain ideas of individuals within institutions become more thinkable and actionable than others. Sociologists have insisted that the mission and practices of an institution help to set the categories of thought and action, in what some call a "thought style." See Douglas, *How Institutions Think*, 27.

21. See Mark L. Wilson, *Destructive Creation: American Business and the Winning of World War II* (Philadelphia: University of Pennsylvania Press, 2016); James Sparrow, *The Warfare State: World War II Americans and the Age of Big Government* (New York: Oxford University Press, 2013).

22. Department of Agriculture personnel working overseas, for example, figure in Cullather, *The Hungry World*.

23. Interior was the source of so many other agencies that officials dubbed it the "Mother of Departments." U.S. Department of the Interior, *Information Concerning the United States Department of the Interior, Assembled in Question and Answer Form for Ready Reference* (Washington, DC: U.S. Government Printing Office, 1939), III. Henceforth U.S. Government Printing Office will be abbreviated to USGPO. Cited in Norman Forness, "The Origins and Early History of the United States Department of the Interior," PhD dissertation, Pennsylvania State University, 1964, 7.

24. Canada's Department of the Interior was in operation from 1876 to 1936, when it split its functions in natural resource management and indigenous management, unlike the U.S. Interior Department. See Irene M. Spry and Bennett McCardle, "Records of the Department of the Interior and Research Concerning Canada's Western Frontier of Settlement," *Canadian Plains Studies* (Regina: Canadian Plains Research Center, 1993). On the Australian version, in operation from 1939 to 1972, see Bruce Juddery, "Interior Develops in Size and Shape," *Canberra Times,* December 30, 1969, p. 12. For an incisive comparison across the U.S.-Canada border by North American Indian intellectual D'Arcy McNickle, see "Private Intervention," *Human Organization* (1960): 208–216.

25. Daniel Carpenter, *The Forging of the Bureaucratic Autonomy: Reputations, Networks, and Policy Innovation in Executive Agencies, 1862–1928* (Princeton: Princeton University Press, 2001); Brian Balogh, *A Government out of Sight* (New York: Cambridge University Press, 2009); Nicholas Parillo, *Against the Profit Motive: The Salary Revolution in American Government, 1780–1940* (New Haven: Yale University Press, 2013).

26. Charles Maier, *Among Empires: American Ascendancy and its Predecessors* (Cambridge: Harvard University Press, 2007); Jane Burbank and Frederick Cooper, *Empires in World History: Power and the Politics of Difference* (Princeton: Princeton University Press, 2010); Lisa Lowe, *The Intimacies of Four Continents* (Durham: Duke University Press, 2015).

1 · The Closing of the Interior

1. Senator Foote, speaking on the Department of the Interior bill, 30th Cong., 2nd Sess., *Congressional Globe* 674 (March 3, 1849): S: 545.

2. Vernon Northrop, "Interior Role in International Activities," Remarks on United Nations Day, October 24, 1952, Folder: October 1952, box 6721, Publicity (080), RG 70, NARA.

3. Scholarship in American foreign relations history has attempted to bring American Indian policy into the foreign policy frame. For a survey, see the roundtable Brian DeLay, Alexandra Harmon, and Paul C. Rosier, "Forum: American Indians and the History of U.S. Foreign Relations," *Diplomatic History* 39, no. 5 (November 2015).

4. Historians of borderlands and Native American history have striven to balance a critique of structural violence and indigenous agency in continental expansion.

Recent works showcase the systemic oppression that at times conformed to contemporary definitions of genocide, as well as the painstaking diplomatic negotiations spearheaded by indigenous peoples to shape terms of extended U.S. power. See Brian DeLay, "Indian Polities, Empire and the History of American Foreign Relations," *Diplomatic History* 39, no. 5 (2015): 929; Benjamin Madley, *An American Genocide: The United States and the California Indian Catastrophe, 1846–1873* (New Haven: Yale University Press, 2016). Scholars in indigenous studies have exposed how American liberal democracy has from its origins required the erasure of the historic and ongoing displacement of indigenous peoples to maintain the artifice of U.S. sovereignty over the continent. See Jodi Byrd, *The Transit of Empire: Indigenous Critiques of Colonialism* (Minneapolis: University of Minnesota Press, 2011); Alyosha Goldstein, ed., *Formations of United States Colonialism* (Durham: Duke University Press, 2014).

5. Other arms of the U.S. government were also important to this process—including the U.S. Army, the Post Office, state governments, and, most centrally, Congress—along with corporations like those behind railroads and extractive industries.

6. Countless scholars across disciplines have repudiated key terms of Turner's analysis. See Patricia Nelson Limerick, *Legacy of Conquest: The Unbroken Past of the American West* (New York: W. W. Norton, 1987), 25; Robert E. Lang, Deborah Epstein Popper, and Frank J. Popper, "'Progress of the Nation': The Settlement History of the Enduring American Frontier," *Western Historical Quarterly* 26 (Autumn 1995): 289–307; Amy Kaplan, "Left Alone with America," *Cultures of U.S. Imperialism,* ed. Amy Kaplan and Donald Pease (Durham: Duke University Press, 1994). More recently, Frederick E. Hoxie, building on insights in borderlands and postcolonial studies, has argued that Turner's conceptualization patterned troubling tendencies in the process of writing American history itself, reinforcing a problematic telos of continental expansion. See "Retrieving the Red Continent: Settler Colonialism and the History of American Indians in the US," *Ethnic and Racial Studies* 31, no. 6 (2008): 1154.

7. A sampling of works drawing linkages between the closing of the frontier and American foreign relations include William Appleman Williams, *The Tragedy of American Diplomacy,* 22; Walter LaFeber, *The New Empire: An Interpretation of American Expansion, 1860–1898* (Ithaca, NY: Cornell University Press, 1963), 2; Walter L. Williams, "United States Indian Policy and the Debate over Philippine Annexation: Implications for the Origins of American Imperialism," *Journal of American History* 66, no. 4 (March 1980): 817; Amy Kaplan, *The Anarchy of Empire in the Making of U.S. Culture* (Cambridge: Harvard University Press, 2002).

8. Walter Hixson, *American Settler Colonialism: A History* (New York: Palgrave MacMillan, 2013); Michael Adas, *Machine as the Measure of Men: Science, Technology, and Ideologies of Western Dominance* (Ithaca: Cornell University Press, 1989).

9. Anthony F. C. Wallace, *The Long, Bitter Trail: Andrew Jackson and the Indians* (New York: Hill and Wang, 1993).

10. See Kevin Bruyneel, *The Third Space of Sovereignty: The Postcolonial Politics of U.S.-Indigenous Relations* (Minneapolis: University of Minnesota Press, 2007).

11. The Trail of Tears, for example, is estimated to have killed 10,000 Creek Indians alone. See Wallace, *The Long, Bitter Trail*, 87–88.

12. Amy S. Greenberg, *A Wicked War: Polk, Clay, Lincoln, and the 1846 U.S. Invasion of Mexico* (New York: Vintage, 2013).

13. Alban W. Hoopes, *Indian Affairs and Their Administration with Special Reference to the Far West, 1849–1860* (Philadelphia: University of Pennsylvania, 1932), 1. The Louisiana Purchase of 1803 had roughly doubled the size of the nation and had similarly challenged the Treasury Department to integrate the new public domain by creating district land offices and establishing territorial governments. See Malcolm Rohrbough, *The Land Office Business: The Settlement and Administration of American Public Lands, 1789–1837* (New York: Oxford University Press, 1968), 30–31.

14. Norman Forness, "The Origins and Early History of the United States Department of the Interior," PhD dissertation, Pennsylvania State University, 1964, 21, 26. Forness's painstaking research into congressional debates and executive authority behind the creation and development of the Interior Department has shaped this chapter in critical ways.

15. U.S. House of Representatives, "Report of the Secretary of War for 1848," *House Ex. Doc. #1*, 30th Cong., 1st Sess., Serial 537, pp. 84, 407–408. Cited in ibid., 22. On indigenous roles in the Mexican-American War, particularly the Kiowa, Comanche, Navajo, and Apache peoples, see Brian DeLay, "Independent Indians and the U.S.-Mexican War," *American Historical Review* 112, no. 1 (2007): 35. Population estimates come from Hoopes, *Indian Affairs and Their Administration with Special Reference to the Far West*, 2.

16. Forness, "The Origins and Early History of the United States Department of the Interior," 22.

17. Senator Mason, speaking on the Department of the Interior bill, 30th Cong., 2nd Sess., *Congressional Globe* 676 and 672 (March 3, 1849): S: 545.

18. John C. Calhoun, speaking on the Department of the Interior bill, 30th Cong., 2nd Sess., *Congressional Globe* 673 (March 3, 1849): S: 545.

19. Leonard White, *The Republican Era: 1869–1901* (New York: MacMillan Company, 1958), 175; Stephen Skowroneck, *Building a New American State: The Expansion of National Administrative Capacities, 1877–1920* (New York: Cambridge University Press, 1982); Daniel P. Carpenter argues that Interior lacked autonomy and power because it failed to rouse a diverse constituency base in *The Forging of Bureaucratic Autonomy: Reputations, Networks, and Policy Innovation in Executive Agencies, 1862–1928* (Princeton: Princeton University Press, 2001), 352. Balogh calls Interior the "most elaborate bureaucracy" in *A Government Out of Sight*, 358; Richard White analyzes Interior's process of parceling out land to settlers and capitalists, though he does so more by attending to its discrete bureaus of the GLO, Bureau of Indian Affairs, and Geological Survey separately. See *"It's Your Misfortune and None of My Own": A History of the American West* (Norman: University of Oklahoma Press, 1991).

20. Carpenter, *The Forging of Bureaucratic Autonomy*, 47.

21. Nicholas Parillo, *Against the Profit Motive: The Salary Revolution in American Government, 1780–1940* (New Haven, Yale University Press, 2013), 3.

22. This is the account given by the first secretary of the Interior Thomas Ewing in "Report of the Secretary of the Interior," *American Quarterly Register and Magazine* 3, no. 2 (1849): 552.

23. A noted exception is Indian Territory, which remained intact through the early twentieth century. On the history of the public domain, see Rohrbough, *The Land Office Business,* ix–xii.

24. Rather than swift incorporation through statehood, territories remained hinterlands of natural resources to shore up the nation's industrial development. Carpenter, *The Forging of Bureaucratic Autonomy,* 50. For one list of governors of the territories, see *Official Register of the United States, Containing a List of Officers and Employees in the Civil, Military, and Naval Service in the United States on the Thirtieth of September, 1877* (Washington, DC: USGPO, 1878), 294.

25. The Jeffersonian vision of officials in the Land Office never kept pace with the desires of settlers to claim land, public domain or Indian reserves, as their own as an extension of their rights as citizens. See Limerick, *Legacy of Conquest,* 60–62.

26. At its founding, Interior managed mines on the enlarged public domain, especially lead mines, to ensure supplies of materials necessary to national defense. See Forness, "The Origins and Early History of the United States Department of the Interior," 232.

27. Robert Swenson, "Legal Aspects of Mineral Resources Exploitation," *History of Public Law Development,* ed. Paul W. Gates (Washington, DC: USGPO, 1968), 707.

28. As with the railroad corporations, the government heavily subsidized and supported the expansion of mining in the West, but then drew public ire when private companies and land speculators acquired lands in ways that cut against the individual homesteader, eliciting charges of opportunism, corruption, and guile. White, *Railroaded,* xxiii, 39–40.

29. Alex Stuart, "Annual Report of the Secretary of the Interior," *New York Times,* December 11, 1852, p. 7.

30. Swenson, "Legal Aspects of Mineral Resources Exploitation," 717–723.

31. Wallace, *The Long, Bitter Trail;* Watson Parker, *Gold in the Black Hills* (Norman: University of Oklahoma Press, 1966); Jeffrey Ostler, *The Lakotas and the Black Hills: The Struggle for Sacred Ground* (New York: Viking, 2010); David Roberts, *Once They Moved Like the Wind: Cochise, Geronimo, and the Apache Wars* (New York: Simon & Schuster, 1993); Ramón Ruiz, *The People of Sonora and Yankee Capitalists* (Tucson: University of Arizona Press, 1988); Benjamin Madley, *An American Genocide: The United States and the California Indian Catastrophe, 1846–1873* (New Haven: Yale University Press, 2017).

32. Carpenter, *The Forging of the American Bureaucracy,* 51–52.

33. *Annual Report of the Secretary of the Interior for the Fiscal Year ending June 1, 1854* (Washington, DC: USGPO, 1854), 475.

34. In 1864, in one of the most harrowing examples, officers in the Colorado militia massacred over 130 men, women, and children in the Sand Creek village in Colorado, inciting the outrage of a broader American public. Richard White, *"It's Your Misfortune and None of My Own,"* 96–97. Another notorious case involved the forcible march of the Navajo people to a reservation in Bosque Redondo, a torturous

journey marked by starvation, disease, and exposure—what became known as "the Long Walk." See Marsha Weisiger, *Dreaming of Sheep in Navajo Country* (Seattle: University of Washington Press, 2009), 21–22.

35. See Marjane Ambler, *Breaking the Iron Bonds: Indian Control of Energy Development* (Lawrence: University of Kansas Press, 1991), chap. 1.

36. Quoted in Forness, "The Origins and Early History of the United States Department of the Interior," 27.

37. Brooke L. Blower, "Nation of Outposts: Forts, Factories, Bases, and the Making of American Power," *Diplomatic History* 41, no. 3 (2017): 439–459.

38. Hoxie, *A Final Promise,* 88–89; Ambler, *Breaking the Iron Bonds,* 9.

39. Employment in the Indian Service increased dramatically in the second half of the nineteenth century. There were approximately 600 employees in the Office of Indian Affairs in 1867, approximately 900 in 1877, and approximately 2,400 in 1887. See *Official Register of the United States, Containing a List of Officers and Employees in the Civil, Military, and Naval Service in the United States on the Thirtieth of September* (Washington, DC: USGPO, 1868), 152–160; *Official Register of the United States* (Washington, DC: USGPO, 1878), 281–293; *Official Register of the United States, 1888* (Washington, DC: USGPO, 1888), 544–576.

40. On the census, see Forness, "The Origins and Early History of the United States Department of the Interior," 69, 80, 104.

41. "The New Indian War," *Harper's Weekly,* December 21, 1878, p. 1.

42. See Francis Paul Prucha, *Documents of United States Indian Policy,* Third Edition (Lincoln: University of Nebraska Press, 2000), 145–146.

43. Donald Worster, *A River Running West: The Life of John Wesley Powell* (Oxford: Oxford University Press, 2001), 207; see also *Annual Report of the Secretary of the Interior for the Fiscal Year Ending June 1, 1866* (Washington, DC: USGPO, 1867), 101; *Annual Report of the Secretary of the Interior for the Fiscal Year Ending June 1, 1871* (Washington, DC: USGPO, 1872), 16–17. The quote is from John Wesley Powell's "From Barbarism to Civilization," cited in Worster, 465.

44. Kevin Robert Hart, "Government Geologists and the Early Man Controversy: The Problem of 'Official' Science in America, 1879–1907," PhD dissertation, Kansas State University, 1976, 68.

45. Worster, *A River Running West,* 363.

46. Quoted in Hart, "Government Geologists and the Early Man Controversy," 92–93.

47. Chief Alaskan Geologist to Loughlin, November 9, 1939, Folder: Reports: Monthly and Annual, 1939, box 1, Central Files of the Alaskan Branch, 1899–1947, Records of the Geological Survey, NARA.

48. Tariffs protected domestic mineral producers by placing a duty on foreign minerals. Despite a recurrent surge of such protectionist sensibilities in the twentieth century, the United States continually looked outward for sources of minerals. G. R. Hawke, "United States Tariff and Industrial Protection in the Late Nineteenth Century," *Economic History Review* 28, no. 1 (February 1975): 84–99. The Geological Survey's efforts were heralded at international conferences in theoretical and practical geology. See *Annual Report of the Secretary of the Interior for the Fiscal Year Ending June 1, 1891* (Washington, DC: USGPO, 1891), xc–xci.

49. Hoopes, *Indian Affairs and Their Administration with Special Reference to the Far West,* 158, 193. Indian Service employees could also swindle and even murder their charges. See Hoopes, 195. *Annual Report of the Secretary of the Interior for the Fiscal Year ending June 1, 1888* (Washington, DC: USGPO), xxii. See, for example, William A. Winder, U.S. Special Allotting Agent, "Map Prepared for U.S. Indian Inspector Jas. McLaughlin Showing Allotments in Gregory County on the Rosebud Indian Reservation South Dakota," prepared by Charles Reiter, September 14, 1901; N. Boardman, U.S. Surveyor, "Plats of the Oneida Indian Reservation, Wis., showing surveys of claims and allotments," December 11, 1890.

50. Mark David Spence, *Dispossessing Wilderness: Indian Removal and the Making of the National Parks* (New York: Oxford University Press, 1999), 3–4, 164.

51. Indian agents tallied, for example, the number of Indians wearing clothes, occupying houses, speaking English, and attending schools, as well as the number of acres cultivated, berries foraged, and butter churned. See *Annual Report of the Secretary of the Interior for the Fiscal Year Ending June 1, 1887* (Washington, DC: USGPO), 25; *Annual Report of the Secretary of the Interior for the Fiscal Year Ending June 1, 1888,* 15.

52. Charles F. Wilkinson and Eric R. Biggs, "The Evolution of the Termination Policy," *American Indian Law Review* (1977): 142; Hoxie, *A Final Promise,* 44. In advancing the allotment agenda, Henry Dawes believed that current leaders among Indian nations lacked the type of selfishness that drove worthy civilizations. See Ambler, 10. An important legal precedent for this enforcement of property laws in indigenous land was the 1823 Supreme Court case *Johnson v. M'Intosh.* See Eric Cheyfitz, "Savage Law: The Plot Against American Indians in *Johnson and Graham's Lessee v. M'Intosh* and *The Pioneers,*" *Cultures of United States Imperialism,* ed. Amy Kaplan and Donald E. Pease (Durham: Duke University Press, 1993), 113.

53. Ambler, *Breaking the Iron Bonds,* 37.

54. Quoted in Joy Porter, "Progressivism and Native American Self-Expression in the Late Nineteenth and Early Twentieth Century," in *Native Diasporas: Indigenous Identities and Settler Colonialism in the Americas,* ed. Gregory D. Smithers and Brooke N. Newman (Lincoln: University of Nebraska Press, 2013), 275.

55. The tabulator was invented by a former Census Office employee in 1888, legally trademarked by the Patent Office in 1889, and first used by the Census Office in 1890. Jon Agar, *The Government Machine: A Revolutionary History of the Computer* (Cambridge, MA: MIT Press, 2004), 264.

56. Robert Porter, Henry Gannett, and William Hunt, "Progress of the Nation," in *Report on Population of the United States at the Eleventh Census: 1890, Part I,* Bureau of the Census (Washington, DC: 1895), xviii–xxxiv; Robert E. Lang, Deborah Epstein Popper, and Frank J. Popper, "'Progress of the Nation': The Settlement History of the Enduring American Frontier," *Western Historical Quarterly* 26, no. 3 (Autumn 1995): 289–307.

57. Porter, Gannett, and Hunt, "Progress of the Nation," xxvii.

58. Ian Tyrrell, *The Crisis of the Wasteful Nation: Conservation and Empire in Teddy Roosevelt's America* (Chicago: University of Chicago Press, 2015), 11.

59. *Annual Report of the Secretary of the Interior for the Fiscal Year ending June 1, 1891* (Washington, DC: USGPO, 1891), ix; *Annual Report of the Secretary of the Interior for the Fiscal Year Ending June 1, 1896* (Washington, DC: USGPO, 1896), 11.

60. On the popular faith in the frontier's closing, see Matthew Frye Jacobson, *Barbarian Virtues: The United States Encounters Foreign Peoples at Home and Abroad, 1876–1917* (New Haven: Yale University Press, 2000), 21. Interior annual reports described efforts to manage and protect settlements and settlers of the "frontier" against Indian belligerents. *Annual Report of the Secretary of the Interior, 1864–5*, 8; *Annual Report of the Secretary of the Interior for the Fiscal Year Ending June 1, 1872* (Washington, DC: USGPO, 1872), 8; *Annual Report of the Secretary of the Interior for the Fiscal Year Ending June 1, 1888*, iii.

61. *Annual Report of the Secretary of the Interior for the Fiscal Year Ending June 1, 1896*, 11.

62. Merrill, *Public Lands and Political Meaning*, 167.

63. Although the sources of this ethos are manifold, and encompass a field of thought from George Perkins Marsh and John Muir to squatters and poachers, scholars widely agree that the movement reached its fever pitch with its embrace by the administration of Theodore Roosevelt. See Hays, *Conservation and the Gospel of Efficiency*, 2; Karl Jacoby, *Crimes Against Nature*, 1; Gifford Pinchot, *Breaking New Ground* (New York: Harcourt Brace, 1947); Kurkpatrick Dorsey, *The Dawn of Conservation Diplomacy: US-Canadian Wildlife Protection Treaties in the Progressive Era* (Seattle: University of Washington Press, 1998).

64. Swenson, "Legal Aspects of Mineral Resources Exploitation," 725; White, *"It's Your Misfortune and None of My Own,"* 117.

65. Hays, *Conservation and the Gospel of Efficiency*, 36. On the land base of the Forest Service, see Merrill, *Public Lands and Political Meaning*, 29.

66. Skowroneck, *Building a New American State*, 184; Bruce Schulman, "Governing Nature, Nurturing Government: Resource Management and the Development of the American State, 1900–1912," *Journal of Policy History* 17, no. 4 (2005): 383. On the birth of the Department of Agriculture, see Carpenter, *The Forging of Bureaucratic Autonomy*, 180; Courtney Fullilove, *The Profit of the Earth: The Global Seeds of American Agriculture* (Chicago: University of Chicago Press, 2017).

67. Carpenter, *The Forging of Bureaucratic Autonomy*, 1; Schulman, "Governing Nature, Nurturing Government," 383; Skowroneck, *Building a New American State*, 190.

68. Carpenter, *The Forging of Bureaucratic Autonomy*, 53–55

69. Schulman, "Governing Nature, Nurturing Government," 389. Emphasis added.

70. *Annual Report of the Secretary of the Interior for the Fiscal Year ending June 1, 1906* (Washington, DC: USGPO, 1906), 4.

71. Paul Sabin, *Crude Politics: The California Oil Market, 1900–1940* (Berkeley: University of California Press, 2005), 19; Jacobson, *Barbarian Virtues*, 19–20.

72. Moreover, although the first Secretary of the Interior under Roosevelt, Ethan Hitchcock, initially resisted key facets of conservationism, the appointment of James R. Garfield to the post in 1907 lent crucial support at the top of the organizational chart.

Garfield, the son of a former president and a member of the Keep Commission, became a an ally of Gifford Pinchot. Hays, *Conservation and the Gospel of Efficiency,* 7–9, 61, 72; on the funds, see Carpenter, 326.

73. Tyrrell, *Crisis of the Wasteful Nation,* 234–240.

74. Parillo, *Against the Profit Motive,* 3; Schulman, "Governing Nature, Nurturing Government," 375. On legibility, see James C. Scott, *Seeing Like a State: How Certain Schemes to Improve the Human Condition Have Failed* (New Haven: Yale University Press, 1998).

75. Gifford Pinchot, *Breaking New Ground* (New York: Harcourt, Brace and Company, 1947), 23. Emphasis added.

76. See Donald Worster, *Rivers of Empire: Water, Aridity, and the Growth of the American West* (New York: Oxford University Press, 1992).

77. Rare works examining the connections between empire and expansion include Tyrrell, *The Crisis of the Wasteful Nation;* Donna Haraway, "Teddy Bear Patriarchy: Taxidermy in the Garden of Eden, New York City, 1908–1936," in *Cultures of United States Imperialism,* ed. Amy Kaplan and Donald Pease (Durham: Duke University Press, 1993), 237–291; and Greg Bankoff, "Breaking New Ground? Gifford Pinchot and the Birth of 'Empire Forestry' in the Philippines, 1900–1905," *Environment and History* 15, no. 3 (August 2009): 369–393. Tyrrell focuses on the intellectual lineage of conservation rather than its institutional and procedural sources.

78. The distance between disposal and conservation was not always as clear as the debates suggested. See Schulman, "Governing Nature, Nurturing Government," 389.

79. Obituary, "Dr. George F. Becker Dead: Member of Geological Survey Since 1879," *Washington Post,* April 12, 1919, p. 12; George F. Becker, *Summary of the Geology of the Quicksilver Deposits of the Pacific Slope* (Washington, DC: USGPO, 1896).

80. George F. Becker, "Conditions Requisite to Our Success in the Philippine Islands," *Bulletin of the American Geographical Society* 33, no. 2 (1901): 112–123.

81. Theodore Roosevelt to George Becker, September 6, 1899, Folder: Becker–T. Roosevelt Correspondence, box 21, Papers of George F. Becker, Manuscripts Division, Library of Congress, Washington, DC.

82. *Annual Report of the United States Geological Survey to the Secretary of the Interior, 1899–1900* (Washington, DC: USGPO, 1900), 56.

83. Ibid., 54.

84. Walter L. Williams, "United States Indian Policy and the Debate over Philippine Annexation: Implications for the Origins of American Imperialism," *Journal of American History* 66, no. 4 (March 1980): 817. On the contingency of racial forms, see Paul Kramer, *The Blood of Government: Race, Empire, the United States, and the Philippines* (Chapel Hill: University of North Carolina Press, 2007).

85. George F. Becker, "Civil Governor of the Philippines Islands, June 10, 1903," Folder: Philippine Commission, box 24, Papers of George F. Becker, Manuscripts Division, Library of Congress, Washington, DC. Genevieve Clutario charts the influence of the Bureau of Indian Affairs on the Bureau of Education in the Philippines; see "The Appearance of Filipina Nationalism: Body, Nation, Empire," PhD dissertation, University of Illinois at Urbana-Champaign, 2014.

86. *Annual Report of the United States Geological Survey to the Secretary of the Interior, 1899–1900*, 54.

87. See Jacobson, *Barbarian Virtues*, 18–21; Tyrrell, *Crisis of the Wasteful Nation*, 45–7. On territory, natural resources, and the scramble for Africa as markers of America's supposedly exceptional empire, see Thomas Bender, "The American Way of Empire," *World Policy Journal* (Spring 2006): 45–61.

88. "Mineral Resources of Porto Rico: Clays and Stone," *Brick* 11, no. 1 (July 1, 1899): 29.

89. Carl Schurz, "For the Republic of Washington and Lincoln: An Address Delivered at the Philadelphia Conference," February 22, 1900 (Chicago: American Anti-Imperialist League, 1900); "Anti-Imperialists in Mass Meeting," *New York Times*, May 25, 1900, p. 1.

90. George F. Becker, "Are the Philippines Worth Having?" *Scribners* 27 (1900): 748; George F. Becker, *Brief Memorandum on the Geology of the Philippines* (Washington, DC: USGPO, 1899), 7.

91. Becker claimed the only meaningful competitor in the region came from China. Becker, "Are the Philippines Worth Having?," 744–746.

92. George F. Becker, "Conditions Requisite to Our Success in the Philippine Islands," *Bulletin of the American Geographical Society* 33, no. 2 (1901): 112–123, at 120–121, 123.

93. George Becker to Theodore Roosevelt, August 27, 1900, Folder: Becker–T. Roosevelt Correspondence, box 21, Papers of George F. Becker, Manuscripts Division, Library of Congress, Washington, DC.

94. *Annual Report of the United States Geological Survey to the Secretary of the Interior, 1899–1900*, 54.

95. Becker, "Are the Philippines Worth Having?," 748.

96. Ibid., 744.

97. Ibid., 748.

98. Becker, "Conditions Requisite to Our Success in the Philippine Islands."

99. George F. Becker, "De Como Tratan á los Indios en la America del Norte," *Filipina Republica*, December 17, 1898, 2. Translation mine. On the Osage murders, see Alexandra Harmon, *Rich Indians: Native People and the Problem of Wealth* (Chapel Hill: University of North Carolina Press, 2010), chap. 5.

100. Becker, "De Como Tratan á los Indios en la America del Norte." On the genocide of California Indians, see Madley, *An American Genocide*, 2–3.

101. In Wood's fifteen-volume report on the state of Cuba, the geological reconnaissance of the island was the only nonmilitary report to be featured in the first installment. C. Willard Hayes, "Report on a Geological Reconnaissance of Cuba," in Leonard Wood, *Civil Report of the Military Governor, 1901*, Vol. I (Washington: USGPO, 1902), 6.

102. Ibid., 69.

103. The other American-owned companies were the Spanish-American Iron Company and the Juragua Iron Company. Hayes, "Report on a Geological Reconnaissance of Cuba," 70–71. See also Bethlehem Steel Corporation Annual Report, 1905, 8, *America's Corporate Foundation*, ProQuest Historical Annual Reports; Bethlehem Steel

Corporation Annual Report, 1917, 16, *America's Corporate Foundation,* ProQuest Historical Annual Reports.

104. After the outbreak of hostilities between the Spanish and the Cubans, the companies maintained "neutrality" and stayed in operation until the U.S. declaration of war. Hayes, "Report on a Geological Reconnaissance of Cuba," in Wood, *Civil Report of the Military Governor, 1901,* 72.

105. David T. Day, "Mineral Resource of Cuba in 1901 for Brigadier-General Leonard Wood," prepared by Harriet Connor Brown (Baltimore: Guggenheier Weil &Co: 1902), 7.

106. Ibid., 8.

107. Ibid., 8–9.

108. Ibid., 8.

109. Ibid., 7.

110. George F. Becker, *Scientific Surveys of the Philippine Islands* (Washington, DC: USGPO, 1903), 3–4.

111. "Coal for Alaska Gold Fields," *New York Times,* September 4, 1901, p. 8; Ruth Hampton to Gilbert Leisinger, January 5, 1944, Folder: Industries—Mining and Minerals—Chromite, box 755, Records of the Office of Territories, NARA.

112. Bankoff, "Breaking New Ground?," 370.

113. Day, "Mineral Resource of Cuba in 1901," 7.

114. Canada was also distinct in its ongoing ties to the British commonwealth, which simultaneously extended its reach across the globe. Canadian firms, moreover, have a decidedly global presence. On the closing of the Canadian Interior Department, see Irene M. Spry and Bennett McCardle, *The Records of the Department of the Interior and Research Concerning Canada's Western Frontier of Settlement* (Regina, SK: Canadian Plains Research Center, 1993), 3.

115. Ibid., 9.

116. LaFeber rather used them to signal a bundling of political and economic interests. See LaFeber, *The New Empire,* 67. This is not to reinforce the Weberian vision of bureaucracy begetting bureaucracy, but rather historical contingency and forks in the road. On Weber and the American state, see Schulman, "Governing Nature, Nurturing Government," 375.

2 · New Jewels in the Crown of American Empire

1. Ernest Gruening, *Many Battles: The Autobiography of Ernest Gruening* (New York: Liveright, 1973), 245. For a vivid account of the accumulating environmental and social impacts of Kennecott's exploitation of the mountain, see William Cronon, "Kennecott Journey: The Paths out of Town," *Under an Open Sky: Rethinking America's Western Past,* ed. William Cronon, George Miles, and Jay Gitlin (New York: W. W. Norton, 1992), 32–43.

2. Gruening, *Many Battles,* 218–221.

3. Brooke L. Blower develops this argument in "From Isolationism to Neutrality: A New Framework for Understanding American Political Culture, 1919–1941," *Diplomatic History* 38, no. 2 (2014): 345–376.

4. Department of the Interior, "Interior 100 Years Old," February 27, 1949, Folder: 1949, box 5945, Publicity and Public Relations, RG 70, NARA.

5. Harold Ickes, "2nd Draft," undated, Folder: Article for the Journal of the Izaak Walton League, box 105, Secretary of the Interior Files, Papers of Harold L. Ickes, Manuscripts Division, Library of Congress, Washington, DC.

6. Analyses of U.S. imperialism include Paul Kramer, *The Blood of Government: Race, Empire, the United States, and the Philippines* (Chapel Hill: University of North Carolina Press, 2007); Matthew Frye Jacobson, *Barbarian Virtues: The United States Encounters Foreign Peoples at Home and Abroad, 1876–1917* (New Haven: Yale University Press, 2000); Eric T. Love, *Race over Empire: Racism and U.S. Imperialism, 1865–1900* (Chapel Hill: University of North Carolina Press, 2004). Analyses of modernization and development that consider this earlier time period include David Ekbladh, *Great American Mission: Modernization and the Construction of an American World Order* (Princeton: Princeton University Press, 2010); Nick Cullather, *The Hungry World: America's Cold War Battle Against Poverty in Asia* (Cambridge: Harvard University Press, 2010).

7. Paul Sabin, *Crude Politics: The California Oil Market, 1900–1940* (Berkeley: University of California Press, 2005), 30.

8. Daniel Yergin, *The Prize: The Epic Quest for Oil, Money, and Power* (New York: Simon & Schuster, 1991), 212–213.

9. Tyler Priest, *Global Gambits: Big Steel and the U.S. Quest for Manganese* (New York: Praeger, 2003).

10. David H. Stratton, *Tempest over Teapot Dome: The Story of Albert B. Fall* (Norman: University of Oklahoma Press, 1998), 21.

11. Mark T. Gilderhus, "Senator Albert B. Fall and the 'Plot against Mexico,'" *New Mexico Historical Review* 48, no. 4 (1973): 304.

12. On Doheny's ties with Fall in Mexico, see Stratton, *Tempest over Teapot Dome*, 23. On Doheny and Sinclair, see Yergin, *The Prize*, 212–213, 229. On the murders of Osage peoples at the hands of white Americans desirous of the titles to oil lands and with the help of Indian officials, see Alexandra Harmon, *Rich Indians: Native People and the Problem of Wealth* (Chapel Hill, NC: University of North Carolina Press, 2010), chap. 5.

13. Stratton, *Tempest over Teapot Dome*, 5.

14. Jeremy Mouat and Ian Phimister, "The Engineering of Herbert Hoover," *Pacific Historical Review* 77, no. 4 (November 2008): 581; Steven Tuffnell, "Engineering Inter-Imperialism: American Miners and the Transformation of Global Mining, 1871–1910," *Journal of Global History* 10, no. 1 (2015): 53–76.

15. On Hoover's associational state and the oil industry, see David Painter, *Oil and the American Century: Political Economy and American Foreign Oil Policy, 1941–1954* (Baltimore: Johns Hopkins University Press, 1986).

16. See Erich Zimmerman, *World Resources and Industries: A Functional Appraisal of the Availability of Agricultural and Industrial Resources* (New York: Harper & Brothers, 1933).

17. Graham White and John Maze, *Harold Ickes of the New Deal: His Private Life and Public Career* (Cambridge: Harvard University Press, 1985), 104.

18. Allen Brinkley, *The End of Reform: New Deal Liberalism in Recession and War* (New York: Alfred A. Knopf, 1995).

19. *Annual Report of the Secretary of the Interior for the Fiscal Year Ending June 1, 1936* (Washington, DC: USGPO, 1936), xvii.

20. Neil Maher, *Nature's New Deal: The Civilian Conservation Corps and the Roots of the American Environmental Movement* (New York: Oxford University Press, 2009).

21. Statement by Ickes, May 2, 1937, Folder: Pinchot Ickes Controversy, box 226, Secretary of the Interior Files, Papers of Harold L. Ickes, Manuscripts Division, Library of Congress, Washington, DC.

22. Ickes, "Gifford Pinchot," undated, Folder: Article for the Journal of the Izaak Walton League, box 105, Secretary of the Interior Files, Papers of Harold L. Ickes, Manuscripts Division, Library of Congress, Washington, DC.

23. Harold Ickes, "Save Our Natural Resources," *The Democratic Digest* April 1938, Folder: Articles: "Save Our National Resources," box 105, Secretary of the Interior Files, Papers of Harold L. Ickes, Manuscripts Division, Library of Congress, Washington, DC.

24. Quoted in Karen Merrill, *Public Lands and Political Meaning: Ranchers, the Government, and the Property between Them* (Berkeley: University of California Press, 2002), 175.

25. *Annual Report from the Secretary of the Interior, Fiscal Year ended June 30, 1931* (Washington, DC: USGPO, 1931), 26, and *Annual Report from the Secretary of the Interior, Fiscal Year ended June 30, 1934,* 309.

26. *Annual Report from the Secretary of the Interior, Fiscal Year ended June 30, 1933* (Washington, DC: USGPO, 1933), vi.

27. On Ickes's self-appointment to petroleum administrator, see White and Maze, *Harold Ickes of the New Deal,* 120. On the transition from coal to oil as the main energy source in America and the world, see David Painter, "Oil and the American Century," *Journal of American History* 99 (June 2012): 24–40; Timothy Mitchell, *Carbon Democracy: Political Power in the Age of Oil* (New York: Verso Press, 2011), 5–7.

28. Sabin, *Crude Politics,* 147.

29. White and Maze, *Harold Ickes and the New Deal,* 116. Nevertheless, years later, Ickes would build from this previous platform to dictate rationing, production quotas, and other restrictions, righteously blaming wartime shortages on his detractors and their shortsightedness.

30. Sabin, *Crude Politics,* 148.

31. Ibid., 148.

32. Quoted in Robert David Johnson, *Ernest Gruening and the American Dissenting Tradition* (Cambridge: Belknap, 1998), 121.

33. On Mexican oil, see Ernest Gruening, *Many Battles,* 107. On Middle Eastern oil, see Robert Vitalis, *America's Kingdom: Mythmaking on the Saudi Oil Frontier* (London: Verso, 2008), 63–68, 77–85.

34. The President's Reorganization Plan No. 2 of July 1, 1939, transferred the Philippines from the Department of War to DTIP. A series of executive orders added

Canton and Enderbury Islands to DTIP and transferred Guam and American Samoa from the navy to DTIP. See Johnson, *Ernest Gruening and the American Dissenting Tradition*, 114.

35. Department of the Interior, "Interior 100 Years Old," February 27, 1949, Folder: 1949, box 5945, Publicity and Public Relations, RG 70, NARA.

36. Love, *Race over Empire*, xviii.

37. Penny von Eschen, *Race Against Empire: Black Americans and Anticolonialism, 1937–1957* (Ithaca: Cornell University Press), 1–4; Thomas Borstelmann, *Apartheid's Reluctant Uncle: The United States and Southern Africa in the Early Cold War* (New York: Oxford University Press, 1993), 12–14; Frederik Logevall, *Embers of War: The Fall of an Empire and the Making of America's Vietnam* (New York: Random House, 2014), 12–19; Charles A. Beard, *The Idea of National Interest: An Analytical Study in American Foreign Policy* (New York: Macmillan, 1934).

38. See Johnson, *Ernest Gruening and the American Dissenting Tradition*, 1.

39. Gruening, *Many Battles*, 158–159.

40. Ibid., 170.

41. Ernest Gruening, "Our Era of 'Imperialism' Nears its End," *New York Times*, June 10, 1934, p. SM4. Emphasis added.

42. Ibid.

43. Gruening, *Many Battles*, 181. Really, Roosevelt hoped that the new DTIP director would help bolster support among anti-imperialists at "minimal political cost," as one historian has claimed. Johnson, *Ernest Gruening and the American Dissenting Tradition*, 123.

44. Gruening, *Many Battles*, 68. Arthur Conan Doyle, *The Crime of the Congo* (New York: Doubleday, Page & Company, 1909), 46–55, 75–80. On the abolitionists, human rights activists, and missionaries who used mass culture to bring the atrocities of the Congo to light, see Kevin Grant, *A Civilized Savagery: Britain and the New Slaveries in Africa, 1884–1926* (New York: Taylor & Francis Books, 2005), 39–78.

45. Gail Bederman, *Manliness and Civilization: A Cultural History of Gender and Race in the United States, 1880–1917* (Chicago: University of Chicago Press, 1996).

46. Kramer, *The Blood of Government*, 219–220.

47. Ernest Gruening edits of Harold Ickes, "Alaska as a Reality," 1938?, Folder: "Alaska as a Reality," box 105, Secretary of the Interior Files, Papers of Harold L. Ickes, Manuscripts Division, Library of Congress, Washington, DC. Emphasis added.

48. Terrence M. Cole, "Jim Crow in Alaska: The Passage of the Alaska Equal Rights Act of 1945," *Western Historical Quarterly* 23 (1992): 429–449.

49. See *Ernest Gruening and the American Dissenting Tradition*, 49.

50. Memo from Ernest Gruening to Harold Ickes, March 13, 1936, Folder: Puerto Rico 2, box 255, Secretary of the Interior Files, Papers of Harold L. Ickes, Manuscripts Division, Library of Congress, Washington, DC.

51. E. K. Burlew to Harold Ickes, June 3, 1937, Folder: Puerto Rico 8, box 257, Secretary of the Interior Files, Papers of Harold L. Ickes, Manuscripts Division, Library of Congress, Washington, DC. See also Daniel Immerwahr, "The Greater United States: Territory and Empire in US History," *Diplomatic History* 40, no. 3 (2016): 373–374.

52. Ickes, "Let's be fair to PR," undated, Folder: Puerto Rico 8, box 257, Secretary of the Interior Files, Papers of Harold L. Ickes, Manuscripts Division, Library of Congress, Washington, DC.

53. *Annual Report from the Secretary of the Interior, Fiscal Year ended June 30, 1933* (Washington, DC: USGPO, 1933), 68.

54. He would eventually claim that God "made no distinction of race, or creed, or color." See White and Maze, *Harold Ickes and the New Deal*, 1. He also oversaw the employment of over 1,000 African Americans; see Harold Ickes, "Should Negroes Quit Roosevelt?" 1944, Folder: "Negro Digest," box 116, Secretary of the Interior Files, Papers of Harold L. Ickes, Manuscripts Division, Library of Congress, Washington, DC.

55. On the Wheeler-Howard Act and John Collier's advocacy on behalf of indigenous sovereignty, see Daniel M. Cobb, "American Indian Politics in Cold War America: Parallel & Contradiction," *Princeton University Library Chronicle* LXVII, no. 2 (Winter 2006): 400; Paul C. Rosier, *Serving Their Country: American Indian Politics and Patriotism in the Twentieth Century* (Cambridge: Harvard University Press, 2012), 73.

56. Marjane Ambler, *Breaking the Iron Bonds: Indian Control of Energy Development* (Lawrence: University of Kansas Press, 1991), 16–17.

57. For example, in one report Collier remarked upon Native Americans' intrinsic tendency to be happy in adversity, a quality he condescendingly feared would cut against the life-saving efforts of the federal government. See *Annual Report from the Secretary of the Interior, Fiscal Year ended June 30, 1935* (Washington, DC: USGPO, 1935), 113.

58. Harold L. Ickes, "Puerto Rico," August 27, 1935, Folder: Puerto Rico 1, box 255, Secretary of the Interior Files, Papers of Harold L. Ickes, Manuscripts Division, Library of Congress, Washington, DC.

59. Memorandum for Secretary of the Interior, July 7, 1936, Folder: Surveys Geological & Topographical—General, box 340, Records of the Office of Territories, NARA.

60. Gruening, *Many Battles*, 194.

61. *Annual Report from the Secretary of the Interior, Fiscal Year ended June 30, 1941* (Washington, DC: USGPO, 1941), 461; the appropriation was $177 million. See "Interior Bill Reported," *New York Times*, May 1, 1941, p. 12.

62. William Atherton Du Puy, "Exploring Alaskan Wilds," *National Republic* (February 1929): 15. The Geological Survey had sent individuals to investigate deposits in this earlier period but did not have a systematized collection of data until 1905. See Philip Smith, *Past Lode-Gold Production from Alaska* (Washington, DC: USGPO, 1938), 163, 168.

63. "Senate Group Votes $522,857,808 for Navy," *New York Times*, March 19, 1937, p. 3; "War Bill Sets Up Mineral Preserve: May's Measure Would Stimulate Output Here of Needed 'Strategic Metals,'" *New York Times*, January 21, 1939, p. 7; U.S. Bureau of Mines, *Mineral Raw Materials: Survey of Commerce and Sources in Major Industrial Countries* (New York: McGraw-Hill, 1937).

64. "Senate Group Votes $522,857,808 for Navy," *New York Times*; "War Bill Sets up Mineral Preserve," *New York Times*.

65. See *Annual Report from the Secretary of the Interior, Fiscal Year ended June 30, 1939* (Washington, DC: USGPO, 1939), 232.

66. Ibid.

67. Charles Hines to Harold Ickes, October 5, 1939, Folder: Industry—Minerals—Mining, box 884, Records of the Office of Territories, NARA; Public No 117—76th Congress, Chapter 190—1st Session (S. 572), Folder: Industry—Minerals—Mining, box 884, Records of the Office of Territories, NARA.

68. Harold Ickes, unnamed article beginning "Were I called upon . . . ," p. 1, Folder: Articles—Miscellaneous Articles on Oil, box 120, Secretary of the Interior Files, Papers of Harold L. Ickes, Secretary of the Interior Files, Manuscripts Division, Library of Congress, Washington, DC. Ickes made such statements undoubtedly to justify the period of rationing that American consumers had to endure. Harold Ickes, unnamed article beginning "Just as will be the case . . . ," p. 1, Folder: Articles—Miscellaneous Articles on Oil, box 120, Secretary of the Interior Files, Papers of Harold L. Ickes, Secretary of the Interior Files, Manuscripts Division, Library of Congress, Washington, DC.

69. Ickes, "Oil at War," July 20, 1940, Folder: Articles: "Oil at War," box 112, Secretary of the Interior Files, Papers of Harold L. Ickes, Manuscripts Division, Library of Congress, Washington, DC.

70. Charles Hines to Harold Ickes, October 5, 1939, Folder: Industry—Minerals—Mining, box 884, Records of the Office of Territories, NARA; Public No 117—76th Congress, Chapter 190—1st Session (S. 572), Folder: Industry—Minerals—Mining, box 884, Records of the Office of Territories, NARA.

71. Ernest Gruening to Anthony Dimond, May 13, 1939, Folder: Surveys Geological & Topographical—Legislation-General, box 340, Records of the Office of Territories, NARA. On "virgin" land, see Memorandum from Philip Smith on the Geological Survey's program in Alaska development, January 10, 1934, Folder: Surveys Geological & Topographical-General, box 340, Records of the Office of Territories, NARA.

72. Harriet Connor Brown transcribed David T. Day, "Mineral Resources of Cuba in 1901 for Brigadier-General Leonard Wood" (Baltimore: Guggenheier Weil & Co, 1902), and Martha Hallman joined a team of women who supported Philip Smith and the Alaskan Branch with mapmaking as seen in "Alaskan Geologists in World War II," Prints and Photographs, Library of Congress, Washington, DC. Feminist Marxist critics have long noted the discursive connections between "virgin" women and land, which underscored metaphors and tactics of rape in conquest. See the introduction of Anne McClintock, *Imperial Leather: Race, Gender and Sexuality in the Colonial Contest* (New York: Routledge, 1995).

73. Programs recounted in *Annual Report from the Secretary of the Interior, 1941,* 99.

74. Ibid.

75. House Joint Memorial No. 57 In the Legislature of the Territory of Alaska, March 10, 1937, Folder: Development of Resources, Tin, box 427, Records of the Office of Territories, NARA.

76. *Annual Report from the Secretary of the Interior, 1941, 467.*

77. "Capital Advised to Develop Alaska," *New York Times,* August 16, 1939, p. 7.

78. "Vast Development of Minerals Urged," *New York Times*, February 16, 1942, p. 34.

79. Memorandum to Governor William Leahy, "Manganese Production in Puerto Rico," September 15, 1939, Folder: Industry—Minerals—Mining, box 884, Records of the Office of Territories, NARA; William Leahy to Harold Ickes, September 20, 1939, Folder: Industry—Minerals—Mining, box 884, Records of the Office of Territories, NARA; Ernest Gruening to William Leahy, October 10, 1939, Folder: Industry—Minerals—Mining, box 884, Records of the Office of Territories, National Archives and Records Administration, College Park, MD; Ernest Gruening to W. C. Mendenall, USGS, October 10, 1939, Folder: Industry—Minerals—Mining, box 884, Records of the Office of Territories, NARA.

80. John Van N. Dorr, USGS, Report on a Reconnaissance of the Manganese Deposits of Puerto Rico, 1943, p. 1, Folder: Minerals and Mining, box 884, Records of the Office of Territories, NARA.

81. R. R. Sayers to B. W. Thoron, June 28, 1943, Folder: Minerals and Mining, box 884, Records of the Office of Territories, NARA.

82. B. W. Thoron to Teodoro Moscoso, Jr., May 27, 1943, Folder: Minerals and Mining, box 884, Records of the Office of Territories, NARA.

83. Teodoro Moscoso to B. W. Thoron, May 11, 1943, Folder: Minerals and Mining, box 884, Records of the Office of Territories, NARA.

84. John Van N. Dorr, USGS, Report on a Reconnaissance of the Manganese Deposits of Puerto Rico, 1943, Folder: Minerals and Mining, box 884, Records of the Office of Territories, NARA.

85. Courtney Whitney to the Secretary of the Navy, September 18, 1937, box 2553, Foreign Issues, Records of the Bureau of Mines, NARA. Emphasis added.

86. Ruth Hampton to Gilbert Leisinger, January 5, 1944, Folder: Industries—Mining and Minerals—Chromite, box 755, Records of the Office of Territories, NARA. ("Of importations, 8 percent came from our possessions in the Orient, the balance being made up from South Africa, Turkey, India, Cuba, and New Caledonia.")

87. Oil, Paint, and Drug Reporter Washington Bureau, Strategic Materials Stock-Pile inventoried, January 13, 1941, Folder: Chromite—General, box 4, Records Concerning Strategic Minerals, 1940–1950, Records of the Geological Survey (RG 57), NARA. Chrome ore ordered: 25,000 L.T. ordered from Alaska (compared to 20,000 Turkey, 19,500 Rhodesia); 31,500 from the Philippines (compared to 27,500 from Cuba, 7,500 from the US, and 20,000 from India).

88. Ruth Hampton to Gilbert Leisinger, January 5, 1944. Ruth Hampton, assistant director for the Division of Territories and Island Possessions, was one of few women in leadership roles in the department and overseeing minerals.

89. Courtney Whitney to the Secretary of the Navy, September 18, 1937. Whitney explained the company invested 1.5 million pesos in developing the chromite in "the largest known single mass of the material in the world."

90. L. R. Nielson, Nielson and Company, to High Commissioner, PI, July 10, 1941, Folder: Industries—Mining and Minerals—Copper, box 755, Records of the Office of Territories, NARA.

91. Richard Ely to Colonel McDonald, August 31, 1942, Folder: Industries—Mining and Minerals—Copper, box 755, Records of the Office of Territories, NARA.

92. Parsons's report was then circulated to Interior and other departments. See J. Bartlett Richards, "Conditions in Philippines after Japanese Occupation," September 2, 1942, Folder: Philippines 1, box 226, Secretary of the Interior Files, Papers of Harold L. Ickes, Manuscripts Division, Library of Congress, Washington, DC.

93. DOI Memo by Undersecretary Fortas for Files, December 5, 1942, Folder: Philippines 1, box 226, Secretary of the Interior Files, Papers of Harold L. Ickes, Manuscripts Division, Library of Congress, Washington, DC.

94. Ruth Hampton to Gilbert Leisinger, January 5, 1944. Hampton's report also noted how the chairman of Consolidated Mining Company had placed its properties "unreservedly at the disposal of the American government."

95. Harold Ickes to FDR, June 2, 1941, Folder: Puerto Rico 6, box 256, Secretary of the Interior Files, Papers of Harold L. Ickes, Manuscripts Division, Library of Congress, Washington, DC.

96. Ickes to John Lord, January 25, 1945, Folder: Philippines 3, box 226, Secretary of the Interior Files, Papers of Harold L. Ickes, Manuscripts Division, Library of Congress, Washington, DC. The insular case *Downes v. Bidwell* is quoted in Alvita Akiboh, "Pocket-Sized Imperialism: US Designs on Colonial Currency," *Diplomatic History* (March 2017): 875.

97. Philip Smith to George Gates, June 9, 1942, Folder: George C. Gates, box 5, Central Files of the Alaskan Branch, 1899–1947, Records of the Geological Survey, NARA.

98. See Wallace Cady to Kathleen Waldron, June 1, 1944, and Wallace Cady to Kathleen Waldron, September 13, 1944, Folder: Alaskan Branch: Correspondence with Employees (Cady), box 5, Central Files of the Alaskan Branch, 1899–1947, Records of the Geological Survey, NARA.

99. George Gates to Philip Smith, June 5, 1943, Folder: George C. Gates, box 5, Central Files of the Alaskan Branch, 1899–1947, Records of the Geological Survey, NARA.

100. George Gates to Philip Smith, August 6, 1943, Folder: George C. Gates, box 5, Central Files of the Alaskan Branch, 1899–1947, Records of the Geological Survey, NARA.

101. Philip Smith to George Gates, June 9, 1942. Smith explained that with recent strategic mineral appropriations, geologists had more than enough funds and must consequently produce results that would directly aid war plans.

102. Ernest Gruening to Harold Ickes, February 20, 1943, Folder: Development of Resources, Coal, box 385, Records of the Office of Territories, NARA; DE Thomas, DTIP to Swope, "Shipment of coal from the States to Alaska," August 5, 1942, Folder: Development of Resources, Coal, box 385, Records of the Office of Territories, NARA.

103. Juneau Alaska to War, Thoron Territories to Department of Interior, Signed Gruening, Governor of Alaska, June 29, 1943, Folder: Development of Resources, Coal, box 385, Records of the Office of Territories, NARA.

104. Ernest Gruening to Harold Ickes, February 20, 1943. Other efforts to stimulate mining included opening new properties, rehabilitating operating mines, and loans from the Reconstruction Finance Corporation. See George Gates to Philip Smith, August 6, 1943, Folder: George C. Gates, box 5, Central Files of the Alaskan Branch, 1899–1947, Records of the Geological Survey, NARA.

105. B. W. Thoron to War Department, June 29, 1943, Folder: Development of Resources, Coal, box 385, Records of the Office of Territories, NARA.

106. At the time of his transfer to Alaska, Gruening had been to the territory only twice, compared to the sixty trips to Puerto Rico. See Johnson, *Ernest Gruening and the American Dissenting Tradition,* 153–154.

107. Ernest Gruening to Harold Ickes, January 15, 1944, Folder: Development of Resources, Coal, box 385, Records of the Office of Territories, NARA. On temperatures, see Robert S. Sanford and Harold C. Pierce, "Exploration of Coal Deposits of the Point Barrow and Wainwright Areas, Northern Alaska," R.I. 3934 (Washington, DC: USGPO, 1946), 5.

108. Sanford and Pierce, "Exploration of Coal Deposits of the Point Barrow and Wainwright Areas, Northern Alaska," 2; General Superintendent Alaska Indian Affairs, January 3, 1944, Folder: Development of Resources, Coal, box 385, Records of the Office of Territories, NARA.

109. Sanford and Pierce, "Exploration of Coal Deposits of the Point Barrow and Wainwright Areas, Northern Alaska," 6–7.

110. Interior's Fish and Wildlife Service similarly conscripted indigenous locals, including Aleutians dislocated with the Japanese invasion, into coercive labor regimes. See Ryan T. Madden, "The Government's Industry: Alaska Natives and Pribilof Sealing during World War II," *Pacific Northwest Quarterly* 91 (2000): 202–209.

111. See "New Ickes Grab for Power Stirs Alaskans' Fears," April 11, 1941, and "Alaska Piles up its Grievances Against Ickes," *Reno Gazette,* April 2, 1941, Folder: Alaska 1934–1941, box 93, Secretary of the Interior Files, Papers of Harold L. Ickes, Manuscripts Division, Library of Congress, Washington, DC. See also George Tagge, "Alaskan Blasts Propaganda by Secretary Ickes," *Chicago Tribune,* April 14, 1941, Folder: Alaska 1934–1941, box 93, Secretary of the Interior Files, Papers of Harold L. Ickes, Manuscripts Division, Library of Congress, Washington, DC; Golden Zone Mining Company to Ernest Gruening, April 20, 1942, Folder: Development of Resources, Coal, box 385, Records of the Office of Territories, NARA.

112. Ernest Gruening to Harold Ickes, April 21, 1941, Folder: Alaska 1934–1941, box 93, Secretary of the Interior Files, Papers of Harold L. Ickes, Manuscripts Division, Library of Congress, Washington, DC.

113. These cynics included a store of Interior Department officials who protested that General MacArthur had used his power to arrange a post-independence rule by a corrupt ruling class. Harold Ickes, "The Philippines Comes of Age," Folder: Philippines 3, box 226, Secretary of the Interior Files, Papers of Harold L. Ickes, Manuscripts Division, Library of Congress, Washington, DC.

114. Ibid.

115. These modest efforts to locate saleable wells laid a groundwork for the discovery of the Swanson River oil field in the Kenai Peninsula, which would catalyze a new bonanza in the region in the next decade, attracting major oil companies Richfield, Philips, Marathon, Unocal, Shell, Mobil, Chevron, and Texaco. Field activities of the Geological Survey in Alaska, Season of 1946, Folder: Surveys Geological & Topographical-General, box 340, Records of the Office of Territories, NARA.

116. Sanford and Pierce, "Exploration of Coal Deposits of the Point Barrow and Wain-wright Areas, Northern Alaska," 2; Alan Probert to C. E. Bartlett, December 6, 1954, Folder: Cuba, box 7205, Technical Assistance (026), RG 70, NARA. According to an Interior publication, the Afghan cabinet said that Sanford's contribution was "the finest thing the United States has ever done for Afghanistan." See *Point 4 in Action: The Interior Department's Role* (Washington, DC: USGPO, 1950), 8.

3 · The Treasure of the Western Hemisphere

1. The Compañia Minera de Oruro, owned by the German tin baron Moritz Hochs-child, was one ally. See *Compañia Minera de Oruro* (Santiago: Imprenta Chile, 1940), Folder: Oruro District, 1940s, box 3, General Materials 1924–1988, Papers of Eu-gene Callaghan, Manuscripts Division, Marriott Library, University of Utah, Salt Lake City, UT; Eugene Callaghan, "Tin Resources of the Santa Teresa Placer, negro Pabellón District Bolivia," 1941, p. 1, Folder: Writings, box 6, General Materials 1924–1988, Papers of Eugene Callaghan, Manuscripts Division, Marriott Library, University of Utah, Salt Lake City, UT.

2. Eugene Callaghan, "Tin Resources of the Llallagua District Bolivia," 1941, p. 7, box 6, General Materials 1924–1988, Papers of Eugene Callaghan, Manuscripts Division, Marriott Library, University of Utah, Salt Lake City, UT.

3. On American intervention and capitalist development in Latin America and the Caribbean, see Greg Grandin, *A Century of Revolution: Insurgent and Counterin-surgent Violence During Latin America's Long Cold War* (Durham: Duke Univer-sity Press, 2010); Greg Grandin, *Empire's Workshop: Latin America, the United States, and the Rise of the New Imperialism* (New York: Metropolitan Books, 2006); Greg Grandin, *Fordlandia: The Rise and Fall of Henry Ford's Forgotten Jungle City* (New York: Picador, 2009); Elizabeth A. Cobbs, *The Rich Neighbor Policy: Rockefeller and Kaiser in Brazil* (New Haven: Yale University Press, 1992); Thomas O'Brien, *The Revolutionary Mission: American Enterprise in Latin Amer-ica* (New York: Cambridge University Press, 1996); Steve Striffler, *In the Shadows of State and Capital* (Durham: Duke University Press, 2002); Peter H. Smith, *Talons of the Eagle: Dynamics of US–Latin American Relations* (Oxford: Oxford Univer-sity Press, 1996); Emily S. Rosenberg, *Financial Missionaries to the World: The Politics and Culture of Dollar Diplomacy, 1900–1930* (Cambridge: Harvard Uni-versity Press, 1999); Mary A. Renda, *Taking Haiti: Military Occupation and the Culture of U.S. Imperialism* (Chapel Hill: University of North Carolina Press, 2001); Jason Colby, *The Business of Empire: United Fruit, Race, and U.S. Expan-sion in Central America* (Ithaca: Cornell University Press, 2012); April Merleaux, *Sugar and Civilization: American Empire and the Cultural Politics of Sweetness* (Chapel Hill: University of North Carolina Press, 2015), 1–27.

4. On the Monroe Doctrine in U.S. history, see Jay Sexton, *The Monroe Doctrine: Em-pire and Nation in Nineteenth Century America* (New York: Hill and Wang, 2012).

5. Charles Kenneth Leith, "Minerals and the Monroe Doctrine," *Proceedings of the Eighth American Scientific Congress, Held in Washington May 10–18, 1940* (Wash-ington, DC: USGPO, 1942), 649–650.

6. Daniel Yergin, *The Prize: The Epic Quest for Oil, Money and Power* (New York: Free Press, 1993); Stephen Krasner, *Defending National Interest: Raw Materials Investments and U.S. Foreign Policy* (Princeton: Princeton University Press, 1978); Alfred Eckes, *The United States and the Global Struggle for Minerals* (Austin: University of Texas Press, 1979). On the arsenal of democracy, see A. J. Brown, *The Arsenal of Democracy* (London: Oxford University Press, 1941) and Julian Zelizer, *Arsenal of Democracy: The Politics of National Security from World War II to the War on Terrorism* (New York: Basic Books, 2009). On pro-tariff sentiments after the First World War, see Tyler Priest, *Global Gambits: Big Steel and the U.S. Quest for Manganese* (New York: Praeger, 2003), 121. Priest acknowledges the role of Interior's geological branches in acquiring minerals under the Interdepartmental Committee on Scientific and Cultural Cooperation, though he understates the importance of the framework of cooperation to these activities. See Priest, *Global Gambits,* chap. 3.

7. It constituted a long-held community value shared by officials and workers alike, both of whom were spearheading the movement against outside exploitation. Thomas O'Brien, *The Revolutionary Mission: American Enterprise in Latin America* (New York: Cambridge University Press, 1996), 5.

8. In the realm of energy, the U.S. consumed 86 percent of the coal, oil, and water power of the Western Hemisphere, and 54 percent when compared to the entire world. Charles Kenneth Leith, "Minerals and the Monroe Doctrine," *Proceedings of the Eighth American Scientific Congress, Held in Washington May 10–18, 1940* (Washington, DC: USGPO, 1942), 649.

9. American Scientific Congress, *Eighth American Scientific Congress, Washington, DC, May 10–18, 1940, Vol. I* (Washington, DC: USGPO, 1940), 11.

10. Pan American Union, *Bulletin of the Pan American Union, Volume LXXIV* (Washington, DC: USGPO, 1940), 514.

11. Justin Hart, *Empire of Ideas: The Origins of Public Diplomacy and the Transformation of U.S. Foreign Policy* (New York: Cambridge University Press, 2013), 3; Grandin, *Empire's Workshop,* 27.

12. Smith, *Talons of the Eagle,* 65–66.

13. On Albert Fall's involvement in Mexico, see Ernest Gruening, *Many Battles: The Autobiography of Ernest Gruening* (New York: Liverlight, 1973), 107. On the Mexican expropriation, see Jonathan C. Brown and Alan Knight, eds., *The Mexican Petroleum Industry in the Twentieth Century* (Austin: University of Texas Press, 1992), xiii.

14. Memorandum from H. Gordon Poole, BOM, to Horace Braun, Attaché, "Minerals Program—Mexico," June 13, 1949, Folder: 1941, box 1, Records Relating to International Aid and Technical Activities, 1941–1952, Records of the Bureau of Mines, NARA.

15. Pan American Union, *Bulletin of the Pan American Union, Volume LXXIV,* 512.

16. Ibid., 526.

17. Ibid., 512.

18. Ibid., 519.

19. Ibid., 515–521.

20. Ibid., 521.

21. Ibid., 527.

22. Leith had been one of a cohort of geologists in World War I who helped centralize minerals in global relations. He was joined by George Otis Smith, a Geological Survey director, and Josiah E. Spurr, the president of the Mining and Metallurgical Society of America. See Eckes, *The United States and the Global Struggle for Minerals*, 4–5.

23. See U.S. State Department, *Proceedings of the Eighth American Scientific Congress, Held in Washington May 10–18, 1940* (Washington, DC: USGPO, 1941), 113–115. On Everette DeGolyer and James Terry Duce, see Nathan J. Citino, "Internationalist Oilmen, the Middle East, and the Remaking of American Liberalism, 1945–1953," *Business History Review* 84 (Summer 2010): 227–251.

24. The Bureau's foreign mineral specialist traveled to Italy, Germany, Poland, Czechoslovakia, Bulgaria, Rumania, Austria, Hungary, Yugoslavia, and Greece. U.S. Bureau of Mines, *Mineral Raw Materials: Survey of Commerce and Sources in Major Industrial Countries* (New York: McGraw-Hill, 1937); *Annual Report from the Secretary of the Interior, Fiscal Year ended June 30, 1936* (Washington, DC: USGPO, 1936), 135–142.

25. Memo from R. S. Dean to Harold Ickes, May 24, 1943, Folder: Bureau of Mines (4), box 140, Secretary of the Interior Files, Papers of Harold L. Ickes, Manuscripts Division, Library of Congress, Washington, DC.

26. *Annual Report from the Secretary of the Interior, Fiscal Year ended June 30, 1940* (Washington, DC: USGPO, 1940), 30.

27. Ibid., 6.

28. Also in attendance were War Production Board consultant Morris L. Cooke, Undersecretary of Agriculture M. L. Wilson, archaeologist Matthew Wilson, and Tennessee Valley Authority advisor Huston Thompson. See U.S. Office of Indian Affairs, *Final Act of the First Inter-American Conference on Indian Life: Held at Pátzcuaro, State of Michoacán, Mexico, April 14–24, 1940* (Washington, DC: USGPO, 1941), 8.

29. U.S. Office of Indian Affairs, *Final Act of the First Inter-American Conference on Indian Life,* 11. Cárdenas also was in the midst of leading agrarian reforms in Mexico. See Nick Cullather, *The Hungry World: America's Cold War Battle Against Poverty in Asia* (Cambridge: Harvard University Press, 2010), chap. 2.

30. On Leith, see Priest, *Global Gambits,* 136–140, 196; Eckes, *United States and Global Struggle for Minerals,* 191.

31. Leith, for example, served on the War Industries Board in World War I and the President's Materials Policy Commission during the Cold War. Priest, *Global Gambits,* 85.

32. Leith, "Minerals and the Monroe Doctrine," 649–650.

33. Ibid.

34. Pan American Union, *Bulletin of the Pan American Union, Volume LXXIV,* 527. Resolutions were adopted across natural resources, including agricultural ones.

35. O'Brien, *The Revolutionary Mission,* 4.

36. See Department of State, *The Department of State Bulletin: July 1–December 30, 1939,* Vol. 1 (London: Forgotten Books, 1940), 45–46; Pan American Union, *Bulletin of the Pan American Union, Volume LXXIV,* 514.

37. W. C. Mendenhall, "Preface," *Geological Investigations in the American Republics, 1941–1943* (Washington, DC: USGPO, 1947), iii. Emphasis added.

38. Priest, *Global Gambits,* 168–176.

39. *Annual Report from the Secretary of the Interior, Fiscal Year ended June 30, 1941* (Washington, DC: USGPO, 1941), vii, xix.

40. Mendenhall, "Preface," iii; W. D. Johnston, "Speech on History of USGS work in Technical Assistance," before the Geological Society of America, November 14, 1952, box 4, Country Mission Files to Saudi Arabia, Records of the Foreign Assistance Agencies (RG 469), NARA. The Board of Economic Warfare was later reorganized as the Federal Economic Administration.

41. Johnston, "Speech on History of USGS work in Technical Assistance." When Johnston was acting as head of foreign minerals programs in international development in the 1950s, he pursued strategic minerals even when admitting ethical shortcomings.

42. On King, see Robert Wilson, *The Explorer King: Adventure, Science, and the Great Diamond Hoax* (New York: Scribner, 2006), 10–11.

43. E. N. Goddard, L. S. Gardner, and W. S. Burbank, "Manganese Deposits of the Republic of Haiti," *Geologic Investigations in the American Republics, 1945* (Washington, DC: USGPO, 1945), 51; William F. Foshag and Carl Fries, Jr., "Tin Deposits of the Republic of Mexico," *Geologic Investigations in the American Republics, 1941–42* (Washington, DC: USGPO, 1942), 99; William T. Pecora, "Nickel-Silicate and Associated Nickel-Cobalt-Manganese-Oxide Deposits Near São Jose Do Tocantins, Goiaz, Brazil," Bulletin 935-A, *Geologic Investigations in the American Republics, 1941–42* (Washington, DC: USGPO, 1942), 282.

44. See, for example, the bibliography of Eugene Callaghan, which cites work in Utah, Idaho, Oregon, and Nevada. Callaghan, "Tin Resources of the Santa Fé Mine Bolivia," 1941, Folder: Report Tin of Santa Fe Mine, box 2, General Materials 1924–1988, Papers of Eugene Callaghan, Manuscripts Division, Marriott Library, University of Utah, Salt Lake City, UT.

45. *Annual Report from the Secretary of the Interior, Fiscal Year ended June 30, 1941,* 89.

46. Eugene Callaghan, "Tin Resources of the Llallagua District Bolivia," 110. As just one example of this widespread trend, Callaghan, like Robert Sanford before him, referred to the earth as "virgin," in highly gendered terms.

47. Joe Webb Peoples to Francis G. Wells, September 28, 1943, Folder: Chomite [*sic*] Letters to Field Men, box 4, Records Concerning Strategic Minerals, 1940–1940, Misc. Correspondence, 1940–1949, Records of the Geological Survey, NARA.

48. William F. Foshag and Carl Fries, Jr., "Tin Deposits of the Republic of Mexico," *Geologic Investigations in the American Republics, 1941–42* (Washington, DC: USGPO, 1942), 103.

49. Luis Soux, "The Potosi Hill," undated, Folder: Potosi, box 3, General Materials 1924–1988, Papers of Eugene Callaghan, Manuscripts Division, Marriott Library, University of Utah, Salt Lake City, UT.

50. O'Brien, *The Revolutionary Mission,* 4. Rural communities resisted these interventions in their land from violent conquest to hegemonic legal and political regimes.

51. Quentin D. Singewald, "Mineral Resources of Colombia (Other than Petroleum),"
    Geologic Investigations in the American Republics, 1949 (Washington, DC: USGPO,
    1950), 172.

52. Ibid., 61.

53. Peoples to Phil Guild, June 9, 1944, Folder: Chromite—(Outside US) Cuba, box 4,
    Records Concerning Strategic Minerals, 1940–1940, Misc. Correspondence, 1940–
    1949, Records of the Geological Survey, NARA.

54. The company had been owned by German tin baron Moritz Hochschild, but re-
    tained much local control. See Compañia Minera de Oruro (Santiago: Imprenta
    Chile, 1940), Folder: Oruro District, 1940s, box 3, General Materials 1924–1988, Pa-
    pers of Eugene Callaghan, Manuscripts Division, Marriott Library, University of
    Utah, Salt Lake City, UT.

55. William T. Pecora, M. R. Klepper, and D. M. Larrabee, USGS, and A. L. M. Bar-
    bosa and Resk Frayha, Divisão de Fomento, Brazil, *Mica Deposits in Minas Gerais,
    Brazil* (Washington, DC: USGPO, 1950), 207.

56. Singewald, "Mineral Resources of Colombia," 169.

57. Ibid., 172.

58. Phil Guild to T. P. Thayer, December 22, 1942, Folder: Chromite—(Outside US)
    Cuba, box 4, Records Concerning Strategic Minerals, 1940–1940, Misc. Correspon-
    dence, 1940–1949, Records of the Geological Survey, NARA.

59. Michael Taussig, *The Devil and Commodity Fetishism in South America* (Chapel
    Hill: University of North Carolina Press, 1986), 19.

60. Taussig argues that as their way of life was being supplanted through the imposition
    of a system that alienated workers from the produce of their labor, workers conjured
    "devil-beliefs" that signaled the changing social relations. See Taussig, *The Devil
    and Commodity Fetishism,* 17.

61. Eugene Callaghan, "Antimony Resources of the Tronchiri (San Luis) Mine, Bolivia,"
    1941, Folder: Writings, box 6, General Materials 1924–1988, Papers of Eugene Callaghan,
    Manuscripts Division, Marriott Library, University of Utah, Salt Lake City, UT.

62. Eugene Callaghan, "Tin Resources of the Huanuni District, Bolivia," 1941, box 6,
    General Materials 1924–1988, Papers of Eugene Callaghan, Manuscripts Division,
    Marriott Library, University of Utah, Salt Lake City, UT.

63. Eugene Callaghan, "Tin Resources of the Santa Teresa Placer, Negro Pabellón Dis-
    trict Bolivia," 1941, p. 1, Folder: Writings, box 6, General Materials 1924–1988, Pa-
    pers of Eugene Callaghan, Manuscripts Division, Marriott Library, University of
    Utah, Salt Lake City, UT.

64. Ralph J. Roberts, "Manganese Deposits in Costa Rica," *Geologic Investigations in
    the American Republics, 1941–1943* (Washington, DC: USGPO, 1944), 391.

65. E. N. Goddard, L. S. Gardner, and W. S. Burbank, "Manganese Deposits of the Re-
    public of Haiti," *Geologic Investigations in the American Republics, 1945* (Wash-
    ington, DC: USGPO, 1945), 30.

66. Ibid.

67. Parker D. Trask and José Rodríguez Cabo, Jr., "Manganese Deposits of Mexico,"
    Geologic Investigations in the American Republics, 1946 (Washington, DC: USGPO,
    1948), 217.

68. Johnston, "Speech on History of USGS work in Technical Assistance." The reports formed the basis of an impressive and wide-ranging bibliography of U.S. Geological Work publications that would be compiled after the Point Four program.

69. Mendenhall, "Preface," iii.

70. Ibid.

71. See Eugene Callaghan, "Tin Resources of the Santa Fé Mine Bolivia," 1941, p. 13, Folder: Report Tin of Santa Fe Mine, box 2, General Materials 1924–1988, Papers of Eugene Callaghan, Manuscripts Division, Marriott Library, University of Utah, Salt Lake City, UT.

72. Singewald, "Mineral Resources of Colombia," 58.

73. Pecora, "Nickel-Silicate and Associated Nickel-Cobalt-Manganese-Oxide Deposits Near São Jose Do Tocantins, Goiaz, Brazil," 286; Eugene Callaghan, "Tin Resources of the Colquiri District Bolivia," 1941, Folder: Writings, box 6, General Materials 1924–1988, Papers of Eugene Callaghan, Manuscripts Division, Marriott Library, University of Utah, Salt Lake City, UT. The report on which he drew was Charles W. Wright, "Mineral Resources, Production, and Trade of Bolivia," *Foreign Mining Quarterly* 2, no. 4 (1939): 42.

74. *Annual Report from the Secretary of the Interior, Fiscal Year ended June 30, 1941,* 145; Memo from R. S. Dean to Harold Ickes, May 24, 1943, Folder: Bureau of Mines (4), box 140, Secretary of the Interior Files, Papers of Harold L. Ickes, Manuscripts Division, Library of Congress, Washington, DC. Because the Bureau of Mines files from the period between 1942–1945 no longer appear to exist, the workings of the Foreign Minerals Bureau beyond published reports remain secretive. See the gap in documentation between Folder: 1941 and Folder: 1946, box 1, Records Relating to International Aid and Technical Activities 1941–1952, Records of the Bureau of Mines RG 70, NARA.

75. *Annual Report from the Secretary of the Interior, Fiscal Year ended June 30, 1942* (Washington, DC: USGPO, 1942), iii.

76. Ibid.

77. Memo from R. S. Dean to Harold Ickes, May 24, 1943, Folder: Bureau of Mines (4), box 140, Secretary of the Interior Files, Papers of Harold L. Ickes, Manuscripts Division, Library of Congress, Washington, DC.

78. Pecora et al., *Mica Deposits in Minas Gerais, Brazil,* 281.

79. Ibid., 213.

80. Ibid., 277–279.

81. Ibid., 219.

82. Charles F. Park Jr., "Manganese Deposits of Cuba," Bulletin 935-B, *Geologic Investigations in the American Republics, 1941–42* (Washington, DC: USGPO, 1942), 75.

83. Goddard, Gardner, and Burbank, "Manganese Deposits of the Republic of Haiti," 30.

84. Roberts, "Manganese Deposits in Costa Rica," 388.

85. John Van N. Dorr, 2d, *Manganese and Iron Deposits of Morro Do Urucum, Mato Grosso, Brazil* (Washington, DC: USGPO, 1945), 34.

86. Thomas P. Thayer to Joe Webb Peoples, June 13, 1942, Folder: Chromite—General, box 4, Records Concerning Strategic Minerals, 1940–1940, Misc. Correspondence, 1940–1949, Records of the Geological Survey, NARA; Thomas Thayer to D. F. Hewett, April 16, 1942, Folder: Chromite—(Outside US) Cuba, box 4, Records Concerning Strategic Minerals, 1940–1940, Misc. Correspondence, 1940–1949, Records of the Geological Survey, NARA.

87. Thayer to Hewett, April 16, 1942. Thayer added that to ensure collegial relations with President Fulgencia Batista and his government, Geological Survey personnel were encouraged to send monthly summaries of their activities, emphasizing their transparency.

88. Sigmund Hammer, L. L. Nettleton, and W. K. Hastings, "Gravimeter Prospecting for Chromite in Cuba," *Geophysics* 10, no. 1 (January 1945): 34; See also Joe Webb Peoples to L. L. Nettleton, June 9, 1944, Folder: Chromite—General, box 4, Records Concerning Strategic Minerals, 1940–1940, Misc. Correspondence, 1940–1949, Records of the Geological Survey, NARA.

89. Bethlehem Steel Annual Report, 1941, 26, ProQuest Historical Annual Reports.

90. Thomas P. Thayer, "Chrome Resources of Cuba," Bulletin 935-A, *Geologic Investigations in the American Republics, 1941–42* (Washington, DC: USGPO, 1942), 36. Comments by Thayer, Folder: Chromite—General, box 4, Records Concerning Strategic Minerals, 1940–1940, Misc. Correspondence, 1940–1949, Records of the Geological Survey, NARA.

91. Herbert Hawkes to Don Fraser, Bethlehem Steel, May 5, 1942, Folder: Chromite—(Outside US) Cuba, box 4, Records Concerning Strategic Minerals, 1940–1940, Misc. Correspondence, 1940–1949, Records of the Geological Survey, NARA.

92. Thayer to Hewett, October 24, 1942, Folder: Chromite—(Outside US) Cuba, box 4, Records Concerning Strategic Minerals, 1940–1940, Misc. Correspondence, 1940–1949, Records of the Geological Survey, NARA; Thayer to Hewett, April 16, 1942. In the absence of corporate correspondence on the matter, we are left to speculate as to the full range of reasons Interior geologists lamented the "uncooperative" attitude of some Bethlehem company geologists.

93. Thomas P. Thayer to Joe Webb Peoples, July 6, 1942, Folder: Chromite—General, box 4, Records Concerning Strategic Minerals, 1940–1940, Misc. Correspondence, 1940–1949, Records of the Geological Survey, NARA.

94. Thomas P. Thayer to Joe Webb Peoples, June 26, 1942, Folder: Chromite—General, box 4, Records Concerning Strategic Minerals, 1940–1940, Misc. Correspondence, 1940–1949, Records of the Geological Survey, NARA.

95. Ward C. Smith and E. M Gonzalez, "Tungsten Investigations in the Republic of Argentina, 1942–43," *Geologic Investigations in American Republics, 1946* (Washington, DC: USGPO, 1946), 13.

96. Park, Jr., "Manganese Deposits of Cuba," 95–97.

97. Thayer, "Chrome Resources of Cuba," 1. The quoted material is from T. P. Thayer to Fred Cater, December 13, 1944, Folder: Chomite [*sic*] Letters to Field Men, box 4, Records Concerning Strategic Minerals, 1940–1940, Misc. Correspondence, 1940–1949, Records of the Geological Survey, NARA.

98. Pecora et al., *Mica Deposits in Minas Gerais, Brazil,* 205.

99. Ibid.

100. Ibid., 213–214.

101. Ibid., 215.

102. Trask and Cabo, Jr., "Manganese Deposits of Mexico," 209.

103. Ibid.

104. On the ecological impacts of extraction, see Richard P. Tucker, *Insatiable Appetite: The United States and the Ecological Degradation of the Tropical World* (Berkeley: University of California Press, 2000); Seth Garfield, "The Brazilian Amazon and the Transnational Environment, 1940–1990," *Nation-States and the Global Environment: New Approaches to International Environmental History,* ed. Erika Marie Bsumek, David Kinkela, and Mark Atwood Lawrence (New York: Oxford University Press, 2013), 245–246.

105. Boucas to Vargas, 23 February 1942, Rio de Janeiro, Centro de Pesquisa e Documentação de História Contemporânea, Fundação Getúlio Vargas, Arquivo Getúlio Vargas. Cited and translated from Portuguese by Tyler Priest in "Banking on Development: Brazil in the United States's Search for Strategic Minerals, 1945–1953," *International History Review* 21, no. 2 (1999): 297.

106. Ibid., 205.

107. Harold Ickes, "Hitler Reaches for the World's Oil Supply," Folder: "Hitler Reaches for the World's Oil Supply," box 113, Secretary of the Interior Files, Papers of Harold Ickes, Manuscript Division, Library of Congress, Washington, DC. Harold L. Ickes, "Hitler Reaches for the World's Oil Supply," *Collier's,* August 15, 1942, pp. 18–20.

108. Ibid.

109. Thayer to Hewett, October 24, 1942, Folder: Chromite—(Outside US) Cuba, box 4, Records Concerning Strategic Minerals, 1940–1940, Misc. Correspondence, 1940–1949, Records of the Geological Survey, NARA.

110. Mendenhall, "Preface," iii.

111. Johnston, "Speech on History of USGS Work in Technical Assistance." It was during these cooperative wartime initiatives, Johnston argued, that the technical assistance approach to mineral programs took form that would underpin international development.

112. One report that synthesizes some mineral programs from wartime efforts to the U.S. Agency for International Development is *Bibliography of Reports Resulting from U.S. Geological Survey Participation in the United States Technical Assistance Program, 1940–67,* ed. Jo Ann Heath and Nancy B. Tabacchi (Washington, DC: U.S. Department of the Interior and Department of State, 1968).

113. Memo from George Sweeney, Arthur D. Little, to Files, "Trip to Sinai Peninsula," January 8, 1954, Folder: Minerals, box 6, Mission to Egypt Industry and Mining, Subject Files, 1954–56, Records of the Foreign Assistance Agencies, 1948–1961, NARA.

114. President Tubman of Liberia would eventually thank Thomas Thayer by conferring the Order of the Star of Africa. Johnston, "Speech on History of USGS work in Technical Assistance." For an account of Thayer's collaborations with Tubman

and American financiers, see Herbert Solow, "Three-Way Payoff in Liberia," *Fortune*, February 1953, 130.

4 · Unearthing Development

1. William E. Warne, *Mission for Peace: Point 4 in Iran* (Indianapolis: Bobbs-Merrill Company, 1956), 18.
2. Ibid., 19.
3. Ibid., 20–21.
4. In the Point Four years, nations formerly of the colonial world forged an identity as the Third World, choosing a third way rather than accepting the bifurcated terms of the U.S-Soviet conflict in the Cold War. On the Point Four program, see Gilbert Rist, *The History of Development: From Western Origins to Global Faith, Third Edition* (London: Zed Books, 2008), 4.
5. See David Ekbladh, *Great American Mission: Modernization and the Construction of an American World Order* (Princeton: Princeton University Press, 2010), 77–82; Daniel Immerwahr, *Thinking Small: The United States and the Lure of Community Development* (Cambridge: Harvard University Press, 2015); Immerwahr, "Modernization and Development in U.S. Foreign Relations," *Passport* (September 2012): 22–25; Nick Cullather, *The Hungry World: America's Cold War Battle Against Poverty in Asia* (Cambridge: Harvard University Press, 2010); Edward Miller, *Misalliance: Ngo Dinh Diem, the United States, and the Fate of South Vietnam* (Cambridge: Harvard University Press, 2013), 54–67; Nils Gilman, *Mandarins of the Future: Modernization Theory in Cold War America* (Baltimore: Johns Hopkins University Press, 2003), 3; Stuart Schrader, "To Secure the Global Great Society: Participation in Pacification," *Humanity* 7, no. 2 (2016): 225–253; Arturo Escobar, *Encountering Development: The Making and Unmaking of the Third World* (Princeton: Princeton University Press, 1995); Laura Briggs, *Reproducing Empire: Race, Sex, Science, and U.S. Imperialism in Puerto Rico* (Berkeley: University of California Press, 2002), 110–121.
6. I have made this argument elsewhere, in Megan Black, "Interior's Exterior: The State, Mining Companies, and Resource Ideologies in the Point Four Program," *Diplomatic History* 40, no. 1 (2016): 81–110.
7. On U.S. mineral pursuits abroad as a form of intervention conforming to understandings of "hard" power, see Stephen Krasner, *Defending National Interest: Raw Materials Investments and U.S. Foreign Policy* (Princeton: Princeton University Press, 1978); Michael T. Klare, *Resource Wars: The New Landscape of Global Conflict* (New York: Metropolitan Books, 2001); Daniel Yergin, *The Prize: The Epic Quest for Oil, Money and Power* (New York: Free Press, 1993). Alfred Eckes argued that Point Four aimed to increase access to raw materials but did not examine the Interior Department's role. See Eckes, *The United States and the Global Struggle for Minerals* (Austin: University of Texas Press, 1979), 160–161. Tyler Priest, in contrast, argued that although the Point Four program sought strategic minerals, it ultimately failed because of infrastructure and transportation deficiencies. See Priest,

Global Gambits: Big Steel and the U.S. Quest for Manganese (New York: Praeger, 2003), 232.

8. This was especially true of firms that, unlike the handful of petroleum and mining firms with storied international portfolios, had yet to break into the international scene. See "Point IV," *Fortune,* February 1950, 90–96.

9. Scholars showing public-private collaborations in trade liberalization include Emily S. Rosenberg, *Financial Missionaries to the World: The Politics and Culture of Dollar Diplomacy* (Cambridge: Harvard University Press, 1999); Greta Krippner, *Capitalizing on Crisis: The Political Origins of the Rise of Finance* (Cambridge: Harvard University Press, 2011). Amanda Kay McVety, focusing more on planners and trade than technicians and earth-moving, has argued that Point Four helped promote investments abroad. See McVety, *Enlightened Aid: U.S. Development as Foreign Policy in Ethiopia* (New York: Oxford University Press, 2012), chap. 4.

10. Priest examines resource internationalism (also referred to as globalism) after World War I in *Global Gambits,* 82–85.

11. William Warne, "U.S. Bureau of Mines Films," Dispatch, March 24, 1954, Iran, Technical Assistance, Records of the Bureau of Mines, RG 70, NARA. Warne also requested films on copper, steel, tin, and zinc.

12. Department of the Interior Circular, "Krug Stresses Urgent Need for Conservation," March 28, 1949, Folder: 1949, box 5944, Public Relations, RG 70, NARA.

13. See James Boyd, "Reports and Addresses at the Thirtieth Annual Meeting, St. Louis, Missouri, April 15–16," *Journal of the American Zinc Institute, Inc.* 26 (1948): 45; James Boyd, "Our Strategic Minerals," *Engineering and Science* 14, no. 8 (May 1951): 18–24. Mineral output increased from $9 billion in 1946 to $12 billion in 1947. Despite popular impressions that the war exceptionally drained petroleum resources, experts instead insisted that consumption was "just about on a straight line." Statement of Oscar Chapman on Anglo-American Petroleum Relations, June 9, 1947, Folder: Public Addresses and Statements, Vol 4, Box 75, Papers of Oscar Chapman, Harry S. Truman Library, Independence, MO (hereafter shortened to HSTL).

14. See Lizabeth Cohen, *A Consumers' Republic: The Politics of Mass Consumption in the Postwar Era* (New York: Vintage Press, 2004), 70–74. On the rise of petroleum over coal as the main source of fuel in the postwar era, see David Painter, "Oil and the American Century" *Journal of American History* 99, no. 1 (2012): 24–40. Such material rewards for the previous wartime austerity seemed reasonable, particularly as citizens had sacrificed for and invested in the state through armed service and war bonds with the promise of this future bounty. See Robert Westbrook, "Fighting for the American Family: Private Interests and Political Obligation in World War II," in *The Power of Culture: Critical Essays in American History,* ed. Richard Wightman Fox and T. J. Jackson Lears (Chicago: University of Chicago Press, 1993).

15. Priest, *Global Gambits,* 194–195. See also Glenn H. Snyder, *Stockpiling Strategic Materials: Politics and National Defense,* (San Francisco: Chandler Publishing, 1966), 106–117. On the 1948 Senate Appropriations Committee debates about Interior's part in excessive taxation, see A. C. Fieldner to W. E. Rice, February 2, 1948, box 5619, RG 70, NARA.

16. These timelines of domestic resource depletion were wrong, and the fears, much like those issuing from the overstated threat posed by the Soviet Union, were exaggerated. See Melvin Leffler, *A Preponderance of Power: National Security, the Truman Administration, and the Cold War* (Stanford: Stanford University Press, 1992).

17. Supplements to Statement by James Boyd, Senate Committee on Interior and Insular Affairs, 1949, Folder: Speech, 1951, Box 6495, Publicity, RG 70, NARA.

18. Julius A. Krug, *National Resources and Foreign Aid: Report of J. A. Krug, Secretary of the Interior, October 9, 1947* (Washington, DC: USGPO, 1947). Marshall's speech was the product of contentious debate among the Allies and several junior officials in various bureaus of the U.S. government regarding the best way to facilitate European recovery. Michael Hogan, *The Marshall Plan: America, Britain, and the Reconstruction of Western Europe, 1947–1952* (New York: Cambridge University Press, 1987), 43–53.

19. Krug, *National Resources and Foreign Aid,* iii. Emphasis added.

20. Daniel L. Goldy to Assistant Secretary Davidson, October 13, 1947, Folder: International Foreign Policy, Box 43, Papers of Daniel L. Goldy, HSTL. Also included in the memo were James Boyd, whose contributions in procurement were celebrated, and Assistant Secretary William Warne, who later worked in Iran.

21. Inaugural address, January 20, 1949, Folder: Inaugural Address January 20, 1949, box 14, SMOF: David D. Lloyd Files, Presidential Speech and Message File, Papers of Harry S. Truman, HSTL.

22. See Benjamin Hardy to Francis Russell, November 23, 1948, Folder: Point IV, 1/3 Box 1, Papers of Benjamin H. Hardy, HSTL; Walter Salant, "Foreign Investment and American Private Capital," January 11, 1949, Folder: Point IV File, box 2, Papers of Walter Salant, HSTL; David Lloyd, "Memoranda for the President," December 20, 1948, Folder: Inaugural Address, Box 14, Papers of David Lloyd, HSTL. McVety discusses these debates at length in Enlightened Aid, 91.

23. On Rhodes's empire and expansionism, see Hannah Arendt, "Nationalism, Imperialism, and Chauvinism," *The Review of Politics* 7, no. 4 (1945): 441–463.

24. Boyd, "Reports and Addresses at the Thirtieth Annual Meeting."

25. In his written edits on the draft, David Lloyd transformed the line about the "old imperialism" to its recognizable form, though Secretary of State Dean Acheson appears to have made almost identical edits. See Inaugural Address draft labeled "Acheson," January 15, 1949, p. 10, Folder: Inaugural Address January 20, 1949, box 14, SMOF: David D. Lloyd Files, Presidential Speech and Message File, Papers of Harry S. Truman, HSTL.

26. Snyder, *Stockpiling Strategic Minerals,* 40.

27. In fact, the chairman of the NRSB, Stuart Symington, had convinced Truman to launch the adjunct Paley Commission. Eckes, *Global Struggle for Minerals,* 175.

28. Krug, *National Resources and Foreign Aid,* iii–iv. On executive authority, see Priest, *Global Gambits,* 199.

29. Eckes, *Global Struggle for Minerals,* 194–195.

30. William Paley to Henry Bennett, May 10, 1951, Folder: General Records—Foreign Resources, box 1, RG 220, HSTL. Philip Coombs to Henry Bennett, June 7, 1951,

Folder: Correspondence—Departmental, Point Four Program, box 59, RG 220, HSTL; Henry Bennett to Philip Coombs, June 26, 1951, Folder: Correspondence—Departmental, Point Four Program, box 125, RG 220, HSTL. Emphasis added. On other links between resource scarcity panics, the Point Four program, and the Paley Commission, see Thomas Robertson, *The Malthusian Moment: Global Population Growth and the Birth of American Environmentalism* (New Brunswick: Rutgers University Press, 2012), 57–63.

31. "Present Status and Proposed Extension of the Foreign Minerals Program of the Department of the Interior," 10–13, August 23, 1951, Folder: Projects—Interior—Exploration, box 125, RG 220, HSTL.

32. "The spearhead" hints at the deeper coercion. "Minerals and Metals Meeting," December 12, 1951, p. 131, Folder: Minerals and Metals Meeting, box 7, RG 220, HSTL.

33. "Geologists Meeting," May 10, 1951, Folder: Mining Geologists Meeting, box 126, RG 220, HSTL. Emphasis added.

34. On Leith and mineral internationalism in the interwar and postwar era, see Priest, *Global Gambits*, 126–128; Mats Ingulstad, "The Interdependent Hegemon: The United States and the Quest for Strategic Raw Materials during the Early Cold War," *International History Review* 37, no. 1 (2015): 59–79.

35. "Minerals and Metals Meeting," p. 131.

36. *Resources for Freedom: A Report to the President,* Vols. 1 to 5 (Washington, DC: President's Materials Policy Commission, 1952).

37. J. A. Krug, Address at Colorado School of Mines, September 29, 1949, Folder: 1949, box 5942, Publicity, RG 70, NARA.

38. J. A. Krug, "Resource Development for the World," Folder: 1949, box 5942, Publicity, RG 70, NARA See also Oscar Chapman, "Resources and Our Future," Commencement Exercises of the Colorado Agricultural and Mechanical College in Fort Collins, Colorado, June 10, 1949, Folder: 1949, box 5943, Publicity (080), RG 70, NARA.

39. Melani McAlister, *Epic Encounters: Culture, Media, and U.S. Interests in the Middle East, 1945–2000* (Berkeley: University of California Press, 2005), 129.

40. Vernon Northrop, "Interior Role in International Activities," Remarks on United Nations Day, October 24, 1952, Folder: October 1952, box 6721, Publicity (080), RG 70, NARA.

41. These attitudes were conveyed in a multipage spread, "Point IV," *Fortune,* February 1950, 94.

42. See Eckes, United States and the Global Struggle for Minerals, 186–187. See also "Point IV," 89.

43. See "Point IV," 182.

44. As 10 percent of returned surveys, these twelve respondents represented major extractive companies and complete survey responses: Aluminum Company of America, Anaconda Copper, Kennecott Copper, National Lead Company, Union Carbide, St. Joseph's Lead, Texas Gulf Sulphur Company, Freeport Sulphur, General Electric, U.S. Steel Company, DuPont, and Phelps Dodge Corporation. All but Phelps Dodge Corporation supported the government assistance. See PMPC Questionnaires, pp. 12–14, boxes 38–47, RG 220, HSTL. Nevertheless, Phelps Dodge

opened its first international offices in Point Four countries like Cuba, Peru, Colombia, the Philippines, and Venezuela in 1955, suggesting that they benefited from the arrangement. See Carlos A. Schwantes, *Vision and Enterprise: Exploring the History of Phelps Dodge Corporation* (Tucson: University of Arizona Press, 2000), 237, 382.

45. On critics of government involvement in markets, see Thomas Ferguson, "Industrial Conflict and the Coming of the New Deal: The Triumph of Multinational Liberalism in America," in *The Rise and Fall of the New Deal Order, 1930–1980*, ed. Steve Fraser and Gary Gerstle (Princeton: Princeton University Press, 1989), 7; and Kim Phillips-Fein, *Invisible Hands: The Businessmen's Crusade Against the New Deal* (New York: W. W. Norton, 2010), 3–28.

46. These measures are suggested in Bennett to Coombs, June 26, 1951; "Present Status and Proposed Extension of the Foreign Minerals Program of the Department of the Interior," 10–13, August 23, 1951, Folder: Projects—Interior—Exploration, box 127, RG 220, HSTL; "Government Encouragement of Private Investment in Materials Development Abroad," 1–4, September 16, 1951, Folder: Second Draft—Foreign Resources, box 16, RG 220, HSTL.

47. Some Interior personnel joined Point Four in 1950. See Draft, "Point Four and Foreign Raw Materials Development," January 24, 1952, Folder: Point Four program, box 104, RG 220, HSTL. On Interior's suitability to the endeavor, see PMPC, "Present Status and Proposed Extension of the Foreign Minerals Program," 10–13, and "Government Encouragement of Private Investment," 1–4. On the allocations, see Draft, "Technical and Financial Assistance in Support of Foreign Materials Development," September 19, 1951, Draft—Foreign Resources, box 16, RG 220, HSTL. Congressional approval is described in William Warne, "Guide for Point 4 Mineral Resources Exploration and Development," July 29, 1952, Folder: Point IV—General, box 4, U.S. Mission to Iran, RG 469, NARA. Projects began in Afghanistan, Bolivia, Brazil, Colombia, India, Mexico, Nepal, the Philippines, and Saudi Arabia. See Technical Cooperation Administration, Point Four Projects in Operation, July 1, 1950, to December 31, 1951, Folder: Point Four Program, box 6, Mission to Peru, RG 469, NARA. Projects expanded to countries including Thailand, China, Greece, Israel, Chile, Peru, Egypt, Jordan, Lebanon, Iraq, Burma, Liberia, Pakistan, Iran, and Cuba by 1956. See International Cooperation Administration, Office of Industrial Resources, *Quarterly Report, Fiscal Year 1956* (4th Quarter), Folder: Reports, box 11, U.S. Mission to Israel, RG 469, NARA.

48. Northrop, "Interior Role in International Activities."

49. On primitivism, see Gail Bederman, *Manliness and Civilization: A Cultural History of Gender and Race in the United States, 1880–1917* (Chicago: University of Chicago Press, 1995), 34–38.

50. PMPC, "Present Status and Proposed Extension of the Foreign Minerals program," 12.

51. Department of the Interior, *Point 4 in Action: The Interior Department's Role* (Washington, DC, 1950), 9; Paul C. Rosier, *Serving Their Country: American Indian Politics and Patriotism in the Twentieth Century* (Cambridge: Harvard University Press, 2012), 138–142. On Fryer's advice, see Warne, *Mission for Peace*, 18.

52. Rosier, *Serving Their Country*, 138–142.

53. Department of the Interior, *Point 4 in Action*, 9.

54. This challenges the bifurcated historical understandings of state- and business-led culture industries. For analyses of U.S. state cultural production for propaganda purposes overseas during the Cold War, see Laura Belmonte, *Selling the American Way: U.S. Propaganda and the Cold War* (Philadelphia: University of Pennsylvania Press, 2008); Andrew L. Yarrow, "Selling a New Vision of America to the World: Changing Messages in Early U.S. Cold War Print Propaganda," *Journal of Cold War Studies* 11, no. 4 (Fall 2009): 3–45; Penny Von Eschen illuminates the failures of the state to legislate meaning in *Satchmo Blows up the World: Jazz Ambassadors Play the Cold War* (Cambridge: Harvard University Press, 2004). On U.S. state cultural production concerned with domestic issues, see Lauren Rebecca Sklaroff, *Black Culture and the New Deal: The Quest for Civil Rights in the Roosevelt Era* (Chapel Hill: University of North Carolina Press, 2009); Barbara Dianne Savage, *Broadcasting Freedom: Radio, War, and the Politics of Race, 1938–1948* (Chapel Hill: University of North Carolina Press, 1999). Meanwhile, big business during the same years undertook cultural production to advance corporate public relations. Karen Miller, *The Voice of Business: Hill & Knowlton and Postwar Public Relations* (Chapel Hill: University of North Carolina Press, 1999); Roland Marchard, *Creating the Corporate Soul: The Rise of Public Relations and Corporate Imagery in American Big Business* (Berkeley: University of California Press, 1998).

55. The history of the film library is recounted in Department of the Interior Information Circular, "M. F. Leopold, Mines Bureau Motion Picture Chief, Dies" December 12, 1951, Folder: Dec. 1951, box 6489, Publicity (080), RG 70, NARA. The quote is taken from Allan Sherman to Osgood Nichols, November 4, 1954, Folder: Nov. 1954, box 7242, Motion Pictures (087.2), RG 70, NARA.

56. Jason C. Parker argues that Point Four indoctrination films from the Technical Cooperation Administration were geared toward "training hands" more than changing hearts and minds. See Parker, *Hearts, Minds, Voices: U.S. Cold War Public Diplomacy and the Formation of the Third World* (New York: Oxford University Press, 2016), 35.

57. U.S. Department of the Interior, *Annual Report from the Secretary of the Interior, Fiscal Year ended June 30, 1956* (Washington, DC:, 1957), 174. For comparison, the highest grossing commercial feature of 1956 was *The Ten Commandments* with an audience of 68 million. Box office returns are cited in McAlister, *Epic Encounters*, n. 321.

58. *The Evolution of the Oil Industry*, 1951, Motion Pictures, RG 70, NARA.

59. *A Story of Copper*, 1953, Motion Pictures, RG 70, NARA.

60. The films rehash tropes of the popular Western genre, which promoted Anglo racial supremacy to justify the conquest of other races. Richard Slotkin, *Gunfighter Nation: The Myth of the Frontier in Twentieth-Century America* (Norman: University of Oklahoma Press, 1993).

61. *Arizona and Its Natural Resources*, 1955, Motion Pictures, RG 70, NARA. A 1948 version of *Arizona and Its Natural Resources* mentioned but did not extensively visualize the previous indigenous inhabitants.

62. Allan Sherman to Frederick Rocket, July 20, 1955, Folder: July 1955, box 7499, Motion Pictures (087.2), RG 70, NARA. Emphasis added.

63. "Present Status and Proposed Extension of the Foreign Minerals Program," August 23, 1951, 12.

64. Alan Probert to E. P. Shoub, October 5, 1954, Folder: 1954, box 7242, Motion Picture Files, Records of the Bureau of Mines, NARA.

65. Alan Probert to Allan Sherman, August 9, 1954, Folder: Cuba, box 7205, Technical Assistance (026), RG 70, NARA.

66. Ibid.

67. Warne, *Mission for Peace,* 97.

68. George M. Potter to Paul Hamer, January 22, 1954, Folder: Afghanistan, box 7205, Technical Assistance (026), RG 70, NARA; Lester G. Morrell to Robert P. Willing, June 29, 1955, Folder: June 1955, box 7499, Motion Pictures (087.2), RG 70, NARA. Some titles in circulation included *The Evolution of the Oil Industry, A Story of Copper, Texas and Its Natural Resources, Oklahoma and Its Natural Resources, Arizona and Its Natural Resources, A Story of Lead,* and *The Drama of Steel.*

69. "U.S. Geological Survey and Bureau of Mines in Cuba and Mexico," April 11, 1956, Folder: Projects, box 23, Mission to Cuba, RG 469, NARA.

70. "U.S. Geological Survey and Bureau of Mines in Cuba and Mexico," April 11, 1956, Folder: Projects, box 23, Mission to Cuba, RG 469, NARA.

71. Ibid.

72. As the administration of President Dwight Eisenhower took the reins of technical assistance, the imperative of bolstering "security" through aid only heightened. The Mutual Security Agency took on a broader role in defining the scope and purpose of assistance in 1953. See Ekbladh, *The Great American Mission,* 110, 137.

73. Point Four technicians developed projects that overtly furthered national economies and quietly would help the United States. See William Warne, "Guide for Point 4 Mineral Resources Exploration and Development," July 29, 1952, Point IV—General, box 4, U.S. Mission to Iran, RG 469, NARA. Alan Probert to Frank Noe, May 8, 1953, Folder: Peru, box 6934, Technical Assistance (026), RG 70, NARA.

74. Department of State, Point Four Projects in Operation (1952), December 31, 1951, Folder: Point Four Program, box 6, Mission to Peru, RG 469, NARA; Division of Foreign Activities Bureau of Mines Monthly Report, April 1957–April 1958, Folder: Projects [1 of 2], box 23, Mission to Cuba, RG 469, NARA; Earl Irving to Mr. Whittington, May 19, 1953, Folder: Commodities—Iron, box 7, Mission to the Philippines, RG 469, NARA; Interior Department, *Point 4 in Action,* 8; Geologic Quarterly Reports in Cuba, October 1955–November 1956, Folder: Reports—Quarterly Reports, box 25, Mission to Cuba, RG 469, NARA. On columbite, cobalt, and tungsten, see Summary of Bureau of Mines Program in Brazil, November 3, 1955, Folder: Brazil, box 7458, Technical Assistance (026), RG 70, NARA; Vija Srasthupatra and W. D. Johnston, "A Geological Reconnaissance of the Mineral Deposits of Thailand," November 30, 1951, Folder: Commodities, box 7, Mission to Thailand, RG 469, NARA; Alan Probert to Benison Lockwood, August 1, 1953, Folder: 1953, box 6932, Technical Assistance (026), RG 70, NARA.

75. Eckes, *United States and the Global Struggle for Minerals,* 160–161.

76. "Gross-Domestic-Product-(GDP) by Industry Data," Bureau of Economic Analysis, Department of Commerce. https://www.bea.gov/industry/gdpbyind_data.htm.

77. A Study of Technical Assistance in Peru, November 10, 1953, Folder: Point IV Technical Cooperation, box 7, Mission to Peru, RG 469, NARA.

78. Ibid.

79. Joseph Harrington, "Minerals in Colombia's Industrial Development," 1954, pp. 2–3, Folder: Geological Survey Project, box 9, Mission to Colombia, RG 469, NARA. On obstacles to aerial surveys, see U.S. Geological Survey, Annual Report for 1952, Folder: Geological Survey, box 12, Mission to Peru, RG 469, NARA.

80. Circular, "Geological Survey to Philippines for Point Four," April 6, 1951, Folder: April 1951, box 6491, Publicity (080), RG 70, NARA. Irving and Sorem arrived in the Philippines in 1946 and 1949, respectively (Irving initially under the Interdepartmental Committee on Scientific and Cultural Cooperation).

81. Joseph Harrington, "Minerals in Colombia's Industrial Development," 1954, pp. 2–3, Folder: Geological Survey Project, box 9, Mission to Colombia, RG 469, NARA. On obstacles to aerial surveys, see U.S. Geological Survey, Annual Report for 1952, Folder: Geological Survey, box 12, Mission to Peru, RG 469, NARA.

82. Glen Brown to John Dunaway, March 1953, Folder: Natural Resources—Mineral Surveys, box 4, Mission to Saudi Arabia, RG 469, NARA. In this letter, Brown alleged that published reports were received by all mining companies and the best way to interest them in foreign investments. *Bibliography of Reports Resulting from U.S. Geological Survey Participation in the United States Technical Assistance Program, 1940–67,* ed. Jo Ann Heath and Nancy B. Tabacchi (Washington, DC: U.S. Department of the Interior and Department of State, 1968).

83. U.S. Geological Survey, T. P. Thayer, "Geology and Iron Deposits in Liberia," 1952, Folder: Geological Survey, box 24, Mission to Liberia, RG 469, NARA.

84. "U.S.-Liberian Point 4 Organization," Folder: Information—Point Four, box 24, Mission to Liberia, RG 469, NARA; Herbert Solow, "Three-Way Payoff in Liberia," *Fortune,* February 1953, 130.

85. Alan Probert to Benoni Lockwood, August 1, 1953, Folder: 1953, box 6932, Technical Assistance (026), RG 70, NARA.

86. George Potter to A. Dor, June 23, 1953, Folder: Minerals—Mining, box 4, Mission to Israel, RG 469, NARA.

87. J. Marvin Weller to Louis A. Turnbull, October 26, 1953, Folder: Commodities—Coal, box 7, Mission to the Philippines, RG 469, NARA. On Egypt and Nepal, see Cooperative Agreement Mineral Research Laboratory, May 24, 1954, Folder: Agreements, box 1, Mission to Egypt, RG 469, NARA; George Potter to A. Dor, June 23, 1953; John R. Welch to Louis Turnbull, August 10, 1956, Folder: Nepal, box 7684, Technical Assistance (026), RG 70, NARA. See Geologic Quarterly Report, October 11, 1955 and April 10, 1956, Folder: Reports—Quarterly Reports, box 25, Mission to Cuba, RG 469, NARA.

88. Frank Noe to Jack Archibald, November 8, 1954, Folder: Mexico, box 7205, Technical Assistance (026), RG 70, NARA.

89. Glen Brown, "Low Grade Copper Discovered in Saudi Arabia by USGS," July 3, 1954, Folder: Natural Resources, box 4, Mission to Saudi Arabia, RG 469, NARA.

90. Memo from Walter Howe to Joseph Harrington, December 14, 1954, Folder: Geological Survey Project, box 9, Mission to Colombia, RG 469, NARA; Joseph Harrington, "Minerals in Colombia's Industrial Development," 1954, Folder: Geological Survey Project, box 9, Mission to Colombia, RG 469, NARA; Airgram, "Preliminary Results of Coal Investigations," July 3, 1953, Folder: Commodities—Coal, box 7, Mission to the Philippines, RG 469, NARA; Brief Description of Technical Cooperation Projects, May 3, 1953.

91. Afghanistan bought a "Denver Hoist" machine from the Vulcan Iron Works Company of America. See George Potter to Paul Hamer, April 1, 1954, Folder: Afghanistan, box 7204, Technical Assistance, RG 70, NARA.

92. Brief Description of Technical Cooperation Projects, May 3, 1953; Alan Probert to Benoni Lockwood, August 1, 1953, Folder: 1953, box 6932, Technical Assistance, RG 70, NARA.

93. On beryl, see Jesse Auvil to Alan Probert, October 18, 1954, Folder: Afghanistan, box 7204, Technical Assistance (026), RG 70, NARA; Louis Turnbull to Paul Hamer, April 20, 1955, Folder: Afghanistan, box 7458, Technical Assistance (026), RG 70, NARA; Paul Hamer to Louis Turnbull, October 4, 1956, Folder: Afghanistan, box 7683, Technical Assistance (026), RG 70, NARA.

94. Although transportation and infrastructure had been consistent obstacles as U.S. mining companies attempted to venture abroad, the situation in Jordan shows that some countries successfully offset the problems posed to the transport of raw materials. "Progress Report on Mineral Deposit Investigations," June 12, 1952, Folder: Minerals, box 1, Mission to Jordan, RG 469, NARA. See also Priest, *Global Gambits*, 230–232.

95. Norman E. Thompson to H. E., Minister of the Economy, November 15, 1954, Folder: Mineral Development, box 1, Mission to Jordan, RG 469, NARA.

96. Alan Probert to C. E. Bartlett, December 6, 1954, Folder: Cuba, box 7205, Technical Assistance (026), RG 70, NARA.

97. See Memo from W. J. Fene to Alan Probert, "Manganese Poisoning," November 16, 1954, Folder: Cuba, box 7205, Technical Assistance (026), RG 70, NARA; E. W. Pehrson to Jerry Marcus, December 30, 1955, Folder: Chile, box 7458, Technical Assistance (026), RG 70, NARA.

98. W. D. Johnston to Joseph Harrington, April 19, 1956, Folder: United States Geological Survey—USBOM Letters, box 12, Mission to Egypt Industry and Mining, Subject Files, 1954–56, Records of U.S. Foreign Assistance Agencies, 1948–1961, NARA.

99. "Circular Private Investment in TCA Countries," October 23, 1952, Folder: Finance—Investments [2 of 3], box 14, Mission to Iraq, RG 469, NARA.

100. In Liberia, the revised mineral code of 1954 expanded prospecting and exploring rights for individuals. See T. C. Denton to E. W. Pehrson, August 26, 1954, Folder: Liberia, box 7205, Technical Assistance (026), RG 70, NARA; On Colombia's changed mining codes, see Randolph Monteith to Ralph A Visbal, December 8, 1956, Folder: Colombia, box 7683, Technical Assistance (026), RG 70, NARA; On Interior's changing mining codes in Afghanistan, Turkey, and Lebanon, see Louis Turnbull to Paul Hamer, November 22, 1955, Folder: Afghanistan, box 7458, Technical Assistance (026), RG 70, NARA. Through Point Four, new mining codes in

Turkey and Lebanon went into effect, as well as petroleum laws in Costa Rica, though it is less clear if Interior technicians were the key architects. On Turkey and Lebanon, see Louis Turnbull to Paul Hamer, November 22, 1955, Folder: Afghanistan, box 7458, Technical Assistance (026), RG 70, NARA; "Laws on Exploration and Development of Oil Fields," March 15, 1956, Folder: United States Geological Survey—General, box 39, Mission to Peru, RG 469, NARA.

101. "Call for Reforms in Mines, Quarries Law," *Egyptian Gazette,* November 27, 1953.

102. Alan Probert to James Hook, March 18, 1953, Folder: Egypt, box 6933, Technical Assistance (026), RG 70, NARA.

103. See "Call for Reforms in Mines," *Egyptian Gazette;* "Committee's Report on Egypt's Mining Policy," April 13, 1953, Folder: Mining and Petroleum Committee—Egypt Mining Policy, box 7, Mission to Egypt, RG 469, NARA.

104. A lease for the exploration of the Ras Matarma field, discovered by Standard Vacuum and Anglo-Egyptian (Royal Dutch Shell) in 1948, was only issued in 1954 after the new law went into effect. One report observed of this transformation, "The activities of the . . . companies are no longer restricted by any major difficulty." See Chamber of Mining, Quarrying and Petroleum Industries—Annual Report for 1954, Folder: Minerals, box 6, Mission to Egypt, RG 469, NARA.

105. Alan Probert to William Young, August 9, 1954, Folder: Colombia, box 7205, Technical Assistance (026), RG 70, NARA; W. D. Johnston to Glen Brown, January 8, 1954, Folder: Natural Resources—Mineral Surveys, box 4, Mission to Saudi Arabia, RG 469, NARA.

106. Richard Bogue, "Report on the Trip to Showings of Iron Formation Northeast of Diba, Saudi Arabia," June 2, 1953, Folder: Natural Resources—Mineral Survey, box 4, Mission to Saudi Arabia, RG 469, NARA.

107. Clifton Day to Admiral Harold Stevens, February 4, 1956, Folder: Industry and Mining, box 5, Mission to Egypt, RG 469, NARA; Joseph Harrington to Charles Hooper, Magnet Cove Barium Corporation, March 12, 1956, Folder: Foreign Capital Investment, box 3, Mission to Egypt, RG 469, NARA. On the sulfur companies, see PMPC Questionnaires, p. 3, box 41 and 46, RG 220, HSTL. Domestic sulfur was reported by PMPC to be exhausted, explaining the urgency of these particular companies moving abroad. See PMPC, "Meeting and Proceedings of PMPC," 22, April 9, 1951, Folder: Proceedings of the PMPC, p. 10, box 134, RG 220, HSTL.

108. Oral History Interview with William E. Warne, Independence, MO, May 21, 1988, HSTL (emphasis added); see also Howard Page to American Embassy, October 28, 1954, Folder: Oil—1954, box 13, Mission to Iran, RG 469, NARA. Warne is absent in Yergin's account of the creation of consortium in *The Prize,* 471.

109. On the mining projects in Iran, see Richard Bogue to William Warne, October 30, 1954, Folder: Mining, box 21, Mission to Iran, RG 469, NARA; Russell Gibson to William Warne, June 16, 1954, Folder: Mining, box 21, Mission to Iran, RG 469, NARA; Russell Gibson to Thomas E. Kilcrease, November 6, 1954, Folder: Mining, box 21, Mission to Iran, RG 469, NARA.

110. Beginning in 1961 and carrying through the 1980s, Interior geologists continued foreign operations under the new U.S. Agency for International Development but were fewer in number. See Charles K. Paul to Dean Alter, "USGS Office of Inter-

national Geology (OIG) and Remote Sensing Dealings with AID," March 3, 1982, Folder: Chronological File—Charles K. Paul, January 1, 1982–March 31, 1981, box 1, USAID/Bureau for Science and Technology/Office of Forestry, RG 286, NARA. See also Eckes, *United States and the Global Struggle for Minerals,* 230, 239.

5 · The Bounty of the Seas

1. Harold L. Ickes, "Our New Frontiers," January 10, 1946, Folder: Articles: "Our New Frontiers," box 118, Secretary of the Interior Files, Papers of Harold L. Ickes, Manuscripts Division, Library of Congress, Washington, DC. Although Harold Ickes, like most of his contemporaries, referred to this region in proper noun form, "Continental Shelf" and "Outer Continental Shelf," a tendency that highlights the parity with which they treated this zone and those defined by political borders like the Middle East, I follow historians' more recent habit of using its common noun form, "continental shelf" and "outer continental shelf."

2. See Lauren Benton, *A Search for Sovereignty: Law and Geography in European Empires, 1400–1900* (New York: Cambridge University Press, 2009); Helen Rozwadowski, *Fathoming the Ocean: The Discovery and Exploration of the Deep Sea* (Cambridge: Belknap Press of Harvard University, 2008); Clyde Sanger, *Ordering the Oceans: The Making of the Law of the Sea* (Toronto: University of Toronto Press, 1986); Kurkpatrick Dorsey, *Whales and Nations: Environmental Diplomacy on the High Seas* (Seattle: University of Washington Press, 2013); Carmel Finley, *All the Fish in the Sea* (Chicago: University of Chicago Press, 2011).

3. The move to the continental shelf does not register in traditional diplomatic histories of American expansionism. As a sampling, see William Appleman Williams, *The Tragedy of American Diplomacy* (New York: W. W. Norton, 1972); Walter LaFeber, *The New Empire: An Interpretation of American Expansion, 1860–1898* (Ithaca: Cornell University Press, 1963); Paul Kramer, "Power and Connection: Imperial Histories of the United States in the World," *American Historical Review* 116, no. 5 (2011): 1348–1391.

4. Historians of oil make reference to the shift offshore, but do not analyze the significance of this territorial acquisition. See, as a sample, David Painter, *Oil and the American Century: Political Economy and American Foreign Oil Policy, 1941–1954* (Baltimore: Johns Hopkins University Press, 1986); Daniel Yergin, *The Prize: The Epic Quest for Oil, Money and Power* (New York: Free Press, 2008). Those who consider the move as a new frontier for business include Tyler Priest, *The Offshore Imperative: Shell Oil's Search for Petroleum in Postwar America* (College Station: Texas A&M University Press, 2007); Tyler Priest, "Extraction Not Creation: The History of Offshore Petroleum in the Gulf of Mexico," *Enterprise & Society* 8, no. 2 (2007): 227–267; Joseph A. Pratt, *Offshore Pioneers: Brown & Root and the History of Offshore Oil and Gas* (Houston: Gulf Publishing Company, 1997).

5. In the postwar era, the U.S. government invested heavily in the ocean's capacities to further national defense and militarism, even as it undertook policies to make the ocean an object of international cooperation. On the tension between national interest and international cooperation, symbolized by U.S. participation in the International Geophysical Year of 1957, see Jacob Darwin Hamblin, *Oceanographers and*

the Cold War: Disciples of Marine Science (Seattle: University of Washington Press, 2005), xvii.

6. Timothy Mitchell, *Carbon Democracy: Political Power in the Age of Oil* (London: Verso Press, 2011), 175.

7. On the Santa Barbara oil spill's influence on environmental action, see Adam Rome, "'Give Earth a Chance': The Environmental Movement and the Sixties," *Journal of American History* 90, no. 2 (2003): 525–554. A growing number of environmental organizations, including the Save the Wales movement, arose in protest, framing the problem as a mandate to better steward the global commons, a call that harmonized with Udall's own in the previous years. See Kurkpatrick Dorsey, "National Sovereignty, the International Whaling Commission, and the Save the Whales Movement," in *Nation-States and the Global Environment: New Approaches to International Environmental History*, ed. Erika Marie Bsumek, David Kinkela, and Mark A. Lawrence (New York: Oxford University Press, 2013), 43–61.

8. Jacob Darwin Hamblin has shown how the ocean by virtue of its scope had long been an object of international collaboration. See Hamblin, *Oceanographers and the Cold War*, xx. On the global commons, see also Richard Peet and Michael Watts, eds., *Liberation Ecologies: Environment, Development, Social Movements*, 2nd ed. (New York: Routledge, 2004), xvi–xviii.

9. Ickes, "Our New Frontiers," January 10, 1946, pp. 11–12. Oil increased in importance to military power and industrial modernity over the twentieth century, shoring up American power. See David Painter, "Oil and the American Century," *Journal of American History* 99, no. 1 (2012): 24. Tom McCarthy argues that desire for "automobility" drove both consumption of oil and environmental degradation in *Auto Mania: Cars, Consumers, and the Environment* (New Haven: Yale University Press, 2007).

10. On Ickes's negotiations in Saudi Arabia, see Robert Vitalis, *America's Kingdom: Mythmaking on the Saudi Oil Frontier* (London: Verso, 2008), 63–68, 77–85; Yergin, *The Prize*, 408.

11. Ickes, "Our New Frontiers," January 10, 1946, pp. 11–12. Companies like Shell Oil were vital to locating the oil potential of the Gulf of Mexico in the 1930s with experimental drilling operations especially in Louisiana. See Priest, *The Offshore Imperative*, 30–31, 35.

12. Finley, *All the Fish in the Sea*, 50.

13. See Donald Cameron Watt, "First Steps in the Enclosure of the Oceans: The Origins of Truman's Proclamation on the Resources of the Continental Shelf, 28 September 1945," *Marine Policy* 3, no. 3 (1979): 213.

14. Ibid., 211–224.

15. Arthur W. Schatz, "The Anglo-American Trade Agreements and Cordell Hull's Search for Peace, 1936–1958," *Journal of American History* 1, no. 1 (1970): 85.

16. Tyler Priest, *Global Gambits: Big Steel and the U.S. Quest for Manganese* (New York, 2003), 136–140.

17. Watt, "First Steps in the Enclosure of the Oceans," 213.

18. Priest, *The Offshore Imperative*, 31.

19. Watt, "First Steps in the Enclosure of the Oceans," 211–224.

20. Harry S. Truman, "Proclamation 2667—Policy of the United States with Respect to the Natural Resources of the Subsoil and Sea Bed of the Continental Shelf," September 28, 1945. Online by Gerhard Peters and John T. Woolley, *The American Presidency Project*. http://www.presidency.ucsb.edu/ws/?pid=12332.

21. *Annual Report of the Secretary of the Interior for the Fiscal Year ending June 1, 1946* (Washington, DC: USGPO, 1946), 10.

22. "Federal Rule Urged for Submerged Oil," *New York Times*, February 7, 1948, p. 3. "Tidelands Veto Urged: Krug Says High Court and Not Congress Should Decide Issue," *New York Times*, July 27, 1946, p. 15.

23. Edward A. Fitzgerald, "The Tidelands Controversy Revisited," *Environmental Law* 19 (1988): 209–210.

24. The Department of the Interior during the Administration of President Lyndon B. Johnson, November 1963–January 1969, Vol. I, Folder: Administrative History, box 151, Secretary of the Interior Files, Stewart L. Udall Papers, Special Collections, University of Arizona Library, Tucson, AZ.

25. *Annual Report of the Secretary of the Interior for the Fiscal Year Ending June 1, 1954* (Washington, DC: USGPO, 1955), xviii.

26. Ibid.

27. *Annual Report of the Secretary of the Interior for the Fiscal Year Ending June 1, 1956* (Washington, DC: USGPO, 1957), 122, 265.

28. Priest, *The Offshore Imperative*, 218.

29. Ickes, "Our New Frontiers," January 10, 1946. Ickes claimed the shelf extended 250 miles off New England, 20 miles off Miami, 60 miles off the Gulf of Mexico, and up to 50 miles off the Pacific, varying by depth.

30. Seth S. King, "Brownell Hails Offshore Oil Acts: He Tells State Officials that Continental Shelf Measure Provides Guide for the World," *New York Times*, August 12, 1953, p. 18.

31. Peter Nolan, "Imperial Archipelagos: China, Western Colonialism and the Law of the Sea," *New Left Review* 80 (March 2013): 77–95; Jeffrey D. Wilson, "Mining the Deep Seabed: Domestic Regulation, International Law, and UNCLOS III," *Tulsa Law Journal* (1982), 207–260.

32. United States Senate, Committee on Interior and Insular Affairs, *Hearings, Pursuant to S. Res. 45: A National Fuels and Energy Policy Study, Ninety-Second Congress, Second Session* (Washington, DC: USGPO, 1972), 451.

33. Samuel P. Hays, *Conservation and the Gospel of Efficiency: The Progressive Conservation Movement, 1890–1920* (Cambridge: Harvard University Press, 1959).

34. Thomas Smith, "John Kennedy, Stewart Udall, and New Frontier Conservation," *Pacific Historical Review* 64 (August 1995): 329–362.

35. See Thomas Robertson, *The Malthusian Moment: Global Population Growth and the Birth of American Environmentalism* (New Brunswick: Rutgers University Press, 2012), 1–8.

36. Stewart L. Udall, *The Quiet Crisis* (New York, 1964); Rachel Carson, *Silent Spring* (New York: Penguin, 1962); Douglas Strong, "The Rise of American Esthetic

Conservation: Muir, Mather, and Udall," *National Parks Magazine* 44 (February 1970): 5–9. See also James Morton Thomas, *The Promise of Wilderness: American Environmental Politics Since 1964* (Seattle, 2012).

37. Smith, "John Kennedy, Stewart Udall, and New Frontier Conservation," 342.

38. Laura J. Martin, "Proving Grounds: Ecological Fieldwork in the Pacific and the Materialization of Ecosystems," *Environmental History* 23, no. 3 (July 2018); N. O. Hines, *Proving Ground: An Account of the Radiobiological Studies in the Pacific, 1946–1962* (Seattle: University of Washington Press). The Trust Territories and Island Possessions had passed from rule by Spain, Germany, and Japan between the two World Wars and were home to 78,000 Micronesian and Polynesian peoples. Guam and Samoa transferred to Interior's jurisdiction in 1951, as Hawai'i and Alaska inched closer to statehood.

39. DOI, "Accelerated Development Program for Pacific Islands Cited by Udall Following 25,000 Mile Inspection Tour," July 25, 1962, Folder: June–Aug. 1962, box 103, Secretary of the Interior Files, Stewart L. Udall Papers, Special Collections, University of Arizona Library, Tucson, AZ.

40. "Department of the Interior," 1962, Folder: Dept. of the Interior (misc.), box 88, Secretary of the Interior Files, Stewart L. Udall Papers, Special Collections, University of Arizona Library, Tucson, AZ.

41. Udall-Khrushchev Talk, Folder: SLU's Visit with Khrushchev, box 105, Secretary of the Interior Files, Stewart L. Udall Papers, Special Collections, University of Arizona Library, Tucson, AZ.

42. Guillermo Leon Valencia to Stewart Udall, October 10, 1962, Folder: Trip to Colombia: Inauguration of President G. Leon Valencia, Folder: June–Aug. 1962, box 103, Secretary of the Interior Files, Stewart L. Udall Papers, Special Collections, University of Arizona Library, Tucson, AZ; Arrival Statement by Sec. Udall-Kenya Independence Nairobi, Kenya, December 10, 1963, Folder: Sept. 4–16, 1963 Trip to Africa (Corres., Itinerary, Speeches, etc.), box 111, Secretary of the Interior Files, Stewart L. Udall Papers, Special Collections, University of Arizona Library, Tucson, AZ.

43. Arrival Statement by Secretary Udall, Santiago, Chile, Folder: Oct. 16–23, 1965, Trip to South America (Chile), box 125, Secretary of the Interior Files, Stewart L. Udall Papers, Special Collections, University of Arizona Library, Tucson, AZ.

44. "Remarks by Secretary of the Interior Stewart L. Udall to the Inter-American Specialized Conference," Mar del Plata, Argentina, October 18, 1965, Folder: Oct. 16–23, 1965, Trip to South America (Argentina), box 125, Secretary of the Interior Files, Stewart L. Udall Papers, Special Collections, University of Arizona Library, Tucson, AZ.

45. DOI, "Sec. Udall Commends Conservation Gains in Latin America; Urges Attention to Overall Environment in Dealing with Resources," October 19, 1965, Folder: Oct. 16–23, 1965, Trip to South America (Argentina), box 125, Secretary of the Interior Files, Stewart L. Udall Papers, Special Collections, University of Arizona Library, Tucson, AZ. Emphasis added.

46. Udall's Visit to East Africa (schedule), Folder: Sept. 4–16, 1963 Trip to Africa (Corres., Itinerary, Speeches, etc.), box 111, Secretary of the Interior Files, Stewart L. Udall Papers, Special Collections, University of Arizona Library, Tucson, AZ.

47. "Remarks by Secretary of the Interior Stewart L. Udall to the Inter-American Specialized Conference," Mar del Plata, Argentina, October 18, 1965, Folder: Oct. 16–23, 1965, Trip to South America (Argentina), box 125, Secretary of the Interior Files, Stewart L. Udall Papers, Special Collections, University of Arizona Library, Tucson, AZ.

48. Laura Martin, "Mathematizing Nature's Messiness: Graphical Representations of Variation in Ecology, 1930–Present," *Environmental Humanities* 7 (2015): 59–88; Sharon Kingsland, *The Evolution of Ecology, 1890–2000* (Baltimore: Johns Hopkins University Press, 2005).

49. Garrett Hardin claimed the problem required the extension of private property to prevent neglect by diffusion of responsibility, which Udall would not emphasize so explicitly. See "The Tragedy of the Commons," *Science* 162 (December 1968): 1243–1248.

50. Arrival Statement by Secretary Udall, Santiago, Chile. Udall added that nations could "either compete ruthlessly for resources, in a context of scarcity," or they could "respect the laws of nature and share its abundance."

51. "Sec. Udall Says Conservation of Resources May Prove to Be a 'Gyroscopic Force' in World Politics," September 16, 1963, Folder: Sept. 4–16, 1963 Trip to Africa (Corres., Itinerary, Speeches, etc.), box 111, Secretary of the Interior Files, Stewart L. Udall Papers, Special Collections, University of Arizona Library, Tucson, AZ.

52. Address of Secretary of the Interior Stewart L. Udall at the First World Conference on Parks at Seattle, Washington, July 4, 1962, Folder: June–Aug. 1962, box 103, Secretary of the Interior Files, Stewart L. Udall Papers, Special Collections, University of Arizona Library, Tucson, AZ.

53. See Odd Arne Westad, *The Global Cold War* (New York: Cambridge University Press, 2007), 122–123, 138, 146.

54. Eckes, *United States and the Global Struggle for Minerals*, 239.

55. Samuel P. Hays, *Beauty, Health, and Permanence: Environmental Politics in the United States, 1955–1985* (Cambridge: Cambridge University Press, 1987); Rome, "'Give Earth a Chance': The Environmental Movement and the Sixties"; Michael Egan, *Barry Commoner and the Science of Survival: The Remaking of American Environmentalism* (Cambridge: MIT Press, 2009). Levels of carbon dioxide were expected to increase by 25 percent by 2000 (in reality, it increased by 40 percent). See Mitchell, *Carbon Democracy*, 7. Strip mining, for example, had adverse effects on topography, vegetation, and water resources.

56. Udall's shift was a complex one. After initially supporting hydroelectric power, Udall bent to the protestations of the Sierra Club against dams that would interfere with scenic wonders. He then eagerly embraced strip mining on the Navajo reservation. See Andrew Needham, *Power Lines: Phoenix and the Making of the Modern Southwest* (Princeton: Princeton University Press, 2014), 208–209.

57. American Embassy to Department of State, "Visit of the Secretary of Interior Stewart Udall, Oct. 20–23, 1965," November 3, 1965, Folder: Oct. 16–23, 1965, Trip to South America (Chile), box 125, Secretary of the Interior Files, Stewart L. Udall Papers, Special Collections, University of Arizona Library, Tucson, AZ.

58. Udall's Visit to East Africa (schedule), Folder: Sept. 4–16, 1963 Trip to Africa (Corres., Itinerary, Speeches, etc.), box 111, Secretary of the Interior Files, Stewart L. Udall Papers, Special Collections, University of Arizona Library, Tucson, AZ.

59. "Press Conference of the Honorable Stewart L. Udall, Secretary of the Interior," January 18, 1967, Folder: Press Conferences Jan.–March 1967, box 134, Secretary of the Interior Files, Stewart L. Udall Papers, Special Collections, University of Arizona Library, Tucson, AZ.

60. Ibid. After giving limited details about the Middle East trip in his press statement, Udall pivoted to a range of topics, including the Redwood Forest, before the press corps returned to the matter of Saudi Arabia, probing about any significance. Udall dismissed this suggestion.

61. Special, Confidential, "US Secretary of the Interior on Secret Security Mission," February 7, 1967, Folder: Feb. 2–12, 1967 Trip to Middle East (Plans, Corres., Itinerary), box 136, Secretary of the Interior Files, Stewart L. Udall Papers, Special Collections, University of Arizona Library, Tucson, AZ.

62. Ibid. The 1967 protests against Aramco operations were hardly the first. A long legacy of the company's Jim Crow segregation practices toward laborers from across the world consistently compelled workers to organize and fight for rights and redistribution. See Vitalis, *America's Kingdom*.

63. Telegram, State Department, "Secretary Udall's Visit," January 26, 1967, Folder: Feb. 2–12, 1967 Trip to the Middle East (Plans, Corres., Itinerary), box 136, Secretary of Interior Files, Stewart L. Udall Papers, Special Collections of the University of Arizona Library, Tucson, AZ.

64. Schedule of Activities, Saudi Arabia, February 4–8, 1967, Folder: Feb. 2–12, 1967 Trip to Middle East (Plans, Corres., Itinerary), box 136, Secretary of the Interior Files, Stewart L. Udall Papers, Special Collections, University of Arizona Library, Tucson, AZ.

65. Memorandum for Secretary Rusk from Stewart Udall, "South Arabia—a Report on Conversations with King Faisal and U.K. Minister Healey," February 15, 1967, Folder: Feb. 2–12, 1967 Trip to Middle East (Plans, Corres., Itinerary), box 136, Secretary of the Interior Files, Stewart L. Udall Papers, Special Collections, University of Arizona Library, Tucson, AZ.

66. Report to the President, "Middle East Impressions of an Itinerant Traveler," February 14, 1967, Folder: Feb. 2–12, 1967 Trip to Middle East (Plans, Corres., Itinerary), box 136, Secretary of the Interior Files, Stewart L. Udall Papers, Special Collections, University of Arizona Library, Tucson, AZ.

67. Ibid. Udall's use of the term "natives" betrays a conflation of foreign peoples with indigenous peoples under his supervision. This conflation is one company leaders made in moving extractive operations from the American West to Saudi Arabia. See Vitalis, *America's Kingdom*, 58–59.

68. Udall's Visit to East Africa (schedule), Folder: Sept. 4–16, 1963 Trip to Africa (Corres., Itinerary, Speeches, etc.), box 111, Secretary of the Interior Files, Stewart L. Udall Papers, Special Collections, University of Arizona Library, Tucson, AZ.

69. Remarks by the Honorable Stewart L. Udall on February 10, 1967, Folder: Feb. 2–12, 1967 Trip to Middle East (Plans, Corres., Itinerary), box 136, Secretary of the

Interior Files, Stewart L. Udall Papers, Special Collections, University of Arizona Library, Tucson, AZ. Emphasis added.

70. Eckes, *The United States and the Global Struggle for Minerals,* 239.

71. Secretary's Advisory Committee on the Geological Survey to Fred Seaton, December 27, 1960, Folder: Dept. of Interior (misc., Reports from Various Divisions), box 88, Secretary of the Interior Files, Stewart L. Udall Papers, Special Collections, University of Arizona Library, Tucson, AZ.

72. Edward Wenk to Joseph A. Califano, "Marine Science Initiative—Marine Safety," December 1, 1967, Folder: Marine Sciences Program for 1968, box 19, Office Files of James Gaither, Presidential Task Forces, Lyndon B. Johnson Library, Austin, TX.

73. Press Briefings, U.S. Department of the Interior, May 22, 1968, pp. 1, 19, Folder: Press Conferences, June–Aug. 1968, box 139, Secretary of the Interior Files, Stewart L. Udall Papers, Special Collections, University of Arizona Library, Tucson, AZ. On self-sufficiency and national security, see DOI Press Conference of Stewart Udall, July 30, 1968, Folder: Press Conferences, June–Aug. 1968, box 139, Secretary of the Interior Files, Stewart L. Udall Papers, Special Collections, University of Arizona Library, Tucson, AZ.

74. Press Briefings, U.S. Department of the Interior, May 22, 1968. Udall did offer in these statements that the enormity of this resource frontier should note be taken lightly and that officials "ought to sit back and absorb this, and see what the significance of it is." However, caution took a backseat as the shelf bidding began.

75. News and Possible News Makers, June 13, 1968, Folder: "News and Possible News Makers" (Memorandum to the President), box 134, Secretary of the Interior Files, Stewart L. Udall Papers, Special Collections, University of Arizona Library, Tucson, AZ.

76. The Department of the Interior during the Administration of President Lyndon B. Johnson, November 1963–January 1969, Vol. I, "Mineral Resources," p. 16, Folder: Administrative History, box 151, Secretary of the Interior Files, Stewart L. Udall Papers, Special Collections, University of Arizona Library, Tucson, AZ.

77. Ibid., 18. Within twenty years, major strides were made as international ocean drilling funds stemming from Johnson's ocean policies quadrupled from $20 million in 1970 to $80 million in 1980. National Research Council, *Global Ocean Science: Toward an Integrated Approach* (Washington, DC: National Academies Press, 1999), 18–19.

78. On manganese nodules, see Alfred Eckes, *The Global Struggle for Minerals,* 252. On the difficulty of adapting terrestrial mining technologies to ocean contexts in comparison with oil, see The Department of the Interior during the Administration of President Lyndon B. Johnson, November 1963–January 1969, Vol. I, "Mineral Resources," p. 18, Folder: Administrative History, box 151, Secretary of the Interior Files, Stewart L. Udall Papers, Special Collections, University of Arizona Library, Tucson, AZ.

79. Assistant Secretary J. Cordell Moore to Sec. of Interior, October 8, 1965, Folder: Undersecretary (Reports), box 122, Secretary of the Interior Files, Stewart L. Udall Papers, Special Collections, University of Arizona Library, Tucson, AZ.

80. News and Possible News Makers, August 1, 1968, Folder: "News and Possible News Makers" (Memorandum to the President), box 134, Secretary of the Interior

Files, Stewart L. Udall Papers, Special Collections, University of Arizona Library, Tucson, AZ.

81. Shaeffer, Science Adviser to Udall, December 1, 1967, Folder: Dept. of the Interior (Misc. Reports from Various Divisions), box 134, Secretary of the Interior Files, Stewart L. Udall Papers, Special Collections, University of Arizona Library, Tucson, AZ.

82. Thomas F. Bates to Stewart Udall, September 24, 1965, Folder: Undersecretary (Reports), box 122, Secretary of the Interior Files, Stewart L. Udall Papers, Special Collections, University of Arizona Library, Tucson, AZ.

83. Thomas F. Bates to Stewart Udall, October 15, 1965, Folder: Undersecretary (Reports), box 122, Secretary of the Interior Files, Stewart L. Udall Papers, Special Collections, University of Arizona Library, Tucson, AZ.

84. The Department of the Interior during the Administration of President Lyndon B. Johnson, November 1963–January 1969, Vol. I, "Mineral Resources," p. 15. The act also helped to clarify the Interior Department's "objectives, functions, and responsibilities" concerning marine resources.

85. Meeting on Report of Marine Science Commission, Ed Wenk and Matt Nimetz, and Public Law 89–454, 89th Congress, S. 944, June 17, 1966, Folder: Marine Sciences Program for 1968, box 19, Office Files of James Gaither, Presidential Task Forces, Lyndon B. Johnson Library, Austin, TX. The Council consisted of Vice President Hubert Humphrey, Secretary of State Dean Rusk, Secretary of the Navy Paul Ignatius, Secretary of the Interior Stewart L. Udall, Secretary of Commerce C. R. Smith, Secretary of Health, Education, and Welfare Wilber Cohen, Secretary of Transportation Alan S. Boyd, Atomic Energy Commission chairman Glen T. Seaborg, and National Science Foundation director Leland J. Haworth. Observers included NASA administrator James Webb, Smithsonian director S. Dillon Ripley, administrator for Agency for International Development William S. Gaud, Bureau of the Budget director Charles Zwick, Council of Economic Advisers chairman Arthur Okun, Office of Science and Technology director Donald Hornig, and Edward Wenk, Jr., who served as executive secretary of the council. Mention of "the wet NASA" is in Edward Wenk to Joseph A. Califano, "Marine Sciences," December 14, 1967, Folder: Marine Sciences Program for 1968, box 19, Office Files of James Gaither, Presidential Task Forces, Lyndon B. Johnson Library, Austin, TX.

86. The Department of the Interior during the Administration of President Lyndon B. Johnson, November 1963–January 1969, Vol. I, p. 16. The entire enterprise would be aided greatly by the creation of satellites that could newly see indicators of the resource potential of the seas. In this sense, the Interior Department's pursuit of an important role in the oceans dovetailed with its pursuit of a central role in space exploration. As the State Department summarized in 1967, "We have a lead in space-ocean technology," and this technology had "a rich potential for enhancing our capabilities to investigate the oceans and their resources." Glenn E. Schweitzer to James Simsarian, IO / OES, State, "IOC Request for Short Statement on the Application of Spacecraft Technology to Investigations of the Oceans," May 25, 1967, Folder: Space Oceanography, box 26, National Security File—Files of

Charles E. Johnson, Lyndon B. Johnson Library, Austin, TX. Lyndon B. Johnson's NASA report further highlighted this growing convergence of space and ocean technology.

87. Senate Resolution, November 17, 1967, Folder: Space Oceanography, box 26, National Security File—Files of Charles E. Johnson, Lyndon B. Johnson Library, Austin, TX.

88. Assistant Secretary J. Cordell Moore to Sec. of Interior, October 8, 1965, Folder: Undersecretary (Reports), box 122, Secretary of the Interior Files, Stewart L. Udall Papers, Special Collections, University of Arizona Library, Tucson, AZ.

89. The collaboration between Interior and private firms in this instance marked, to borrow from Udall, a reversal of "the familiar situation in which the Federal Government provides research funds to private organizations." Assistant to the Secretary and Director of Information to Lyndon B. Johnson, September 24, 1965, Folder: FG 145 8/1/65–11/23/65, box 205, Executive Files of the Federal Government, Lyndon B. Johnson Library, Austin, TX; R. O. Swenarton to Charles K. Boatner, Director, Office of Information, "Weekly Report on Upcoming Press Releases," September 23, 1965, Folder: 1965, box 9475, General Files, Records of the Bureau of Mines, RG 70, NARA; Allan Sherman, Chief, Office of Mineral Reports, to Charles K. Boatner, Director, Office of Information, "Weekly Report on Upcoming Press Releases," July 22, 1965, Folder: 1965, box 9475, General Files, Records of the Bureau of Mines, RG 70, NARA.

90. News and Possible News Makers, April 25, 1968, Folder: "News and Possible News Makers" (Memorandum to the President), box 134, Secretary of the Interior Files, Stewart L. Udall Papers, Special Collections, University of Arizona Library, Tucson, AZ.

91. They were debating the relative economic merits of two systems: 350 kilometers (200 miles) distance from the shore with 500 meters depth (whichever was greater) and 350 kilometers distance from the shore with 1,000 meters depth. Schaeffer to Stewart Udall, "Weekly Activities Report," December 22, 1967, Folder: Dept. of the Interior (Misc. Reports from Various Divisions), box 134, Secretary of the Interior Files, Stewart L. Udall Papers, Special Collections, University of Arizona Library Tucson, AZ.

92. M. B. Schaeffer, Science Adviser, to Stewart Udall, January 26, 1968, Folder: Dept. of the Interior (Misc. Reports from Various Divisions), box 139, Secretary of the Interior Files, Stewart L. Udall Papers, Special Collections, University of Arizona Library, Tucson, AZ.

93. Ted L. McDorman, *Salt Water Neighbors* (New York: Oxford University Press, 2009), chap. 4; Jeffrey D. Wilson, "Mining the Deep Seabed: Domestic Regulation, International Law, and UNCLOS III," *Tulsa Law Journal* (1982), 207–260.

94. National Council on Marine Resources and Engineering Development, "An Elaboration of President Johnson's Proposal of March 8, 1968 for an International Decade of Ocean Exploration," May 9, 1968, Folder: Marine Sciences Program for 1968, box 19, Office Files of James Gaither, Presidential Task Forces, Lyndon B. Johnson Library, Austin, TX.

95. Ibid. Johnson stated this goal following first, promoting cooperative efforts by scientists to interrogate the ocean's many mysteries, and second, increasing knowledge of food resources to combat world hunger. Minerals were thus rarely positioned as the first priority among international audiences, even as they were the central preoccupation of U.S. officials.

96. Malta proposed ocean exploration as a way to access more resources for developing countries. The State Department encouraged the Johnson administration to make this gesture. On Malta, see Nicholas Katzenbach, the White House, to Joseph Califano, Jr., November 30, 1967, Folder: Marine Sciences Program for 1968, box 19, Office Files of James Gaither, Presidential Task Forces, Lyndon B. Johnson Library, Austin, TX. On the potential profits, see Wilfred Rommel, Bureau of Budget to Nimetz, "Paper to you from Dr. Wenk on the International Decade of Ocean Exploration," January 17, 1968, Folder: Marine Sciences Program for 1968, box 19, Office Files of James Gaither, Presidential Task Forces, Lyndon B. Johnson Library, Austin, TX.

97. After winning the 1968 election, President Richard Nixon renewed commitments to the effort, and the International Decade of Ocean Exploration continued through the 1970s, changing forever the way ocean science was organized. Richard Nixon to Edward Wenk, November 26, 1968, Folder: Marine Sciences Program for 1968, box 19, Office Files of James Gaither, Presidential Task Forces, Lyndon B. Johnson Library, Austin, TX. On the impact of the International Decade on ocean science and the increasing investments therein, see National Research Council, *Global Ocean Science,* 17–20.

98. The Quality of the Environment, Folder: SLU and the President's Staff, box 133, Secretary of the Interior Files, Stewart L. Udall Papers, Special Collections, University of Arizona Library, Tucson, AZ.

99. The department had responsibility in oil spill emergencies because of the Oil Pollution Act of 1924. The continental shelf surrounding the United States had been brought into Interior's sphere as result of the Outer Continental Shelf Lands Act of 1953. See Memo from Lyndon B. Johnson to Clark Clifford, Stewart Udall, Alan Boyd, and Donald Hornig, "Federal Plans for Oil Spill Emergencies," June 7, 1968, Folder: FG 145 8/1/65–11/23/65, box 205, Executive Files of the Federal Government, Lyndon B. Johnson Library, Austin, TX.

100. Stewart Udall to President Johnson, April 21, 1967, Folder: SLU and President Johnson, box 133, Secretary of the Interior Files, Stewart L. Udall Papers, Special Collections, University of Arizona Library, Tucson, AZ.

101. The Department of the Interior during the Administration of President Lyndon B. Johnson, November 1963–January 1969, Vol. I, "Water Pollution Control," p. 32, Folder: Administrative History, box 151, Secretary of the Interior Files, Stewart L. Udall Papers, Special Collections, University of Arizona Library, Tucson, AZ.

102. Malcolm F. Baldwin, "The Santa Barbara Oil Spill," *University of Colorado Law Review* 42 (1970): 41.

103. In 1965, of the $238 million in mineral leases supervised by the Geological Survey, $127 million were in the continental shelf. See Report to President, December 30,

1966, Folder: Reports to President, box 126, Secretary of the Interior Files, Stewart L. Udall Papers, Special Collections, University of Arizona Library, Tucson, AZ.

104. Baldwin, "The Santa Barbara Oil Spill," 50.

105. "Secretary Udall Announces a Program for Offshore Oil and Gas leasing in Gulf of Alaska," November 22, 1967, Folder: Alaska (Misc. and General, 1960–1968), box 153, Secretary of the Interior Files, Stewart L. Udall Papers, Special Collections, University of Arizona Library, Tucson, AZ.

106. Baldwin, "The Santa Barbara Oil Spill," 38.

107. News and Possible News Makers, February 6, 1968, Folder: "News and Possible News Makers" (Memorandum to the President), box 134, Secretary of the Interior Files, Stewart L. Udall Papers, Special Collections, University of Arizona Library, Tucson, AZ.

108. News and Possible News Makers, May 23, 1968, Folder: "News and Possible News Makers" (Memorandum to the President), box 134, Secretary of the Interior Files, Stewart L. Udall Papers, Special Collections, University of Arizona Library, Tucson, AZ.

109. Press Briefings, U.S. Department of the Interior, May 22, 1968, p. 19, Folder: Press Conferences, June–Aug. 1968, box 139, Secretary of the Interior Files, Stewart L. Udall Papers, Special Collections, University of Arizona Library, Tucson, AZ. DOI Press Conference of Stewart Udall, July 30, 1968, p. 6, Folder: Press Conferences, June–Aug. 1968, box 139, Secretary of the Interior Files, Stewart L. Udall Papers, Special Collections, University of Arizona Library, Tucson, AZ.

110. Baldwin, "The Santa Barbara Oil Spill," 34. Map, Results of OCS Sale, February 6, 1968, Folder: Santa Barbara Channel Oil Spill, box 2, Office of the Solicitor, Records Relating to the Santa Barbara Oil Spill, 1969–1975, Records of the Office of the Secretary of the Interior, NARA.

111. John Glude, "Observations on the Effects of the Santa Barbara Oil Spill on Intertidal Species," April 10, 1969. Same folder as above. The leak was likely greater.

112. Baldwin, "The Santa Barbara Oil Spill," 36.

113. Ibid., 34.

114. DOI Circular, "Report Issued on Marine Mammals on San Miguel Island," June 29, 1969, Folder: Legal—Claims, Santa Barbara Channel Oil Spill, box 1, Office of the Solicitor, Records Relating to the Santa Barbara Oil Spill, 1969–1975, Records of the Office of the Secretary of the Interior, NARA.

115. Federal Water Quality Administration, Santa Barbara Oil Incident—Draft, Folder: Santa Barbara Channel Oil Spill, box 2, Office of the Solicitor, Records Relating to the Santa Barbara Oil Spill, 1969–1975, Records of the Office of the Secretary of the Interior, NARA; Baldwin, "The Santa Barbara Oil Spill," 37. On the dangers of Corexit, used extensively in the recent *Deepwater Horizon* oil spill, see Mark Hertsgaard, "What BP Doesn't Want You to Know About the 2010 Gulf Spill," *Newsweek,* April 22, 2013.

116. Robert H. Phelps, "Udall Criticizes Own Role in Drilling," *New York Times,* February 9, 1969, p. 1.

117. Dick Main, "Procedure to Settle Oil Damage Suits Set," *Los Angeles Times,* December 17, 1969.

118. Claim for Damage or Injury, Submitted to Sec. of Interior, Folder: Legal—Claims, Santa Barbara Channel Oil Spill, box 1, Office of the Solicitor, Records Relating to the Santa Barbara Oil Spill, 1969–1975, Records of the Office of the Secretary of the Interior, NARA.

119. U.S. Court of Claims, Pauley Petroleum, Colorado Oil and Gas, Mesa Petroleum, McCulloch Oil Corp of California, JM Huber Corporation, Husky Oil Co. of Delaware, April 9, 1969, Folder: Legal—Claims, Santa Barbara Channel Oil Spill, box 1, Office of the Solicitor, Records Relating to the Santa Barbara Oil Spill, 1969–1975, Records of the Office of the Secretary of the Interior, NARA. Secretary Hickel ultimately denied all claims by August 1969, and claimants took their suits to federal court where they had all made settlements by 1975. See David Lindgren to Shiro Kashiwa, December 8, 1969, Folder: Legal—Claims, Santa Barbara Channel Oil Spill, box 1, Office of the Solicitor, Records Relating to the Santa Barbara Oil Spill, 1969–1975, Records of the Office of the Secretary of the Interior, NARA.

120. Statement by Secretary of the Interior Walter J. Hickel, March 21, 1969, Folder: Santa Barbara Channel Oil Spill, box 2, Office of the Solicitor, Records Relating to the Santa Barbara Oil Spill, 1969–1975, Records of the Office of the Secretary of the Interior, NARA.

121. E. W. Kenworthy, "Nixon to Propose Pollution Agency," *New York Times,* June 1970, p. 1.

122. Phelps, "Udall Criticizes Own Role in Drilling."

6 · Prospecting the Final Frontier

1. Excerpts from Remarks by Secretary of the Interior Stewart L. Udall at Symposium of American Society of Oceanography, Houston, Texas, April 6, 1967, Folder: April 1967, box 136, Secretary of the Interior Files, Stewart L. Udall Papers, Special Collections, University of Arizona Library, Tucson, AZ. Emphasis added.

2. John F. Kennedy, "1960 Democratic National Convention," July 15, 1960, transcript, John F. Kennedy Presidential Library and Museum, http://www.jfklibrary.org/Asset-Viewer/ASo8q50YzoSFUZg9uOi4iw.aspx; John F. Kennedy, "President Kennedy's Inaugural Address," January 20, 1961, transcript, John F. Kennedy Presidential Library and Museum, http://www.jfklibrary.org/Research/Research-Aids/Ready-Reference/JFK-Quotations/Inaugural-Address.aspx.

3. Excerpts from Remarks by Secretary of the Interior Stewart L. Udall at Symposium of American Society of Oceanography. This claim resonated with earlier claims by Interior officials that the experiences of the Interior Department in overseeing expansion had prepared it for international development.

4. The definitive and richly researched account of the low-profile satellite, Pamela Mack's *Viewing the Earth,* similarly positions Landsat as a thing of unfulfilled potential. Mack maintains that key decision makers failed to work effectively with potential users of Landsat data and therefore sealed its fate as a tool that, in trying to appease the many, ultimately dazzled few. See Mack, *Viewing the Earth: The Social Construction of the Landsat Satellite System* (Cambridge, MA: MIT Press, 1990).

Neil Maher has recently considered Landsat's role as a public relations tool for the United States that helped Third World nations develop their natural resources, in keeping with the stated objectives. See Maher, *Apollo in the Age of Aquarius* (Cambridge: Harvard University Press, 2017). For other analyses of the Landsat program, see Pamela Gerald Thomas, "Analyzing Environmental Policy Change: U.S. Landsat Policy, 1964–1998," doctoral dissertation, Colorado State University, 1998; Dorothy Harper, *Eye in the Sky: Introduction to Remote Sensing* (Montreal: Multiscience Publications, 1976). The recent dissertation work of Brian Jirout tells a new history of Landsat and its commercialization and role in agricultural development home and abroad. See Jirout, "One Space Age Development for the World: The American Landsat Civil Remote Sensing Program in Use, 1964–2014," doctoral dissertation, Georgia Technical Institute, 2016. The role of Landsat is downplayed in relation to other important programs in histories of space. See Walter MacDougall, . . . *the Heavens and the Earth: A Political History of the Space Age* (Baltimore: Johns Hopkins University Press, 1985); Roger D. Launius, "Compelling Rationales for Spaceflight? History and the Search for Relevance," in *Critical Issues in the History of Spaceflight*, ed. Steven J. Dick and Roger D. Launius, NASA Sp-200604702 (Washington, DC: NASA, 2008): 55–57; Audra J. Wolfe, *Competing with the Soviets: Science, Technology, and the State in Cold War America* (Baltimore: Johns Hopkins University Press, 2013); Asif A. Siddiqi, *The Soviet Space Race with Apollo* (Gainesville: University Press of Florida, 2003).

5. Scholars examining earthbound pathways for the United States to minerals of the Third World include Odd Arne Westad, *The Global Cold War: The Third World and the Making of Our Times* (New York: Cambridge University Press, 2007); Daniel Yergin, *The Prize: The Epic Quest for Oil, Money and Power* (New York: Free Press, 1991); David Painter, *Oil and the American Century* (Baltimore: Johns Hopkins University Press, 1986); Stephen Krasner, *Defending National Interest: Raw Materials Investments and U.S. Foreign Policy* (Princeton: Princeton University Press, 1978); Alfred Eckes, *The United States and the Global Struggle for Minerals* (Austin: University of Texas Press, 1979); Tyler Priest, *Global Gambits: Big Steel and the U.S. Quest for Manganese* (New York: Praeger, 2003); Timothy Mitchell, *Carbon Democracy: Political Power in the Age of Oil* (London: Verso, 2011); Sebastian Herbstreuth, *Oil and American Identity: A Culture of Dependency and U.S. Foreign Policy* (London: I. B. Tauris, 2016); and Robert Vitalis, *America's Kingdom: Mythmaking on the Saudi Oil Frontier* (New York: Verso, 2009). Although some have portrayed the 1960s, the era of Landsat's early planning stage, as a placeholder interval between the material panics of the 1950s and the energy crises of the 1970s, in which supply of most important industrial resources like iron, copper, and petroleum outstripped demand, many U.S. officials and mining firms continued to believe in the importance of pursuing and maintaining foreign investments in the face of Third World nationalism. See Eckes, *The United States and the Global Struggle for Minerals*, 230.

6. Excerpts from Remarks by Secretary of the Interior Stewart L. Udall at Symposium of American Society of Oceanography, Houston, Texas, April 6, 1967, Folder: April 1967, box 136, Secretary of the Interior Files, Stewart L. Udall Papers, Special Collections, University of Arizona Library, Tucson, AZ.

7. On post-1970s globalization, see Daniel J. Sargent, *A Superpower Transformed: The Remaking of American Foreign Relations in the 1970s* (New York: Oxford University Press, 2014); Thomas Borstelmann, *The 1970s: A New Global History from Civil Rights to Economic Inequality* (Princeton: Princeton University Press, 2012); Saskia Sassen, *Losing Control? Sovereignty in an Age of Globalization* (New York: Columbia University Press, 1995); David Harvey, *The Condition of Postmodernity: An Enquiry into the Origins of Cultural Change* (Oxford: Basil Blackwell, 1989); Arjun Appadurai, *Modernity at Large: Cultural Dimensions of Globalization* (Minneapolis: University of Minnesota Press, 1996).

8. See Eugene M. Shoemaker to V. R. Wilmarth, "Monthly report for Director and Secretary," January 31, 1964, Monthly Reports, 01/1963–01/1969, Records of the U.S. Geological Survey, RG 57, National Archives at Riverside, Perris, CA; D. P. Elston to V. E. McKelvey, "Monthly report for Director and Secretary," January 30, 1963, Monthly Reports, 01/1963–01/1969, Records of the U.S. Geological Survey, RG 57, National Archives at Riverside, Perris, CA. NASA outfitted Apollo missions with 150 pounds of geological tools. Memorandum for President from E. C. Welsh, "Space Activities," February 4, 1966, Folder: Outer Space 1/29/66–3/10/66, box 2, Executive Office Files on Outer Space, Lyndon B. Johnson Library, Austin, TX.

9. Comptroller General, "Review of Development of Certain Scientific Instruments for the Surveyor Project," May 1966, p. 1, Folder: Outer Space, box 293, Executive Office, Files of the Federal Government, Lyndon B. Johnson Library, Austin, TX.

10. On the branch of Astrogeology's role advising the Jet Propulsion Laboratory on geological aspects of Surveyor, see Eugene M. Shoemaker to V. R. Wilmarth, "Monthly report for Director and Secretary," January 31, 1964; Acting Chief, Branch of Astrogeology to Assistant Chief Geologist for Engineering Geology, "Monthly report for Director and Secretary," April 28, 1967, Monthly Reports, 01/1963–01/1969, Records of the U.S. Geological Survey, RG 57, National Archives at Riverside, Perris, CA.

11. See Lyndon B. Johnson, *Report to Congress from the President of the United States: United States Aeronautics and Space Activities,* 1967, Folder: Outer Space, box 294, Executive Office, Files of the Federal Government, Lyndon B. Johnson Library, Austin, TX. On Surveyor's many missions and their incremental findings, see Memo from E. C. Welsh to Lyndon B. Johnson, February 16, 1968, Folder: Outer Space 11/1/67–6/30/68, box 3, Executive Office Files on Outer Space, Lyndon B. Johnson Library, Austin, TX; Memo from E. C. Welsh to Lyndon B. Johnson, June 2, 1967, Folder: Outer Space 5/18/67–7/31/67, box 3, Executive Office Files on Outer Space, Lyndon B. Johnson Library, Austin, TX; Memo from E. C. Welsh to Lyndon B. Johnson, October 6, 1967, Folder: Outer Space 8/1/67–10/31/67, box 3, Executive Office Files on Outer Space, Lyndon B. Johnson Library, Austin, TX; Memo from E. C. Welsh to Lyndon B. Johnson, September 29, 1967, Folder: Outer Space 8/1/67–10/31/67, box 3, Executive Office Files on Outer Space, Lyndon B. Johnson Library, Austin, TX; NASA, Press Kit: Surveyor E, August 31, 1967, Folder: Aeronautical and Space Research, box 7, Executive Office Files on Outer Space, Lyndon B. Johnson Library, Austin, TX.

12. Memorandum for President from E. C. Welsh, "Space Activities," May 22, 1964, Folder: Outer Space 11/22/63–6/19/64, box 1, Executive Office Files on Outer Space, Lyndon B. Johnson Library, Austin, TX.

13. Barry Goldwater, "A Realistic Space Program for America," *Science and Mechanics,* July 21, 1964; Republican Citizens, Release, May 28, 1964, Folder: Outer Space 6/20/64–9/21/64, box 1, Executive Office Files on Outer Space, Lyndon B. Johnson Library, Austin, TX.

14. James Webb to Lyndon B. Johnson, August 21, 1964, Folder: Outer Space 2/27/65–6/10/65, box 1, Executive Office Files on Outer Space, Lyndon B. Johnson Library, Austin, TX; Lyndon B. Johnson, *Report to the Congress from the President of the United States.* Tensions between the civilian and military uses of space plagued the space bureaucracy and also served as competing rationales for its continuation. On the importance of space age management to legitimating NASA, see Roger D. Launius, "Managing the Unmanageable: Apollo, Space Management, and American Social Problems," *Space Policy* 24 (2008): 158–165.

15. Hugh Dryden, "No Tourists on the Moon," *New York Times,* April 19, 1964, p. SMA102.

16. He was invited to speak at the first Earth Day in April 1970. See Brian Herbert, *Dreamer of Dune: The Biography of Frank Herbert* (New York: Tor Books, 2003), 94–99, 522–523; Frank Herbert, *Dune,* 40th Anniversary Edition (New York: Ace Books, 2005).

17. Department of the Interior, "Bureau of Mines Scientists Begin First Moon-Mining Research," July 4, 1965, Folder: 1965, box 9475, Publicity, Records of the Bureau of Mines, NARA.

18. Ibid.

19. John Noble Wilford, "Space Planners Debating Next Stop After the Moon: Mars, Venus and . . . ," *New York Times,* January 22, 1967, p. 1.

20. As one editorial critical of NASA's lunar resource investigations later harshly summarized, "To mine and ship gold from the moon, assuming it's to be found there, would cost a thousand times its earth-value." Ralph E. Lapp, "A Critic's View of Apollo," *New York Times,* July 17, 1969, p. 40. Responding to the successful Apollo 11 landing, the article challenges the "earthly value of these exploits" when the United States spends $40 million a year for the Bureau of Mines and about $95 million for the U.S. Geological Survey.

21. Wolfe, *Competing with the Soviets,* 91. This precedent enabled the United States to place myriad satellites in orbit.

22. Richard N. Gardner, "Outer Space: A Breakthrough for International Law," *American Bar Association Journal* (January 1964).

23. Bill Moyers to Lyndon B. Johnson, May 6, 1966, Folder: Outer Space, box 74, Confidential File, Lyndon B. Johnson Library, Austin, TX.

24. "Treaty on the Principles Governing the Activities of States in the Exploration and Use of Outer Space, Including the Moon and Other Celestial Bodies," Folder: Outer Space 1/21/67–1/30/67, box 2, Executive Office Files on Outer Space, Lyndon B. Johnson Library, Austin, TX; The adoption of the American principles in the U.N.

was swift and unsurprising; the United States had overwhelmingly set the terms of space exploration, and then, as a measure of goodwill, if in reality only a formality, invited the international community to grant their approval. John M. Logsdon, "The Development of International Space Cooperation," in *Exploring the Unknown: Selected Documents in the History of the U.S. Civil Space Program*, ed. John M. Logsdon, with Dwayne A. Day and Roger D. Launius, *Vol. 2, External Relationships* (Washington, DC: NASA SP-4407, 1996), 4.

25. Mack, *Viewing the Earth*, 42.

26. Although the broader scientific community had collectively developed interest in remote sensing, a point evident in the first symposium on remote sensing hosted by the Environmental Research Institute of Michigan (ERIM), which convened geologists from Interior alongside others in academia and private industry, the geologists in the central hub of NASA's innovation had the lead role shaping the satellite. Some of these scientists apparently drew upon findings emerging from the secret CORONA program. See Mack, *Viewing the Earth*, 31; Thomas, "Analyzing Environmental Policy Change," 71–72; Ray Williamson, "The Landsat Legacy: Remote Sensing Policy and the Development of Commercial Remote Sensing," *Physical Environment & Remote Sensing* (July 1997): 887; Donald T. Lauer, Stanley A. Morain, and Vincent V. Salomonson, "The Landsat Program: Its Origins, Evolution, and Impacts," *Physical Environment & Remote Sensing* (July 1997): 832; Curtis Peebles, *The CORONA Project: America's First Spy Satellites* (Annapolis: Naval Institute Press, 1997).

27. Mack, *Viewing the Earth*, 53, 59. Experimentation on lunar geology in NASA programs had produced new technologies that could perform resource prospecting from afar: multispectral scanners and other remote sensors adept at locating mineralized zones and deposits. Homer E. Newell, "Practical Results from the NASA Space Science," 38–39, Folder: 2, box 1, Records of Dr. Homer Newell, Associate NASA Administrator, Records of the National Aeronautics and Space Administration, RG 255, NARA.

28. William T. Pecora nomination, August 10, 1965, Folder: SLU and President Johnson, Folder: Appointment Schedule, box 121, Secretary of the Interior Files, Stewart L. Udall Papers, Special Collections, University of Arizona Library, Tucson, AZ.

29. See "Major Activities of the Bureau of Mines Division of International Activities," Folder: 1965, box 9475, General Files, Records of the Bureau of Mines, RG 70, NARA.

30. On Minas Gerais, see Mack, *Viewing the Earth*, 184. Memorandum for President from E. C. Welsh, "Space Activities," January 14, 1966, Folder: Outer Space 8/8/65–1/28/66, box 1, Executive Office Files on Outer Space, Lyndon B. Johnson Library, Austin, TX; Meeting at the U.S. Geological Survey (USGS), 10 A.M., August 25, 1966, featured in John M. Logsdon, Roger D. Launius, David H. Onkst, and Stephen Garber, eds., *Exploring the Unknown: Selected Documents in the History of U.S. Civilian Space Program, Volume III: Using Space* (Washington, DC: NASA, 1996), 243; Meeting at the U.S. Geological Survey (USGS), August 25, 1966, regarding Remote Sensing and South America, Logsdon, Launius, Onkst, and Garber, *Exploring the Unknown*, 241.

31. Science Advisor to Stewart Udall, September 7, 1966, Folder: Dept. of the Interior (misc. reports from various divisions), box 127, Secretary of the Interior Files, Stewart L. Udall Papers, Special Collections, University of Arizona Library, Tucson, AZ.

32. Excerpts from Remarks by Secretary of the Interior Stewart L. Udall at Symposium of American Society of Oceanography, Houston, Texas, April 6, 1967, Folder: April 1967, box 136, Secretary of the Interior Files, Stewart L. Udall Papers, Special Collections, University of Arizona Library, Tucson, AZ. Emphasis added.

33. Dean McGee to Lyndon B. Johnson, October 8, 1965, Folder: "Ex SO 2/9–30–65, box 6, Subject File SO—Social Affairs, White House Central File, Lyndon B. Johnson Library, Austin, TX; Stewart Udall to Dean McGee, November 5, 1965, Folder: FG 145 8/1/65-11/23/65, box 205, Executive Files of the Federal Government, Lyndon B. Johnson Library, Austin, TX.

34. Department of State, "The Frontiers of South America: Appendix VII, The Use of Satellites for Resource Studies in South America," Folder: Earth Resources Observation Satellite (EROS), Interior Dept., box 14, National Security Files of Charles E. Johnson, Lyndon B. Johnson Library, Austin, TX; Walt Rostow to Mr. Gordon, August 8, 1966, Folder: Earth Resources Observation Satellite (EROS), Interior Dept., box 14, National Security Files of Charles E. Johnson, Lyndon B. Johnson Library, Austin, TX. On Rostow's role in modernization, see Michael Latham, *Modernization as Ideology: American Social Science and 'Nation Building' in the Kennedy Era* (Chapel Hill: University of North Carolina Press, 2000), 45.

35. Memorandum from Walt Rostow to Lyndon B. Johnson, May 27, 1966, Folder: Space Flight, box 74, Confidential File, Lyndon B. Johnson Library, Austin, TX.

36. Eckes, *The United States and the Global Struggle for Minerals,* 239.

37. The founding of the Organization of Petroleum Exporting Countries (OPEC) was a response to oil price cuts originating in the United States that negatively impacted host countries, and while it would take a decade for the organization to reach its full strength, it nevertheless made a resounding statement about growing power and solidarity in the Third World. See Vitalis, *America's Kingdom,* 209; Mitchell, *Carbon Democracy,* 168. It also represented an important iteration of a broader resource sovereignty movement helmed by anticolonial elites. See Christopher Dietrich, *Oil Revolution: Anticolonial Elites, Sovereign Rights, and the Economic Culture of Decolonization* (New York: Cambridge University Press, 2017).

38. Meeting at the U.S. Geological Survey (USGS), 10 A.M., August 25, 1966, featured in Logsdon, Launius, Onkst, and Garber, *Exploring the Unknown,* 241–242; Mack, *Viewing the Earth,* 61.

39. Memo from Charles E. Johnson to Lyndon B. Johnson, September 20, 1966, Folder: Earth Resources Observation Satellite (EROS), Interior Dept., box 14, National Security Files of Charles E. Johnson, Lyndon B. Johnson Library, Austin, TX; Department of State, "The Frontiers of South America." The report elaborated that if "agitation made significant headway," the satellite program could damage U.S. interests. It thus encouraged delicacy, ensuring "the South American governments not only give their consent but also actively cooperate."

40. On the Open Skies accords, see MacDougall, . . . *the Heavens and the Earth,* 186–187. The Soviets established a precedent for international use of space objects for civilian purposes. The reality was that the framework provided what Wolfe calls "legal cover" for military surveillance activities in *Competing with the Soviets,* 90–92.

41. Department of the Interior, "Earth's Resources to Be Studied from Space," September 21, 1966, Folder: Earth Resources Observation Satellite (EROS), Interior Dept., box 14, National Security Files of Charles E. Johnson, Lyndon B. Johnson Library, Austin, TX.

42. Department of the Interior Geological Survey, *Earth Resources Observation Satellite* (1966), Folder: Earth Resources Observation Satellite (EROS), Interior Dept., box 14, National Security Files of Charles E. Johnson, Lyndon B. Johnson Library, Austin, TX. Emphasis added.

43. Charles E. Johnson to E. C. Welsh, November 10, 1966, Folder: Earth Resources Observation Satellite (EROS), Interior Dept., box 14, National Security Files of Charles E. Johnson, Lyndon B. Johnson Library, Austin, TX; Mack, *Viewing the Earth,* 61.

44. Draft NSAM, "Coordination of Civilian Programs Using Earth Sensing Satellites and Clearance of Public Statements Related Thereto," November 25, 1966, Folder: Earth Resources Observation Satellite (EROS), Interior Dept., box 14, National Security Files of Charles E. Johnson, Lyndon B. Johnson Library, Austin, TX; Mack, *Viewing the Earth,* 60.

45. Robert Seamans to Arnold Frutkin, September 27, 1966, Folder: Earth Resources Observation Satellite (EROS), Interior Dept., box 14, National Security Files of Charles E. Johnson, Lyndon B. Johnson Library, Austin, TX.

46. Draft, "A Cooperative Research Program for Brazilian and Mexican Participation in the U.S. Earth Resources Survey Program," November 16, 1966, Folder: Earth Resources Surveying with Brazil and Mexico, box 15, National Security File—Files of Charles E. Johnson, Lyndon B. Johnson Library, Austin, TX.

47. Charles F. Luce, Undersecretary, U.S. Department of the Interior, to Dr. Robert C. Seamans, Jr., Deputy Administrator, NASA, October 21, 1966, with attached "Operational Requirements for Global Resource Surveys by Earth-Orbital Satellites EROS Program." Source: Department of the Interior Library, DOI, WDC, featured in Logsdon, Launius, Onkst, and Garber, *Exploring the Unknown,* 246–247.

48. Charles Johnson to Robert Seamans, 1966, Folder: Earth Resources Surveying with Brazil and Mexico, box 15, National Security File—Files of Charles E. Johnson, Lyndon B. Johnson Library, Austin, TX.

49. "Space Goals and Foreign Policy Priorities," May 10, 1967, Folder: Post-Apollo (Outer Space Goals after Lunar Landing), box 16, National Security File—Files of Charles E. Johnson, Lyndon B. Johnson Library, Austin, TX.

50. Memo from E. C. Welsh to Lyndon B. Johnson, March 29, 1968, Folder: Outer Space 11/1/67–6/30/68, box 3, Executive Office Files on Outer Space, Lyndon B. Johnson Library, Austin, TX.

51. Logsdon, Launius, Onkst, and Garber, *Exploring the Unknown,* 257–262.

52. Excerpts from Remarks by Secretary of the Interior Stewart L. Udall at Symposium of American Society of Oceanography, Houston, Texas, April 6, 1967, Folder: April 1967, box 136, Secretary of the Interior Files, Stewart L. Udall Papers, Special Collections, University of Arizona Library, Tucson, AZ.

53. Address by President Richard Nixon to the UN General Assembly, September 18, 1969, www.presidency.ucsb.edu/ws/index.php?pid=2236. On Vietnam's undercutting the "Pax Americana," a period of American ascendance buoyed by its claims to moral leadership, as well as the Nixon administration's attempts to deal with global visions, see Sargent, *A Superpower Transformed*, 10, 41–42.

54. The governments of Ghana, Mali, Brazil, Egypt, and Thailand offered ringing endorsements of earth resource satellites. Logsdon, Launius, Onkst, and Garber, *Exploring the Unknown*, 257–262.

55. Cited in Mack, *Viewing the Earth*, 187.

56. Excerpts from Remarks by Secretary of the Interior Stewart L. Udall at Symposium of American Society of Oceanography. Udall insisted that raising remote sensing devices to this height would allow officials to "detect and study the earth's mineral and oil structures."

57. Mack, *Viewing the Earth*, 110–115; Thomas, "Analyzing Environmental Policy Change," 63; Minutes of the Landsat Follow-on Interagency Decision Team Meeting, August 18, 1976, NASA Headquarters, Folder: Interagency Decision Team—NASA, box 9, Records of the Agency for International Development, National Archives, College Park, MD.

58. John Noble Wilford, "Mapping in the Space Age," *New York Times*, June 5, 1983, p. SM46.

59. Mack, *Viewing the Earth*, 123, 172; *Mission to Earth: Landsat Views the World* (Washington, DC: Scientific and Technical Information Office National Aeronautics and Space Administration, 1976), 327.

60. Mack, *Viewing the Earth*, 110–115; Thomas, "Analyzing Environmental Policy Change," 63; Minutes of the Landsat Follow-on Interagency Decision Team Meeting, August 18, 1976, NASA Headquarters, Folder: Interagency Decision Team—NASA, box 9, Records of the Agency for International Development, National Archives, College Park, MD.

61. Excerpts from Remarks by Secretary of the Interior Stewart L. Udall at Symposium of American Society of Oceanography. Udall cited the recent Gemini photographs that in just one pass visualized 80 percent of Peru with great accuracy in the span of three minutes.

62. On the piecemeal surveys conducted by the U.S. government in the Cold War, see Megan Black, "Interior's Exterior: The State, Mining Companies, and Resource Ideologies in the Point Four Program," *Diplomatic History* 40, no. 1 (January 2016): 21–23.

63. Mack, *Viewing the Earth*, 27; Minutes of the Landsat Follow-on Interagency Decision Team Meeting, August 18, 1976, NASA Headquarters, Folder: Interagency Decision Team—NASA, box 9, Records of the Agency for International Development, National Archives, College Park, MD.

64. Order Form, Landsat Standard Products, U.S. Department of the Interior Geological Survey, undated, Folder: EROS Data Center-#RSSA-Int. USGS-1-17, box 2, Records of the Agency for International Development, National Archives, College Park, MD. On the cost of images, see Thomas, "Analyzing Environmental Policy Change," 81.

65. Early in the experimental phase, the Geological Survey kept prices low to incentivize participation in the remote-sensing agenda—a goal closely tied to international development. On Landsat revenues, see Minutes of the Landsat Follow-on Interagency Decision Team Meeting, July 7, 1976, NASA Headquarters, Folder: Interagency Decision Team—NASA, box 9, Records of the Agency for International Development, National Archives, College Park, MD.

66. After Udall's tenure had ended, Interior officials of the 1970s recapitulated such claims, citing the way that the technology helped with newly required environmental impact statements and with monitoring strip-mining and reclamation operations from the sky. Merrill Conitz, TA/OST, Summary Statement of AID Requirements for Landsat Follow-on System, July 6, 1976, Folder: Interagency Decision Team—NASA, box 9, Records of the Agency for International Development, National Archives, College Park, MD.

67. On the many voices in the environmental movement, particularly among students, liberals, and women, see Adam Rome, "'Give Earth a Chance': The Environmental Movement and the Sixties," *Journal of American History* 90, no. 2 (2003): 527. On the increasingly global shape of environmentalism, see Richard Peet and Michael Watts, eds., *Liberation Ecologies: Environment, Development, Social Movements* (New York: Routledge, 2004), 3–4. On the environmental movement's push against the nation-state and for transnational solutions, see Kurkpatrick Dorsey, "National Sovereignty, the International Whaling Commission, and the Save the Whales Movement," in *Nation-States and the Global Environment,* ed. Erika Marie Bsumek, David Kinkela, and Mark Atwood Lawrence (New York: Oxford University Press, 2013), 43–61; Frank Zelko, *Make It a Green Peace! The Rise of Countercultural Environmentalism* (New York: Oxford University Press, 2013); David Kinkela, *DDT and the American Century: Global Health, Environmental Politics, and the Pesticide that Changed the World* (Chapel Hill: University of North Carolina Press, 2011); Sheila Jasanoff, "Heaven and Earth: The Politics of Environmental Images," in *Local and Global in Environmental Governance*, ed. Sheila Jasanoff and Marybeth Long Martello (Cambridge: MIT Press, 2004), 32–33; Andrew G. Kirk, *Counterculture Green: The Whole Earth Catalog and American Environmentalism* (Lawrence: University Press of Kansas, 2007).

68. "Remote Sensing in Development," *Science* (1982), Folder: Chronological File—Charles K. Paul, RG 286, January 1, 1982–March 31, 1982, box 1, Records of the Agency for International Development, National Archives, College Park, MD.

69. Merrill Conitz, TA/OST, Summary Statement of AID Requirements for Landsat Follow-on System, July 6, 1976, Folder: Interagency Decision Team—NASA, box 9, Records of the Agency for International Development, National Archives, College Park, MD.

70. Minutes of the Landsat Follow-on Interagency Decision Team Meeting, July 7, 1976, NASA Headquarters, Folder: Interagency Decision Team—NASA, box 9, Records

of the Agency for International Development, National Archives, College Park, MD. Most often, foreign nations had to rely not on local ground stations, which cost an average of $6 million to construct, but rather on the EROS Data Center for data about their resources.

71. Speech of President Marcos at the Opening Ceremony of the Twelfth International Symposium on Remote Sensing of Environment, Folder: 12th International Symposium Remote Sensing of Environment, April 20–26, box 2, Records of the Agency for International Development, National Archives, College Park, MD.

72. Mack, *Viewing the Earth*, 192.

73. An examination of the schedule for the International Symposium on Remote Sensing reveals the geological slant of the early programming. Of the 223 papers presented, 43 dealt directly with minerals, 20 with water resources and hydrology, 19 with agricultural crops and vegetation, and 18 with forestry. Moreover, every summary of national programs indicated that there was geological work under way. *Proceedings of the Twelfth International Symposium on Remote Sensing of Environment, April 20–26, 1978* (Ann Arbor: Environmental Research Institute of Michigan, 1978), vii–xix.

74. Charles K. Paul to William M. Feldman, "Remote Sensing and Global Petroleum Reserves," June 5, 1980; N. C. Brady to ES, "AID's Involvement with Satellites," January 27, 1982, Folder: Chronological File—Charles K. Paul, RG 286, January 1, 1982–March 31, 1982, box 1, Records of the Agency for International Development, National Archives, College Park, MD.

75. *Proceedings of the Twelfth International Symposium on Remote Sensing of Environment*, 191.

76. Ibid., 192. See also Seth Fletcher, *Bottled Lighting: Superbatteries, Electric Cars, and the New Lithium Economy* (New York: Hill and Wang, 2011).

77. *Proceedings of the Twelfth International Symposium on Remote Sensing of Environment*, 2227. Emphasis added.

78. Ibid., 1513, quote from 1517.

79. Problems arose, however, as the international geology unit expressed interest only in geological mapping, and not, as Geological Survey and Landsat supporters behind it hoped, the more practical "goal of finding and bringing up minerals." Charles K. Paul (S&T / FNR) to Dean Alter (NE / PD), "USGS Office of International Geology (OIG) and Remote Sensing Dealings with AID," March 3, 1982, Folder: Chronological File—Charles K. Paul, RG 286, January 1, 1982–March 31, 1982, box 1, Records of the Agency for International Development, National Archives, College Park, MD. On Bokassa, see "Bokassa Crowns Himself Emperor in Rich Central African Pageant," *New York Times*, December 17, 1977, p. 77.

80. Elizabeth Fuller Collins, *Indonesia Betrayed: How Development Fails* (Honolulu: University of Hawaii Press), 10–11.

81. *Proceedings of the Twelfth International Symposium on Remote Sensing of Environment*, 1037–1038.

82. Arthur A. Brant, "Report: The Geosat Committee, Inc.," *Geophysics* 42, no. 4 (1977): 887–889. For NASA's statistics, see *International Journal of Remote Sensing* 1, no. 3 (1980): 314.

83. See *International Journal of Remote Sensing* 1, no. 3 (1980): 314.

84. On Chevron's Landsat allocation, see Mack, *Viewing the Earth,* 175. On the broad purposes to which companies put Landsat to use, see Agenda, IDT Working Group Meeting, June 25, 1976, 1:30–4:30, Directors Conference Room USGS National Center, Reston, Virginia, Folder: Interagency Decision Team—NASA, box 9, Records of the Agency for International Development, National Archives, College Park, MD.

85. Charles K. Paul to William M. Feldman, "Remote Sensing and Global Petroleum Reserves," June 5, 1980. According to the report, the consultant used Landsat with aerial photography to identify anticlines at intersections of wrench faults and initiate wells that produced 20–100 barrels a day.

86. Mack, *Viewing the Earth,* 175.

87. Merrill Conitz, TA/OST, Summary Statement of AID Requirements for Landsat Follow-on System, July 6, 1976, Folder: Interagency Decision Team—NASA, box 9, Records of the Agency for International Development, National Archives, College Park, MD. Emphasis added.

88. Historians have long shown the deep interdependence of the government and corporations in projects as varied as infrastructure, the welfare state, and trade liberalization. Landsat represents the outer limits of a publicly funded infrastructure enabling private gain, one that reached inconspicuously into the heavens. See Jennifer Klein, *For All These Rights: Business, Labor, and the Shaping of America's Public-Private Welfare State* (Princeton: Princeton University Press, 2003); Richard White, *Railroaded: The Transcontinentals and the Making of Modern America* (New York: W. W. Norton, 2011); Christopher F. Jones, *Routes of Power: Energy and Modern America* (Cambridge: Harvard University Press, 2014); David Nye, *Consuming Power: A Social History of American Energies* (Cambridge: MIT Press, 2001).

89. Mack, *Viewing the Earth,* 172–176.

90. See Mitchell, *Carbon Democracy,* 177–181; Herbstreuth, *Oil and American Identity,* 57, 82; Meg Jacobs, "The Conservative Struggle and the Energy Crisis," in *Rightward Bound: Making America Conservative in the 1970s,* ed. Bruce J. Schulman and Julian E. Zelizer (Cambridge: Harvard University Press, 2008), 196–197.

91. Jacobs, "The Conservative Struggle and the Energy Crisis," 196–197; Borstelmann, *The 1970s,* 55–60.

92. John Darnton, "Diplomatic Realignment in Africa Makes Americans Welcome in Sudan," *New York Times,* June 27, 1977, p. 3.

93. Ibid.

94. Charles K. Paul to Merril Conitz, "Remote Sensing Oil Discovery in Sudan," June 2, 1980, Folder: Chronological File—Paul and Withington, April 1–June 30, 1980, box 1, Records of the Agency for International Development, National Archives, College Park, MD.

95. Luke Patey, *The New Kings of Crude: China, India, and the Struggle for Oil in Sudan and South Sudan* (London: Hurst, 2014), 1–3. On the history of oil conflicts in Sudan, see Foreign Affairs, Defense, and Trade Division (CRS), "Sudan: Humanitarian Crisis, Peace Talks, Terrorism, and U.S. Policy," September 27, 2004, p. 11, IB98043, ProQuest CRS Report, February 22, 2015.

96. Charles K. Paul to William M. Feldman, "Remote Sensing and Global Petroleum Reserves," June 5, 1980.

97. *Proceedings of the Twelfth International Symposium on Remote Sensing of Environment,* 404.

98. Ibid., 404. Emphasis Added.

99. Speech of President Marcos at the opening ceremony of the Twelfth International Symposium on Remote Sensing of Environment. Other countries represented at the symposium included Argentina, Australia, Bangladesh, Bolivia, Canada, Costa Rica, Czechoslovakia, England, East and West Germany, France, Greece, Hong Kong, India, Indonesia, Iraq, Italy, Japan, Kenya, Malaysia, New Zealand, Oman, China, Peru, Philippines, Poland, Qatar, Sierra Leone, Singapore, South Korea, Sri Lanka, Surinam, Switzerland, Turkey, Uganda, and the United States.

100. J. Troughton, "News Section: United Nations and Remote Sensing," *International Journal of Remote Sensing* 1, no. 3 (1980): 316.

101. Joanne Irene Gabrynowicz, ed., *The UN Principles Relating to Remote Sensing of the Earth from Space: A Legislative History—Interviews of Members of the United States Delegation* (Oxford: University of Mississippi School of Law, 2002), 13, 27.

102. Troughton, "News Section: United Nations and Remote Sensing," 316.

103. This latter system was characterized by such diffuse chains of production and supply that workers could not strike and shut down the operations of far-flung oil installations as easily in the continual struggle for rights. Mitchell, *Carbon Democracy,* 7.

104. Stephani Yanchinski, "Thorny Questions over Remote Sensing," *The New Scientist,* April 17, 1980, p. 150.

105. Edward Said, *Orientalism* (New York: Penguin Books, 1978), 12–14.

106. Charles K. Paul to Dean Alter, "USGS Office of International Geology (OIG) and Remote Sensing Dealings with AID," March 3, 1982, Folder: Chronological File—Charles K. Paul, RG 286, January 1, 1982–March 31, 1982, box 1, Records of the Agency for International Development, National Archives, College Park, MD.

107. See Deborah Mackenzie, "Cutbacks Jeopardise Landsat Work," *The New Scientist,* October 11, 1984, p. 4; Mack, *Viewing the Earth,* 3.

108. The eventual and temporary transfer of control from the U.S. government to private operators in the late 1980s ultimately drove up prices and alienated users, including a mining sector that already had an arsenal of data that would remain relevant long into the future. See Thomas, "Analyzing Environmental Policy Change," 134–140; Committee on Science, Space, and Technology (HR), "Landsat Program: Management, Funding, and Policy Decisions," November 26, 1991, p. 1, 92-H701-42, ProQuest Hearings Published, March 28, 2015.

109. See Seth Garfield, "The Brazilian Amazon and the Transnational Environment, 1940–1990," in Bsumek, Kinkela, and Lawrence, *Nation-States and the Global Environment,* 235, 239.

7 · The Wealth of the Wastelands

1. David F. Salisbury, "American Indians Intend to Use Own Energy Wealth," *Christian Science Monitor,* November 16, 1977.

2. The Geological Survey shifted these figures in the next five years, so that by 1980, the assessments of tribal uranium holdings in particular were more modest at 37 percent. Marjane Ambler, *Breaking the Iron Bonds: Indian Control of Energy Development* (Lawrence: University of Kansas Press, 1991), 94.

3. Roger Cohn, "Energy Gives Indians New Potential Clout," *Philadelphia Inquirer,* September 8, 1980, p. 1.

4. Special to the *New York Times*, "Navajo Leader Is Guilty in a Tribal Bribery Trial," *New York Times,* October 18, 1990, A16.

5. Peter MacDonald, "The Bottom Line," Folder: Council of Energy Resource Tribes, box 264, Indian Rights Association records (Collection 1523), Historical Society of Pennsylvania, Philadelphia, PA.

6. OPEC had earlier posited such a transnational imaginary, but the *Indian* OPEC did so in ways that called attention to the porosity of nation-states and the internal colonies therein. On imaginaries, see Benedict Anderson, *Imagined Communities* (London: Verso Press, 1991), 6–7, 37–40. Fernando Coronil revises this theory to insist that imagined political communities are equally dependent on "the very materiality of the nation as a life-sustaining habit." See Coronil, *The Magical State: Nature, Money, and Modernity in Venezuela* (Chicago: University of Chicago Press, 1997), 8.

7. Ambler, *Breaking the Iron Bonds;* Alexandra Harmon, *Rich Indians: Native People and the Problem of Wealth* (Chapel Hill, NC: University of North Carolina Press, 2010); Donald Fixico, *The Invasion of Indian Country in the Twentieth Century* (Niwot: University Press of Colorado, 1998); Sherry L. Smith and Brian Frehner, eds., *Indians & Energy: Exploitation and Opportunity in the American Southwest* (Santa Fe, NM: School for Advanced Research, 2010); Traci Brynne Voyles, *Wastelanding: Legacies of Uranium Mining in Navajo Country* (Minneapolis: University of Minnesota Press, 2015); James Robert Allison, *Sovereignty for Survival: American Energy Development and Indian Self-Determination* (New Haven: Yale University Press, 2015). On U.S. energy policy outside of Native American reservations, see Daniel Yergin, *The Prize: The Epic Quest for Oil, Money and Power* (New York: Free Press, 2008); Richard Vietor, *Energy Policy in America Since 1945: The Study of Business-Government Relations* (New York: Cambridge University Press, 1987); David E. Nye, *Consuming Power: A Social History of American Energies* (Cambridge: MIT Press, 2001); Daniel J. Sargent, *A Superpower Transformed: The Remaking of American Foreign Relations in the 1970s* (New York: Oxford University Press, 2014), chap. 5; Michael T. Klare, *Blood and Oil: The Dangers and Consequences of America's Growing Petroleum Dependency* (New York: Metropolitan Books, 2004); Bruce A. Beaubouef, *The Strategic Petroleum Reserve: U.S. Energy Security and Oil Politics, 1975–2005* (College Station: Texas A&M University Press, 2007). This chapter therefore enters only in a narrow and limited way the rich and varied historiography on Native American experience and activism. In showing the connections between indigenous policy and foreign policy, it falls short of a nuanced account of negotiations within and between indigenous nations.

8. Timothy Mitchell, *Carbon Democracy: Political Power in the Age of Oil* (London: Verso, 2011), 180.

9. Meg Jacobs, "The Conservative Struggle and the Energy Crisis," in *Rightward Bound: Making America Conservative in the 1970s,* ed. Bruce J. Schulman and Julian E. Zelizer (Cambridge: Harvard University Press, 2008), 196–197; Bruce Schulman, *The Seventies: The Great Shift in American Culture, Society, and Politics* (New York: Free Press, 2001), 127.

10. Richard Vietor, *Energy Policy in America since 1945: A Study of Business-Government Relations* (New York: Cambridge University Press, 1987), chaps. 5 and 6.

11. On U.S. foreign policy and material interest in the developing world, see Melvyn P. Leffler, *A Preponderance of Power: National Security, the Truman Administration, and the Cold War* (Stanford: Stanford University Press, 1992); Odd Arne Westad, *The Global Cold War: Third World Interventions and the Making of Our Times* (New York: Cambridge University Press, 2007); David Painter, "Oil and the American Century" *Journal of American History* 99 (June 2012): 24–40.

12. On OPEC's founding, see Robert Vitalis, *America's Kingdom: Mythmaking on the Saudi Oil Frontier* (New York: Verso, 2009) and Siba Grovugu, "A Revolution Nonetheless: The Global South in International Relations," *Global South* 5, no. 1 (Spring 2011): 175–190.

13. The Arab OPEC members sought, as Timothy Mitchell has argued, to tie availability of oil from producer nations to U.S. support for Palestine. The event came to be more simplistically understood as an embargo tied to a price hike, which in turn was labeled a "crisis" of energy. However, the limitation of oil from some Middle Eastern nations, excluding Iran and other oil producers that would continue to supply oil to the United States and its trade partners, was never as total as it seemed. Consumer panic and government overcompensation fueled the deteriorating situation. Mitchell, *Carbon Democracy,* 175–176.

14. Jacobs, "The Conservative Struggle and the Energy Crisis," 196–197; Thomas Borstelmann, *The 1970s: A New Global History from Civil Rights to Economic Inequality* (Princeton: Princeton University Press, 2012), 55–60.

15. Everette DeGolyer declared after World War II that the "center of gravity of world oil production" shifted from the Caribbean and U.S. Gulf Coast to the Middle East, as cited in Nathan J. Citino, "Internationalist Oilmen, the Middle East, and the Remaking of American Liberalism, 1945–1953," *Business History Review* 84 (Summer 2010): 233.

16. Borstelmann, *The 1970s,* 55–60; Jacobs, "The Conservative Struggle and the Energy Crisis," 194–199; Allison, *Sovereignty for Survival,* 39–41.

17. William Endicott, "Indians Seek Help from OPEC," *Los Angeles Times,* October 16, 1977, p. A3.

18. Ambler, *Breaking the Iron Bonds,* 13; MacDonald, "The Bottom Line." MacDonald argued that three centuries before, Indians "gave a continent," while in the 1970s, they were once again giving so much without receiving fair compensation.

19. Daniel M. Cobb, *Native Activism in Cold War America: The Struggle for Sovereignty* (Lawrence: University Press of Kansas, 2008), 11–13, 76.

20. On the National Congress of American Indians' agitation for a domestic Point Four, see Paul C. Rosier, *Serving Their Country: American Indian Politics and Patriotism in the Twentieth Century* (Cambridge: Harvard University Press, 2012), 191–200, and Alyosha Goldstein, *The Politics of Community Action During the American Century*

(Durham: Duke University Press, 2012), 78. On the Association on American Indian Affairs' involvement, see Daniel M. Cobb, "American Indian Politics in Cold War America: Parallel & Contradiction," *Princeton University Library Chronicle* 67, no. 2 (Winter 2006): 407.

21. On the Atomic West, see Arthur R. Gomez, *Quest for the Golden Circle: The Four Corners and the Metropolitan West, 1945–1970* (Lawrence: University Press of Kansas, 2000). On the BIA, see Ambler, *Breaking the Iron Bonds,* 58.

22. Winona LaDuke, "Native America: The Economics of Radioactive Colonization," *Review of Radical Political Economies* 15, no. 9 (1983): 12.

23. Voyles, *Wastelanding,* 4.

24. Ambler, *Breaking the Iron Bonds,* 58.

25. Ibid., 53, 63.

26. Ann Crittenden, "Tribes Tap Iranian's Fuel Expertise," *New York Times,* August 7, 1979, p. D1.

27. LaDuke, "Native America," 14.

28. Phileo Nash, Commissioner of Indian Affairs, to Stewart Udall, "Coal Reserves on the Navajo Indian Reservation in New Mexico," August 26, 1965, Folder: Indian Affairs (Economic Development), box 154, Secretary of the Interior Files, Stewart L. Udall Papers, Special Collections, University of Arizona Library, Tucson, AZ.

29. Stewart Udall to Bennett, August 10, 1967, Folder: Indian Affairs (Economic Development), box 154, Secretary of the Interior Files, Stewart L. Udall Papers, Special Collections, University of Arizona Library, Tucson, AZ.

30. It became an early symbol of the unequal distribution of economic benefits and environmental tolls across the geography of the American West. Andrew Needham, *Power Lines: Phoenix and the Making of the Modern Southwest* (Princeton: Princeton University Press, 2014), 213; William Greider, "Indians Organize own Energy Combine," *Washington Post,* July 17, 1977, p. 2.

31. Needham, *Power Lines,* 245.

32. This history of legal vacillation on tribes' sovereign status is recounted in Kevin Bruyneel, *The Third Space of Sovereignty: The Postcolonial Politics of U.S.-Indigenous Relations* (Minneapolis: University of Minnesota Press, 2007). On termination policies and activism, see Cobb, "American Indian Politics in Cold War America," 393–394; Sherry L. Smith, *Hippies, Indians, and the Fight for Red Power* (New York: Oxford University Press, 2012), 4–5.

33. Joseph G. Jorgensen, "A Century of Political Economic Effects on American Indian Society, 1880–1980," *Journal of Ethnic Studies* 6, no. 3 (Fall 1978): 50–52.

34. MacDonald, "The Bottom Line." MacDonald frequently identified both energy firms and the Interior Department as antagonists, but ultimately portrayed the firms as the lesser of two evils.

35. Ambler, *Breaking the Iron Bonds,* 92–93.

36. Indian Affairs New Priority for Interior, Folder: Bureau of Indian Affairs, box 76, Office of Public Liaison—Costanza, Jimmy Carter Library, Atlanta, GA.

37. See, for example, MacDonald, "The Bottom Line."

38. Mark and Judith Miller, "The Politics of Energy v. the American Indian," *USA Today,* March 1979, reprinted in *Akwesasne Notes* 11, no. 2 (May 1979): 20–21.

39. White House, "CERT Agenda / Proposal," February 13, 1978, Folder: Indian Energy Meeting, box 78, Office of Public Liaison—Costanza, Jimmy Carter Library, Atlanta, GA.

40. Lou Cannon, "Insurance Company Offers to Invest in Indian Energy," *Washington Post,* November 18, 1978, p. A2.

41. Jack Watson, "Indians," January 6, 1978, Folder: Indian Meeting 10/77–3/78, box 78, Office of Public Liaison—Costanza, Jimmy Carter Library, Atlanta, GA.

42. On OPEC's commitments to give aid in the Global South as a counterbalance to Israeli aid, see Paul Hallwood and Stuart Sinclair, "OPEC's Developing Relationships with the Third World," *International Affairs* (Spring 1982): 272.

43. It was not until the coalition framed their struggle as a global one, forging connections to the much-despised OPEC, that it established a national reputation. Although pan-tribal activism of the 1960s and 1970s, including the National Congress of American Indians (NCAI), National Indian Youth Council (NIYC), and American Indian Movement (AIM), had been—by the nature of tribal sovereignty— "transnational," CERT became transnational in new global directions as well.

44. Bill Strabala, "Indian Tribes Seek to Form OPEC-Style Energy Cartel," *Denver Post,* July 10, 1977, p. 1.

45. Ibid. This imagined community does not conform to what Benedict Anderson outlined, but nevertheless shares certain meaningful qualities, like the need to create a shared past. See Anderson, *Imagined Communities* (London: Verso Press, 1991), 6–7.

46. Crittenden, "Tribes Tap Iranian's Fuel Expertise"; Endicott, "Indians Seek Help from OPEC."

47. Greider, "Indians Organize own Energy Combine."

48. Cited in Vitalis, *America's Kingdom,* epigraph. See also Rob Nixon, *Slow Violence and the Environmentalism of the Poor* (Cambridge: Harvard University Press, 2011), 68.

49. Hallwood and Sinclair, "OPEC's Developing Relationships with the Third World," 271.

50. Associated Press, "Ex-Iranian Official Named to U.S. Indian Energy Post," *Albuquerque Journal,* August 9, 1979.

51. Ambler, *Breaking the Iron Bonds,* 97.

52. Crittenden, "Tribes Tap Iranian's Fuel Expertise."

53. Associated Press, "Ex-Iranian Official Named to U.S. Indian Energy Post"; Associated Press, "Indians Offer Energy Plan," *Reading Eagle,* August 9, 1979.

54. Carolyn Niethammer, "The First Americans: Trading Energy for a Piece of the Pie," *Los Angeles Times,* August 26, 1979.

55. Peter MacDonald, "Statement by Peter MacDonald at CERT 1981 Annual Meeting," Denver, CO, October 26, 1981, Folder: Council of Energy Resource Tribes, box 264, Files of the Indian Rights Association Record 1523, Historical Society of Pennsylvania, Philadelphia, PA.

56. In February 1978, the Carter administration scheduled a meeting with Peter MacDonald and the council. MacDonald claimed the purpose was to explain CERT's precarious position and to discuss the historic mismanagement of leases and information related to tribal resources by the Interior Department. The White House

agreed to take the meeting in large part because Interior's BIA had assured them that the meetings with OPEC the previous summer were purely technical—on matters of pricing and resource availability. This was the opinion they shared with Jack Watson, Carter's White House staff assigned to the case, who seemed similarly unconcerned about the OPEC contacts, despite the vitriol playing out in the press. Watson explained that an economic alliance would be "impossible." See Jack Watson, "Indians," January 6, 1978, p. 6, Folder: Indian Meeting 10/77–3/78, box 78, Office of Public Liaison—Costanza, Jimmy Carter Library, Atlanta, GA.

57. Endicott, "Indians Seek Help from OPEC."

58. Jack Watson, "Indians," January 6, 1978, p. 6, Folder: Indian Meeting 10/77–3/78, box 78, Office of Public Liaison—Costanza, Jimmy Carter Library, Atlanta, GA.

59. "American Indians Seek OPEC Aid," *Christian Science Monitor,* July 19, 1977.

60. For scholarship on reverse discrimination, affirmative action, and white (ethnic) grievance, see Ronald P. Formisano, *Boston Against Busing: Race, Class, and Ethnicity in 1960s and 1970s* (Chapel Hill: University of North Carolina Press, 1991); Robert O. Self, *American Babylon: Race and the Struggle for Postwar Oakland* (Princeton: Princeton University Press, 2003); Kevin Kruse, *White Flight: Atlanta and the Making of Modern Conservatism* (Princeton: Princeton University Press, 2007); Joseph Crespino, *In Search of Another Country: Mississippi and the Conservative Counterrevolution* (Princeton: Princeton University Press, 2007). Scholars have begun to move beyond the black-white binary and urban center of this narrative. See Lawrence D. Bobo and Mia Tuan, *Prejudice in Politics: Group Position, Public Opinion, and the Wisconsin Treaty Rights Dispute* (Cambridge: Harvard University Press, 2006).

61. Kevin P. Phillips, "The Potential Problems of Indian Sovereignty," *Arizona Republic,* September 4, 1977.

62. Pat Oliphant, *Washington Star,* July 22, 1977, p. A-11. The syndicated political cartoon was featured two weeks later along with the Kevin P. Phillips editorial in the *Arizona Republic,* September 4, 1977. For another article in which Indians were depicted as rich, see the cartoon accompanying Associated Press, "Hard Bargains," *Sumter Daily Item,* September 6, 1978.

63. Melani McAlister, *Epic Encounters: Culture, Media, and U.S. Interests in the Middle East, 1945–2000* (Berkeley, University of California Press, 2001), 136.

64. Greider, "Indians Organize own Energy Combine"; *Washington Post* News Service, "Indian OPEC? Navajos Join Push to Control Natural Riches," *Tucson Citizen,* July 18, 1977; *Washington Post* News Service "Indians Forming New Energy Cartel," *Tuscaloosa News,* July 21, 1977.

65. On connections between welfare queens and oil sheiks in the energy crisis, see Natasha Zaretsky, *No Direction Home: The American Family and the Fear of National Decline, 1968–1980* (Chapel Hill: University of North Carolina Press, 2007), 80.

66. "Indians in OPEC?" *Denver Post,* August 13, 1979.

67. Zaretsky, *No Direction Home,* 80.

68. Interstate Congress for Equal Rights and Responsibilities (ICERR), "Are We Giving Back America to the Indians?," Folder: Backlash—Articles, Publications, etc. (1977–

1980), box 296, Files of the Indian Rights Association Record 1523, Historical Society of Pennsylvania, Philadelphia, PA.

69. Reportage across the nation toward the end of the 1970s increasingly identified a "toughening mood of an American majority disenchanted with the doctrine of white guilt." See Howell Raines, "American Indians Struggling for Power and Identity," *New York Times*, February 11, 1979.

70. Endicott, "Indians Seek Help from OPEC." Alongside H.R. 9054, eleven like-minded bills before Congress aimed to deprive Native Americans of their rights.

71. Scholars have offered different frameworks to understand indigenous agency since earliest European settlement. See Richard White, *The Middle Ground: Indians, Empires, and Republics in the Great Lakes Region, 1650–1815, Anniversary Edition* (New York: Cambridge University Press, 2010); Frederick Hoxie, "Retrieving the Red Continent: Settler Colonialism and the History of American Indians in the US," *Ethnic and Racial Studies* 31, no. 6 (2008); Audra Simpson, *Mohawk Interruptus* (Durham: Duke University Press, 2014).

72. Mike Meyers, "Ahmed Kooros: A Discussion," *Akwesasne Notes*, May 1980, 27.

73. Russell Means, Speech at Black Hills International Survival Gathering, July 19, 1980, Folder: Means, Russell (1976–1980), box 311, Files of the Indian Rights Association Record 1523, Historical Society of Pennsylvania, Philadelphia, PA. The speech was transcribed and printed in *Mother Jones*, December 1, 1980, pp. 26–38. See also Toby McLeod, "Has CERT Sold Out?," *Mother Jones*, December 1, 1980, p. 31.

74. On OPEC's straddling the boundary between a status as "developing" and "industrialized," see Mary Ann Tetreault, *The Organization of Arab Petroleum Exporting Countries: History, Policies, and Prospects* (Westport, CT: Greenwood Press, 1981), 1–5. On developing world disillusionment with OPEC, see Hallwood and Sinclair, "OPEC's Developing Relationships with the Third World," 273.

75. Hallwood and Sinclair, "OPEC's Developing Relationships with the Third World," 275.

76. Denise Tessier, "United Nuclear Will Reopen Its Mill Today," *Albuquerque Journal*, October 29, 1979.

77. Voyles, *Wastelanding*, 4.

78. Winona LaDuke, "CERT: An Outsider's Perspective," *Akwesasne Notes* 12, no. 3 (1980): 19–22.

79. Finis Dunaway, "Gas Masks, Pogo, and the Ecological Indian: Earth Day and the Visual Politics of American Environmentalism," *American Quarterly* 60, no. 1 (March 2008): 67–99.

80. Merrill Sheils, "The Rich Indians," *Newsweek*, March 20, 1978, p. 63.

81. Niethammer, "The First Americans."

82. Mark Potts, "Energy Resources Bring Change," *Chicago Tribune*, February 3, 1980, p. W1.

83. Judith Cummings, "Indian Tribes Seek to Increase Income in Mineral Leases," *New York Times*, June 8, 1978, p. A11.

84. "Mine Development on US Indian Lands," *Engineering and Mining Journal* (January 1980).

85. National Congress of American Indians, "Capitol Hill Review," July 30, 1979, Folder: Congress—BIA Hearings Schedule, Legislative Reports (1979), box 259, Files of the Indian Rights Association Record 1523, Historical Society of Pennsylvania, Philadelphia, PA.

86. The Interior Department through its BIA and Geological Survey at times advocated terms favorable to tribes, as with the Laguna and Northern Cheyenne in 1980 rulings that favored environmental impact statements on the one hand and terminated unequal leases on the other. See "Laguna," *The CERT Report,* June 27, 1980, p. 3; "Carter cancels N. Cheyenne Peabody Coal Co coal leases," *The CERT Report,* October 31, 1980, p. 4.

87. See "In this Issue," *The CERT Report,* February 11, 1980, p. 1; "Conpaso Mine," *The CERT Report,* December 10, 1979, p. 5; "In this Issue," *The CERT Report,* July 20, 1979, p. 1.

88. "Mine Development on US Indian Lands," *E&MJ,* January 1980, 66–70.

89. Cohn, "Energy Gives Indians New Potential Clout"; Ronald Reagan to Peter MacDonald, September 4, 1980, Folder: Council of Energy Resource Tribes, box 264, Indian Rights Association records (Collection 1523), Historical Society of Pennsylvania, Philadelphia, PA.

90. CERT News Release, "Tribal Energy Coalition Ends 1980 Annual Meeting with Call for Tribal-Federal Energy Partnership," Folder: Council of Energy Resource Tribes, box 264, Files of the Indian Rights Association Record 1523, Historical Society of Pennsylvania, Philadelphia, PA.

91. Stewart Udall to Cecil Andrus, December 29, 1976, Folder: Speeches, 1975, box 187, Secretary of the Interior Files, Stewart L. Udall Papers, Special Collections, University of Arizona Library, Tucson, AZ. Emphasis added.

92. Ibid.

93. Yergin, *The Prize,* 252–255.

94. "Text of President's Statement on Dealing with Nation's Energy Problem," *New York Times,* June 30, 1973, p. 20.

95. Stewart Udall to Cecil Andrus, December 29, 1976. Emphasizing minerals and environmental management mirrored Harold Ickes' earlier priorities in rebuilding the Interior Department in the New Deal.

96. Edward Cowan, "Nixon Will Create an Energy Agency in Major Shake-up," *New York Times,* December 2. 1973, p. 1.

97. Cecil D. Andrus and Jim Schlesinger to Jimmy Carter, February 16, 1977, Folder: Energy Reorganization, box 201, Staff Offices Domestic Policy Staff—Stuart Eizenstat, Jimmy Carter Library, Atlanta, GA.

98. The Bureau of Mines' remaining functions were distributed among the Department of Energy and other Interior agencies like the Bureau of Land Management and the Geological Survey. See Sandra Blakesale, "Babbitt Likens Move to Kill Science Agencies to 'Book Burning,'" *New York Times,* February 17, 1995; Robert Pear, "With New Budget, Domestic Spending is Cut $24 Million," *New York Times,* April 27, 1996.

99. Cecil D. Andrus and Jim Schlesinger to Jimmy Carter, February 16, 1977. The watchdog relationship between the two departments carried over to the controversial matter of nuclear energy management.

100. Both agendas were tied to important environmental legislation in the 1960s and 1970s. See "Statement of Cecil D. Andrus, Secretary of the Interior, Before the Senate Committee on Governmental Affairs, March 9, 1977," Folder: Speeches, 1975, box 187, Secretary of the Interior Files, Stewart L. Udall Papers, Special Collections, University of Arizona Library, Tucson, AZ.

101. Daniel T. Rodgers, *Age of Fracture* (London: Harvard University Press, 2011), 35.

102. *The CERT Report,* December 19, 1980, pp. 1–2; Folder: Council of Energy Resource Tribes, box 264, Indian Rights Association records (Collection 1523), Historical Society of Pennsylvania, Philadelphia, PA.

103. George Cameron Coggins and Doris K. Nagel, "'Nothing Beside Remains': The Legal Legacy of James G. Watt's Tenure as Secretary of the Interior on Federal Land Law and Policy," *Boston College Environmental Affairs Law Review* 17, no. 3 (Spring 1990): 489.

104. T. R. B., "Watt's Teapot Dome," *New Republic,* June 6, 1983, 6.

105. Coggins and Nagel, "'Nothing Beside Remains.'"

106. James G. Watt had written an amicus brief challenging the Jicarilla Apache tribes' right to tax energy companies on its lands. See *The CERT Report,* December 19, 1980, p. 3.

107. Aaron Epstein, "Reagan's 'Lightning Rod' Watt Keeps Critics Seething," *Philadelphia Inquirer,* January 21, 1983, p. 5-A.

108. See "Whose Economic Development?" *Akwesasne Notes,* Autumn 1980, p. 16.

109. Hazel W. Hertzberg, "Reaganomics on the Reservation," *New Republic,* November 22, 1982.

110. Elizabeth Hinton, *From the War on Poverty to the War on Drugs: The Making of Mass Incarceration in America* (Cambridge: Harvard University Press, 2016), 4.

111. Philip Jenkins, *Decade of Nightmares: The End of the Sixties and the Making of Eighties America* (New York: Oxford University Press, 2006), 213.

112. Rodgers, *Age of Fracture,* 37.

113. "Ex-Navajo Leader Draws a Jail Term: Tribal Court Orders 450-Day Term in Bribery Conviction," *New York Times,* February 7, 1991.

114. See Ambler, *Breaking the Iron Bonds,* 98; Harmon, *Rich Indians,* 231–240; Smith and Frehner, eds., *Indians & Energy;* Fixico, *The Invasion of Indian Country in the Twentieth Century.*

115. Jenkins, *Decade of Nightmares,* 218.

116. See David Harvey, *The Spaces of Global Capitalism: Towards a Theory of Uneven Geographical Development* (London: Verso Press, 2006); Leo Panitch and Sam Gindin, *The Making of Global Capitalism: The Political Economy of American Empire* (London: Verso, 2012).

Epilogue

1. James Risen, "U.S. Identifies Vast Mineral Riches in Afghanistan," *New York Times,* June 13, 2010.

2. U.S. Geological Survey, *Preliminary Non-Fuel Mineral Resource Assessment of Afghanistan* (Washington, DC: USGPO, 2004), 2. On the long-standing role of the

United States and Soviet Union in development projects in Afghanistan, see Timothy Nunan, *Humanitarian Invasion: Global Development in Cold War Afghanistan* (New York: Cambridge University Press, 2016); Linda Nash, "Traveling Technology? American Water Engineers in the Columbia Basin and the Helmand Valley," in *Where Minds and Matters Meet: Technology in California and the West*, ed. Volker Janssen (Berkeley: University of California Press, 2012), 135–158.

3. M. G. Volin, *Chromite Deposits in Logar Valley, Kabul Province, Afghanistan* (Washington, DC: USGPO, 1950).

4. Brief Description of Technical Cooperation Projects, May 3, 1953; Alan Probert to Benoni Lockwood, August 1, 1953, Folder: 1953, box 6932, Technical Assistance, RG 70, NARA; Risen, "U.S. Identifies Vast Mineral Riches in Afghanistan."

5. *Assisting Development in a Changing World: The Harvard Institute for International Development, 1980–1995* (Cambridge: Harvard University Press, 1997).

6. Michael Watts, "Violent Environments: Petroleum Conflict and the Political Ecology of Rule in the Niger Delta, Nigeria," in *Liberation Ecologies: Environment, Development, Social Movements,* 2nd ed., ed. Richard Peet and Michael Watts (New York: Routledge, 2004), 275–276.

7. Michael T. Klare, *Blood and Oil: The Dangers and Consequences of America's Growing Petroleum Dependency* (New York: Metropolitan Books, 2004), xii.

8. Didier Fassin, "Heart of Humanness: The Moral Economy of Humanitarian Intervention," in *Contemporary States of Emergency: The Politics of Military and Humanitarian Interventions* (Brooklyn: Zone Books, 2010), 269–294; Andrew Bacevich, *The Limits of Power: The End of American Exceptionalism* (New York: Holt Publications, 2009).

9. John M. Broder, "U.S. Revises Rules for Drilling Ban," *New York Times,* July 13, 2010, A15.

10. J. R. McNeill, *The Great Acceleration: An Environmental History of the Anthropocene since 1945* (Cambridge: Harvard University Press, 2015); Dipesh Chakrabarty, "The Climate of History: Four Theses," *Critical Inquiry* 35, no. 2 (2009): 197–222.

11. Megan Black, "Interior Imperialism: Fossil Fuels, American Expansion, and Rebel Park Rangers," *n+1*, March 28, 2017.

12. "No Filter: Interior Tweets America the Beautiful," *NPR Blog,* July 19, 2014, www.npr.org/blogs/itsallpolitics/2014/07/08/329883587/no-filter-interior-tweets-america-the-beautiful.

Acknowledgments

In writing this book on ever-widening frontiers, I got by with more than a little help from my colleagues and friends. At the University of Nebraska–Lincoln, friends stoked my curiosities about American global power and helped me to see it in unexpected places, especially Elizabeth Tarvin, whose phenomenal artistry and family involvements in the indigenous sovereignty movement provided early and ongoing inspiration. In the classroom, committed educators across departments, including Stephen Buhler, Wheeler Winston Dixon, Gwendolyn Audrey Foster, and Patrick McBride, encouraged me to cross intellectual borders. Tim Borstelmann, the ringleader, instilled in me a passion for archives along with the unendingly helpful entreaty to "be weird"—advice I took to heart in pursuing an unconventional project in an interdisciplinary field. I thank my professors in the American Studies Department at the George Washington University for encouraging the mischief, teaching me to think and to write: Thomas Guglielmo, Andrew Zimmerman, Libby Anker, Suleiman Osman, Jamie Cohen-Cole, Dara Orenstein, Kip Kosek, Elaine Peña, Jennifer Nash, and Chad Heap. My greatest debt is to my fearless advisor Melani McAlister, a model scholar, a devoted teacher, and my mentor-hero.

Numerous archivists helped me survey the terrain of the Interior Department's activities. Early in the process, David Clark of the Truman Library directed me to the files of the President's Materials Policy Commission, while Maureen Booth of the Department of the Interior Library provided pivotal moorings in the institution's history. At the later stages of my research, Barbara Cline of the Johnson Library went above and beyond in retrieving scattered traces of space race correspondence. Year after year, Joseph Schwarz of the National Archives and Records Administration demonstrated great patience as I sought Interior Department personnel across numerous, seemingly disconnected, files. These archivists and more at places like the Jimmy Carter Library, University of Arizona Special Collections, Marriott Library at the University of Utah, Manuscripts Division of the Library of Congress, and Tamiment Library at New York University were instrumental in connecting the dots. Research would not have been possible without funding from the

George Washington University, Society for Historians of American Foreign Relations, Lyndon B. Johnson Library, Harry S. Truman Library, and Historical Society of Pennsylvania.

I completed important research and writing on the manuscript while a postdoctoral fellow in Global American Studies at the Charles Warren Center for Studies in American History at Harvard University. Throughout, I had formative conversations with our spirited director, Walter Johnson, as well as an incredible group of fellows who converged at Harvard: Laura Martin, Abby Spinak, Ann Jones, Paul Adler, Amy Offner, Lily Geismer, Rebecca Marchiel, Katherine Marino, Justin Leroy, Samantha Iyer, Destin Jenkins, Christopher Clements, Nicolas Barreyre, Martin Giraudeau, Gabrielle Clark, Noam Maggor, Tracy Neumann, Paul Kershaw, Sarah Horowitz, Jessie Wilkerson, and Timothy Nunan. From my first day at the Warren Center, Stuart Schrader was the consummate cohort mate. Harvard faculty and staff across departments also generously donated time and offered feedback, including Genevieve Clutario, who deserves special recognition for the length and regularity of those exchanges, as well as Frederick Logevall, Erez Manela, Joyce Chaplin, Sven Beckert, Kirsten Weld, Neil Brenner, Daniel Carpenter, and Arthur Patton Hock. Oliver Curtis, a friend training at Harvard's Graduate School of Design, schematized the maps for the book. In one of the greatest gifts of this postdoctoral experience, Richard White, Timothy Mitchell, Paul Kramer, and Beverly Gage were brought on to review the manuscript. Their incisive marginal comments and overarching questions integrally shaped the penultimate draft of the book.

This manuscript has also greatly benefited from the opportunity to workshop it in intellectual communities across institutions and borders. I received influential feedback from Sheila Jasanoff and the Science and Technology Studies Colloquium at the John F. Kennedy School of Government at Harvard University; Tehila Sassen and the Sovereignty, Economy and the Global Histories of Natural Resources Symposium at Cambridge University; Bruce Schulman and the American Political History Institute at Boston University; Randal Hall and the Andrew W. Mellon Seminar on Environment, Culture, and Limits at Rice University; Thomas Robertson and Jenny Leigh Smith and the National Science Foundation workshop on Transplanting Modernity at Georgetown University; and Imre Szeman and Sheena Wilson and the Petrocultures Symposium at the University of Alberta. In the pivotal final stages of writing, the International History Department at the London School of Economics, where I teach, has provided considerable support. Colleagues Matthew Jones, Imaobong Umoren, Tanya Harmer, Taylor Sherman, Ronald Po, David Motadel, Paul Stock, Paul Keenan, Padraic Scanlan, and Demetra Frini engaged critically with my work and cheered me along as I inched through the final edits.

Along the way, I received razor-sharp feedback on drafts and presentations from colleagues: Robert Vitalis, Brian DeLay, Paul Rosier, Daniel Immerwahr, Kate Brown, David Engerman, Brooke Blower, Sarah Phillips, Daniel Horowitz, Helen Horowitz, Glenda Sluga, Alyosha Goldstein, Penny Von Eschen, Paul Sutter, Josh Howe, Tyler Priest, David Painter, Thomas Blake Earle, Brian Jirout, Nathan Citino, Andrew Needham, Edward Miller, Andrew Friedman, Vanessa Ogle, Chris Dietrich, Christy Thornton, Linda Nash, Daniel Margolies, Mark Lytle, Nils Gilman, Fredrik Albritton Jonsson, Mats Ingulstad, and Sebastian Herbstreuth. My editor at Harvard, Kathleen McDermott, helped bring all the strands together.

Finally, I thank those colleagues, friends, and family who irrevocably shaped this project by lending an ear and providing support at pivotal stages: Lindsay Davis (my work wife) and Justin Mann (my everyday superhero), as well as Kimberly Probolus, Kathleen M. Brian, Kathryn Gaskill, Julie Chamberlain, Shannon Davies Mancus, Patrick Nugent, Deb Ziems, Mary May, Dan May, Donna Lathrop, Craig Lathrop, Gary Thompson, Linda Thompson, Ed Thompson, Lindsey Hanson, Alexa Gryzwa, Shannon Killion, Danny Girard, Michaela Cerrato, Megan Balogh, Stefanie Hall, Claire O'Connor, Emily Thornton, Amanda Barker, Trevor Nieveen, Margaret Goll, Carson Vaughan, Molly Thomas, Julie Skinner Manegold, Laura Dziorny, and Alex Grayson. I dedicate this book to the memory of my father, Steve Black, and to my mother, Ann Black, and brother, Ryan Black, for their endless support, love, and imagination.

Index